THE SALTWATER FRONTIER

The Saltwater Frontier

Indians and the Contest for the
American Coast

ANDREW LIPMAN

Yale

UNIVERSITY PRESS

NEW HAVEN AND LONDON

Yale University Press books may be purchased in quantity for educational, business,
or promotional use. For information, please e-mail sales.press@yale.edu (U.S. office)
or sales@yaleup.co.uk (U.K. office).

Set in Electra type by IDS Infotech, Ltd.
Printed in the United States of America.

Library of Congress Control Number: 2015939464
ISBN: 978-0-300-20766-8 (cloth : alk. paper)

A catalogue record for this book is available from the British Library.

This paper meets the requirements of ANSI/NISO Z39.48-1992
(Permanence of Paper).

10 9 8 7 6 5 4 3 2 1

To Mom, in memory

Sepagehommaûta. | Let us saile.
—Roger Williams, *A Key Into the Language of America*

CONTENTS

Prologue: October 29, 2012   ix

Acknowledgments   xv

A Note on the Text   xix

Introduction   1

ONE

The Giants' Shore   19

TWO

Watercraft and Watermen   54

THREE

The Landless Borderland, 1600–1633   85

FOUR

Blood in the Water, 1634–1646   125

FIVE

Acts of Navigation, 1647–1674   165

CONTENTS

SIX
Sea Changes, 1675–1750   203

Epilogue: "What Need Is There to Speak of the Past?"   244

List of Abbreviations   252
Notes   255
Index   329

October 29, 2012

I was living in Brooklyn, writing this book, when the Atlantic Ocean made an unexpected visit. It came in the form of a tropical system that gathered south of the West Indies in late October 2012. After ripping roofs off houses and flooding streets across Jamaica, Hispaniola, and Cuba, Tropical Storm Sandy became Hurricane Sandy and veered north. On the night of October 29, 2012, it slammed New York City with a thirteen-foot wall of water. The surge shredded boardwalks, flipped cars on their sides, and lifted beach houses off their foundations. As avenues became filthy estuaries, a flooded power substation on the East River exploded and lit up my apartment with a sputtering, eerie flash. A third of Manhattan's twinkling skyline went dark. On Staten Island, people drowned in their living rooms. Fires raged across whole blocks of the Rockaways in Queens. All told, Sandy killed a hundred and forty-eight people across the Northeast, contributed to the deaths of a hundred more, and left tens of thousands homeless.

Over the next few days it felt like the city was slipping out of the modern world and into a postapocalyptic future. Subways shut down and traffic onto bridges stretched for miles, effectively severing the borough's lifelines to the mainland. Having no way to get to the research library on the Upper West Side that was sponsoring my year of leave, I spent time walking around my neighborhood. Near my building a tangle of branches and downed wires blocked the sidewalk. Snapped trees leaned lazily against brownstones, while entire metal-frame store awnings had fallen dejectedly onto the pavement. Unlit buildings across the river created the illusion that the heart of the metropolis had been abandoned. As the days wore on, ATMs started to run out of cash. Gasoline rationing, a wartime relic I had never seen in my lifetime, went into effect. I started getting nervous when I noticed that the shelves of my corner bodega were becoming alarmingly bare.

It was as though Sandy had opened up a brief tear in space-time. Soon it became a cliché for commentators to suggest that the storm's aftermath was an ominous preview of the century of global warming to come. But it seemed to me more like a peek at a century long gone. I was realizing, in a way I had not truly grasped before, that I was on an island next to other islands. Stripped of its modern infrastructure, Gotham revealed its origins as a group of settlements oriented around the sea—and at its mercy. Flooding on Manhattan exposed the island's long-lost face, as the high waterline traced the contours of the seventeenth-century coastline. Near my apartment, the Gowanus Canal similarly tried to reclaim its irregular, marshy course. It was soon clear that those hit hardest were also economically marginalized: some were uninsured folks unable to recoup their losses, others were elderly or infirm and thus isolated in a crippled city. Parts of the coast were without power for weeks, forcing people in the most stricken areas to cook over fires and get their water by the bucket. I heard more than one reporter compare the storm-ravaged districts of the Tri-State area to the Wild West. It seemed like my own titular conceit, "the saltwater frontier," had leapt from the page.

Obviously, the trials of modern urban people facing climate change in the twenty-first century are vastly different from the events discussed in this book, which reexamines how coastal Algonquians from the Hudson River to Cape Cod faced the colonial invasion in the seventeenth century. Indeed, these events may appear to have little in common other than bringing death and dislocation to the same corner of North America. But when seen together in a long view of this region's history, the seemingly dissimilar processes of global warming and European colonization draw our attention to some of the same things. They remind us that we all live on a single ball of rock that is mostly covered with water. They illustrate how profit-seeking activities often create unintended and lasting consequences for people and the environment. They reveal that political boundaries are mostly an illusion and offer little protection from troublesome planet-wide trends. And they demonstrate that so much of what appears permanent is in fact precarious.

We share more than we think with the Native, English, and Dutch people whose stories fill the following pages. Like us, they lived in an age of environmental crises, exploitive global trade, far-reaching wars, and frightening pandemics. They also believed storms could be powerful omens or the dire consequences of human actions. Witnessing a dramatic transformation of this coast and thinking of more catastrophic changes to come certainly convinced me that events in our rearview are closer than they appear. My intent is not to draw overly simple parallels to the colonial period but to point out its surprising immediacy in a region that seldom wants to dwell on its violent past or the global processes that created its current boundaries.

In American popular culture the shore from Manhattan to Nantucket seems quite remote from the bloody realities of the seventeenth century, as it is so often depicted as a placid place defined by leisure. The congested western side features the country's richest city while the bucolic eastern side is perceived as an exclusive playground for elites. Though in truth much of the coast — home to some twenty million people — is now a densely packed swath of modest-sized houses and car-friendly retail strips, with impoverished factory towns perched at the falls of retired rivers. F. Scott Fitzgerald fittingly described the region's largest bay, Long Island Sound, as "the most domesticated body of salt water in the Western Hemisphere."

But even suburbanized, deindustrialized places can remain contested. Between the brick and cement grids of New York City and the precious clusters of gray-shingled beach houses there are Native villages standing. Not as many as in 1600 but probably more than you think. Thousands of people from the region belong to over a dozen indigenous communities. Some live on soil that their ancestors never ceded in federal- and state-recognized reservations, others live among the vast non-Native population. Thousands more people whose ancestors came from this coast now belong to tribal nations located deep in the American and Canadian interior. These

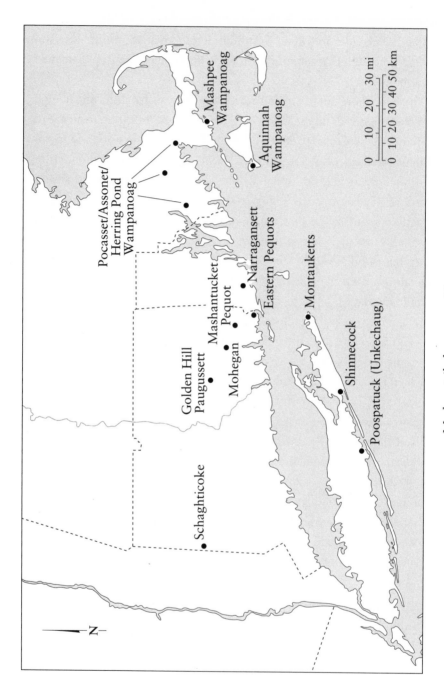

Modern tribal communities.

communities need no reminders of the frontier's modern relevance. While all sides long ago laid down their weapons, Indians from the region are still entangled in fraught cultural and political negotiations with their neighbors. For them, the colonial period is far from over.

This book returns to the years in which catastrophic Atlantic arrivals first ruptured the social fabric of this shore. It is not just a narrative of devastation but also one of navigation. For although those indigenous people lost most of their lands, in the process they discovered an ocean.

ACKNOWLEDGMENTS

Many people made this book possible and made it better. I am grateful for the teachers who, whether they realized it or not, inspired this project in classes they taught years ago. At Vassar College, James H. Merrell was my first mentor and is still one of my most trusted. Jim shared with me, as he does with so many of his students, his infectious enthusiasm for the early American past and his reverence for the power of words. At the Maritime Studies Program of Williams College and Mystic Seaport, James T. Carlton taught me that human actions must always be seen within a larger ecological web. Glenn Gordinier was my guide to the Seaport's collections, showing me how objects—from entire whaleships to simple clay pipes—are valuable primary sources. When I was a master's student at the University of Oxford, Richard Carwardine and Benjamin Marsh got me reading more deeply and widely in early American history, further compelling me to join the scholarly conversation. At the University of Pennsylvania, Daniel K. Richter was an ideal adviser—patient, available, and challenging. Most of all, I valued Dan's insistence that an active imagination and a sense of humor should always be part of the historian's toolkit.

Other faculty members at Penn, especially Richard Beeman, Kathleen Brown, Robert Blair St. George, Bruce Kuklick, Robert Naborn, Kathy Peiss, and Michael Zuckerman, were all excellent teachers who each encouraged my research. Penn was also where I made lasting friends with whom I shared many chapter drafts and laughs: Joanna Cohen, Aida

Gureghian, Andrew Heath, Katherine Hill, Erik Mathisen, Matthew Karp, John Kenney, William Kuby, Jaffa Panken, Brian Rouleau, Matthew Schauer, Alison Scheiderer, Laura Keenan Spero, Patrick Spero, and Catherine Styer. And as a frequenter of the McNeil Center for Early American Studies, I remain grateful for the friends and collaborators I met there, especially Zara Anishanslin, Christopher Bilodeau, Paul Conrad, Simon Finger, Jaap Jacobs, Alyssa Mount Pleasant, and Dawn Peterson.

At Syracuse, I have enjoyed the friendship of many folks who truly lived up to the title of colleague, especially Susan Branson, Andrew Cohen, Carol Faulkner, Samantha Kahn Herrick, Norman Kutcher, Chris Kyle, Laurie Marhoefer, Mark Schmeller, David Stam, Junko Takeda, and John Western. Other upstate neighbors have also offered me constructive feedback, particularly Paul Moyer, Richard Newman, Michael Oberg, Holly Rine, and Erik Seeman. And I am grateful to the seminar conveners who invited me to workshop several chapter drafts: Philip D. Morgan at The Johns Hopkins University, Douglas Bradburn and the Upstate Early American History Workshop at Binghamton University, Alison Parker and the Rochester United States History workshop, Conrad Wright and Kate Viens at the Boston Early American History Seminar, and the McNeil Center for Early American Studies' Friday Seminar. As I finished revisions, I was further heartened by the enthusiastic and warm welcomes I received from so many of my new colleagues at Barnard College and Columbia University.

My Williams–Mystic classmate Lauren Morgens, now the captain of the SSV *Kalmar Nyckel*, a gorgeous replica of a Dutch-built, Swedish-run pinnace based in Wilmington, Delaware, gave me an eye-opening tour of her ship in the spring of 2009. I have also gained critically valuable feedback and insights from a number of fellow scholars I came to know either through research trips, residential fellowships, conferences, or simply through digital correspondence: Edward Andrews, Matthew Bahar, Catherine Cangany, Kelly Chaves, Megan Lindsay Cherry, Matthew Crawford, Christine DeLucia, Claire Gherini, Katherine Grandjean, Daragh Grant, Robert Grumet, Julie Fisher, Linford Fisher, Karen Kupperman, Ned Landsman, Jason Mancini, Kevin McBride, Simon Middleton, Alison Tubini Miner,

Andrew Newman, Paul Otto, Susanah Shaw Romney, Nancy Shoemaker, William Simmons, Danielle Skeehan, William Starna, John Strong, Jerusha Westbury, Laurie Wood, and Joanne van der Woude. Amy Turner Bushnell deserves a special thanks, as she too came up with the title "the saltwater frontier" and graciously yielded it to this junior scholar.

Several scholarly initiatives made the regional ambitions of this project possible. All students of the colonial Northeast owe a particular thanks to Charles Ghering for his stewardship of the New Netherland Institute's ongoing forty-year translation project, which prods more early Americanists to include the Dutch colony in their interpretations with new and revised translations. Several works of digital scholarship were also a major help in allowing me to tell a richly sourced story that wandered across both colonial and disciplinary boundaries. Led by Paul Grant-Costa, the New England Indian Papers Project at Yale University is the finest online archive I have ever used, a boon to scholars of the region. I have also learned a lot from the finely grained research being led by Jason Mancini for his Indian Mariners Project and the excavations led by Kevin McBride and the Battlefields of the Pequot War project, both supported by the Mashantucket Pequot Museum and Research Center.

A few institutions made this book a reality with their generous financial support, first and foremost my principal employers over the past decade: the University of Pennsylvania and Syracuse University. The New-York Historical Society Museum and Library hosted me for a year-long Andrew W. Mellon Foundation Fellowship that allowed me to make significant progress on my writing. And I appreciated the other kind of fellowship I enjoyed at the N-YHS, thanks to Kevin Butterfield, Catherine McNeur, Nina Nazionale, Dael Norwood, Valerie Paley, and Robin Vandome. My research and writing also benefited enormously from fellowships and grants from the Massachusetts Historical Society, the John Carter Brown Library, the American Philosophical Society, and the International Seminar for the Study of the Atlantic World at Harvard University.

Additionally, I want to thank the research staffs at the American Antiquarian Society, Bird Library at Syracuse University, Boston Public Library, Brooklyn Historical Society, Brooklyn Public Library, British

National Archives, John Hay Library at Brown University, Mashantucket Pequot Research Center and Museum, Massachusetts Historical Society, New York Municipal Archives, New York Public Library, Pilgrim Hall Museum, and Van Pelt Library at the University of Pennsylvania. The *William and Mary Quarterly* allowed me to reprint revised portions of my article "'A meanes to knitt them togeather': The Exchange of Body Parts in the Pequot War" (2008), and *Early American Studies: An Interdisciplinary Journal* granted the same for passages from my article "Murder on the Saltwater Frontier: The Death of John Oldham" (2011). Chris Rogers at Yale University Press and John Demos and Aaron Sachs have been steady believers in this project. Chris's incisive suggestions as well as those of David Silverman and Neal Salisbury greatly improved the final draft. I am also grateful to Erica Hanson and Annie Imbornoni for leading me through the editorial process, to Lawrence Kenney for copyediting, to Bill Nelson for drawing the maps, and to Mary Valencia for creating the jacket design.

Several close friends have been priceless to me through various stages of writing, especially Peter Wagner, Peter Coco, Adrienne Phelps-Coco, and Clara Platter. My larger family through blood and marriage—Katherine Lipman, Jake Lipman, Roger Lipman, Jasmine Lipman, Philip Rothman, and Nancy Isherwood—have always encouraged me along the way, as did my grandmother Dora Michaelson. My father, Stephen Lipman, taught me to sail along the same shores featured in this book and first told me the story of King Philip's War as we sailed by Mount Hope. He has always been unfailingly enthusiastic about my dreams of becoming a professional historian. Last, I dedicate this book to my mother, Marguerite Jordan Lipman. A self-declared citizen of the world and widely published travel writer who saw more of the planet than most people ever will, she taught me that seeing is a way of learning, writing is a way of thinking, and exploring a place means exploring its past. She died shortly before I began this project, but I hope a part of her lives on in these pages.

For ease of reading, archaic shorthand marks such as thorns, ampersands, the long *s*, interchangeable *u/v* or *i/j* usage, double *f,* and all superscript abbreviations from primary texts are silently corrected to modern usage, though all other original spellings are maintained. "Old style" Julian dating favored by the English is also corrected to the years of the modern "New style" Gregorian calendar favored by the Dutch in the main text, though the original date as it appears in the source is retained in the notes.

L and looms large in the American Indian past. The continent itself is a document for indigenous peoples, a vast page with a deep concentration of stories. Colonial historians study how Natives shared ground and lost it, fought for ground and held on to it. Still, land was not the only setting for Indian history or its sole defining issue.[1]

This book covers territory that we Americans might think we know all too well: the Northeast in the seventeenth century. It is safe to say that the history of Indians in this region is well-trodden ground. The English and Dutch invasions of the coast were, by the colonists' own admissions, aggressive and brutal. Yet today, the same region that witnessed multiple colonial-led massacres that literally scorched the earth is now home to one of the densest concentrations of Indian reservations on the eastern seaboard. Why was this first century of colonization so violent? And how did some indigenous peoples survive the onslaught and remain in their homelands for centuries to come? This book argues that the answers to both those questions can be found simply by flipping our traditional westward-facing picture around. What if we considered this contested region not just as a part of the continent but also as part of the ocean?

When towering ships first appeared off North America, the coast and sea became a space that Natives had to share and fight for. Tens of thousands of Algonquian-speaking people made their homes on the sandy margin between the later sites of Plymouth and New Amsterdam. Though the coast was divided into more than twenty independent polities, its chain of bays served as a cohesive, connecting space. After years of brief visits to these waters, English and Dutch colonists built their first settlements at the eastern and western ends of the coast in the 1620s. They eventually converged along Long Island Sound as the century wore on. In fact, at no other spot on mainland North America did two competing empires place so many villages so close together. The foreigners audaciously renamed this region as part of New England and Nieu Nederlandt, each claiming the entire shore belonged to them.

The beginnings of these twin colonial intrusions are fabled events in Americans' national memory. We see the colonial arrival as a heroic act of *Mayflower* passengers striding on Plymouth Rock or we remember it slightly more cynically in the legend that Dutchmen bought Manhattan on the

Michel Felice Corné, "The Landing of the Pilgrims." Courtesy of Pilgrim Hall Museum, Plymouth, Massachusetts.

Jennie A. Brownscome, "The First Thanksgiving at Plymouth." Courtesy of Pilgrim Hall Museum, Plymouth, Massachusetts.

Alfred Fredericks, "The Purchase of Manhattan Island by Peter Minuit."

cheap for mere baubles. These myths are primarily about colonists' initial seizure of land, zeroing in on the instant Native dispossession began. They celebrate the uncanny luck of the fair-skinned folks in buckled hats, offering little concern for the fates of the people with feathers on their heads lurking at the edge of the frame. The fact that these tales are misremembered only seems to add to their longevity—the very act of debunking falsehoods requires repeating them. Images of colonial destiny have a more sticky hold on the public consciousness than scholars' depressing, nitpicky claims of complexity.[2]

Thankfully there are other versions of this past that are not so triumphant—Native and non-Native historians have been telling them for quite a while. But even nuanced accounts can share the same blind spots as the legends. Too often we suppose that the story started when colonists left their ships. We forget that Indians met Europeans as fellow mariners. We allow colonists' artificial borders to stand to this day, telling two unrelated English and Dutch stories. And we therefore assume that colonization was a process that happened only on soil.[3]

By looking toward the sea rather than the land, this book offers a new way of thinking about Indian history and a new way of understanding this all-too-familiar region. Throughout this retelling, the physical shore plays a formative role. Its geological quirks, economic resources, and ecological changes all shaped the fates of those who inhabited it in the seventeenth century. Early New England and New Netherland should be seen as overlapping maritime zones with a shared history rather than as discrete territories with separate pasts. Colonial bounds were shifting and porous, unable to contain either people or events. Over the seventeenth century, Algonquian *sachems* (chiefs) and colonial governors engaged in a multidirectional struggle for control of the coast. This contest was a fight for waters and territories, a fight between European seaborne empires, and a fight for Native independence. It also was a complex meeting of maritime cultures that would transform the region and its people. And in some ways this contest is not over.

The following pages offer a novel explanation of how the English came to dominate the region in part by emphasizing the intentions of Indians and Dutchmen. The book argues that neither group of colonists were solely responsible for their colonies' fates, as Native decisions and opinions were crucial at every stage of conquest. Viewing the overlap of two empires through a single frame uncovers curious similarities and differences between these abutting colonial projects. The meeting of indigenous and foreign seafaring traditions drove many physical changes along the shore, while rivalries between Native leaders and between the English and Dutch seaborne empires spurred its political realignments. However, the *saltwater* in this book's title is not strictly literal. After all, territory *is* a key part of this story, especially in the later chapters. Instead, *saltwater* refers to the many kinds of maritime and Atlantic connections—cultural, political, martial, ecological, and material—that formed this borderland that was not entirely based on land.[4]

This is also a history that focuses on the use of deadly force. Our sunny pictures of Europeans and Indians gathering by calm seas to swap goods or dine on turkey are not entirely wrong—these folks did sometimes trade and feast in peace. But an honest view of this shore's past must also feature darker scenes of captive taking, shipboard stabbings, attempted piracy, intentional drownings, mass incinerations, and ritual dismemberments. Not incidentally, most of these acts of mayhem and bloodshed occurred on the water or at the water's edge. European soldiers would kill several thousand coastal Indians over the century, while tens of thousands more would die of introduced diseases. Still, Natives were not mere passive victims. In resisting the English and Dutch invasions, they would slay as many as a thousand colonists—no small toll but far fewer than the number they lost. Algonquian peoples in conflict with each other would also kill a considerable but hard-to-quantify number of their neighbors, totaling over a few hundred more dead.[5]

The dueling nations of foreigners did not settle this shore: they *unsettled* it. In the grimmest moments of the century, parts of the once-thriving indigenous shoreline would become a nightmarish landscape of death, pocked with freshly dug graves and the charred remains of entire towns. Many combatants likened the sporadic bursts of violence to sea squalls. One veteran compared the bravery it took to fight Indians to the courage of sailors, summing up his narrative of a frontier war with the wry aphorism "more men would goe to Sea, if they were sure to meet with no stormes."

Another Englishman poetically referred to the same confrontation as "the Ocean of Troubles and Trials wherein we saile." And in at least one coastal language, Indian fighters would "wittily speake of" conflicts as "*Chépewess & Mishittâshin*," or the "Northerne storm of war," associating warfare with the bad weather created by a malicious spirit.[6]

Despite all this turbulence, coastal Algonquians encountered Europeans in ways that were constructive, inventive even. Looking at exchanges between ships and canoes, one discovers that soon after they met, the locals and invaders began a cross-cultural trade in seagoing skills that would further bind the region together. Colonists eagerly followed the advice of Native mariners, hired them as ferrymen and couriers, and adopted their canoes as everyday vessels. Indians also bought, borrowed, and stole colonial boats and became talented sailors of European-style craft. The coast remained a central setting for frontier interaction well into the century. Abundant local clams and whelks became the raw material for the sacred shell beads known as *wampum* that doubled as trade currency through much of the colonial Northeast. These shells were just one resource of many that made nearshore waters a shared commons, as seafood was a staple of daily meals fixed in both wigwams and cottages.

At the same time, this region was also becoming part of a grand imperial contest that spanned the ocean. By midcentury the civil competition between the two European neighbors was turning into a hostile showdown between emerging global powers. The rivalry between England and the Netherlands started to overshadow frontier dealings throughout the region. It was soon apparent that the fates of all villages along the shore were tied to the outcomes of distant naval battles in the Caribbean and North Seas and of domestic upheavals in London and Amsterdam. And American events could have consequences in Europe, too. The English and Dutch long feared the other would ally with coastal Indians to overwhelm their colonial competitors; their mutual suspicions would only heighten in the years before James, Duke of York, first seized New Netherland and renamed it in honor of himself. Sensing their neighbors' shared fear of conspiracies, Native sachems would traffic in rumors to use the Europeans' quarrels for their own gain. The constant specter of conquest gave the shore a paranoid character. That famous wall that once stood where Wall Street is today was one of several dozen wooden stockades raised near European and Algonquian villages, as all braced for the seemingly inevitable Atlantic tempest headed their way.

The rise of a single empire over the coast was a fitful but bloodless process, at least from the colonial perspective. Starting in 1664 the English and Dutch traded possession of Manhattan and its hinterlands three times in ten years. Each handoff was swift and never escalated into a full-on war. But just a year after the final Dutch surrender, Indians who were furious at overreaching English authorities began a conflict in 1675 that would become the deadliest conflict ever fought on these shores. We know it as King Philip's War, so-named after the Wampanoag sachem Metacom, whom the English called Philip, who acted as the symbolic head of the Indian campaign. Historians often describe the fighting as Natives' last attempt to drive colonists back into the sea. That common summary of indigenous motives ignores the fact that the English victory ultimately pushed Indians, not colonists, toward the ocean. During the fighting, hundreds of Native captives were sold as slaves on distant tropical islands and in European cities, joining the larger diaspora of Indians across the Atlantic rim.

Other Algonquians set sail willingly, turning to seafaring as a living. Low-paying, risky jobs in maritime industries were hardly romantic or easy, but the work let Native men become acquainted with a changing watery world. Even as workers their actions would have far-reaching consequences, as indigenous whalers played a role in the boom-and-bust cycles of the American whale fishery. And as Indian communities formed links to the port towns of New York, Sag Harbor, New London, Newport, New Bedford, Nantucket, and Boston, they often intermarried with freed and enslaved black people, forming enduring multiracial families that are the core of the modern tribal communities along this shore. A few of these seasoned travelers would become well known on both sides of the ocean during the revolutionary era and early republic for their advocacy of Christianity, Native rights, and the abolition of slavery.

Ultimately, viewing saltwater as the primary stage of cultural encounters changes our simple narratives of colonization. The sea, unlike territory, could never quite be won or lost. Entering the Atlantic economy would transform Native societies, but Natives would likewise alter the history of the larger ocean. Despite the physical perils of engaging with ships that carried horrific diseases and hostile invaders and the threats to their cultural and political independence that came with remaining inside colonial bounds, coastal peoples did not retreat from the surf. Just as Europeans stood awestruck on their decks surveying the mysterious green continent before them, Indians faced an expanding blue horizon.

The Frontier, the Atlantic, and Natives

European vessels could cross the ocean and indigenous ones could not. That simple fact goes a long way toward explaining why some scholars, to this day, view Natives as spectators rather than actors in maritime and global history. But there are other reasons we erased Indians from the sea, reasons that are rooted in the old ways we used to think about geography, indigenous people, and the writing of history. Americans have a long national tradition of imagining the oceans around us as a protective moat and assuming our past is always grounded. This terrestrial habit of thinking was ascendant in the nineteenth century, the century that saw the birth of history as a proper academic field and the spread of those misleading myths that fetishized the moment colonial feet touched dirt. The single best articulation of this idea came in a talk given by a mustachioed young professor named Frederick Jackson Turner on a Chicago summer evening in 1893.

To understand our nation's origins, Turner told a crowd of well-fed faces, we had to face inland, toward a space he called the frontier. His term described a westerly moving "wave" of progress, a near-unstoppable flood of conquest and innovation that made America America. Each advance into the "free land" of the "wilderness," each triumph over its "uncivilized" aboriginals would force Euro-American pioneers to reinvigorate their democratic institutions and come together as a people. Though Turner acknowledged that "at first, the frontier was the Atlantic coast" making it "the frontier of Europe in a very real sense," he also insisted that "the true point of view in American history . . . is the Great West." In the years after Turner finished his speech, his "frontier thesis" would become a dominant, long-lasting interpretation of the nation's past, not because it was so original but because it was such an elegant synthesis of so many things that white scholars and citizens wanted to believe were true.[7]

Turner was born in Portage, Wisconsin, a town only one generation removed from its former life as a fur-trading outpost. He had been trained at the first American university to offer doctoral degrees in history, The Johns Hopkins University in Baltimore. His tendency to see land as the defining feature of the American past was personal and political. Like so many of his countrymen from the Revolution onward, he subscribed to the popular small-*r* republican idea that farming was the nation's truest occupation. Anglo-Saxon writers like Turner loved to valorize their forefathers who broke sod with humble plows, but they were less comfortable talking about the ones who funded grand ships, engaged in high-risk, high-profit gambles of trade, and became ensnared in debt and foreign affairs. The sea brought luxuries and the temptation to form a global empire. It needed to be deemphasized, depicted as a barrier between continents. By favoring ground over water, these historians actively created the myth of American exceptionalism. Once colonists untethered themselves from the aristocracies and miseries of Europe, the story went, they would craft a society that was fundamentally more free than the ones they left behind, thanks to all their abundant land. And should America expand its territory after its continental frontier was closed, the nation's pioneer origins could keep its intentions pure.[8]

Modern historians consider Turner problematic. Some find the very word *frontier* so distasteful, so easily conflated with justifications for white supremacy, Native dispossession, and American imperialism that they jokingly call it the *f*-word. An early critique came from one of Turner's own students, a fellow Wisconsinite named Herbert Eugene Bolton. Unlike his mentor, Bolton actually spent part of his childhood in a covered wagon as his family headed out to a plot in the Nebraska prairie, only to soon retreat to the wooded upper Midwest. In his research Bolton saw that the concept of a westward-moving wave implicitly privileged the perspective of English-speaking peoples over all others, effectively vanishing the Native peoples and rival empires who came before them. He memorably described the region north and west of the Gulf of Mexico as a zone of *borderlands,* contested by Native, Spanish, French, and American powers.[9]

Bolton's ideas have enjoyed a renaissance in the past two decades, as historians discard those textbook maps that showed rigid, Anglo-drawn lines expanding into blank space. This shift is in part due to American scholars finally admitting to their blatant East Coast bias, dropping their Anglo-centric blinders, and starting to study non-English colonists in depth. And this new picture of the past also comes thanks to an explosion of research on Natives that has turned cigar-store caricatures into splinters. We are reimag-ining the American old world, mapping the medieval continent's landscape of farming villages, far-ranging hunting peoples, monumental earthworks, and trading towns. We keep learning more about the stunning diversity of Native experiences in the colonial period, when indigenous people were pioneers and refugees, slaves and slaveholders, evangelical Christians and traditional revivalists, anti-imperial fighters and perhaps even architects of their own empires. Historians now see the continent during the colonial advance as a worn and messy patchwork: crisscrossed with uncertain borders, ripped in many spots. And we use the word *frontier* more thought-fully, redefining it to mean the combative and collaborative spaces that formed between Indian country and European colonies. The break between Turner the teacher and his student Bolton seems to have been resolved, and the *f*-word can once again be uttered in polite company. Still, even scholars who would never dream of reviving his moribund thesis share Turner's fondness for land, using territorial metaphors to frame their studies.[10]

Other thinkers challenge Turner from the opposite angle. Maritime and imperial historians have long pointed out that the Atlantic Ocean was actu-ally a connector of continents, not a partition. To a cohort writing after the Second World War, including a few men coming straight from the services into universities, the winning alliances of the last two wars demonstrated a profound bond between the United States and Western Europe. Following the urgings of the American journalist Walter Lippmann and a number of French and British scholars, they looked to affirm the shared values of the emerging anti-Communist partnership by writing a history of the "Atlantic Community" that emphasized links between continents' political and cultural evolutions. They saw the United States not as a uniquely superior nation but as part of an exclusive team of wealthy, white-majority, Christian nations that together were better than all others.[11]

Like work on the frontier, in recent decades Atlantic history has grown far beyond its beginnings as a triumphant project designed to flatter the powerful and justify their expanding rule. The field is no longer about elite intellectual links or simple diagrams of Triangle Trade. Rather, Atlantic historians are creating a kaleidoscopic picture of how the ocean connected the histories of the Americas, Africa, and Europe. Bridged by several entangled empires, crossed by millions of enslaved and free peoples, habitat for fishermen, sailors, merchants, and pirates, the ocean would become the main stage for the ages of revolution and abolition and ultimately for the rise of the nation-state and industrial capitalism. Yet in most Atlantic studies indigenous Americans are still landbound onlookers with little reach beyond their immediate shores.[12]

Historians are only slowly breaking the habit of leaving Natives high and dry. Quite recently research on the ocean and continent has started to blend together into a new, amphibious genre of "surf and turf" histories. Scholars argue that the sudden linkage of Indians' exchange networks to global ones could transform distant parts of the world at the same time. Some studies of the Atlantic World now range far inland; others trace Native stories all the way to Europe. Native maritime history is becoming a genuine subfield. An overlapping group of scholars pays close attention to coastlines, islands, even offshore banks, pointing out that in periods of Western expansion from antiquity to the present these seemingly peripheral places were often the center of the action. It is getting harder for scholars to ignore the prominent role indigenous peoples played in the larger epic of how this wet planet became connected and how the modern era began.[13]

Though this book owes much to this cutting-edge work, its most basic idea is actually almost as old as the frontier thesis. Just five years after Turner gave his talk in Chicago, a historian named Olivia Bush-Banks proposed that the Native past could be seen as a sea story. Bush-Banks was born Olivia Ward in 1869 in Sag Harbor on Long Island. Both of her parents were Montauketts of African ancestry, and her father, Abraham, was likely a fisherman. Bush-Banks would go on to become the tribal historian for the

Montaukett nation, where she met with elders and worked in the archives of Long Island's east end to recover the story of her ancestors. She joined a cohort of other indigenous writers publishing in the nineteenth century, whose narratives defied the ongoing erasure of Indians' past and presence on the continent. Later in life she also became a minor but respected figure in the Harlem Renaissance. But back in the 1890s, at the same time her contemporary Professor Turner achieved national prominence, she was a divorced woman struggling to raise her two daughters while looking for work as a seamstress in New England's gritty port cities.[14]

It was then she wrote what would become her most famous poem, "Driftwood." Her verses articulated the idea that the ocean was a frontier—a simultaneously destructive and generative space—for indigenous cultures. To Bush-Banks, Turner was correct in imagining the colonial advance as a wave, but in her eyes the wave was not a civilizing flood: it was a hurricane-force surge that carried off her ancestors' property, tore their communities apart, washed away their languages, stripped them of their political independence and personal freedom. It was an especially fitting metaphor given that her ancestors used storms as metaphors for violence.

"Driftwood" opened with an image of poor children collecting worn timbers off a beach to use as firewood. The following stanzas suggested that the histories of Natives and African Americans resembled the fate of a ship smashed to pieces in a storm. The essence of this and other lost vessels lived on in battered fragments that could still heat humble homes and light the way for passing voyagers. Driftwood was a source of hope to the Montaukett poet, not despair:

> Within my mind there dwells this lingering thought,
> How oft from ill the greatest good is wrought,
> Perhaps some shattered wreck along the strand,
> Will help to make the fire burn more bright,
> And for some weary traveller to-night,
> 'Twill serve the purpose of a guiding hand.
>
> Ah yes, and thus it is with these our lives,
> Some poor misshapen remnant still survives,

Of what was once a fair and beauteous form,
And yet some dwelling may be made more bright,
Some one afar may catch a gleam of light,
After the fury of the blighting storm.

Written in the absolute bleakest decade of American Indian history, when tribal populations and power were at their lowest, "Driftwood" was nonetheless an ode to cultural persistence. Even the most dissonant line, the reference to a "poor misshapen remnant" that echoes how most white writers insultingly described Indians in the 1890s, is countered by the following verses that recast the surviving elements of Native traditions as glowing beacons.[15]

Bush-Banks's imagery was also subtler than most coastal metaphors of cultural contact. She avoided the easy Turnerian cliché of likening her Indian forebears to the weathered margin of the continent and colonists to the dissolving sea. She chose a ship, a human-made structure that operates under human command, to represent the towering civilizations of her ancestors, while using natural imagery to evoke the Euro-American onslaught. Ships brought more than just the devastation wrought by first encounters or the Middle Passage. They could also be vessels of economic opportunity, structures that fostered new connections between people of color in a white-dominated society. The world of her ancestors now existed only in fragments, but the pieces retained their buoyancy. Even in flames, lost watercraft lived on as aids to navigation. In just eleven stanzas that long predated many reams of scholarship, Bush-Banks offered a maritime version of frontier history that neither ignored the violence Natives faced nor condemned them to drown in the currents of modernity.[16]

Methods, Limits, and Terms

This book draws evidence from English and Dutch letters, diaries, laws, administrative minutes, estate inventories, travel accounts, war narratives, and court records as well as from Native traditions, archaeological site reports, maps, and historic images of vessels and forts. These sources offer valuable quotations, and they also draw our attention to compelling artifacts, in both physical and written evidence that evokes the material world. Looking closely at physical objects helps create as vivid a picture as possible of the watery setting that Natives and colonists shared. Particular attention is given to watercraft, shell beads, wartime trophies, and forts, as the changing uses of these artifacts redefined relations between frontier neighbors. Anthropologists have long been interested in "the social life of things," that is, following the path of objects from person to person or from one society to another to uncover ideas held by the people who touched them.[17]

Biographies of things in contested regions can reveal the dense entanglements of societies in conflict, the strange ways in which seemingly opposing technologies, economies, and polities ended up overlapping. And there is no better way to understand an abstraction like a frontier than to envision how it really looked, to picture colonists hungrily eating freshly cooked meals served by Native women, coveting their stores of shell beads, and solemnly accepting grisly wartime trophies from their allies. Or to imagine Algonquians raising the walls of their own European-inspired forts, sewing shell jewelry onto imported woolen cloth, and placing their hands on the tillers of colonial vessels. Archaeological evidence also lets one peek behind the shoulders of elite Native men to catch glimpses of the larger indigenous communities they spoke for. The first two chapters in the book also rely on other methods borrowed from anthropologists: sidestreaming, which means combining evidence from neighboring culturally akin peoples, and upstreaming, that is, compressing accounts from different times. Despite the obvious perils of these slippery methods, they are helpful for discerning trends that crossed boundaries and for making informed guesses about how Indians perceived European actions.[18]

The following narrative is intended to be concise and provocative rather than magisterial or definitive. It is primarily about how three things– seafaring, violence, and Atlantic geopolitics–shaped one place. My use of such a tight focus to survey an entire region over a whole century inevitably leaves some peoples, problems, and events in the blurry background. For example, maritime encounters on freshwater lakes and rivers are seldom discussed, as the book is explicitly not about following colonists' inland creep but about tracing the processes that moved in the opposite direction.

Furthermore, the Dutch further up the Hudson at Fort Orange and the English north of Boston and south by Chesapeake Bay are only minor figures in this telling because they were peripheral to the chain of maritime events that connected the fates of New England and New Netherland. The same is true of many neighboring Iroquoian and Algonquian peoples as well as nearby French and Swedish colonists. Readers seeking biographies of major Native and colonial figures, histories of specific sachemships and colonies, and studies of the region that focus on gender, slavery, religion, communication, trade networks, and ecology can turn to the endnotes for a long reading list.[19]

Another limit of this book comes from using just one language to write about a place where more than seven were spoken. Snippets of Algonquian dialects and Dutch appear throughout, reminders of the many tongues that coexisted along this coast. Rather than chase the impossible goal of ridding American English of its colonial legacies, the aim is to acknowledge complexity but favor clarity. Sometimes indigenous peoples appear generically as *locals*, *Natives*, and *Indians*, but whenever possible they appear with the names they called themselves, such as Raritans, Wampanoags, Hackensacks, Montauketts. Naming the people from the eastern side of the Atlantic is also complicated. The use of terms like *foreigners*, *invaders*, *Europeans*, and *colonists* is straightforward; slightly trickier is the occasional use of *Christian*, which was their preferred generic term to differentiate themselves from locals. It becomes problematic later in the seventeenth century as some Algonquian people would also become followers of Jesus Christ. Not every English-speaking colonist was a hardline Calvinist who wished to purify the Church of England; nonetheless, *Puritan* is an accurate descriptor of most of those colonies' elites, especially those of Massachusetts Bay, Connecticut, and New Haven. Calling the New Netherland colonists *Dutch* is a stretch in the same way *Puritan* is for New England: it is the correct term for most authorities but not the ordinary people, as the colony's population was a diverse mix of various European and African ethnicities.

When it comes to describing physical American geography, the present-day place-names sometimes used serve to keep the reader oriented.

Native names for this shore are surely the most intriguing, as they represent the most ancient, detailed map but also the most difficult to get right. Typically rendered in multiple spellings by colonists with varying degrees of familiarity with Native languages, Algonquian place-names were themselves changed by encounters with Europeans or corrupted by generations of English and Dutch speakers, then often given spurious etymologies by well-meaning local historians. Even experts in Algonquian dialects find the task of translating place-names difficult. Still, the dominant theme in Native names is intensive description of the usefulness and variety of this coast. For example, *Sewanhacky*, a name for Long Island, referred to the island's reputation as a place rich with shells and apt for bead making; *Connecticut*, a place on both the island and mainland, referred to a settlement by a long tidal river. Algonquian place-names could function as a set of detailed directions and a travel guide, evoking the shore as it looked from the hold of a canoe. Natives' geographical imagination was not the same as Europeans', so labels do not always match up tidily, the invaders coining new terms for major features while retaining local words for smaller ones.[20]

Dutch explorers often described terrain in the simplest, most functional adjectives, as in *'t Lange* (The Long) *Eylandt*, *Varsche* (Fresh) *Rivier*, *Noord* (North) *Rivier*, *Oost* (East) *Rivier*, *Roodt* (Red) *Eylandt*, while the English also liked to adopt Native names or include slightly more poetic references to local wildlife, such as *Oyster Bay*, *Buzzards Bay*, and *Cape Cod*. Both were apt to litter their maps with references to European peoples and locales, as in *Adriaen Blocx Eylandt*, *Elizabeth's Island*, *Nieuw Amsterdam*, and *Plymouth*. Even some seemingly Native-inspired place-names were pretty much colonial inventions. *Tappan Zee*, for instance, is a Munsee-Dutch mash-up: Tappans were the people who lived near this wide point in the Hudson that Netherlanders likened to a sea. *Narragansett Bay*, another hybrid term, was more English than Algonquian, as Indians did not see that particular confluence of estuaries as one feature, and the bay was divided almost equally between Wampanoags and Narragansetts. For that matter, even the colonists who named it could not agree on where it ended and began.[21]

Throughout the following chapters there are plenty of reminders that we should think of Indian sachemships, English colonies, and Dutch colonies

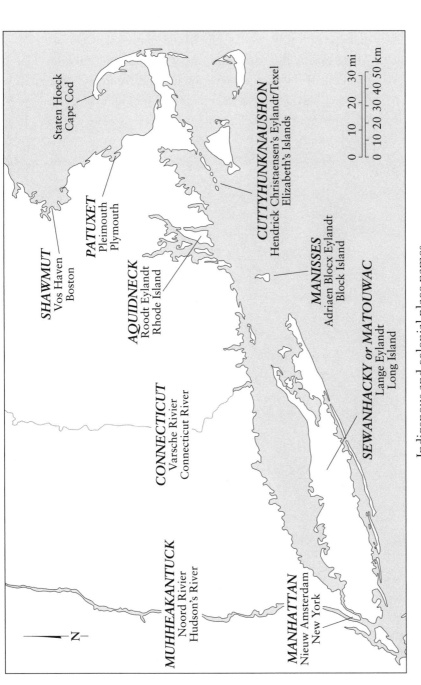

MUHHEAKANTUCK
Noord Rivier
Hudson's River

MANHATTAN
Nieuw Amsterdam
New York

CONNECTICUT
Varsche Rivier
Connecticut River

SHAWMUT
Vos Haven
Boston

PATUXET
Pleimouth
Plymouth

AQUIDNECK
Roodt Eylandt
Rhode Island

Staten Hoeck
Cape Cod

CUTTYHUNK/NAUSHON
Hendrick Christaensen's Eylandt/Texel
Elizabeth's Islands

MANISSES
Adriaen Blocx Eylandt
Block Island

SEWANHACKY or MATOUWAC
Lange Eylandt
Long Island

0   10   20   30 mi

0 10 20 30 40 50 km

N

Indigenous and colonial place-names.

as porous, elastic realms rather than as concrete parts of the continent. Colonists and Indians alike would experience many moments of being unsure of where exactly they were and who was in control. All knew that names and borders could change suddenly. Perhaps we should, like mariners, become accustomed to constant motion and mind the things beneath the surface that cannot be seen. Then we can start to explore this coast in the seventeenth century.

ONE

The Giants' Shore

Once there was a moody giant who roamed the waters from the Hudson River to Cape Cod and ate roasted whales for breakfast. When he enjoyed a pipe, the smoke became fogbanks that shrouded the coast for miles. With taps of ash from his pipe's bowl, he created the two sandy lumps we now call Martha's Vineyard and Nantucket. In his amphibious adventures he was sometimes graceful, sometimes clumsy, and always emotional. In one story a crab bit his hand just as he was rolling boulders across the waters west of Cape Cod, causing him to abandon his rocks and fling the pinching crustacean all the way to Nantucket to spawn a local crab fishery. In another fit of pique he transformed his wife into a wave-swept cluster of tiny islands near the mouth of Narragansett Bay and morphed his children into fierce killer whales.[1]

The stories often ended with the towering man disappearing into the deep. In various tellings he made an angry dash toward the open ocean, pelting various bays with massive boulders and creating several chains of stepping-stones across the region. Just before he dove into the sea he left massive footprints on the mainland and islands as though the stone were mud. Munsees called the pacing titan Maughkampoe; Narragansetts, Pequots, and Mohegans knew him as Weetucks; Wampanoags named him Maushop. Later English-speaking Christian Natives at times referred to him as the Evil Spirit or the Devil, though a devout colonist who listened to "many strange Relations of one Wétucks" fixed on the stories in which he strode upon water and suggested he bore "some kind of broken Resemblance to the Sonne of God."[2]

Yet this brooding colossus was quite unlike the only child Europeans worshipped. He shared a crowded land-and-seascape with many other spirits, including little people, magical animals, and capricious gods who needed constant reminders of humans' gratitude through gifts of food and tobacco. These immortal actors' fluid spiritual power, which Natives called *menutto* or *manitou*, could shape or influence all things, living and inanimate. And few places were more obviously sites of manitou than the sea, with its constant creation and destruction. Water itself could be seen as "the threshold to the underworld," the cusp of the known and the unknown. Creatures that crossed this dangerous boundary were especially potent. Thus stranded whales, whose bodies were rich with meat and oil, were seen as prized gifts from Maushop or Weetucks, while beads fashioned from whelks and hard-shelled clams were treasured. The giant's tantrums also accounted for a number of the region's geological oddities: the sandier soil in outlying peninsulas and islands, the erratic strings of wayward boulders and rocky islets scattered from west to east, the deep grooves where it looked like something huge had scoured the earth.[3]

Modern geologists have another explanation for these features, and their story stars an icy giant. About twenty-five thousand years ago, in the midst of the last Ice Age, a mile-thick glacial sheet plowing south from the Arctic reached the site of these shores. This part of the earth was not a shoreline then. The global sea level was four hundred feet lower, placing the ancient coast well to the south and east. The glacier advanced and retreated several times in its long life, scraping the land like an enormous rusty razor, leaving deep scars on the continent's face, and tilling a vast wake of soil and rock in front of it.

Some eighteen thousand to ten thousand years ago, as the ice sheet made its slow, final retreat, it left behind two long belts of glacial debris running west to east called moraines. As the Atlantic Ocean rose to its present level, it drowned these leftover rinds of dirt. The moraines gave shape to the sandy masses of islands and peninsulas that stretched in an east–west chain from Sandy Hook to Cape Cod. While frozen water gave this shore its rough

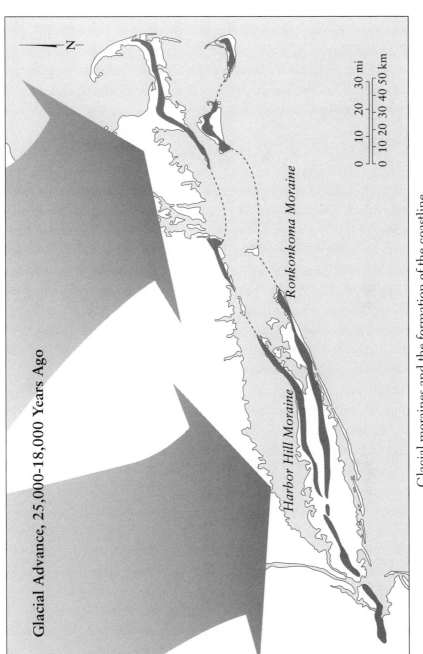

Glacial moraines and the formation of the coastline.

shape, the liquid sea is constantly refining it. The exchange of sand with waves and tides can swiftly build and demolish beaches, barrier islands, and underwater shoals. As sea levels continue to rise, the ocean will swallow chunks of the shore whole. The outermost island of Nantucket, for example, may exist only for another seven hundred years before waves wear it down to a mere sandbank.[4]

A Connected Coast

The tracks of these massive bodies trace the outline of a coherent region. Geographers have long seen something distinctive about the geology and ecology of the area's strand of connected bays. Seeking a term that transcends the artificial frames of *New York* and *New England,* the nature writer Dorothy Sterling coined the title "outer lands" for the sandy archipelago and peninsulas that stand between the main and the ocean. She pointed out that this shore's shared glacial ancestor makes it unlike the rest of the seaboard to the north and south. The east–west slope of this coastline is contained in fewer than two degrees of latitude, giving it a nearly uniform climate and range of land and marine species.[5]

While the ice sheet was the architect of the shore, the mythic man is a fitting symbol of its peoples. In his travels the giant illustrates the subtle shifts in local traditions, as there was not one giant but several. His feats changed from west to east to suit the immediate coastline, while his name switched from Maughkampoe to Weetucks to Maushop. The gradual shift in languages was obvious to the traveler who remarked that among the region's Natives "every Countrey doe something differ in their Speech." The peoples living along the lower Hudson spoke Munsee Algonquian dialects that were distinct from the languages spoken to the east. Differences between dialects also coincided loosely with some distinctions in local politics and geographies.[6]

Though his various guises demonstrate the region's continuum of cultures, the giant is a unifying figure as well. His fame ranged far and wide: as one colonist reported, "The Indians for 100 miles about" the Hudson "all agreed in one Story of a Gyant." These recurring stories of a huge spirit in

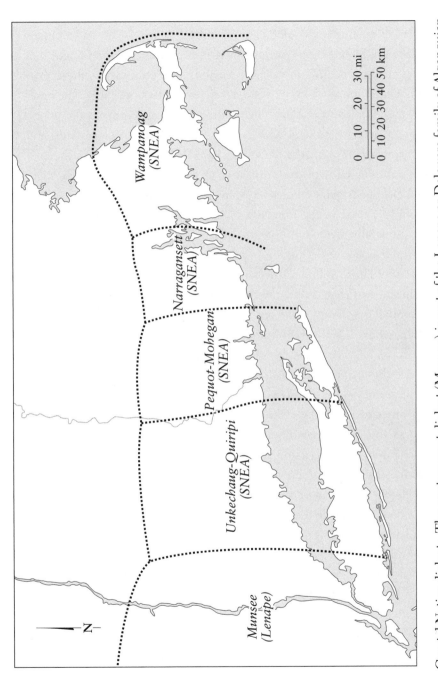

Coastal Native dialects. The westernmost dialect (Munsee) is part of the Lenape or Delaware family of Algonquian languages; the rest belong to the Southern New England Algonquian (SNEA) family.

the water were one of many ways these peoples resembled each other. The similar diets, buildings, clothes, and beliefs of proximate Algonquians impressed a Dutch colonist who visited Plymouth in 1628 and found that "tribes in their neighborhood have all the same customs" as those near Manhattan, though he noted a few exceptions to that sweeping statement. Later anthropologists also have few qualms about using observations of one group to make inferences about others, noting that constant trade and marriages between villages made it certain that many people in the area were multilingual. However, in a strange coincidence later Dutch-Anglo colonial bounds came close to a Native dialect border, which has served to split this coast in the minds of some historians. For too long scholars have artificially divided a shoreline that had many points of cultural and political overlap.[7]

What did this region look like around 1600, when only a tiny number of Europeans had ever visited and their cultural influence was minimal? To answer that question, I will focus first on the broad-stroke cultural similarities shared by all Natives, from their diets to their politics, then switch to a finer brush to trace the local differences in their political bodies. Unlike other studies that typically favor either Dutch or English sources, this sightseeing journey relies on both, looking for moments when the texts echo each other to help us see through anachronistic colonial boundaries to uncover the Native coastline. This view relies as well on upstreaming, drawing from accounts dating from as early as 1524 to as late as the 1720s.

Ecologists and environmental historians offer further clues as to how the economies of the Native coast worked. Their insights suggest that the shore's indigenous cultures and environments cannot be considered separately, as each had a profound impact on the other. And though this is just a snapshot, the work of archaeologists and anthropologists keeps the subjects from standing too still. Numerous digs have shown that coastal peoples were reckoning with sweeping economic and cultural transformations that had been under way for centuries, and these changes were subtly altering the flow of power within their households and among their villages. Together, these many streams of evidence reveal a shore of neighboring societies that were both dynamic and maritime well before foreign ships appeared on the horizon.

It is hard to say for sure how many people lived here in 1600. Scholars only have a handful of fuzzy colonial estimates to plug into tricky demographic equations, and given the many variables, they often disagree. The best guess is around ninety thousand people, a sparse number by modern standards but not by global norms of the time.[8] Indeed, the first foreigner to write about this coast described it as being densely populated; later colonists characterized the same shores as "so populous a Country" that a traveler "shall come to many Townes, some bigger, some lesser," at a density of a dozen villages every twenty miles. The more teeming towns were home to hundreds of residents living in clusters of bark-sided, dome-roofed portable buildings that the English called wigwams. Some settlements surpassed two thousand people during the planting and harvesting seasons. The Narragansetts' bayside capital, for example, contained so many wigwams during the spring of 1636 that one visitor called it a "great Citty." That might sound like a mild exaggeration, but at the time that Narragansett "Citty" was bigger than New Amsterdam and Boston combined. Smaller mobile villages and hamlets with only a hundred people or fewer were also common.[9]

Locals placed their primary settlements near estuaries and surrounded them with sprawling cornfields. They lived near their fields for planting in the wet bloom of spring and for harvesting during the crisp, technicolor autumns. Villagers relocated to more sheltered spots for the snowy winters and moved to the breezy coast at the humid height of summer. Rivers and trails served as busy arteries binding these mobile communities to the rest of the continent, while the protected waters created by the glacier created passages for local fleets of dugout canoes. Linguistic and political maps illustrate that the region's five major dialects and many polities bridged this central chain of bays. This was a place where the sea had long been a conduit, not a barrier.[10]

Corn and Fish, Women and Men

Like all frequent travelers, coastal Algonquians valued hospitality. Newcomers reported that they "invite all Strangers in . . . upon any occasion," "providing the best victuals they could" and insisting that "any one shall eate with them" and "strangers must be first served." "One can hardly ever enter an Indian dwelling" without being offered "wooden dishes" filled with a food that modern Americans would recognize as grits, a wholesome porridge made by boiling coarse, parched cornmeal. Narragansetts called it *aupúminea-nawsaùmp* while Munsees near the Hudson knew it as *sappaen*, and its "use among the Indians is so general that rarely a day passes without their eating it." Cooking their grits in clay pots with conical bottoms suspended over fires, Native women "frequently boil[ed] in this pottage fish and flesh of all sorts." Fish was the most common meat in the summer, and cooks liked to season their stews with "a fatty broth" made from "the naturall liquor" of clams.[11]

Many favorite local delicacies were seafood: villagers "delight[ed] in" littleneck clams, they had a "lascivious" appetite for "a daintie dish" of the heads of striped bass, and they roasted up the meaty tails of whales as a treat and gave whale meat as a gift. Later colonists looking to purchase the Indians' surplus sturgeon found that the locals, "for the goodness and great-ness of it, much prize" the fish, asking so much in trade that the newcomers concluded it would be cheaper to catch their own. Starchy corn grits was also the source of many cravings. As one of their later neighbors observed, "All of them, including women, children, and old people, are so attached and used to" their grits that "when they visit us or one another they first of all ask and look for *sappaen*. Without it one cannot entertain them to their liking, nor can they, so it seems, eat their fill."[12]

Guests who sampled the region's cuisine gave it mixed reviews. One picky traveler faulted his hosts for "dishing it up in a rude manner," griping that they consider "it a great discourtesie not to eat of their high-conceited delicates," which he found hard to stomach, as the meat in the grits could be either nearly raw or else boiled to "a loathed mush." Another fussy fellow complained that Indian women "have no pride or particular fashion in preparing and serving," while another feared the "danger of being choked with fish bones" from their stews. However, some newcomers praised the "delicious flavor" of the "so sweet toothsome and hearty" cornmeal, finding that the "very whole-some" grits promoted regularity and that the popular snack of ash-baked corn-cakes was "excellent eating" and "good bread, but heavy."[13]

Regardless of foreign opinions, these villagers' everyday dishes of starch and meat, when looked at closely, can tell us a lot. There was a good reason

Indian leaders consistently used "the common pot" or "one dish" as a powerful metaphor for shared spaces and alliance: the practice of serving from a single vessel was the simplest way to demonstrate goodwill among peoples. And in light of its environmental sources, this savory, fishy porridge reveals how the region's Natives were constantly combining traditions and innovations, as some practices, especially fishing and shell fishing, were indeed quite ancient, while maize-centered farming had become prevalent just a few centuries earlier. Those servings of cornmeal stew also should be seen as the product of an uneven divide between genders, as much of the work to prepare those meals fell into the hands of women. More broadly, tracing foodways back to their origins divulges how these peoples' economies straddled the land and sea.[14]

The large servings of seafood in Algonquian diets were the product of the shoreline's robust estuarine ecology. There is always an immense flourishing of life in the places where warm, nutrient-rich freshwater mixes with the colder sea, and the region's unique geological features only amplified this effect, making it "one of the most productive landforms in the world, rivaling intensive agricultural lands in food productivity." The rainy American Northeast is laced with river systems that dump millions of gallons of continental runoff into the ocean every second. The glacial remnants of the outer lands act as a kind of staggered gate standing between river mouths and the open ocean, feeding the shore's many river estuaries into the larger bays of New York Harbor, Long Island Sound, Narragansett Bay, Buzzard's Bay, Vineyard Sound, and Nantucket Sound. These bays remain in constant flux between ocean currents and river flows, creating ideal homes for a host of tiny simple creatures like krill, seaweed, and jellyfish that thrive in the slosh of sweet and saltwater. When the dense clusters of microscopic life in estuaries get thick, blooms of bioluminescent plankton make the nighttime surf glow an eerie blue-green.[15]

The abundant tiny plants and animals held in the region's bays were attractive food sources for both shellfish and finfish. Nearer to shore, long-necked waterbirds poked their bills under water to graze and hunt in thickets of seaweed. At the water's edge the glacier had left behind a diverse shore that alternated between rocky, sandy, and marshy stretches. Those meadows of marsh grass teemed with insects and worms, a buzzing and crawling feast for migrating birds, as the whole region sits at a key junction between continental and Atlantic flyways. Shaggy carpets of algae and crusty bands of barnacles covered the rocky shores, while mussels, snails, and crabs thrived in the rocks' cracks and pools. Even the seemingly barren sandy beaches hid rich banks of clams in their mudflats and delicate nests of plovers in their dune grass. These shores were so full of life that they constantly bled streams of nutrients into even deeper waters, nourishing offshore fisheries on banks on the continental shelf and drawing whales that came to swallow clouds of small fish and krill.[16]

Natives knew just how rich their waters were, comparing "their store in the Sea, to the haires of their heads," and newcomers agreed. "There is no countrey known," one stated plainly, "that yeelds more variety of fish." Another wrote of "sea fish and river fish in such great abundance there, that they cannot be sold." The crew of a newly arrived ship in these waters got so carried away loading their deck with codfish they had to toss "numbers of them over-boord againe" and so named the nearby peninsula Cape Cod. Soon thereafter, passing to the north of Martha's Vineyard, they saw beaches littered "with many huge bones and ribbes of Whales." Though colonial promoters typically wrote in a breathless style to lure investors, even they worried that their descriptions of sea life would read as exaggerations. "The aboundance of Sea-Fish are almost beyond beleeving," one remarked, "sure I should scarce have beleeved it except I had seene it with mine owne Eyes." The famed explorer John Smith began his description of the region by apologizing for all the fish that filled his pages, writing "because I speake so much of fishing, if any take mee for such a devote fisher . . . they mistake mee." He simply could not ignore the obvious wealth in the waters.[17]

Shellfish were also plentiful and grew to mammoth sizes, dwarfing what you might find at a modern-day raw bar. Travelers reported "clammes as bigge as a pennie white loafe," oysters in shells "a foot long and correspondingly wide," and even spoke of lobsters that were "five or six feet long," an exaggeration reflecting Europeans' awe at the mature American lobster, which can live a hundred years and grow to a weight of fifty pounds. Noting the locals' expertise as fishermen, newcomers would quiz their Native neighbors about various kinds of sea life. A Connecticut woman curious about strange shells she discovered on the northern shores of Long Island Sound in 1673 learned that "the Indians think" this particular species "does grow in the sound where the water is 20 or 30 fathames deep." To this day the leftovers of Algonquians' coastal feasts are strewn on these shores, as piles of shells are the most obvious telltale of a former village site. Though seafood was a major protein source in all coastal villagers' diet, on the island of Nantucket, where corn and game were often scarce, archaeologists believe two-thirds of the people's daily calorie intake came from marine life.[18]

No matter how bountiful the shore appeared, working its waters was never easy. One writer felt it necessary to append to his description of American fishing the warning that fish would not "leape into the kettle, nor on the drie land, neither are they so plentifull, that you may dipp them up in baskets." Native men caught most of the finfish, as part of the larger pattern of divided labor that kept women closer to hearths and children. These fishermen built stone and wooden gates in rivers to trap spawning schools, hunted their prey with spears and arrows from bark canoes in rivers and bays, launched heavier oceangoing dugouts to haul in offshore species, and went ice fishing on ponds in the winter. "Wild hemp," which more than one colonist character- ized as "a stronger material than our own," could make "a drag net they themselves knit very neatly." To catch striped bass they wove nets "seventy to eighty fathoms in length" (nearly five hundred feet) rigged with stone sinkers and wooden floats and stretched them near river mouths.[19]

These nets were occasionally adorned with reminders of the respect and gratitude the fishermen owed the powerful spirits or manitou who ruled the comings and goings of sea life. One colonist observed "over the purse" of one bass net "a figure made of wood, resembling the Devil"—probably a god of the ocean or fish. "When the fish swim into the net and come to the purse, so that the figure begins to move, they then begin to cry out and call upon the Mannetoe, that is, the Devil, to give them more fish." "The Natives take exceeding great paines in their fishing," another witness wrote, marveling that in search of a good catch men would stay out all night watching for a run or checking to see if anything had landed in their river nets. Europeans praised their techniques as being "very expert," as they were skilled at "fitting sundry baites for severall fishes, and diverse seasons," though sweet lobster meat seems to have been a popular lure. Indian mariners coming back to shore worked alongside their wives to dry their catch "in the Sunne and smoake" so it could be stored and later reconstituted in a simmering pot of cornmeal.[20]

Women and children were responsible for shell fishing, which could be deceptively difficult work. Male colonists pitied women "who trudge to the Clam-bankes," where they raked, dug, and dove for mollusks and periodically hiked "two or three miles with a hundred weight of Lobsters at their backs." Once returned home with their heavy baskets of shellfish, women set about prying shells open and preserving the meat alongside fish fillets in wooden smokehouses. Indian men then fashioned the shells of whelks and hard-shelled clams into the small beads, best known as *wampum*, that became a sacred object given in rituals of diplomacy, condolence, marriage, and trade. Mollusks and crustaceans were certainly an old food source. Heaps of peoples' shell debris on the coast date back at least three millennia, and some archaeologists wonder if clusters of ancient oyster shells found in the nets of modern fishing trawlers may in fact be markers of the campsites of paleo-Indians who foraged along Ice Age shores.[21]

Corn, by contrast, arrived several centuries before colonists. People on this coast started growing it as a major crop only around the year 1000 CE, though the kernels they planted had a long and distant ancestry. Farmers in the tropics of Central America had raised the nutritionally balanced trio of maize, beans, and squash as staples for some two thousand years. These crops, which some Indians called the three sisters, began to spread rapidly from Mexico and the Southwest into the eastern woodlands of North America with the onset of a climate shift that scientists call the Medieval Warm Period (900–1300 CE). The flux in global temperatures extended the growing season and made it less risky to try out new crops, ushering in an agricultural revolution that caused population spikes in parts of the continent and led to the rise of bustling trading towns and cities throughout the Southeast and along the Mississippi and Ohio valleys.[22]

The giants' coast was at the fringe of these continental transformations, and here corn, beans, and squash did not unleash so many dramatic changes.

Those living along fertile river valleys took most quickly to the new crops. While cornfields became widespread on the shores three or four centuries before the first European ship arrived, there were coastal pockets where locals still relied heavily on hunting, gathering, and fishing. The adoption of corn was an ongoing process through the colonial period and was possibly intensified by the arrival of hungry colonists willing to trade for surplus harvests. Some Native historians' accounts of the arrival of tropical crops sounded the same as archaeologists': they recounted that "beans and corn came to them from the southern Indians who had earlier obtained them from people living still farther south." The same informants also remembered a not-too-distant time "before they knew of corn" when "they ate tree bark or roots instead of bread." Others shared a "tradition that the Crow brought them first an Indian Graine of Corne in one Eare, and an Indian or French Beane in another, from the Great God *Kantántouwits* field in the Southwest from whence they hold came all their Corne and Beanes."[23]

The Southwest was both a physical direction and a place that could not be reached via mere earthly canoes or paths. It was the land of the dead, ruled over by an aloof but generous creator god. Indians described it as "a kind of paradise wherein they shall everlastingly abide," filled with "odiferous gardens, fruitful cornfields, green meadows" and "cool streams of pleasant rivers," a place where "one never needs protective covering against the cold, yet not so hot as to be uncomfortable." Visits from thievish, clever crows were links to the mythic Southwest. Indians near the Hudson reported that "when they die they go to a place where they sing like the ravens," while Narragansetts had a taboo against killing crows, even when the birds picked at their ears of corn. Since belief in the "Great God" and reverence for corvids were so closely tied to corn, squash, and beans, perhaps the moment when women first started maize farming was also a spiritual transition as well. The orienting of corn-raising peoples' cosmos toward the maize giver could be seen in numerous grave sites in the area where the dead were buried on their sides, in the fetal position, facing southwest.[24]

The crow's gifts had reordered life as well as death. Following a pattern that was common in villages everywhere east of the Mississippi, women planted corn in "heaps like molehills" with "their natural Howes of shells and

Wood" in April, then added beans in May, and weeded throughout the spring and summer. They shucked and dried the mature corn in late September or early October, storing their harvest in "barnes"—cellars, really—deep pits in dry soil. Farmers packed their harvests in clay pots and "greate baskets," lined their containers with reed mats and "rinds of trees" to keep pests and water out, then sealed the "barne" with a thick layer of topsoil. Indian women raised "so much corn and green beans" that colonists were still trading for their surpluses every autumn as late as the 1650s, sailing away from villages "in fully laden yachts and sloops." Unsurprisingly, Native farmers would "regard their methods as much better" than those of the newcomers.[25]

While the farming of corn, beans, and squash filled villagers' cellars and bowls, the diverse workloads of farmers and hunters revealed a rift between the genders. "The women live a most slavish life," male colonists claimed, being "compelled to work like asses" "above the labour of men," assembling houses, making clothes, harvesting shellfish, planting crops, grinding corn-meal, cooking food, making pottery, raising children, and bearing "mighty Burthens." Part of this critique stemmed from the European notion that farming was men's work, hunting was an aristocratic leisure activity, and therefore Native economies were dangerously backward if men allowed "their Wives [to be] the Husbandmen to till the Land." However distorted the colonial gaze was, though, there is ample evidence that in Algonquian households men were dominant over women. Colonists reported that a husband who caught his wife cheating "thrashes her soundly" "before many witnesses, by many blowes and wounds," even to the point of death. Clearly adult women faced a much greater social stigma for promiscuity than men. And much like European women at the time, Native women had less of a say in public affairs.[26]

In areas where corn was the main staple of the diet, the central, life-providing labor performed by Native women could be seen down to their bones. Female skeletal remains unearthed from seventeenth-century burial sites in the region had noticeably more worn wrist bones than males, and their knees showed evidence of "habitual kneeling," stress injuries from decades spent grinding cornmeal and weeding fields. Their dental remains prove that women ate a maize-heavy, meat-poor diet. Excess sugars in their starchy diet took a toll: old Algonquian women had more cavities and missing teeth than men of the same age. Further, these women were buried with hoes, mortars, and pestles that showed nearly as much hard use as their joints.[27]

Still, Native women had some rights that were unknown to their colonial counterparts. As teenagers they enjoyed a period of sexual freedom before finding a husband, and married women were allowed to "leave their husbands frequently, upon grounds of displeasure or disaffection." "If a woman ha[d] a bad husband" she could not only seek divorce but also move to a neighboring village, "where [women] never come unwelcome: for where are most women, there is greatest plenty." The very act of planting served as a constant reminder of female economic power. The growing season began in "a very loving sociable speedy way" in late March, when "all neighbours, men and Women" in a single village "joyne and come in to help freely" in breaking up the soil of the cornfields. In the months to come, men generally left the crops to women's care, "unless they are very young or very old," or, more rarely, a man might lend a hand "either out of love to his Wife or care for his Children." Still, the cornfields were clearly female spaces: any man deigning to "help the women" did so "under the latter's direction." Farming could be seen as a restrictive force in women's lives, but it also created a zone within villages where female authority was supreme.[28]

Men's primary space on land, the woods, was also more complex than colonists realized — in part because their tendency to stick close to the coast hid the intricate social and ecological spaces of the woodlands. These forests, filled with countless trails, traps, and campsites, were hardly an untouched wilderness, nor were they places of leisure. Indians saw their woodlands as both game reserves and gardens that required regular management. Algonquian men set seasonal fires to clear undergrowth from the forest floor, "an extraordinary and spectacular event," above all "when one sails on the rivers at night while the forest is ablaze on both banks." Regular burning cleared the way for easy foot travel, while ashes became a potent fertilizer, creating an artificial landscape that was highly suited for people's hunting and collecting needs. Fire-enriched soil anchored hardwood forests heavy with maples that leaked sugary sap plus oaks and chestnuts that littered the ground with wholesome, protein-rich nuts. Especially at the edges of recently burned areas, colorful clusters of vitamin-loaded berries flourished in dense bushes, which in turn allowed game populations to spike.[29]

Coastal Algonquians hunted all sorts of furry, feathered, and scaly creatures on land, but their most sought-after catch was the bounding white-tailed deer, a prey that rewarded its hunters with ample cuts of meat and large skins. Herds flourished in the parklike, green-canopied forests and sometimes grew to over two hundred head, making deer "general and wonderfull plenteous hunting" and venison the most common meat after seafood in corn-grit stews. Men stalked deer with arrows, set dozens of traps at a time, drove herds into elaborate corrals, even lassoed swimming whitetails from their canoes as herds swam across rivers. Woodlands were not exclusively male spaces either. Women frequently traveled there in search of berries and nuts and hunted small game. Forest creatures were the main source of clothing. Deerskin and fur mantles were the standard outerwear, though Natives also wove wild turkey feathers into downy, soft coats, made belts of snakeskins, whalebone, and shell beads, and fashioned tanned leather into medicine bags, tobacco pouches, stockings, and moccasins. Underneath they wore a loincloth, the sole covering some men used outdoors in warmer months. English writers delicately described the primary male garment as "Adam's Apron" for "their secret parts." But the Dutch more frankly called it a *clootlap*, or "balls cover." Colonists noted that Indians "smear their bodies and hair with grease," intending these formulas of fish oils and animal fats to function as heat insulators, mosquito repellants, and sunblock. To European noses this anointing made them "smell very rankly."[30]

Natives worked other landscapes of the ecologically diverse patchwork of the Northeast besides seas, fields, and forests. Depending on where they lived, they would have been familiar with the distinct pockets of species around riverine floodplains, bogs, salt marshes, pine barrens, and heath. And there were a number of reciprocal, material links between their work in forests, fields, and saltwater. Wooded hunting grounds near good water could be converted into villages and then back into woods. In clearing of land, stumps of trees could become mortars to grind corn. Trunks could be carved into massive canoes fit to plow through ocean swells. Some forest overgrowth was destined to become fish food. Ash from intentional fires carried by wind or water added phosphorous and potassium to the nutrient load in estuarine waters, fortifying the already robust offshore food webs. Likewise, decomposing fish carcasses became fertilizer for hills of corn while shells became the blades of hoes that cleared cornfields.[31]

Tracing the routes of fish from the sea, corn from the tropics, and venison from the woods into a steaming bowl of porridge does not even come close to portraying a total picture of coastal Native life. Nor can a quick introduction to the temperamental giant and the corn-giving god in the Southwest tell us about the many sources of manitou or spiritual power that shaped the world as these villagers saw it. But as we turn to look at the flow of power within and among villages we can see further regional trends. Algonquian leaders and followers, like Algonquian men and women, formed unequal but negotiated relationships. And the shape and character of their polities, like that of their economies, were tied to the spaces where the continent met the ocean. To understand the structure of local governments, however, we have to start by looking at the elemental links that held these societies together.

Bloodlines and Bloodshed

On these shores ancestry mattered. Colonists noticed that Natives "reckon consanguinity to the eighth degree" and "are carefull to preserve the memory of their families, mentioning Uncles, Grandfathers, and Grandmothers, &c and much studying the advancing of their houses and kindred." Interest in genealogy was more than a hobby. The anthropologist Kathleen Bragdon points out that in this region's languages family terms took on distinct forms depending on the speaker. For instance, Natives had no independent words like *daughter*, *father*, or *brother*. They only had words that, if rendered crudely in English, would sound like *mydaughter, yourfather, hisbrother*. A speaker could not identify a person within a family without explaining that person's connection to either himself or to someone else in that person's family. This pattern of "intimate possession" in Algonquian dialects, which also applied to words for houses and body parts, meant that links between peoples and things that could be hidden in translation were always explicit to indigenous speakers. These word structures reflected a way of speaking and perhaps of thinking in which family ties were inescapable.[32]

Lines of blood and fictive relations were central to how Indians saw the flow of power within and beyond their local villages. Coastal peoples were fond of using their binding, intimate words for family members in a more elastic way to describe political relationships. Algonquian speech was often infused with metaphor, as a colonist who learned the Narragansett dialect commented, "Similitudes greatly please them." The various ways of saying *brother* and *sister* could be stretched to refer to cousins and allies, while *father* and *uncle* could also be used as an honorific rather than literal address. A telling example came in a momentous speech given by the Narragansett sachem Miantonomi, who proposed forming a grand alliance of sachems across the coast. Addressing a gathering of Long Island sachems, "calling them brethren and friends," he urged his fellow leaders to "say brother to one another." Calling a nonrelative brother—or, more accurately, *neémat*, "mybrother"—was no mere sentimental affectation but a firm agreement of mutual accountability. "They hold the band of brotherhood so dear," one colonist marveled, that one brother could be rightfully executed for the other's crime and debts. Political speech was loaded with this sense of obligation, as Algonquian leaders and followers discussed their relations with their imagined brothers in terms of affection and grievance. And those leaders, called *sachemas* or *sachems*, further legitimized their right to rule through bloodlines.[33]

Kinship therefore created a social hierarchy made up of households. "Indians recognize some as noble born and others as commoners," a Dutch colonist wrote, noting that "the oldest and foremost of the households and families, together with the supreme chief, represent the whole nation." An English writer differentiated between Native aristocrats, "whose descent was from Ancestors, who had time out of mind been esteemed," and the commoners, who were further "distinguished by two names or titles, the one signifying subjection and the other Tiller of the Land." Another colonist claimed even that the "two sorts" of Indians, nobles and yeomen, had distinct sets of manners: either they were "sober and grave, and yet chearfull" or else "Rude and Clownish." Though kin and status were linked, when compared to the steep ladder of social stations in Europe, "differences among the Indians are not nearly as great and obvious," while feats of war may have given men some social mobility: "The lowliest person can become the greatest military chief, but the rank dies with the person." The same Dutch account implied that deference toward sachems and their families was truly granted only when earned: "The commoners show little respect for rank unless it is accompanied by courage and energy, and then it really counts."[34]

Sachems' dynasties followed complex rules that modern anthropologists are still trying to work out, but one typical line of succession went from a male sachem to either his son or nephew. Women apparently stepped into the office of *squaw sachem* only if there was no suitable male heir. Male leaders worked to accumulate outward symbols of their spiritual power. Along with other elite men, they often had "two or three Wives," while "Men of ordinary Rank" had one; extra wives could multiply their elite husband's reproductive potential. When appearing before any public meeting, sachems typically brought an entourage of "Attendants" or "a Company of armed men"; in wartime the more weighty sachems traveled with over a hundred escorts at a time, closely trailed by an elite corps that acted as "a special Guard, like unto a Life-Guard."[35]

Leaders lived in large houses fit to hold their multiple wives and broods of children and to host any visiting guests. They sometimes raised ceremonial long houses that stretched up to two hundred feet in length and could accommodate indoor meetings and seasonal gatherings. Though Native officials did not have the paper bureaucracies that Europeans typically associated with government, their politics followed a number of scripts. A yearly calendar of feasts, dances, and prayers led by elite men and shamans helped bind communities together and reinforce sachems' right to rule. A sachem's elite supporters and ordinary villagers gave him tributary gifts, including wampum beads, animal pelts, prized kills, and maize. The leader then redistributed these offerings, creating a continuous orbit of gifts flowing between them and their defenders, thereby fostering a sense of trust and obligation between both and justifying the sachems' claims to greater authority.[36]

Decision making was a collaborative process, involving the elder heads of households, men considered to be holy healers, and the "chiefest champions or men of valor," who debated public affairs along with the lead sachem. In meetings the sachem or a surrogate "gifted with eloquence and a strong, penetrating voice" set the agenda. A speaker would often brandish "a bundle of sticks" as props, his rhetorical "points being represented and remembered by means of wooden tallies," with the aim of building consensus around a decision. These meetings had a tendency to run long, as "they consider everything at great length and spare no time when the matter is of any importance." One impatient colonist who interrupted a Canarsie elder's speech justified his rudeness with an observation that might sound familiar to anyone who has ever sat through a rambling presentation: "This laying down of sticks began to be tedious to me, as I saw that he had many still in his hand." Elders could act as a check on a sachem's power; one such elite adviser told a colonist that his supposedly mighty sachem could not launch any military campaigns or alliances "without the advice and furtherance of men of that rank."[37]

The use of violence could enhance or secure a sachem's realm. When a leader "feared Mutiny," he might dispatch "a secret Executioner, one of his cheifest Warriors to fetch of[f] a head." These slayings were extraordinary events, as a colonist who noted that Indians at times practiced capital punishment was more generally "amazed that a human society can remain in existence where no stronger judicial authority prevails." Though top-down violence imposed by a sachem on his people was rare, bloodshed between rival villages and families was more common. Men were expected to avenge any murder of their kinsfolk, and this expectation could create cycles of retribution between families and whole sachemships, leading colonists to describe them as "very revengeful." Local wars were therefore short series of raids fought to resolve unjust deaths.[38]

Narragansetts' metaphoric terms for armed conflicts, *Chépewessin & Mishittâshin*, or the "Northerne storm of war," envisioned wars as natural manifestations of the darker side of human nature. *Mishittâshin* meant storm, while *Chépewessin* was the cold northeastern wind associated with the troublemaking, chaotic spirit *Cheepi*, the exact opposite of *Sowwánishen*, the southwestern coastal breezes that Indian mariners favored for their warmth and association with the holy direction of the corn-giver and the idyllic afterworld. It was no coincidence that Cheepi was linked to the Northeast, the same prevailing wind direction in the common weather systems that people in the region now call nor'easters. Natives' keen sense of the sea as a potentially destructive space was shaped by occasional visits from tropical hurricanes, like the one that slammed this shore in the late summer of 1635: a "mighty storm of wind and rain" that brought a twenty-foot storm surge, forcing "many of the Indians [to] climb into trees for their safety," knocking down "sundry houses" and "many hundred thousands of trees," and leaving "sign and marks" that would "remain this hundred years in these parts where it was sorest." Though Natives might have described the coming of war as the product of tempests beyond their control, their behavior in battle was highly ordered and tied to deeper cultural ideas.[39]

Rules of bloodshed reinforced beliefs about gender and mortality. Much like their European contemporaries across the ocean, Algonquians some-times subjected their enemies to bodily desecration. Women and children who found themselves captured were usually spared death, as their captors would likely seek a ransom for their return or else assimilate them into their villages. But when a fighting-aged man fell into enemy hands, he could face an excruciating fate. He would be slowly tortured and dismembered in front of his captors' entire village and expected to remain stoic right up to the moment of death. These ceremonies usually included the amputation of hands and feet and culminated in either the beheading or scalping of the captive. The public slaughter of a male captive was a cathartic performance by which Indians could vent their anger for a wrongful slaying and revel in their victory over a bitter enemy. It also gave the enemy warrior a chance to redeem the honor he lost in being captured by demonstrating his fearless-ness toward death.[40]

Colonial observers were often aghast at the torture of captives, but, at the same time, they had to admit that Indian conflicts were far more restrained and short-lived than European wars. One seasoned English soldier who watched Native men in battle scoffed, "They might fight seven years and not kill seven men," while another remarked, "It is a great fight where seven or eight is slain." Killing on a large scale was a wasteful and dangerous act; it served only to perpetuate violence. Coastal Natives much preferred taking the lives of just a few foes in a deliberate fashion to satisfy the mourning families. Indian combatants also performed a symbolic kind of butchery on the bodies of the dead and dying. When "their arrow sticks in the body of their enemie . . . they follow their arrow, and falling upon the person wounded and tearing his head a little aside by his Locke, they in the twinckling of an eye fetch off his head though but with a sorry [dull] knife." Hands and feet were common trophies as well, perhaps because they were key targets in torture rituals; taking them from the dead may have been analogous to performing the ritual on a dead foe. When Indians "returne [as] conquerours they carrie the heads of their chiefe enemies that they slay in the wars: it being the custome to cut off their heads, hands, and feete."[41]

Narragansetts called this act *Timeqúassin*, which a colonist translated as "to cut off or behead," though the term probably also referred to the more famous and widespread Native practice of scalping; the two actions can be viewed as part of the same tradition. Because Indians believed that the free soul—their closest analogue to the Christian concept of an eternal soul— was anchored in the head, scholars have theorized that beheading and scalping were intended to keep the free soul from reaching the Southwest. Colonists were vague in their references to this custom, using the word *head* interchangeably with *scalp* or *head-skin*. Archaeologists have found evidence to support the prevalence of beheading over scalping, including the grave site of a seventeenth-century headless Narragansett woman. By the time of King Philip's War in the 1670s the colonial records had more explicit references to scalping, though this shift may have reflected the vast scale of that conflict. In one account of the war an Englishman observed that Native fighters in the region preferred heads to scalps and only took the latter "when it is too far to carry the heads."[42]

When warriors took heads, scalps, hands, and feet back to their villages, the grisly parts became weighty objects in Algonquian societies. Like any gift, they carried with them unspoken obligations between the giver and the receivers. At times a head changing hands could be an obvious gesture of submission and loyalty. A colonist related the tale of an Indian warrior who, pretending to defect from his people, joined a group of his enemies as they went into battle. As the fighting began he fired an arrow into the enemy sachem and "in a trice fetcht off his head and returned immediatly to his own againe." Delivering trophies reinforced a man's bond to his immediate kinsfolk. As one colonist put it, men were eager to "beare home to their wives and children" the body parts of foes "as true tokens of their renowned victorie."[43]

Trophies could strengthen ties between families, especially as fighters of ordinary rank delivered their prizes to higher-born sachems. By accepting body parts, a sachem demonstrated that he shared the grievances of the person delivering it, making him a kind of imagined kinfolk. Receiving the human fragment also signified his continued commitment to the cause of war since his acceptance of the trophy made him complicit in the act of killing and reinforced the ethos of mutual defense that held all sachemships together. And when sachems gave parts of their foes to each other they extended the bonds of fictive kinship even further. In the same speech in which the Narragansett sachem rallied his neighbors "to say brother to each other," he proposed that they trade the heads and hands of their slain foes to serve as "a meanes to knitt them togeather."[44]

Murders could be resolved peacefully with payments of wampum, as the giving of these shell beads was seen as a soothing, peacemaking gesture. Gifts of beads needed to be exceedingly generous in order to contain violence. In the midst of one war with colonists, some sachems reported that, contrary to their wishes, young Indian men hoped to continue the war on the basis of individual grief for lost family members, "as one had lost his father, another his mother, a third his uncle, and also their friends, and that the presents or recompense were not worth taking up." When northeasterly storms of war blew down the coast, villagers redirected their grief and anger into familiar channels of tradition, using symbolic exchanges of trophies to prolong wars or gifts of shell beads to end them.[45]

Every aspect of coastal Algonquians' political culture—their dynasties, hierarchies, holidays, and practices of consensus building, warfare, and conflict resolution—was structured along the lines of families and discussed in the language of feelings. One colonist attending a meeting presided over by the popular sachem Massasoit watched his elite supporters one by one "brake forth into these speeches, '*Neen womasu Sagimus, neen womasu Sagimus,*'" meaning, "My loving Sachem, my loving Sachem, Many have I known, but never any like thee." When a whole village broke from their head sachem later in the colonial period, the villagers pointed out that "we tock him in our bosom . . . and fout for him and brout ourselves into a great deal of trouble," but when he took land from them without asking and cheated them out of a wampum payment they declared, "We are abused by him and there fore we dis oune him for our sachim." Though this specific schism was entangled with the Indians' relations with colonists, their complaint was couched in terms of love, trust, and betrayal. This source likewise spoke to the contractual, dissolvable quality of sachems' relationships with their followers. Algonquians' political rhetoric had a pattern of expectation and grievance one might expect from people who saw authority and ancestry as tightly linked, making all public affairs family affairs. Though kinship and reciprocity were the common organizing ideas behind all Native powers, their specific governments took on different shapes and sizes depending on where they were along the coast.[46]

In describing the dense webs of relationships that held sachemships together and formed Native power structures, historians run into a central problem. Relying on sources written by colonists, we have little choice but to focus on the predominately male sachems in their retellings, with a tendency to characterize their actions as the decisions of individuals. Since these sachems are among the few Indians we can truly trace the lives of in any detail, there is real value in assessing them as quirky individuals with distinct personalities. Furthermore, some of these Indian politicians could indeed act in transparently self-serving ways. Still, we need to remember how male European writers seldom saw the internal workings of Algonquian societies, the slow formation of opinions at a village level, the everyday ways in which sachems courted their followers, and most of all the role of women in shaping policy. Though there is no easy way to fill this vast hole in our understanding, at the very least we can acknowledge its presence and size. Every time a male sachem appears as an actor in this narrative, readers should always recall his unseen backstory: his elders and other relatives he hoped to please; the long hours of conversation around fires that informed his speeches; the women as well as men who shaped his views before he came to speak to colonists.[47]

Monarchies and Democracies

While the Dutch and English described many similar Algonquian political traditions found in villages across the region, there was a stark divide in how they characterized the extent of sachems' rule. Dutch colonists arriving near the Hudson tended to see Indian politics as highly localized and egalitarian. Some even doubted that sachems' realms had any hierarchy at all, making blanket statements that "there is little authority known," "they have no form of political government," and chiefs had "not much authority and little advantage, unless in their dances and ceremonies." A more careful Dutch observer opined, "Public policy in the proper sense does not exist" but allowed, "There is a glimmer of government and something that in broad terms suggests policy." The same man believed Native "government is of the popular kind," and a fellow countryman agreed that their "government is democratic." The English, by contrast, saw more than "a glimmer of government" on the other side of the shore, reporting that their neighbors had hierarchical power structures. They were quick to call neighboring sachems kings or princes and to describe local governments as "mixed, partly monarchical, and partly aristocratical" or flatly declare them "purely monarchical." But even a colonist who agreed that Natives lived under monarchies had to admit, when a matter arose "that concernes all, either Lawes, or Subsides, or warres," if "the people are adverse" the "absolute Monarchie" of a sachem could yield to "gentle perswasion."[48]

Puritans' fondness for using *monarchy* to describe Indian powers was no doubt complicated by their feelings about the increasingly absolutist regime of Charles I that so many had fled. For that matter, Dutch opinions of supposed democratic or popular rule was colored by the state of affairs in the Netherlands, where seven newly united provinces were working out how to balance representative and hereditary systems of government. Yet no matter how clouded colonial lenses were, they reveal more than just European reflections. Neither *monarchical* nor *democratic* was an accurate description of any coastal Algonquian power, but the two terms serve as useful shorthand for a real distinction. In the early seventeenth century a couple dozen weaker, more consensus-oriented sachems were in control of the western side of the shore, while just three chief sachems seemingly held sway over nearly all eastern villages.[49]

The so-called monarchies, the Wampanoags, Narragansetts, and Pequots, were more like loose constellations of villages that grew and shrank over time. Each of these three large groups was in truth a collection of smaller affiliated sachemships. But the flow of allegiance had a kind of hub-spoke shape, with the head sachem's community at the center, receiving tributes and promises of loyalty from lesser sachems. An early account of the Wampanoags described the sachemship as being made up of "circuits" possessed by "the Imperial Governor Massasoit"; a later description characterized all three chief sachems as holding "dominion over divers petty governours." In reality the Wampanoags were more of an affiliated ethnic grouping bound together by lineages and language who let Massasoit serve as a figurehead when dealing with outsiders. The English tended to exaggerate Native hierarchy and had only a hazy view of the subtle negotiations between sachems. But their mistake is understandable given that eastern sachemships bore a superficial resemblance to the monarchies on their home continent, where dynastically appointed scions cobbled together disparate realms by encouraging marriage between noble bloodlines.[50]

Colonists played a part in expanding these composite sachemships. Trade heightened the production of the key tribute items of wampum and corn, since colonists were eager to barter for both. The three best-known coastal "kings" from this region that appear in the early sources, Massasoit (Wampanoag), Canonicus (Narragansett), and Tatobem (Pequot), owed their sway over their neighbors in no small part to their commerce with foreigners. But the earliest sources that describe these sachemships as formidable powers all predate the boom in colonial trafficking that came in the mid to late 1620s. Giovanni da Verrazzano's account of Narragansett Bay (1524) described an elegantly robed king always accompanied by attendants; he even described a power-sharing co-sachemship between an elder and younger sachem much like the one formed between Canonicus and his

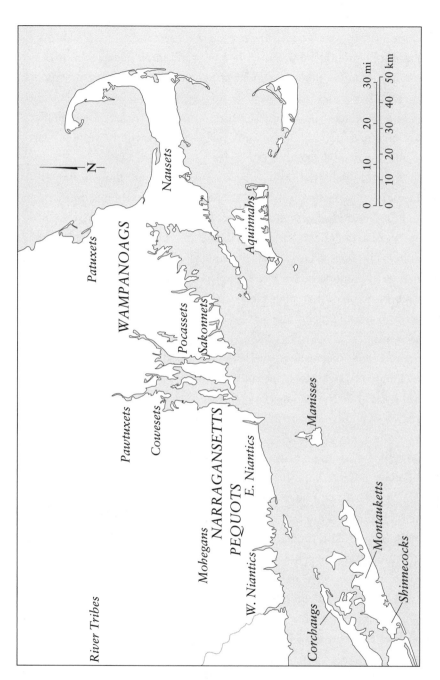

Eastern Native sachemships.

nephew Miantonomi in the 1630s and 1640s, suggesting the elite structure of power among eastern sachemships was well over a century old. In 1621 colonists at Plymouth claimed their neighbor Massasoit had a realm of tributary villages "larger than England and Scotland," a major overstatement but nonetheless clear evidence that he was the head of a composite body of allied villages before sustained trade transformed the region. The colonial market undeniably strengthened and expanded the reach of coastal monarchies, but it did not create them.[51]

To the west side of the shore, where some Dutchmen thought they saw democracies, there were over twenty separate Native sachemships. Living around the lower Hudson were Raritans, Hackensacks, Sinisinks, Tappans, Wappingers, Weichquagesecks, Tankitekes, Siwanoys, Manhattans, Matinnecocks, Massapequas, Nyacks, and Canarsies. Anthropologists use *Munsee* as a broader term for these peoples and some of their inland neighbors, a corruption of the upper Delaware Valley group name Minisink. To the east on the mainland along the Connecticut and Quinnipiac valleys were Quiripis, Potatucks, Schaghticokes, Mattabessecks, Sequins, Wangunks, and Wepawaugs, while in the middle of Long Island were Unkechaugs, Nissequogues, Setuakets, Secatogues; scholars group all these central coast and river peoples as Quiripi–Unkechaug speakers. The mere compiling of all these group names into numbing lists hints at a pattern of intensely local power.[52]

Experts describe these powers as being diffuse and independent-minded. While there were no supreme sachems in the area, western peoples saw a world of brothers and friends that stretched beyond the bounds of any one sachem's control. A Dutch colonist who lived on Staten Island was surprised to run into some of his Indian neighbors "seven leagues" to the east on Long Island and "asked them how they came so far from their dwelling. They answered that they were out a hunting with these [Long Island] Indians, and had friends among them." Plenty of relationships in the area could be fueled by hatred as well as by fondness; early accounts noted an ongoing blood feud between the Manhattans and the Sinisinks along the Hudson that was apparently later resolved. These multidirectional, reciprocal ties created by women looking to trade handicrafts, men looking for hunting

Western Native sachemships.

partners, young adults seeking spouses, and politicians conferring with their brothers were the connecting structures of their world as opposed to the more ordered flow of tribute goods into the hands of a few mighty sachems. The Dutchmen who saw "no authority" and "no form of political government" here were simply oblivious to the invisible lines of kinship, marriage, friendship, commerce, and grievance that laced villages together into various webs but did not center on a single person.[53]

Distinguishing between the larger composite sachemships to the east and the smaller atomized ones to the west offers further insights into the perspectives of coastal Indian leaders after the arrival of colonists. A changing

47

trio of rival Wampanoag, Narragansett–Niantic, and Pequot–Mohegan eastern sachems would look to maintain and expand their realms of subject sachemships, while dozens of Munsee and Quiripi–Unkechaug western sachems would try to preserve their traditions of local independence, while from time to time seeking help from nearby brothers and friends. The intruders into this amphibious world, the English and Dutch, would discover that learning their way around older political contours was the key to forming new ones.

Arrivals and Apocalypses

To consider when and where New England and New Netherland began, we need to turn our gaze to the other side of the ocean, to that craggy western wing of the Eurasian landmass. The differences between the two old worlds of America and Europe were significant, though we often exaggerate them. It helps to step back and glimpse the people of the far side of the Atlantic through the same long-perspective anthropological lens used for Natives.

Fewer than ten centuries before they met Americans many Northern Europeans also lived in localized, nonstate societies and worshipped multiple gods. Even in the early modern era the most striking distinctions between people from opposite sides of the Atlantic were material. Europeans wore more woven plant fibers and wool than hides, ate more farmed foods than foraged and hunted ones, and raised domesticated animals that, unbeknownst to them, infected them with a whole rash of contagious diseases. Their wooden house frames were fashioned from tree trunks rather than tree branches, while their largest ceremonial buildings were made of blocks of stone and baked earth. Europeans' steeply hierarchical governments were like Algonquians' in that leaders often came to power through the ties of kinship, but they differed in their reliance on coercive taxation, majority-rule assemblies, and written laws, a stark contrast to indigenous gift exchanges, consensus-driven meetings, and communal laws. Christianity had centered their spiritual world around the written word and an institutional church staffed by a rarified class of literate priests, but many combined their lettered faith with strong beliefs in folklore and magic. Their fighting men had also used bows and arrows only a few generations ahead of forming Atlantic colonies and had not entirely abandoned archery as a weapon of war in the seventeenth century. As noted earlier, their conflicts were far longer, more destructive, and more lethal than Algonquian ones. And European rulers regularly used rituals of torture and dismemberment to punish criminals and enemies.[54]

Well before English and Dutch ships starting lurking off North America, tremendous changes were going on throughout northwestern Europe. In most places the region's economies had been focused on food production through the early Middle Ages, making them not so unlike the maize-, fish-, and game-centered coastal Algonquian economies. But the same global Medieval Warm Period that made corn more viable in the Northeast and led to the rapid growth of towns along the Mississippi River basin helped foster greater surpluses of grain across Europe. Expanding land and sea trade began to link more regions and nations together. As more people moved away from sustenance farming, manufacturing and trading began to flourish, which in turn fostered ever denser towns and cities, above all along waterways and coasts.[55]

The English kingdom and the Dutch Republic were both ambitious maritime nations whose respective sailors had long shared another choppy, gray arm of the Atlantic, the North Sea. Indeed, they had been in such constant contact that many common English nautical terms—*boom, schooner, skipper, sloop, yacht*—were of Dutch origin. The two countries started their overseas expansion in earnest within a few decades of each other, though the English had been toying with the idea of forming an Atlantic empire for over a century. Henry VII sponsored John Cabot's exploratory voyage to Newfoundland in the precociously early year of 1497, while under Elizabeth I a cohort of improvising adventurers made a failed attempt at permanent settlement on Roanoke Island in the 1580s.[56]

The Dutch had good reasons for lagging behind. Their country, officially known as the Republic of the Seven United Netherlands, was only decades old. Formed from a septet of rebellious former provinces of the Hapsburg Spanish monarchy, the new nation had been mired in a grueling war of independence since 1568. The Netherlands was more a loose union than a coherent nation with a central government. Its chief assembly, the States General, had restricted powers over the highly independent provinces, while the Prince of Orange served as the Dutch Republic's *stadholder*, the national military leader and de facto head of state, though the stadholders from the House of Orange had far fewer rights than those claimed by Tudor and Stuart sovereigns in England.[57]

The new, small, kingless state mirrored its older, larger, monarchical neighbor in a few basic ways. The political cultures of both were strongly shaped by the Protestant Reformation. That revolution in Christian beliefs, practices, and institutions had swept across Europe in the sixteenth century, causing nasty bouts of sectarian violence and inspiring whole countries to break ties with the Roman Catholic Church and form national churches that hewed closer to the teachings of the radical clerics Martin Luther and John Calvin. The Dutch and English alike were involved in ongoing debates over which precise strain of this bold new theology would come to dominate their nations' Sundays. Each country had an outspoken and influential faction of zealous Calvinist believers who remained sharply critical of what they saw as the continued popish corruption of their home nations' houses of worship and halls of power. And many of these "hotter sort of Protestant" would take a special interest in colonial projects, seeing them as social laboratories where a select population could set a more godly example for their respective home countries.[58]

While the elites of the two nations rejected the authority of Italian pontiffs, their merchant fleets were making more and more visits to Mediterranean ports, although here the Netherlands outpaced England. Dutch traders, who had long been middlemen in the "mother trade" of Baltic grain, had begun using routes through the English Channel and the Strait of Gibraltar to compete with Spain during their war of independence. Holland was more practiced in shipping than England, and its shipbuilders and sailors were widely regarded as the best in northern Europe—hence English tars peppered their speech with Dutch, but not the other way around. The English navy, however, proved its mettle by defeating a planned invasion of the island by the Spanish Armada in 1588. Chasing

Iberian warships around the British Isles, Elizabeth I's fleet emerged victorious and the hulls of the would-be invaders broke apart in raging storms off Ireland. This seemingly providential event helped seal the nation's reputation as a major naval force that, like the Netherlands, would have to be reckoned with in the coming century.[59]

For indigenous people the memory of foreign seafarers' arrivals in America was a similarly disruptive event, albeit with darker consequences. When Munsees recalled the moment they first saw a European vessel—perhaps Henry Hudson's storm-battered, Dutch-owned vessel *De Halve Maen* (the half moon) on its futile search for a passage to the Pacific in 1609—they mainly remembered their confusion. "They knew not what to make of it and dreaded that it be a ghostly or similar apparition from heaven or from hell," wrote a colonist who listened to several accounts. "Others wondered whether it might be a rare fish or a sea monster, and those on board devils or humans, and so on, each according to his inclination." In retelling these stories, colonists were often deliberately shaping a story of Native naïveté. They tended to mishear the word *manitou*, a complex word with several definitions, and repurpose these tales as evidence of their own nations' first discovery. Still, the similarities of these accounts from across the coast suggest that indigenous historians also saw the coming of ships as a moment of innocence lost, though they likely imbued their stories with a tone of self-awareness, using metaphors that we should not take too literally.[60]

Algonquians who may have been recalling the short visit of Verrazzano and his French-commissioned caravel *Dauphine* in 1524 or perhaps the more recent appearance of Bartholomew Gosnold and his English-sponsored bark *Concord* in 1602 told a story of colonists' arrival that was rich with simile: "They tooke the first ship they saw for a walking Iland, the Mast to be a Tree, the Saile white Clouds, and the discharging of Ordinance for Lighting and Thunder," but when "this moving Iland steadied with an Anchor, they manned out their cannowes to goe and picke strawberries there." The unnamed storyteller chose imagery that foreshadowed what the "Iland" would bring: its cloudy, thunderous qualities would strike an indigenous listener as omens of violence. And the anticipation of strawberries, a common gift from visitors that was also associated with travel, could be heard as portents of the trade goods offered by foreign vessels. In 1760 a Pequot man reported that when his ancestors "first saw Vessels passing in the Sound off against Paucatuck," perhaps those of Hudson or Adriaen Block, some Pequots "said at first it was Weetucks a coming again," in other words, that the mercurial giant who had once disappeared into the sea had returned. Again, there were notes of irony and prophecy in these stories that may have eluded the colonists who recorded them. For just as the pacing titan had once reshaped this shore, so too would those walking islands.[61]

Ships brought an *apocalypse* in the original sense of the word, meaning the arrival of a profound and world-changing truth. "Strange reports" of the first ship sighting "caused great despondency among the Indians, several of them have declared to me more than once." The revelation came, as Munsees told a Dutch colonist, because "they did not know there were more people in the world than those of their own kind around them, much less people so different in type and appearance as their nation is from ours." That last distinction, that it was the degree of difference between Europeans and other foreigners that was surprising, is telling. After all, Algonquians lived on the edge of a diverse and connected continent. A major portion of seaside peoples' diet came from imported seeds from Central America, they wore jewelry fashioned out of copper and stone that came from the far Great Lakes and Mississippi Valley, while their own soapstone carvings were found as far west as the Plains. By various reports they were well traveled through the Northeast; they spoke knowledgeably about the terrain from the Chesapeake to the St. Lawrence seaway and had both friendly and hostile dealings with inland powers like the five Haudenosaunee nations, who spoke a language as distinct from theirs "as Japanese is from English."[62]

It would be a stretch to call coastal Natives cosmopolitan, but the arrivals of the *Dauphine, Concord,* and *Halve Maen* were not the first time they had encountered foreign peoples, ideas, and things. No doubt the strangely clad Europeans with their bushy faces and elaborate vessels were surprising in their novel appearances, but the real shock came not just from what the aliens looked like but *where* they came from. Even decades after the arrival of ships, when dozens of Native men had made Atlantic journeys themselves, a colonist reported that most locals still could hardly be "brought to believe that the Water is three thousand English mile[s]" across. It took a while for the stunning truth of the ocean's dimensions to sink in. Until that moment of first contact the sea was a closed space shared only with neighbors and spirits, not strangers.[63]

A similar revelatory moment had rocked Europe just a century earlier when a series of cocky Mediterranean navigators returned from long voyages bearing news that the sea was home to far more peoples and places than any Christian had ever dreamed of. Indeed, just as some Algonquians wondered if the arrival was a spiritual reckoning, many Europeans would suspect their discovery of the Americas was a harbinger of their long-anticipated biblical revelations. The historian J. H. Parry called this European revelation the "discovery of the sea," an apt phrase, as Renaissance sailors did not land on any new continents. Their true find was the central stage for engaging this newly connected planet: the single world ocean.[64]

Ships would also bring about the other, more widely used secular definition of *apocalypse*, the term from science fiction meaning the destruction of one world and the dawning of another in its ruins. In the postapocalyptic world to come, the place that delivered devastation was also the home of Algonquians' legendary giant, the same place that fed and linked their communities for centuries. As coastal villagers realized that their familiar waters belonged to more people than just themselves and their immediate neighbors, they witnessed significant changes well before large numbers of Europeans started trudging up American beaches. And foreign sailors would have to make quick adjustments as well, as they found that nearshore waters could be as much a Native space as the land itself.

Watercraft and Watermen

European sailors, overdressed, sunburned, and full of wonder, gawked at the vessels headed their way. A flotilla of thirty boats carrying "innumerable people" appeared off Manhattan when a strange craft entered the harbor in 1524. Days later a similar fleet of boats packed with Native men surrounded the newcomers in Narragansett Bay. The canoes that came up boldly alongside alien ships were heavy craft carved from the trunks of mature trees, stretching an average of twenty to thirty feet long. Natives built even larger dugouts suited to hold "twenty, thirty, forty men" and reaching near sixty feet in length. One colonist claimed he witnessed a sea canoe with eighty people aboard plowing through the waters of Long Island Sound. Even if that account was an exaggeration, it is clear that the grandest Native boats had a longer waterline and could hold more people than the smallest European ships that crossed the Atlantic.[1]

Indians also built light bark canoes for protected passages, but most coastal Algonquians preferred to travel in weightier dugouts. These indigenous craft were not solely powered by oars: crews sometimes raised "poles in their Conoos" that colonists likened to the "Masts in our boats," poles rigged with simple foresails that Narragansetts called *sepâkehig*. An Englishman explicitly noted that Indians had been sailing long before the colonial arrival, commenting that "their owne reason hath taught them" how to sail downwind courses of twenty miles or more. Yet despite the ample evidence of Algonquians' large sailing canoes, these vessels are largely missing from historic images of first contact. Artists often use a lazy iconography of dynamic, seaborne Europeans and static, landbound Indians: indigenes stand awestruck on beaches or paddle ahead in tiny craft overwhelmed by looming ships. If we include confident Native mariners and their hefty boats in our imaginings of early contact, we remember that coastal encounters were formed by two maritime cultures, never just one.[2]

Historians, too, are responsible for creating the old problematic pictures. In one of the most widely read modern accounts of the European invasion of the Americas, Howard Zinn depicted Indians as mere passive reactors who were either "naked, tawny, and full of wonder" when first sighting Christopher Columbus's flotilla off the Bahamas or else "peered out of the forests" to see English sails approaching the American Northeast. Even most recent scholarship on the region, while providing a far more active picture of Indians' responses to European arrivals, simply fails to examine indigenous nautical technology in any depth, leading to small but telling mistakes. Otherwise careful experts conflate bark craft with dugouts, misread descriptions of Native sails, and declare that canoes could only "skirt the coast" when in fact they regularly journeyed over open water to points beyond the horizon.[3]

Some Europeans made the same error of thinking that Native Americans had no real claim to the sea. Writing in 1585, the Englishman Richard Hakluyt the younger imagined that in hostile territories ships could simply stay offshore and "annoy" the Indians, who would be helpless to stop them "by reason that we are lords of navigation and they not so." As Hakluyt wrote those words, Europeans were just beginning to distinguish between the old common practices of coastal, vernacular reckoning and the new techniques that let ships venture around the planet. The colonist Thomas Morton more precisely observed that Indians "have not the use of navigation, whereby they may trafficke as other nations," as the English and Dutch were undoubtedly "lords" of transoceanic travel and the Indians "not so." But these brazen claims of European superiority are quickly undermined if we use the more expansive definition of *navigation* to describe a broad spectrum of marine wayfinding and technology.[4]

Unlike writers and painters who never witnessed indigenous watermen at work, seventeenth-century Dutch and English observers seldom trivialized

Native seafaring. For almost as soon as locals started sharing waters with foreigners, they started sharing watercraft. Before we get to the main narrative, the political, events-driven story of how the colonies took shape, we need to take a more general look at the material world of this coast. An exploration of these saltwater engagements, both in early contact and in the decades after, uncovers a surprising story about the overlap of maritime traditions. There were two groups of watermen in this corner of the ocean. Newcomers were more hirsute than locals and clad in linen and wool; locals fashioned their hair into elaborate scalplocks and wore tanned leather. Soon both types of men would become similarly skilled at trimming canvas sails and balancing canoes.

There was a reason these mariners were all male, as Indians and colonists agreed that the ocean was a distinctly masculine space. From the beginning Native women were excluded from these offshore cross-cultural negotiations. The party of local men who boarded the first strangers' ship sequestered a group of women "in a little light boat to wait on a small island about a quarter

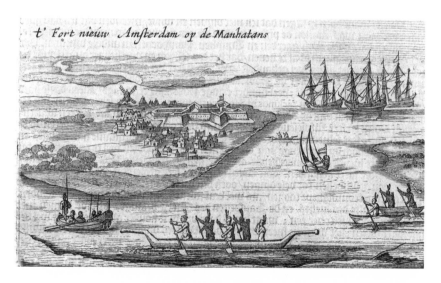

"t' Fort nieuw Amsterdam op de Manhatans" (detail); courtesy of the John Carter Brown Library at Brown University. While the creator of this fanciful depiction of Manhattan in 1628 never actually visited America, the watercraft accurately reflect the variety of vessels that shared these waters.

of a league from" the ship itself, while a later English explorer noted that coastal Wampanoags "seeme to bee somewhat jealous of their women, for we saw not past two of them" in two weeks of trading. Male colonists would do much the same, as European women stayed distant from most early encounters, protected by the defensive wooden structures of anchored ships, forts, and stockades. In one of the rarely recorded instances of a Native woman boarding a colonial ship, a crewman noted approvingly that she "sate so modestly, as any of our countrey women would doe in a strange place." In another mirroring of masculine maritime worlds, both kinds of mariners would make a rough analogy between the offices of captain and sachem. Indians around Massachusetts Bay would "call all Masters of Shippes Sagamore [sachem], or any other man, that they see have a command of men," while the crew of an English sailor identified a Wampanoag sachem as a "lord or captaine."[5]

Looking at alien vessels, local craft, and the moments when those objects changed hands, illustrates how boundaries between powers and cultures stayed in flux. The point here is not to claim that Western and indigenous seafarers possessed equivalent or even similar technologies—no matter their bulk, Indian dugouts were never designed to weather a weeks-long crossing. Noting the asymmetries between ships and canoes leads to the most compelling fact about nautical encounters in this region. Even on the water, the realm where one might reasonably assume that the disparity between tools was the greatest, it would be a long time before colonizers had a clear advantage over the people they hoped to colonize.

European Watercraft

The wooden contraptions that carried the foreigners looked like bizarrely seaborne fortresses, which in some ways they were. European ships sported defensive structures called forecastles and aftcastles that were often decorated with gaily painted carvings. These moving strongholds were products of an increasingly commercial continent, as the expansion of grain, salt, fertilizer, and textile trades in the late Middle Ages compelled people from the Mediterranean to the Baltic to take major leaps in shipbuilding and navigation techniques, leaps that made Atlantic trade possible. The breakthrough in naval architecture came in the fifteenth century with the proliferation of stout caravels like the ones sailed by Columbus. These craft had complex rigs and broad, deep hulls, which made them sturdy enough to brave the open ocean. The most crucial transformation, though, came from a few small gadgets and printed pieces of paper. Shipmasters worked with the most cutting-edge technology for global positioning, including astrolabes and sextants, along with simpler tools of relative positioning like sounding leads, loglines, compasses, and spyglasses. Also crucial were the cheaper published maps and coastal guides known as *rutters* and waggoners that became widely available in the sixteenth century. Together, these innovations allowed sailors to retrace the paths of explorers through distant seas.[6]

European mariners and fishermen were a rough lot. Many were drawn from the urban poor and spent their lives in a dangerous, male-dominated milieu. Landlubberly Christians found their manners wanting. One crew member on the *Mayflower* mocked the passengers for their seasickness, taking great glee in telling "them that he hoped to help cast half of them overboard before they came to their journey's end." Plymouth's governor, William Bradford, seemed to take some wry satisfaction in the sailor's ironic fate, writing that "it pleased God . . . to smite this young man with a grievous disease, of which he died in a desperate manner, and so himself the first that was thrown overboard." Bradford continued to be aghast at the conduct of seamen, like "the master, one Baker," who arrived in 1624 to fish for cod but "proved a very drunken beast, and did nothing (in a manner) but drink and guzzle and consume away the time and his victuals, and most of his company followed his example."[7]

Though they could seem ungovernable on land, these men's floating worlds had a severe hierarchy: the structure of ships worked like a backward body, with lower functions at the head, higher functions in the rear. A ship's front was where waste was expelled. Sailors sat on heads, open toilet holes by the bowsprit that were, in theory at least, self-cleaning, as they were located over the ship's bow, where the wake most vigorously washed the hull. Within the ship's pointed bow was the triangular forward cabin known to the Dutch as the *vooronder* and to the English as the forecastle, fo'c'sle, or simply "before the mast." Here sailors slept on thin mattresses in tight quarters. The number of sleeping spaces was often half the number of crewmen, as most ships worked on a two-watch hot-bunking schedule whereby one watch worked while the other rested, meaning that two men shared one bed. Along the torso-like central deck were useful organs. Two large winches served as the ship's main sources of leverage. The windlass near midships could lift sails and topmasts and move cargo in and out of the hold, while the capstan near the bow had the main job of raising and lowering the anchor. The main deck also anchored the limbs, that is, the masts and sails, the sources of propulsion, while below was the main compartment for cargo and provisions. At the rear, or stern, of the ship was another superstructure called the quarterdeck, aftdeck, or *achterdek*, a towering, narrow cabin that sometimes looked almost comically out of proportion with the rest of the ship. As the highest point of the hull, it served as the center of seeing and decision making. Along with his mates, the captain, or *skipper*, lodged inside this stern castle, which also housed the steering works. The contrast between ordinary and elite accommodations was stark. The captain's cabin often was outfitted with a comparatively spacious bed, glass windows, and a desk for reading charts and keeping a log. In these sailing castles the captain was king.[8]

While seventeenth-century ships were several generations removed from the *Niña*, *Pinta*, and *Santa María*, many features one might expect to find on oceangoing vessels had not yet been invented. There were no steering wheels, for instance. Ships used a whipstaff, a large vertical arm that was hinged to the rudder, the plane of wood at the rear of the ship that pivoted the hull's direction in the sea. The helmsman could not always see where the ship was headed, so steering was an imprecise art that relied on careful communication between the rudder-gang at the stern and those on the forward deck. Ship rigs consisted of square sails rigged from the forward-jutting bowsprit and the two main masts, and sailors rigged a lateen triangular sail on the mizzen rear mast. A useful design long favored by Mediterranean sailors, lateen sails gave ships a broader range of motion by picking up the wind at more angles than the rectangular mainsails and thus making it easier to sail closer to the direction of the wind. But these mast-mounted lateen sails were nowhere near as versatile as jibs and staysails, which allowed even greater range but did not yet exist. Working with this sail plan, the helm could point only to within 60° of the weather, meaning that all courses had to account for at least a 120°-wide no-go zone. And the feature that made these ships ideal for crossing the ocean—their large hulls—was a limitation when they reached American waters.[9]

The unique geological character of the shore between the Hudson and Cape Cod created numerous obstacles for these tubby-bodied craft, especially in the early years. Quirky wind patterns formed in the "many crooked and streight passages" between glacial outlands, and the region's staggered basins of constantly draining and refilling water made difficult going for underpowered ocean vessels that could sail only within a constrained set of compass points. Even in a ship's boat, Verrazzano and his men had to turn back shortly after entering the narrows that now bear his name, for "as often happens in sailing, a violent unfavorable wind blew in from the sea, and we were forced to return to the ship." Conditions were so reliably turbulent where Long Island, Manhattan, and the mainland met that the Dutch dubbed the rocky confluence *Hellegat,* or Hell's Gate. Sailors described the watery intersection as "a most dangerous Catwract" on account of "a rapid violent Stream both upon Flood and Ebb; and in the middle lieth some Islands of Rocks, upon which the Current sets so violently, that it threatens present Shipwreck." Some Dutch sources called the entire East River Hellegat, while later English sailors nicknamed Long Island Sound the Devil's Belt, perhaps in part because of the chain of stony islets that local Indians attributed to their coastal giant but were known to colonists as the Devil's Stepping-Stones.[10]

The trails of glacial debris that shaped the chain of outer lands also stretched underwater, threatening to ground or puncture European hulls that were sailing blind in these uncharted seas. To the east, extensive shoals lurked off Cape Cod, making it "a very dangerous place to fall withall," and as late as 1628 Plymouth colonists were still "afraid to pass" through the forbidding waters. Caution around the "dangerous shoals and roaring breakers" convinced the crew ferrying Plymouth colonists to scrap their original plan to drop their passengers near the Hudson and leave them on the north side of the Cape instead. Sailors named parts of the peninsula

Point Care and Tuckers Terrour after some anxious moments when they narrowly avoided shipwreck. As a result of the Cape's forbidding reputation, the earliest Europeans in this corner of the Atlantic—the Basque, Portuguese, English, and French fishermen that worked offshore banks in the sixteenth century—all gave the sandy arm a wide berth, keeping its southern shore and the coast westward to the Hudson largely free of ships until the early seventeenth century.[11]

Once European vessels began to brave these shores, they tended to be smaller, older craft, as backers were reluctant to send their best vessels on a risky passage for a low-profit haul of fish or fur. The account of the *Concord's* voyage to the region in 1602 stated matter-of-factly, "our barke being weake," "our sailers being few, and they none the best, we bare (except in faire weather) but low saile" so as not to tax the fragile hull and mediocre crew. The quality of seamen headed to this coast did not necessarily improve even as the century wore on. One passenger on a ship bound for Manhattan in 1679 became so frustrated with the "disorderly" and "wretched" sailors that he "took upon myself, out of love of the thing . . . to watch and attend the rudder, as well as to make observations in navigation." Early sponsors of New Netherland voyages complained about "great expenses and damages by loss of ships and other dangers." Their concerns were real. Hudson's *De Halve Maen*, for example, was in such sorry shape that it lost its mainmast in a storm off Iceland. Colonists were constantly reminded of how vulnerable they were in sinkable, flammable structures. The Dutchman Adriaen Block's ship *Tijger* (tiger) caught on fire and burned to the waterline while anchored off Manhattan in the fall of 1613, stranding him and his crew over the winter while they built a smaller replacement.[12]

Passengers on the shabby, twelve-year-old wine hauler *Mayflower* were rightfully worried about it coming apart at sea, as it was "over-masted and too much pressed with sails" and "met with many fierce storms with which the ship was shroudly shaken, and her upper works made very leaky; and one of the main beams in the midships was bowed and cracked." Once arrived off America, the *Mayflower's* passengers became so visibly disgruntled with the "dangerous and almost incureable errors and mistaking" of their pilot Robert Coppin that he had to beg them to "be of good cheere" in the tense days before "he stumbled by accident upon the harbor of Plimoth." An English pinnace attempting to round Cape Cod in 1615 was not so lucky and "run on ground a furlong off the shoare, where we had beene beaten to pieces" had the crew not thrown all their excess cargo overboard, allowing their keel to lift free at the next high tide, "by which meanes we escaped." Afloat in fragile cradles of wood, feeling their way around the margins of an unknown shore, foreigners were keenly aware of the weaknesses of both ships and sailors.[13]

Colonists feared as well that Indians would breach their wooden shells. The captain of the English *Speedwell*, who sailed near Cape Cod in 1602, was "very carefull and circumspect having not past two [Indians] with him in the shippe . . . lest they should have invaded." They would remain suspicious throughout their visit, for just as they weighed anchor to leave the Patuxets' harbor (later Plymouth) "very neere two hundred" locals "came downe to the shoare . . . and would have had us come in again: but we sent them backe," the English preferring to remain safely ensconced in their ship. Even colonists who had more established relations with Native peoples remained suspicious of any offer of hospitality that required them to leave their craft. An English colonist visiting the powerful Narragansetts in 1622 suspected that their "many persuasions to draw us from our shallops to the Indians' houses" were ploys to give the Natives "better advantage."[14]

Surviving an actual attack only heightened the foreign seamen's wariness. When in 1609 Hudson first anchored at the mouth of the river that now bears his name, two Munsee canoes surprised his ship's boat when it was on a reconnaissance mission, probably near Coney Island. In a brief naval exchange Munsees killed one of the strangers with an arrow to his throat. Hudson then fortified his midships' "side with waste boords in defence of our men." Waist boards were planks raised along the midship bend, or waist, of a ship during a naval encounter, as the low rail made it the most vulnerable spot on the deck. From then on out, Hudson usually assumed the appearance of a canoe signified the beginning of an attack. The account of the voyage described three separate Indian approaches with the same phrase: "We suffered none of them to come into our ship." Another explorer, the Englishman Thomas Dermer, did not even bother to detail every last one of the "many accidents" in his difficult passage south of Cape Cod that were "occasioned by treacherie," though he took special note of the time he sailed through a narrow passage in western Long Island Sound, where "the Savages had a great advantage of us" and "a multitude of Indains let flye at us from the banke, but it pleased God to make us victours." Plymouth colonists likewise endured a brief arrow attack when they were first desperately wandering the coast in a small, storm-battered shallop; as a result, some men were adamant that they never let their crippled and demasted craft out of sight. No wonder explorers clung to their vessels as though they were floating fortresses: they felt as though they were under constant siege.[15]

Meetings between canoes and large multimasted ships, whether welcoming or hostile, became rare by the 1620s. Colonists began deploying a variety of smaller, more nimble double- and single-masted vessels — pinnaces, barks, yachts, shallops, and sloops — as their primary vehicles for dealing with Natives. Dutch and English terms for their vessels were frustratingly vague. *Boat*, which modern landlubbers use generically for anything that floats, applied only to small, oar-propelled crafts. *Fluyt*, or flute, was a reasonably precise term, referring to a Dutch-built cargo ship that had a low superstructure, few cannon, a simple rig, and a capacious hold. *Bark* or *barque* could be English synonyms for a generic ship or it could be a more specific term for a modest, single-decked coastal fishing and trading craft with two masts; Dutch *jachts* were often of similar dimensions. *Shallop* usually meant a small, single-masted, sometimes open-decked craft meant for coastal sailing, but it also could apply to a heftier vessel more like a bark. *Pinnace* was one of the most commonly used and vaguest terms of all. It could indicate a ship, often specifically an armed fluyt or a fluyt with a square stern, but more often it referred to minor crafts that were "little more than decked ship's boats." The one thing all these craft had in common was that they were made of pine: the term *pinnace* derives from the Latin *pinus*.[16]

Smaller vessels were easier to build than ships and cheaper to maintain than manned outposts. An early Dutch account noted that trade in some parts was "carried out only in yachts, in order to avoid expense." Compact, shallower boats were less vulnerable to grounding and could be rowed when tides and winds were unfavorable. Furthermore, "tolerable yachts" and other small craft could be fashioned locally seeing as "the country there abounds in timber suited for ship-building." Block was the first sailor to pilot an American-built European-style craft in the region, "a yacht of eight Lasts" that he named *Onrust* (restless); Plymouth colonists would later build a little shallop of local wood solely for the purpose of trading with Natives. By 1630 the new colonists in Massachusetts Bay, in want of "a stronge boat good cheape," built the twenty-four-foot-long *Blessings of the Bay* to trade with their Indian neighbors. Yet despite the abundant raw wood in America, properly made planks remained precious, as there was a general scarcity of milling and hewing tools. In the 1620s ships bound for New Netherland were still importing "a large quantity of timber, fit for the building of the vessels."[17]

Remains of the *Sparrow-Hawk* on Boston Common. Courtesy of Pilgrim Hall Museum, Plymouth, Massachusetts.

Even as colonists began setting up more sawmills, there were never quite enough experts who knew the delicate, hard-to-master art of fashioning straight timbers into something rounded and seaworthy. The Dutch colonial director Willem Kieft was often at odds with the colony's boatswains and master carpenters. Conflicts began as soon as he arrived and learned that every vessel owned by the colony except one was unserviceable. He would later curse one carpenter as a rascal for defecting to the English and fault another for the woefully leaky state of the colony's fleet. English leaders had similar concerns. In 1642 the new colony of Connecticut would begin compelling every colonist who possessed hempseed to begin raising the crop to provide badly needed material for ships' ropes, while several towns banded together to begin raising funds for the colony's first ship. Declaring "the building of ships" to be "a business of great importance to the common good," officials in Massachusetts Bay appointed a ship inspector to monitor the burgeoning industry. The labor of shipwrights was so precious to the Bay colony in early decades that they were exempt from military service.[18]

The shortage of shipyards in the region until midcentury made some watercraft more expensive than houses. In 1642 New Amsterdam the well-used bark *De Hoop* (the hope) sold for the princely sum of ƒ1,100, while just weeks later a housebuilder signed a contract to build a brand-new two-story house with a thatched roof, three windows, and an enclosed staircase for the comparatively modest price of ƒ350. English records reveal that even the smallest boats were worth sizable sums. A diminutive boat of eight tons listed in the property inventory of a deceased Connecticut man was valued at £24, making it the bulk of his estate. Another English colonist who had his small vessel seized wrongfully in 1653 would value its hull and rigging at £52, a greater price than most homes. Even some of the finest buildings were not worth as much as ordinary secondhand watercraft. A well-appointed stone manor and barn built for Director Kieft cost him ƒ600, making it ƒ200 cheaper than the used yacht that one Dirck Corssen Stam sold to Maryn Adriaensen just weeks earlier. Owing to the extraordinary level of skill required to build a decent timber-made boat and the high cost of maintenance, European-style watercraft were about the most valuable single piece of property a colonist could own.[19]

Christians' small craft often carried far fewer crew than indigenous vessels, leading to naval encounters that were quite unlike those distorted images that depict Europeans overwhelming Indians at sea. The boat- and canoe-borne trade was seldom described in detail. But perhaps we can get a rare glimpse by drawing from accounts like that of a bartering appointment off Block Island in 1636. John Oldham's small pinnace was carrying four men in total, two of whom were Indian guides, when they met a Manisses Indian canoe. Oldham's crew was outnumbered at least three to one by the Manisses, who came in a great canoe "full of Indians" that was carrying a dozen crewmen and stretched at least ten feet longer than the colonial craft.[20]

Face-offs like this, in which the balance of power on the water decidedly favored Indians, were easily more common than the other way around, as rowing craft generally needed more men than sailing craft. No matter the respective numbers of Natives and newcomers in any given meeting, mutual paranoia would inform all encounters well into the seventeenth century. And yet the longer these tense floating engagements went on, the more the two maritime cultures began to intermix.

Native Watercraft

Though colonists would often gaze at America's soaring trees and imagine the shipyards all that timber could supply, they were hardly the first to see the forest for the boats. Algonquians had long surveyed their curated woods with canoe building on their minds. Native canoe makers valued silvery waterproof birch bark for the skin of their lightest craft; they liked buoyant, tallow-colored pine for everyday dugouts; they favored darker chestnut wood for its rot-resistant qualities; they sought strong but lightweight ash and maple logs for paddles; and most of all they prized the enormous, straight, largely branchless trunks of the tulip tree for their great canoes. In at least one coastal dialect, the word for tulip tree—which is, not coincidentally, one of the tallest species found in North America—translated literally as "canoe tree."[21]

Making dugouts was hard work, as Native craftsmen felled and hollowed out massive trunks with only fire and stone tools. Roger Williams described the process by which a single Narragansett fisherman made a personal vessel as an arduous regime of "burning and hewing" that took "ten or twelve dayes." No doubt hollowing out a forty-man great canoe would take weeks, if not months. In Pacific Island cultures that built canoes of similar dimensions with similar tools, the process of carving often took a whole year. Algonquians' largest dugouts were surely built a bit more swiftly, as they lacked the detailed woodworking found on the grandest canoes of Oceania. Assembling bark canoes was also a labor-intensive task, as they were "sowed together with strong and tough Oziers or twigs, and the seames covered over with Rozen or Turpentine." Though no colonial observer recorded the same level of attention to Indians' boat construction as that found among many Pacific peoples, there is evidence that canoe making in this corner of the Atlantic was associated with expert craftsmanship and great toil. Coastal peoples had a specialized set of knives reserved only for the task of fashioning bark canoes, while one of the Sisyphean punishments that lost souls endured in the afterworld was "making a canoe with a round stone."[22]

Most adult men in Native communities throughout the region were practiced seamen as well as boatbuilders. Canoeing was an essential skill for all, as seafood made up such a large portion of the coastal Algonquian diet. As we saw earlier, villagers from the Hudson to Cape Cod regularly traded, visited, feasted, fought, and intermarried with neighbors who lived across dozens of miles of saltwater. In Williams's English–Narragansett phrase book there were words for nine points of wind, seven makes of canoes, six stages of the tides, and four kinds of European crafts. He recorded tidbits of nautical folklore, such as Indians' fondness for the local shift of northerly winds to the southwest during sunny days, a "sea turn" they called *sowwánishen*: "This is the pleasingest, warmest wind in the climate, most desired of the *Indians*" because it brought "faire weather" and was a favorable blessing from the *Sowwaníu*, the mythical land in the Southwest. Narragansett also had numerous nautical verb constructions, including "*Sepagehommaûta* / Let us saile," "*Wauaúpunish* / Hoyse up," "*Touwopskhómmke* / Cast anchor," and "*Kspúnsh* / Tie it fast." Williams reported seeing a full-on naval battle between rival sachems' canoe fleets, witnessing "thirty or forty of their

Dugout canoe replicas. Courtesy of the Mashantucket Pequot Museum and Research Center, Archives and Special Collections.

Canowes fill'd with men, and neere as many more of their enemies in a Sea-fight."[23]

Canoe was a Carib loanword the English and Dutch picked up from Spanish sources, but the term slipped into such widespread usage by both colonists and Indians that a visitor in 1678 assumed it was of Native origin. In coastal dialects actual terms for any Native boat, bark or dugout, included *amokol, maushee, mishwe, mishoon,* and *micseh.* Birchbark canoes were most often used to navigate rivers, while dugouts were more favored for open ocean crossings. Canoes varied in their carrying capacity, from the diminutive dugout skiffs Narragansetts called *mishoonémese* that "will not well carry above three or foure" to the heftiest great canoes, or *mishíttou-wand,* which could hold well above thirty men. At each end the body of a *mishíttouwand* narrowed into a protruding point colonists called the nose or the beak head, which, like the beak head on a ship, was meant to break through ocean swells and reduce chop. Birchbark vessels were "sharpe at both ends" too, but "the beake was a little bending roundly upward." Most of what is known of makes of mishoon comes from colonial pens, though small Algonquian dugouts from before and during the colonial era have been discovered by underwater archaeologists. These finds were weighted down with rocks in freshwater ponds in Connecticut and Massachusetts and buried in the soil of Manhattan, and they correspond closely with written descriptions. Since immersed wood warps and cracks when it is removed from water for a prolonged period, the intentional sinking of canoes was the surest way to keep them seaworthy during seasons of disuse.[24]

Native vessels, just like European ones, had serious drawbacks beyond their finicky preference to remain in the water. Overset canoes were such a fact of life that the coastal Indians had established a common law of salvage, as "when any sachem's men are driven or cast ashore, upon any other sachem's jurisdiction . . . the goods are to be restored." Algonquian dugouts lacked stabilizers like outriggers or keels, making them tricky and crude sailing vessels. A colonist noted that they could set sail only "before a wind," though if the crew used their paddles as steering rudders and steadying leeboards a sailing dugout could follow a reasonably precise course, provided the wind was blowing in the general direction of its destination. But a steady wind was crucial for canoe sailing, as an underpowered dugout without an outrigger could be easily capsized by cross waves. Though rarely recorded, indigenous wrecks did happen, such as the tragic loss of a Niantic canoe and all twelve men aboard off the village of Dartmouth in the spring of 1675. Crews of dozens of men on oceangoing canoes were similarly necessary because Natives' paddles, held upright rather than leveraged in locks, did not offer great mechanical advantage. One account described them as scoops and not quite oars, while another described Native "Oares" as "flat at the end like an Oven peel," that is, resembling the wooden paddles used by bread bakers.[25]

Some handy design features brought obvious risks. Bark-sided boats' feather-light weight made them ideal for portages, but their thin hulls could be easily swept away. A colonist related the tragic tale of an Indian trader headed down the Hudson in a birchbark canoe "accompanied by his wife and child and about sixty beaver pelts" at the height of spring flooding. When the Native pilot trusted "his powers too far" and failed to beach his canoe properly, "the rapid flow of water flung him and his little vessel of tree bark" downriver, and his "wife and child were killed, most of his goods lost or damaged, and his craft broken into many pieces, but he survived." Birch canoes' delicate skins were also easily damaged in a direct attack. In a dispute between rival Dutch traders in 1614, sailors rammed their sturdy ship's boat into a Munsee birch canoe "with such a speed that the canoe was smashed to pieces" and then set about hacking at the bark sides with an axe to sink it.[26]

Though Native vessels were unstable when compared to colonial ones, that fact only made foreigners all the more impressed with Algonquians' nautical feats. The earliest captain to record his voyage to these shores marveled that "with only the strength of their arms" coastal watermen "go to sea without any danger, and as swiftly as they please." A century later colonists were still astonished at the Native oarsmen who "will venture to Seas, when an English Shallope dare not bear a knot of sayle; scudding over the overgrown waves as fast as a winde-driven ship." "They will indure an incredible great Sea," echoed another stunned Englishman in 1638, who described indigenous vessels "mounting upon the working billows like a piece of Corke; but they require skilful hands to guide them in rough weather, none but the Indians scarce dare to undertake it." Colonists had to admit that while canoes may have been unassuming, the mariners themselves were "very adventurous in their boats."[27]

A few colonists even squinted at rugged sea canoes and wondered if they were actually looking at relics from the classical or medieval world. Noting parallels between American and European nautical practices, Thomas Morton observed that his Massachusett neighbors "doe divide the windes into eight partes," just like westerners. He was similarly intrigued that Natives saw the North Star as part of a bear-shaped constellation, just like Europeans' Ursa Minor. Weighing these clues, Morton speculated they might be the descendants of "scattered Trojans" who had gone to sea and been caught in "a storme that would carry them out of sight of Land . . . and so might be put upon this Coast." The New Netherland governor Willem Kieft believed in an alternate theory that Indians "draw their Line from Iceland." The thesis of Viking origins posited that "long ago in legendary times a group of people sailed well equipped from parts of Sweden and

Norway to look for a better country, led by a chief named Sachema," and "since all the chiefs in New Netherland who live by waterways and seashores are known as Sachemas, it is concluded that they descend from those settlers." This sort of armchair musing about Native history was largely motivated by Europeans' interest in establishing that "the peopling of America must necessarily have happened by migration and not by creation, or the very foundation of Scripture would be destroyed."[28]

Practical concerns made colonists come to respect Indian craft more than any historical speculations. After all, their livelihoods often depended on the steady traffic of Native cargo vessels laden with furs and surplus corn. And over the seventeenth century colonists increasingly depended on Native watermen to link their expanding social and political worlds. As the historian Katherine Grandjean revealed through a meticulous survey of nearly three thousand letters in the Winthrop Family Papers, English correspondents frequently hired Indian messengers to carry their letters in the holds of their mishoon. A sizable portion of colonial epistles traveled in Native hands, above all for the English living along Long Island Sound. "I understande that you did not receive myne by [the Mohegan sachem] Oncus before the 30th past," one Long Island colonist wrote to a friend on the mainland, noting that his Native postman's "promis was great, he would de[liver] them to you the verie same day" and commenting with some concern that "his passage from hence could not be long." A colonist from Stonington, Connecticut, kept an eye on the comings and goings of a Niantic sachem who acted as a courier across the Sound, speculating that "he is very [possibly sending] to the long Iland for it hath bene his manner every tyme he hath yet put thither to importune me to write for him," noting the sachem brought "a great Canow of his and that takes his men away." In an aside revealing the breadth of connections fostered by Indian dugouts, a New Haven Puritan thanked his friend in New London "for this Intelligence you sent me" but also acknowledged an unnamed "Indian who came from Cannow," carrying the letter fifty miles across the Sound in late January.[29]

Colonists saw Indians' dugouts as more than mail and cargo carriers; they were also handy ferryboats. From some of their earliest contacts Europeans regularly hitched rides with Native pilots. By later in the century ferrying had become a side business for some coastal Algonquians. When Nyacks living near what is now Fort Hamilton, Brooklyn, greeted a ship passing through the Narrows to New York harbor in 1679, "some of the passengers intended to go ashore with them" by canoe, allowing travel-weary colonists to take a shortcut to their ultimate destinations on Long Island or Staten Island; "but the captain would not permit it, as he wished, he said, to carry them, according to his contract, to the Manathans." Some foreigners were understandably hesitant to ride in Indians' tippy boats, where "the edge was not more than a hand's-breadth above the water," but too often the advantage of using Indians as ferrymen was obvious — in one case, taking a canoe instead of walking from one village to another on Long Island "made full three hours difference." Colonists likewise returned the favor of carrying neighbors over water. Egbert von Borsum's ferry across the East River was almost as diverse as the modern subway cars that now follow its route underwater. Operated by one of his slaves, Borsum's boat service carried Natives, Africans, and Europeans alike, forcing peoples from far corners of the world to cram in awkwardly for the quick trip from Breukelen to Manhattan.[30]

Canoe travel could also seem rather daunting to Europeans given that most of them, sailors included, could not swim. Dutch and English alike admired how Indians could "swim a mile, yea two or more," and observed that "from the youngest age" Indians "swim like ducklings." Williams sometimes believed himself to be "in great danger" in his frequent rides aboard Native dugouts. During frequent sea canoe voyages with his neighbors "it hath pleased God to make them many times the instruments of my preservation." Once when he "questioned safety" one of his Narragansett friends calmly reassured him by saying, "Feare not, if we be overset I will carry you safe to Land." The man soothing his white-knuckled passenger hints that, to Indian mariners, Europeans could sometimes seem like unseaworthy companions.[31]

Colonists and Native Watercraft

Tippiness aside, many newcomers openly acknowledged the perks of canoes both by acquiring them from their neighbors and by fashioning their own. One of the first things men from the *Mayflower* and *Arbella* did after arriving on American shores was try to snatch Indian dugouts they believed to be abandoned. The crew of the *Speedwell* were so taken by the "almost incredible" lightness of Patuxet peoples' birchbark craft that they took one back to Bristol with them. And pretty soon colonists were building their own dugouts of identical size and form as Indian ones, as Native boat-building practices were far cheaper and easier to master than European methods. John Josselyn observed that the English used old-growth pines "to make large Canows of 20 feet long, and two and a half over, hollowing them with an Adds, and shaping them like a Boat." William Wood also took note of English-made dugouts of identical dimensions and observed that in Salem "there be more Cannowes in this towne than in all the whole Patent; every household having a water-ho[r]se or two." "I have a lustie Canow," wrote Williams, assuring a fellow colonist that he could easily transport pigs to a nearby island. The craft were so obviously useful to farmers in New Amsterdam that one landlord included a canoe as part of his lease to a tenant. Dutch court records featured casual references to colonists using dugouts to carry loads of lime to outlying farms or taking them on daytrips to go oystering on Ellis Island. Native-style craft also doubled as ship's boats, as indicated by an account from 1650 of an English bark capsizing when the owner's "Canow fell over" off the deck "and was loast his Oare &c."[32]

Though colonists took to Algonquian-style boating quickly, accounts suggest that canoe travel was highly perilous for those who were inept at swimming and fond of booze. The Puritan chronicler William Hubbard almost seemed to relish sharing New England capsizing stories, all of which had the same lesson: drinking and canoeing did not mix. There were the two fishermen who ducked out of a Sunday sermon in 1666 and "drank so much rum that, being intoxicated therewith, they fell out of their canoe as they were going down the river, and were both drowned." And there were the cautionary tales of one "J. S.," who, "having profanely spent the Lord's Day" boating and then imbibing, became "so excessive drunk that he fell over his canoe and was drowned, and his body not found till twelve days after"; and of the woman simply known as "Captain Lockwood's wife," who made the fatal error of "going in a canoe with a drunken fellow" only to be "carried away by the tide, and never heard of more." When a Dutch visitor on Staten Island paid a colonist twelve guilders in wampum to go ring in the New Year in a mainland tavern, he was relieved when a winter rainstorm forced his party to stay the night ashore, for "to be in such weather and darkness upon the water in a canoe, is not without danger." Yet sometimes the weather was so bad that Native boats had clear advantages over European ones, as ice could trap larger craft at anchor while canoes could be launched in all weather. A Dutchman looking to sail from Staten Island to Manhattan in the depth of winter found that since his "boat was frozen up in the kill" he instead paddled his spare dugout "between the cakes of ice, down the river to Fort Amsterdam."[33]

Colonial demand for these versatile and sometimes lethal boats was so great that Indians sometimes sold their vessels to foreign customers. By the 1640s Dutch colonists boasted that they possessed a massive "wooden canoe obtained from the Indians, which will easily carry two hundred schepels of wheat"—a carrying capacity of nine thousand pounds, or, in material terms, nine adult horses. While never as pricey as plank-built boats, the finest canoes were prized possessions: in 1655 a Long Island colonist valued his dugout at the not-insignificant price of ƒ25. Yet persistent worries about the perils of canoe travel inspired some colonial officials to begin a regime of inspection. Noting that "divers cannows, some made of the English, some bought of the Indians, are altogether unfit for the service to which they are putt," New Haven's legislature declared that all dugouts within their bounds needed to be inspected and marked before they could put to sea. After several colonists died in accidents on rivers and at sea, a Plymouth official debated restricting the use of such "smale and naughty cannoos." Later in the century colonial canoe men became so adept and common that even Natives hired them as ferrymen. By merely offering their assistance with rowing, a party of Indians chartered John Dyer's dugout from New London to Saybrook in 1651 with the intent of buying cloth from a visiting Dutch vessel.[34]

A Connecticut man's diary revealed just how crucial Native boats were to European settlers' daily lives. Thomas Minor, a resident of Stonington, revealed in his terse daily log that he owned at least two Indian-made boats, one birchbark and one dugout great canoe. Both vessels had been purchased from his Native neighbors, in one case from the Pequot sachem known as Cashawasset, or Harmon Garrett, and the other from another boatbuilder named Sabiantwosucke. Minor remained highly attentive to the comings and goings of his "Canoows," making them recurring characters in his journal. He took note of the days his neighbors Mr. Chester or "the Irishman" "had the greate Conoow" on loan or a friend "fecthed [home] the Canoow," the days when "our Canoow went to New london with 30 bushels of oates" and when Goodman Parker "Calked the Canoow," the unhappy day his wife "fell out of the Canoow," and the even more unfortunate day that "our Canoow was driven away" in a snowstorm. Minor's diary hints at why farmers living along the countless inlets, creeks, and bays of this drowned coastline would sometimes call their Native-style boats water-horses.[35]

Canoes could strengthen ties between frontier neighbors, but they incited conflicts as well. When Dutch soldiers, "being intoxicated, burnt a small canoe of the Savages" in 1660, the aggrieved Natives "threatened to set fire to an house," seeing the destruction of a dwelling as a comparable loss. Back in the early 1620s the trader Thomas Weston at first had "fared well with the Indians" north of Plymouth by "making them canoes." In manufacturing these welcome gifts, Weston was no doubt using metal tools that felled and hollowed tree trunks faster than any indigenous methods, and the local Massachusett people surely valued the craft more in light of their recent devastating population losses in epidemics. But the boatbuilding partnership soon soured. When some Massachusett men commissioned five more vessels from Weston in 1623 the Englishman soon heard a rumor that his customers were in fact would-be pirates who "intended to kill Mr. Weston's people, and not to delay any longer then till they had two more Canoes or Boats, which Mr. Weston's men would have finished by this time (having made them three already) had not the Captain prevented them." The rumored attack was part of a larger Massachusett conspiracy that English colonists suppressed with the surprise slaying and beheading of the lead conspirator. This exceptional incident demonstrates how the exchange of transportation technologies rather quickly had gone full circle and how canoes were so valuable that they may have been at the center of a murder plot.[36]

More commonly, water-horses triggered legal disputes. Colonies passed laws explicitly forbidding their subjects from taking unmanned canoes without permission, while residents of New Amsterdam, New Haven, Plymouth, and Boston regularly dragged their neighbors into court to accuse them of pinching dugouts. At least one canoe on the open market had to have its title cleared: Minor was called before a magistrate in 1652 to affirm that the Indian vessel he once sold to a neighbor was not stolen property but had been discovered "upon the water adrift" by his son and had lain along a beach for weeks, while "No Indean nor English laid any Claime to it." Lawmakers in Manhattan were so exasperated with ongoing dugout pilferings in 1672 that they proposed that "besides a fine" canoe thieves must also surrender "one of their Ears."[37]

These civil disputes involved Natives as well. During the Pequot War, Williams adjudicated "a grievance about a Pequot canoe" between the soldier Israel Stoughton and his Narragansett partners. In a curious case from 1650, the trader and interpreter Thomas Stanton wrote to the Connecticut governor on behalf of an Indian whose canoe had been stolen by some Dutchmen. The Dutch party, who had been visiting Stanton and sold him a sloop, took the canoe, then sold it to another Englishman on their way back to Manhattan. The Indian, "a verie fayer Conditioned ould man" who had often served as a courier, "is much wronged for want of his Cannow." Stanton helped settle the matter by delivering twenty shillings' worth of "wampam for his Cannow" as "Justies" for the crime. Another peculiar case came from East Hampton in 1659, when the Montaukett sachem Wyandanch sued the colonist Jeremy Daily for negligent care of his "Great Cannow," as Daily had failed to secure the borrowed vessel in a winter storm, leading to serious damage to its body. The dispute resulted in "one of the earliest trials involving an Indian plaintiff and an English defendant in colonial history," a trial that concluded with the colonist paying the Montaukett ten shillings for the cost of repairs.[38]

Natives and Colonial Watercraft

Along with all these scenes of English and Dutch people riding in canoes with Indians, buying canoes from Indian makers, building their canoes after Indian examples, and squabbling among themselves and with Indians over canoes, there were a number of corresponding moments when Indians appeared aboard colonial watercraft. When indigenous mariners took their first steps on those foreign decks, they encountered a place that could be mystifying and terrifying. When Verrazzano invited a local sachem aboard *La Dauphine* in 1524, his guest insisted upon touring the whole ship and "looking at all the ship's equipment, and asking especially about its uses." Just as Natives were first setting eyes on the unfamiliar capstan and whipstaff and decoding the tangle of halyards and sheets, they sometimes met unfamiliar creatures. When a party of Munsees boarded a ship of the Van Tweenhuizen trading company in the early 1610s, they were "very much afraid" when they spotted the captain's enormous dog, a mastiff that dwarfed the small dogs Natives kept. The animal barked at them furiously until they fed him a snack of Indian corncake. Likely many early Native encounters with Europeans' exotic livestock came when they got a first glimpse (or whiff) of them in their shipboard stalls. One Dutch writer assured his readers that while Indians' reactions to initial contact were often skittish and hostile, "when they have seen the ships once or twice, or traded with our people, they become altogether friendly." While coastal Algonquians and their descendants recalled the confusing mixture of fear and amazement they felt at their first sight of ships, colonial accounts imply that Natives pivoted fairly quickly from awe to appraisal.[39]

Besides introducing them to Europeans' peculiar gadgets and creatures, touring the strange ships could give Algonquians clues about the foreigners' social world, as the accommodations revealed an obvious hierarchy. It was not difficult to see that hardworking men who climbed perilous rigging and lived at the cramped bow of the ship were subject to the whims of the finer-dressed captain and his mates, who enjoyed superior lodging in the stern. Indians definitely took note of the discrepancy in wealth at ships' ends: one of the first attacks on *De Halve Maen* targeted the loot-rich aft quarters, where a Munsee thief lifted a "Pillow, and two Shirts, and two Bandeleeres" that belonged to a mate. It seemed that even hostile encounters could reveal the swift process by which colonists and Natives alike became familiar with the basic features of the others' watercraft.[40]

A few Natives were welcomed warmly to the quarterdeck, as newly arrived Christians turned to indigenous mariners for navigational assistance, realizing that having an Indian assist their helmsmen was better than any one device or chart. Contrary to the quips of some Europeans that the locals "lack navigation," these sailors were quite vocal in their appreciation of Native wayfinding. Early English traders valued their kidnapped guides' advice over "the opinion of our best Sea-men of these times," for they "understood the Natives themselves to be exact Pilots for that Coast, having been accustomed to frequent the same, both as Fishermen and in passing along the shoare to seek their enemies." Bradford singled out the former captive Squanto for showing starving Plymouth colonists "where to take fish" and acting as "their pilot to bring them to unknown places for profit." One English colonist praised Indian mariners who acted as spies on the larger Atlantic horizon, offering "certain intelligence" on the "burthen and forces" of "any roving ships," "which is a great privilege and no small advantage."[41]

Newcomers prized Natives' mapmaking abilities. Locals near Cape Ann obliged Samuel de Champlain's request to illustrate "the course of the shore," using a crayon to trace all of Boston Harbor and pebbles to mark the location of various towns. One explorer was highly grateful to the Wampanoag cartographer who alerted him to the existence of Long Island when he "drew mee a Plot with Chalke upon a Chest, whereby I found it a great Iland, parted the two Seas." Indians who met Bartholomew Gosnold's bark *Concord* north of Boston "with a piece of chalk described the coast" and demonstrated familiarity with the nine hundred miles of shoreline from there to Placentia in Newfoundland. To give a sense of terrestrial scale, nine hundred miles is about how far Chicago is from Boston.[42]

Some foreign mariners had to thank the unofficial Algonquian coast guard for saving their lives. A distressed small bark named the *Sparrow-Hawk* wrecked upon a sandbar when it veered too close to Cape Cod in the winter of 1626–27. At first the stranded crew and passengers were alarmed to see Nauset canoes approaching, "but when they heard some of the Indians speak English unto them, they were not a little relieved." Citing their alliance with Plymouth, the Nausets offered to "bring them to the English house or carry their letters" and would ultimately feed the castaways and safely transport them to the English settlement once it was evident the wrecked vessel was unredeemable. The remains of the *Sparrow-Hawk* would be rediscovered in the nineteenth century, and the astonishingly petite frame of this ocean-going vessel now sits in a museum in Plymouth.[43]

Nausets would again rush to the aid of lost Englishmen when they assisted the shipwrecked and hypothermia-stricken Garrett family and redeemed their stranded vessel from freezing waters off Cape Cod in 1630. Long Island Natives similarly discovered a delirious castaway named Flips Jansz. in 1641 and helped nurse him back to health; they assisted Jacob Alrichs and the passengers aboard the ship *Prins Maurits* (Prince Maurice) when they ran aground off Fire Island in 1657. Colonial records include instances of Native peoples finding and returning lost craft to colonists as a means of currying favor. Plymouth colonists were highly grateful to the Nausets who found a missing shallop in 1635, while officials in New Amsterdam generously rewarded one of their Munsee neighbors in 1638 for salvaging a lost yawl. Still, not all shipwreck stories involved heroic Indians. When a bark broke up on western Long Island in 1636, the colonists who came looking to salvage its lost goods were chased off by Indians who had killed two passengers and were jealously guarding the beached hull as they made off with its cargo. Later that same year a vessel bound to Virginia also broke apart "toward the Dutch." The captain, William Hammond, met a similar fate: he was "killed by a giant-like Indian."[44]

Aggressive and opportunistic behavior on the water was hardly limited to Natives. In fact, the first Indian passengers and crewmen aboard foreign vessels were there against their will, as Europeans had been stealing people away from North American shores long before the arrival of the *Mayflower*. The first instances occurred in the eleventh century, a thousand miles north of Cape Cod. Sagas of Vinland, the chain of Norse outposts that briefly claimed the edge of Atlantic Canada around 1000 CE, reported that the Viking invaders brought a couple of coastal Natives back to Greenland. Furthermore, a team of geneticists recently confirmed sexual contact between at least one Norse sailor and an Indian woman with their discovery of distinctly Native American markers in the maternal genes of eighty modern Icelanders. It is thus possible to say with confidence that approximately one thousand years ago either an indigenous woman or else a number of her descendants crossed the ocean eastward on a Viking ship returning to Europe.[45]

Coastal abductions continued when alien fishermen and explorers returned to North American waters in the 1490s. Drawn to the schools of codfish that teemed around the Grand Banks, this second wave of sailors — Basque, Portuguese, French, and English — cruised along the piney shores that Wabanaki peoples in their local dialects called the Dawnland, the present-day international region divided into Maine and the Canadian Maritimes. In their seasonal visits to the Wabanaki homeland's beaches and estuaries over the fifteenth century, foreigners engaged in sporadic captive taking. In his journey up the American coast in 1524, Verrazzano kidnapped a Native boy from the mid-Atlantic shore "to carry back to France," though he found that Europeans' people-stealing ways were already well known. On his visit to Casco Bay the local Indians would trade only at a spot "where the breakers were most violent, while we remained in the little boat, and they sent us what they wanted to give on a rope, continually shouting to us not to approach the land." Apparently, Portuguese explorers had kidnapped several Wabanaki people on a recent visit to the area in an incident that likely informed the Indians' brusque attitude. These same Natives were all too delighted to see Verrazzano go: as he sailed away, the Indians bade the ship farewell by "showing their buttocks and laughing."[46]

Although Wabanakis were among the most vulnerable to sailors' captive raiding, they were in a prime position to take command of European-style vessels. Foreigners sailing in these northern waters typically carried one or two disassembled shallops of Basque design in their holds on far-reaching voyages. The additional boat could be quickly put together to serve as an auxiliary vessel to drag additional nets or to function as a tender for trips ashore. When ships had a particularly good haul of fish or furs, the small boats would take up valuable hull space, so sea captains left them behind in hidden marshes or coves or else bartered them with local peoples for additional cargo. As a result, the peoples living along these highly trafficked waters who purchased or discovered surplus European small craft became regular sailors of the vessels, "which they can manage as well as anie

Christian." This early familiarity with foreign craft would prove to be a key adaptation of the Wabanakis, who would develop "an elaborate extractive economy" as fishermen, merchants, and pirates preying on European vessels well into the eighteenth century.[47]

Wabanaki seafarers would in turn appear further south. Often called Tarentines, they surfaced in the records of the Massachusetts Bay colony making opportunistic raids and trading with their southerly neighbors. On a visit to Boston harbor in 1638 Josselyn witnessed "an *Indian*-Pinnace sailing by us made of *Birch-bark*, sewed together with the roots of *spruse* and white *Cedar* (drawn out into threads), and trimmed with sails top and top gallant very sumptuously." It was almost certainly visitors from the Dawnland who fashioned those "*Birchen-pinnaces.*" Indians were drawn by the increased capacity and range of foreign designs as well as by the labor-saving nature of European-style sails. Yet the energy and time it would take them to master the designing of craft suited for sailpower no doubt partly explain why birchbark sailboats were rare.[48]

While Native boatbuilders emulated the basic architecture of foreign vessels, Native sailors would also borrow the trappings of European sailors' command structure. Shortly after Gosnold's *Concord* dropped anchor near the Isle of Shoals north of Massachusetts Bay in 1602, a party of Wabanakis approached, not in a canoe but in a Basque-style "shallop with mast and saile, an iron grapple, and a kettle of Copper." An Englishman noted that the leader of the Indian crew was "apparelled with a waistcoat and breeches of black serage made after our sea-fashion, hose and shoes on his feet; all the rest (saving one that had a paire of breeches of blue cloth) were naked." The details of this getup, the "sea-fashion" of the materials, the hose and shoes, all hint that this was a deliberate costume. Styling himself as a Native captain, or a sachem of the sea, this man was a classic cultural cross-dresser, a person decking himself out in the garments of another society to improve his standing when dealing with them. In two episodes from the Pequot War, Indians also donned captains' outfits. The Pequot man who killed the roguish English captain John Stone in 1634 was spotted years later proudly wearing Stone's "red scarlet mantle" while piloting a canoe. When the Narragansett sachem Miantonomi proposed chartering an English pinnace to surprise his Pequot enemies in 1637 and sink their dugouts, he made a rather specific wardrobe choice: he planned to "dress as an English man" and stand aboard the pinnace's deck while leading the amphibious attack.[49]

For reasons beyond their control, indigenous people between the Hudson and Cape Cod only rarely adopted foreign vessels. By the 1620s most Dutch and English in the area were permanent settlers engaging in coastal trade, not fishermen or traders headed back to European ports. Unlike the itinerant sailors who appeared off the Dawnland, they were typically piloting modest craft and therefore did not bring many spare boats that Native mariners could either purchase or steal. The early scarcity and resulting expense of small craft were largely what inspired colonists to adopt dugouts, and the same principles of supply and demand applied to Indians as well. Colonists did occasionally allow Indians to borrow their plank-built vessels. Williams granted Narragansett men "use of my boats or pinnace," especially in the Pequot War, though the Dutch also lent their sloops to their Indian partners in Kieft's War. And a pattern of seaborne hijackings in the region suggests that Natives' interest in foreign vessels was indeed strong: there were simply none for sale.[50]

Therefore, like the Wabanakis, Natives southwest of Cape Cod sometimes turned pirate. From their earliest encounters the Dutch and English feared hostile canoe men who "would kill the traders for the sake of the plunder." Besides lifting goods from Dutch and English holds many times over, Natives would sink a handful of colonial boats, and on a few occasions they sailed away with whole European vessels as their prizes. These raids began almost as soon as explorers appeared. A half dozen Munsee and Mahican peoples died in failed attacks on *De Halve Maen* in 1609, while pillaging Munsees would slay the Dutch skipper Pieter Fransz. aboard his ship *Vosje* (little fox) in 1613. In 1619 a former Manhattan Indian captive launched an ambitious vengeful raid on Hendrick Christiaensen's ship *De Swarte Beer* (the black bear) near Governor's Island in New York harbor. The Native pirates succeeded in murdering the captain and nearly claimed the whole ship; the Dutch sailors escaped only by scaring off the raiders with gunshots and killing their ringleader.[51]

Indian naval attacks became a regular feature of wars fought across the region from the earliest skirmishes through King Philip's War. As we will see in later chapters, the raiding and sinking of John Stone's bark in the Connecticut River in 1634 and the murder of John Oldham aboard his pinnace off Block Island in 1636, followed by Natives' theft of the craft, were precipitating events in the Pequot War of 1637. Piracy would inflame the conflicts between the Dutch and Natives, as in the Raritan attack on a Dutch yacht off Staten Island in 1641 and the Munsee raid on a ship taking a leisurely day sail in the midst of the Peach War in 1655, in which Johannes van Beeck was slain at sea, perhaps while trying to flee in a canoe. Esopus Indians made such persistent and unrelenting assaults on colonial vessels along the Hudson during the 1650s and 1660s that the Dutch sent soldiers in canoes to "constantly cruise from one side of the river to the other . . . especially at night, to prevent the coming down of their canoes, or at least to discover them." Later in the war the Dutch started capturing Esopus pirates and forcing them to serve as pilots. As the century wore on, colonists started passing laws that regulated canoe traffic and explicitly forbade the selling of European craft to Indians.[52]

Even in a period of supposed peace colonists remained on guard against offshore attacks. An Englishman sailing off Long Island in 1661 accidently hired his own murderer as a pilot; rather than show the way, the Native navigator "struck his hatchet into [the colonist's] head for his goods sake." Similarly, a party of Nantucket pirates "murdered and pillaged the saylers" in a bark stranded off Nantucket in 1665. Just two years later a man named William Weeks anchored off Naushon Island near Martha's Vineyard only to find that the local Wampanoag people had their eyes on his shallop and everything in it. All told, it was an impressive score for the islanders. The haul included two guns, an axe, a hat, eight pairs of shoes, a green blanket, a woman's cloak, a bushel of tobacco, four barrels of dried pork, and twenty-six bushels of grain and vegetables. And they kept the compact fifteen-ton vessel. Aside from minor damage to its rudder, the shallop was fully loaded with a spare foresail, a lead and line, a cable and anchor, and "all due furniture." Hunger did not seem to be a motive, for Vineyard colonists insisted that "these Indians are not necessitous, for that they have a great store of hogs which may yield satisfaction." It was unclear if Weeks ever recovered his property or if the islanders simply enjoyed their booty and kept sailing their prize for years to come.[53]

Uncovering stories of the cross-cultural fleet of watercraft that carried people, letters, and cargo undermines our simplistic pictures of how and where colonists and Indians met. European ships and navigational aids, while impressive in many ways, were an easily compromised and temperamental set of technologies that hindered as well as enabled colonists' efforts to claim the region. Canoes were much simpler to make and often better suited to the task of quickly crossing bays and rivers, making them an essential part of both Indians' and colonists' daily lives. Like plank-built craft, canoes could be both tools of Native resistance and aids to European expansion. Colonists who could count on making or buying cheap dugouts and hiring the services of Indian sea couriers would be able to scatter their new homesteads along a much greater range of small bays and inlets than just those accessible by ships and small sailcraft and yet still maintain steady links to the larger colonial settlements on the best harbors. And just as Europeans were learning the tricky business of canoe travel, Indians were figuring out how to attack and appropriate the strangers' vessels.

Especially in the first three decades of the seventeenth century, navigating the waters between Algonquian homelands and the small foreign outposts meant reckoning with greater challenges than just tides and shoals. All mariners had to figure out how to broker trade and trust in a world made up of bobbing wooden vessels. Neither Algonquian, nor English, nor Dutch seamen could fully control these floating encounters, making them highly volatile. As the years wore on, seaborne violence became less random but not less common.

THREE

The Landless Borderland, 1600–1633

More than two decades after fleets of Algonquian vessels first greeted English and Dutch ships, New England and New Netherland were more fantasylands invented by mapmakers than real territories. The invasive population was contained in two small towns founded in the 1620s—New Amsterdam and Plymouth—that each clung to opposite sides of the shore. The most consequential new arrivals, the only ones with the power to alter the landscape dramatically, were not the strangers themselves but the microscopic germs they carried in their bloodstreams. Waves of an unknown disease, perhaps the plague or smallpox, swept over the far east side of the coast, leaving vast tracts nearly empty as entire Massachusett and Wampanoag villages perished in the outbreak. By the time Europeans found these abandoned sites, bad weather had torn the dead townsfolks' houses to pieces, while vultures and other scavengers had picked their bones dry. But only the easternmost peoples felt the full force of these outbreaks of 1616–19—most other people in the region were spared their ravages. The invisible, accidental exchange of lethal microbes that reshaped one corner of the coast was an unintended consequence of the visible, intentional trade in colonial wares that transformed Algonquians' lives across the shore.[1]

Still, a traveler visiting the region as late as 1630 would have little doubt that the coast largely belonged to Natives. Estuaries were still crowded with thousands of low-slung, dome-roofed houses that greatly outnumbered the exceedingly rare stands of blocky, gable-roofed colonial homes. The farming families we typically think of as colonists had a minor and sometimes fleeting presence on the continent. And these invaders were, by their own admission, "surrounded on all sides by the Native inhabitants of the country." When Christians wanted to travel from their small compounds they usually took watercraft; if braving inland paths they were often accompanied by enormous dogs or clad in "corslets, headpeeces," bearing "weapons defensive and offensive," and generally looking "like lobsters, all cladd in harnesse."[2]

In these initial days of colonization coastal traders were far more responsible for forging relationships with Native peoples than the seasick families and preachers who sometimes tagged along with them. Trading companies, the sponsors of these ventures, would help shape the outlook and motives of the colonists, but these adventurers were "more zealous of gain than frought with experience [of] how to make it." Neither were they always in control of the process. For Indians the task of dealing with foreigners often fell into the hands of former captives. These decades during which captives and captains held sway were more than an easily skimmed prologue to the "real" events, which happened on land. Indeed, this was the moment when people formed relationships that would definitively link this region of North America to Europe, as all involved would establish strategies and form opinions that persisted well into the century.[3]

Even in early encounters there was a distinction forming between how Natives dealt with the Dutch and how they dealt with the English. Among the independent, atomized Munsee-speaking peoples of the west side of the shore Indians and Dutch alike would find each other to be brusque and commercially minded. Neither Natives nor Netherlanders would work to forge close diplomatic or military partnerships in these early decades. Meanwhile, Indian leaders from the composite, larger powers to the east would gradually come to see English intruders as valuable and potent partners. The Wampanoag sachem Massasoit in particular was quicker to link his realm to a colonial one, largely because of the destabilizing effects of the recent epidemic.

And though the colonists were still too timid to stray far from their vessels, Dutch and English leaders each claimed they had the right to rule the

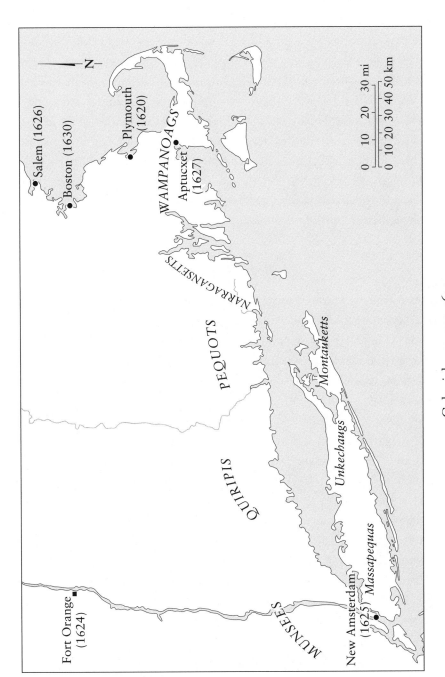

Colonial presence, 1630.

region's lands and seas. But they differed greatly in their methods, as each empire experimented with a distinct mixture of ideological justifications, blanket decrees, and symbolic gestures to assert its claim. These were all acts of legal gamesmanship that any European invader knew could be easily voided through force. Even as their numbers rose, neither colonial power had much in real claims beyond a few patches bought in small sales or wider swaths seized in the aftermath of Indian depopulation from disease. The enduring Native presence southwest of Cape Cod continued to be the main obstacle to territorial expansion. While the English population began to grow rapidly after 1630, the rival empires were first in conflict over where they dropped their anchors, not where they dragged their plows.

Cities and Companies

Each of these colonies existed mainly as optimistic projections of power across waters; to understand their origins one must glance toward the eastern side of the ocean. The booming capitals of England and the Netherlands sat along rivers that emptied into the same body of water: the North Sea. Popular histories might encourage one to see these conurbations on the Thames and Amstel as romantic places, Shakespeare's London and Rembrandt's Amsterdam, the gleaming metropolises of their nations' respective Golden Ages, places where prosperous city folk strode about cobbled streets decked in puffy pantaloons and ruffled collars. But the real Renaissance London was the gritty, plague-ridden, overcrowded epicenter of a developing nation. Its dangerous streets teemed with livestock and vermin. It was a place where homeless orphans were rampant, poor men faced grueling labor conditions in cramped workshops, and poor women sometimes turned to prostitution out of desperation. Amsterdam, though smaller and less poverty stricken than London, was suffering symptoms of rapid growth. Both cities were ruled over by an older set of elite landed families and a newer rising merchant class, both of whom were funding and profiting from the hectic, constant traffic of masts through their waterfronts.[4]

Some of the crucial differences between these two nations lay in just how their new riches were distributed. The concentration of wealth and population along England's estuaries had intensified ever since the manorial system of land tenure broke apart in the fifteenth century. The end of vassalage freed up more land for profitable sheep pastures, leading to the rise of the "middling sort" of yeoman farmers, many of whom would become the most fervent Calvinists and critics of the ideological compromises made by the top Anglican clergy. The nobles and merchants of London were often in tension with Puritan yeomanry, contributing to the ongoing national debates over the extent of the king's authority and the doctrine of the Anglican Church that contributed to the outbreak of the English Civil War in 1639. The new economy had also created a rootless class of vagrant former tenants that gravitated toward cities, causing London to balloon in size. The large population of urban poor and the abundance of highly devout farmers who were discontent with their homeland's rulers would create a vast store of potential colonists.[5]

By contrast, the growth of cities in the Netherlands was more evenly distributed. Even before the nation's tumultuous birth in the revolt against Spain, the waterlogged provinces were among the most densely settled regions in Northern Europe, home to multiple urban centers that served as trading and manufacturing hubs. The Dutch Republic's expanding economy made it a magnet for immigrants, as the Low Countries' high demand for skilled labor and its practical, if sometimes begrudging, tolerance of religious minorities would make the seven provinces attractive destinations. Most famously, a congregation of self-declared pilgrims — Calvinist separatists from Scrooby, England — settled for years in the Dutch university city of Leiden before joining the charter population of Plymouth colonists. The welcoming prosperity of the Netherlands thinned the ranks of potential Dutch colonists. Why hazard a passage in search of economic opportunities or religious freedom in a distant, dangerous land when it all could be found at home? Various political and economic struggles within the cities of England and the Netherlands greatly influenced the flow of funds and migrants toward overseas colonies, further underscoring how urbanization and empire building could be intertwined.[6]

Cities were also where both English and Dutch crafted a crucial instrument of their respective empires: the joint-stock company. The English had invented these organizations with the formation of the Muscovy Company in 1555 in an attempt to monopolize the fur trade in the far Baltic. They later established the East India Company in 1600 and the Virginia Company in 1606. Virginia was, to the English, all the land north of Florida and south of Newfoundland. From its outset the Virginia Company was split into two subcompanies representing England's two leading ports, London and Plymouth. The southern portion of Virginia (N 34° to N 41°) was granted to the London group, while the northern part (N 38° to N 45°) went to the Plymouth faction. To prevent the three degrees of overlap from becoming a source of conflict the company forbade its two internal companies from settling within one hundred miles of each other.[7]

The Dutch followed English examples when they created their own East India Company in 1602. Fur-trading merchants headed for the Hudson River formed rival small companies in the early 1610s, and their claims were later folded into, first, the New Netherland Company and then the West India Company, which was chartered in 1621 and covered all Dutch interests in the Atlantic. Though the Dutch would claim much of the same land as the Plymouth and Virginia companies, in practice New Netherland would eventually come to fill the intentional gap between the two English outfits.[8]

Along with other evolving institutions like banks and commodities markets, companies were central to the rise of mercantile capitalism. These outfits could even be seen as ancestors of the modern multinational, publically traded corporation. In fact, Hudson's Bay Company, an English fur-trading venture founded in 1670, is a going concern to this day, living on as a major Canadian retailer. As tools of empire, companies were distinct from the sixteenth-century Iberian model, in which the crown directly commissioned conquistadors and allowed them to keep a share of the profits from their discoveries and eventual colonies. The English crown and Dutch States General granted companies their charters, but these bodies were fundamentally private ventures. Companies were a direct improvement on the ad hoc ship-by-ship pattern of financing that enabled the long-range expeditions to North American fishing banks and bankrolled early fur-trading voyages. Unlike the process of funding a single ship, joint-stock organizations had more structure and permanence. Most had governing boards, while some maintained posts in foreign harbors and owned their ships outright.

Companies allowed the flourishing ports of Amsterdam and London and, to a lesser extent, places like Plymouth, Bristol, Hoorn, and Haarlem to become nodes in a truly global economy. These firms became lobbying groups for merchant interests in England and the Dutch Republic, influencing their respective states' import and export taxes. Beyond their most immediate goal of rewarding investors, trading companies sought to bolster national pride by taking on the empires of their Catholic Spanish, Portuguese, and French rivals. And although these corporations were primarily formed to foster commerce, investors often mulled the prospect of claiming and managing foreign territories, making them quasi-governmental bodies, a fact that would ultimately create tensions between them and their home states, especially in the case of the Dutch West India Company and its colony of New Netherland.[9]

Companies were partially responsible for encouraging the many published accounts of Atlantic voyages to North America, as such promotional literature could bring more investors and colonists onboard. Despite — or perhaps because of — these reports European knowledge remained spotty and speculative. Some would-be imperialists were entranced with visions of American hills littered with gold and fabulous Indian metropolises built of silver and crystal; others were more dismissive of America's potential, hoping instead that the coast would prove to be a long spit of land that could be circumnavigated and give them a shortcut to the better-documented riches of Asia.[10]

The fuzziness in regard to the shape and potential of the continent was reflected in the vague, generic names both the English and Dutch used for it. The English favored *Virginia* but sometimes *America*, while the Dutch used both terms and sometimes applied *West India* as a catchall term for all the landmasses, whether islands or continents, that stood in the way of *East India*. Not until the early 1600s, when their ships began to converge on the area of temperate coastline generally known to them as Norumbega, or "the Northern part of Virginia," would the sailors begin to meet the acute need for correct, specific local knowledge. Indeed, the greatest motive driving them to capture Natives was their utter ignorance of the local tongues and seashore. Captives would find that information was a treasured resource, one that Europeans lacked.

Captives and Captains

American Indians in the seventeenth century had a similar unawareness of the opposite shore of the Atlantic, though they had no printing presses to reproduce their speculative reports. The first accounts they had came from fellow Natives who made coerced visits to foreign ports and returned to their home shores. Colonists kidnapped at least fifty Native men from the region in the years from 1600 to 1620, while one escaped black sailor would fall into a role similar to that of some former captives. No doubt the survivors' stories of the larger ocean spread from village to village, accumulating ever more fantastic details until they became as wildly distorted as the European accounts of America.

At first glance, kidnapping seemed only to sour European dealings with Natives. Modern scholars argue that it was obvious that captive taking was a "self-defeating," "extraordinarily ill-conceived strategy" that "did not lead to grateful Natives, lasting friendships, or real alliances." Acting out of self-interest rather than a sense of larger colonial goals, the sailors who stole people from these shores left furious communities in their wake. A heart-wrenching protest came from a Nauset woman whom Plymouth colonists "judged to be no lesse then an hundred yeeres old"—though from details she gave about her family, it seems she was probably not much older than sixty. She came to meet the envoy of Englishmen on Cape Cod in 1621 but upon seeing the strange men she "could not behold us without breaking forth into a great passion, weeping and crying excessively." She explained that her three sons had all been stolen by one Captain Thomas Hunt in 1614, meaning "shee was deprived of the comfort of her children in her old age." This woman's losses had taken on new depth of sorrow as she grew older in a society that so valued the bond between generations. And even in their self-serving telling, the Pilgrims' shame at their countryman's deeds was palpable. The example of another avaricious captain, Thomas Jones, further demonstrated the folly of Europeans' stealing people from the very places they hoped to settle in. In 1622 he attempted to raid for slaves off the Massachusetts coast, but his ship *Discovery* would soon run aground "upon the Sands, neere Capecode," perhaps because his Native pilots misled him. Regardless of the cause of the grounding, "the Savages escaped and great exclamacion against the present Planters of New England." News of this protest alarmed colonial backers, who once again denounced the practice of slaving.[11]

Yet captive taking did more than just poison cross-cultural relations. Regardless of the shortsighted intentions of the captors and the obvious moral repugnancy of the practice, it initiated a kind of cutthroat, antagonistic learning process for both Natives and newcomers. There was a cynical logic behind these waterborne abductions. Foreign sailors believed the best gems of Native wisdom either could not be won through mere gifts or persuasion or else would take more effort to extract than they had time to spare. As we saw in the previous chapter, hostages could save sailors' lives with their skills as coastal navigators and lead them to profitable harbors; as interpreters they could give the foreigners a simple vocabulary in their local dialect that would be roughly intelligible across much of the shore. When George Waymouth stole five men from the Maine coast in 1605, he would claim to learn "much of their language" and regularly quizzed them about the riches of their homeland.[12]

Ships were schools for Natives, too. Captives would soon exploit their newly acquired intelligence about Europeans to their own ends. Abducted, disoriented, and often deeply embittered by their ordeals, the cohort of Algonquian men who survived more than one Atlantic crossing would find that once arrived back in America they had meaningful advantages over their captors. Trading on their hard-earned stores of geographic and linguistic knowledge, a select few would learn to survive and even thrive in the cultural spaces forming between canoes and ships. By following the journeys of those accidental go-betweens one can chart the connections forming between the Algonquians' home seas and various other harbors of the world.

English captains seized more Natives than Dutch skippers, and they also left more vivid records of their hostages' exploits. A Wampanoag man named Epenow was one of the earliest abductees for whom we can trace the biography in detail. His Atlantic journey illustrates the unexpected outcomes of maritime captive taking. Tall and well built, Epenow hailed from a place known as both Capawack and Noepe, the island the foreigners named Martha's Vineyard. Most of what is known of his life comes from an account by Ferdinando Gorges, the self-titled adventurer who became Epenow's master in England. The original captor was Captain Edward Harlow, who detained Epenow and his fellow Capawack Native Coneconam on his voyage of 1611 to the "Northern part of Virginia."[13]

Aboard Harlow's vessel, the Vineyard men met a fellow prisoner from neighboring Nantucket named Sakaweston and two Wabanakis named Pekenimme and Monopet. Three of the five men likely died in transit or soon after arrival in London, a not-uncommon fate of kidnapped Americans on forced voyages to the germy cities of Europe. John Smith would sketch out an intriguing fate for the Nantucket man, suggesting that Sakaweston lived in England for several years and eventually became a mercenary soldier in "the warres of Bohemia"; but he offered no further elaboration on the itinerant Indian's continental journeys. Meanwhile Epenow faced his own odyssey. Mystified at what to do with him back in Europe, his owners decided his unusual height and impressive physique offered "the last and best use they could make of him," and they lent him out to be "shown in London as a wonder." In his brief career as a stage performer Epenow was reportedly "stout and sober in his demeanor," learning enough English "as to bid those that wondred at him, welcome, welcome."[14]

Captive Americans were becoming a familiar sight in London. Shakespeare would mention the public display of Indians in both *The Tempest* and *Henry VIII*. The two plays were first performed shortly after Epenow arrived on the Thames, which has led some to suspect it was the lanky Wampanoag whom Shakespeare was thinking of. However, seeing as nearly two dozen Indians had appeared as "wonders" in the English capital by that date, we cannot say with any confidence that Epenow was the true subject of the Bard's pen. And while European crowds would gather to gawk at Indians again and again for centuries to come, Epenow's act itself was short-lived, as his simple gimmick of merely greeting passersby had soon "growne out of the peoples wonder." Moving from London to Plymouth, Epenow came to the attention of Gorges and his fellow entrepreneur Nicholas Hobson, who were still looking to find untold riches in New England even though by the year 1614 "adventurers of that kind were worne out of date."[15]

Colonists were still hoping the forested shores of North America held some easily extracted, lucrative source of wealth. They must have mentioned their near-obsessive interest in a soft, yellowish metal so often that their Wampanoag prisoner hatched an idea. Looking to feed his master's scheming imagination, Epenow intimated that he could "conduct the adventurers to a gold mine" on his home island off Cape Cod. The prospect was too irresistible for the adventurers to pass up, and Hobson outfitted a ship. As the English vessel carrying Epenow and four other Natives (survivors of Waymouth's raid in 1605) arrived back in American waters in 1614, "they were Piloted from place to place by the Natives themselves as well as their hearts could desire." Soon they arrived off the Vineyard, where a party of Epenow's "Brothers" and "Couzens" met the ship with great celebration. The English crew "kindly entertained" the captive and his kinsmen while they "communed" in their mother tongue.[16]

After the locals left with cheerful promises to return the next day and show the way to gold, it began to strike the captors that perhaps they were about to be had. They suspected "Epenow privately (as it appeared) had contracted with his friends, how he might make his escape." Hoping "by all meanes to prevent his escapeing," the sailors dressed Epenow in a long-sleeved shirt and pants to make it easier to restrain him "if occasion should require." Despite these precautions, the next day a fleet of twenty canoes closed in rapidly on the anchored ship, greatly alarming the English crew. After a brief struggle Epenow freed himself and slipped overboard. As the prized captive splashed into the water "the Natives sent such a showre of arrowes, and came withall desperately so neer the Ship that they carried him away in despight of all the Musquetteers aboard." Dodging whistling arrows, the crew watched helplessly as Epenow and the dream of a New England gold mine disappeared across the water.[17]

We can only imagine the triumphant homecoming ashore, with Epenow shedding the soaking "long garments" that had failed to restrain him, congratulating his fellow islanders on their daring rescue, and chuckling about the foolish men whose greed had brought him home. And whatever stories he told about his trying years in England and the peering crowds he once bid welcome, it seems the tale of his redemption became his favorite. Four years later, when the explorer Thomas Dermer dropped anchor off the Vineyard, he "met with Epinew a Sauage that had lived in England, and speakes indifferent good English." "With him I had much conference," Dermer recalled, as the former captive, who had now risen to the rank of sachem, "laughed at his own escape, and reported the story of it" with obvious satisfaction.[18]

As incredible as this tale was, it was not unique. A more spare and obscure Dutch account of two Munsee teenagers tells a story much like Epenow's, featuring a forced visit to Europe and then an American revenge. Known only as Orson and Valentine, the "two sons of the principal sachem" near Manhattan were kidnapped by the Dutch captains Hendrick Christiaensen and Adriaen Block just a couple of years after Epenow was nabbed by Harlow. Their names were a tongue-in-cheek reference to *Valentin et Orson*, a popular French medieval romance that was still well known in both the Netherlands and England in the early seventeenth century. In the play Orson and Valentine were royal twins, separated at birth when the prophetically named Orson was snatched up by a mother bear. Much of the play is about the gradual civilizing and refinement of the furry, savage Orson by his gallant brother.[19]

The drama was a powerful allegory of a long sweep of Northern European history from the Middle Ages to the early modern period. The bear, a major pagan icon, was the target of both literal and ideological campaigns of extermination. The vast expansion of plow agriculture in the medieval period would clear the continent of most of its woodlands and take a heavy toll on its brown bear populations, while at the same time Christian powers looked to eradicate uses of the bear as both a spiritual and royal totem. Embedded in the Dutch sailors' seemingly trifling joke was an arrogant narrative of how more civilized Christian ideas and landscapes were destined to replace savage ones. And engaging whimsical references to a story of educating a

feral child was a funny way for Captain Christiaensen to deflect the fact that
he needed the Munsee teens' tutelage more than they needed his.[20]

On their voyage Orson and Valentine would likely become the first
North American Indians to see the Low Countries' flat, green farms and
walk the paved banks of its cities' busy canals. They apparently never
became a stage attraction, but no doubt they were subject to some of the
same gawking that Epenow endured, perhaps paraded before West India
Company investors. Dutch spectators coming to gape at the young men
would no doubt share a knowing chuckle upon learning their adopted
names. A later chronicler would express a general disdain for these enslaved
young men, remarking, "Though very dull men, they were expert enough
in knavery." His captors would claim Orson in particular was "a thoroughly
wicked fellow," and the lack of any subsequent reference to his brother
Valentine hints that perhaps he died in the Dutch Republic or upon his
return to Manhattan. Orson escaped at some point after returning to
American shores, though the details of his liberation are missing. The brief
account of his life would implicate him as the leader of a raid in 1619 on his
former master Christiaensen's ship, De Swarte Beer (the black bear). In the
ursine-named man's attack on the ursine-named ship, Orson killed
Christiaensen. However, the revenge of the captive-turned-pirate had a
price: Orson "was paid in like coin; he got a bullet as his recompense."[21]

In their scant early records Dutch sailors did not mention any other
Indians taken back to Europe before 1630, but another well-traveled coastal
intermediary does appear in their sources. Juan Rodrigues, "a mulatto born
in St. Domingo," was a paid crewman aboard Thijs Volckertsen Mossel's
ship, Jonge Tobias (young Tobias). Though not technically a captive, much
like Epenow and Orson he would use his seaborne experiences to advance
his own needs. Traveling as a free man, not a slave, he was an archetypical
member of the charter generation of globe-trotters with African ancestry
that the historian Ira Berlin describes as "Atlantic creoles," that is, black
people who were "familiar with the commerce of the Atlantic, fluent in its
new languages, and intimate with its trade and cultures."[22]

In the middle of a dispute between Captain Mossel and his rival Block
on the Hudson in 1613, Rodrigues apparently "had run away from the ship,"

taking with him "eighty hatchets, some knives, a musket and a sword." Soon after Rodrigues stepped out of the river's brackish, chilly waters he was greeted by the local Manhattans. No doubt he was wise to come bearing gifts: that surely would have been a well-received gesture. Likely he would be immediately offered a generous bowl of fish-and-cornmeal stew, then welcomed to lodge in the sachem's ample house. And if the experiences of later Dutch traders are any guide, perhaps he was encouraged to share a bed with one of the sachem's wives or that of a young, unmarried woman.[23]

Although the exact details of his reception are unknown, there is ample evidence Rodrigues found life in America more pleasing than life as a sailor. After residing on the lower Hudson for a year, he "came on board" the vessel *Fortuyn* (fortune) and volunteered his language skills and Native contacts to serve as liaison. Rodrigues reminded the sailors that he "had no business" with any one captain and "was not bound to" any of the Dutch rivals, for "he was a free man and . . . had nothing to do with anybody." Some crewman affirmed that he was indeed never enslaved to his previous captain. After briefly conducting his shipboard business, the Dominican man returned to his new home.[24]

Conversant in Munsee, Dutch, and Spanish, familiar with captains and sachems alike, skilled in seamanship and the handling of firearms, Rodrigues had seemingly created an ideal niche for himself as an indispensable navigator of this fluid frontier. But his switching sides turned out to be a dangerous move. As the internal Dutch trading rivalry flared up again in the spring of 1614, Rodrigues's former crewmates from the *Jonge Tobias* returned to the mouth of the Hudson, where Rodrigues was now working for their rival Christiaensen, the man Orson would later slay. On an April day these mates came upon the scene of a trading liaison between Christiaensen and a party of Indians, probably near the island of Manhattan. The Indians had tethered a bark canoe to the Dutchman's sloop. When Mossel's crew "saw this, they fired at the said canoe," then "put their oars down and got their muskets and rowed towards" the Indians and Christiaensen, plowing into them "with such a speed that the canoe was smashed to pieces." They set about hacking at the canoe's sides to sink it, swinging their hatchets with such recklessness that one of the attacking Dutchmen almost had his head split in the fracas.[25]

Rodrigues tried to protect both his European and Indian partners by firing his musket at Mossel's crew. Four of his former shipmates angrily charged ashore, "took away his musket, drove him into the water, and arrested him by force." Rodrigues's new friends came to his rescue, leaping into the river to wrest him from his attackers and carrying him back to the *Fortuyn*. His ex-shipmates would later curse him as "that black rascal," seeing him as a traitor to their company. The bitter rivalry between Dutch ships was later resolved by the creation of a single New Netherland company that in 1621 was folded into the Amsterdam chamber of the West India Company. Rodrigues apparently lived out his days as the first non-Native permanent resident of the lower Hudson.[26]

By springing themselves from their floating prisons, Rodrigues, Orson, and Epenow each demonstrated the weaknesses of European power in the years when the only true colonial-controlled spaces were the decks of ships. They were finding that the knowledge of tongues and places could be more powerful than mere technology and that the adventurers' own greed was their biggest downfall. Calling Epenow "so cunning," labeling Rodrigues "that black rascal," and declaring Orson to be "a thoroughly wicked fellow," the foreign seamen seethed with a sense of betrayal and anger at the men's total lack of submission. Sailors who might have assumed these men of color would be dumbstruck at their towering rigs and cowed by the authority of the captain were finding that their hostages could see the vulnerabilities of their vessels and the weaknesses of their souls quite clearly.

Natives' dealings with these acquisitive strangers would change with the founding of fledgling colonial outposts in the 1620s. It was then that the most famous captive of all, the man known as Tisquantum, or Squanto, would use his experiences to reconcile the needs of neighbors. There is no shortage of writing devoted to this man who crossed the Atlantic at least twice, learned English along the way, and, after his return, struck up a partnership with the Plymouth colonists, who were so grateful for his help that one declared him "a special instrument sent of God for their good beyond their expectations." Squanto likely saw himself as a divine actor as well, given that his name was the same as that of a powerful figure in Wampanoag mythology and likely was a title of his own choosing. His career as seen in a regional frame reveals key distinctions between the English and Dutch experiences that would only become more evident in decades to come.[27]

Squanto came from the farming and fishing community of Patuxet, which stood along a secure harbor, the same site the English would later rename Plymouth. The Patuxets, like the Nausets on Cape Cod, were tributaries of Massasoit, who lived at the northern side of Narragansett Bay. When Samuel de Champlain visited their main town in 1605 he reported "a great many cabins and gardens," while the Natives would tell later colonists that the bay at its peak was home to two thousand people. Squanto was one of nearly thirty Patuxet and Nauset men captured by one Thomas Hunt in 1614, a fisherman in the employ of Captain John Smith who decided slaves might be worth more than codfish. (Among the thirty were the three sons of that distraught Nauset woman who, with Squanto acting as her translator, would tell colonists about her unrelenting heartache some seven years later.) Hunt had lured the men aboard his vessel and refused to let them go, hoping to sell them on arriving at his eventual destination of Málaga, Spain. For six years Squanto would become an Atlantic wanderer, making at least one round-trip. For reasons long obscure he eventually left the Spanish friars in Málaga and ended up living in the London household of a captain named John Slany. The records of his captive years are vague, but it seems Squanto returned to North America by 1619 by way of the fishing colony of Newfoundland. Then he finally sailed back toward the Wampanoag homeland, departing from St. John aboard Thomas Dermer's vessel.[28]

He would find a coast in chaos. The last decade of captive raiding had made locals deeply suspicious of English sailors, while the impact of fast-spreading diseases left many in despair. Squanto would learn that the once-bustling shores of Patuxet had been hit hard by the recent epidemics and that most of his relatives and friends were dead. Massasoit bore a deep grudge against the English on behalf of the many men stolen away, and he faced a severe challenge to his leadership. His neighbor and rival, the Narragansett sachem Canonicus, could see that Massasoit had lost many warriors to disease and seemed to be plotting to subordinate the Wampanoag leadership in its hour of weakness. Furthermore, a ragtag group of self-declared English pilgrims was squatting on the ruins of his home and dying at an alarming rate.[29]

Squanto would soon realize that he understood the perspectives of all these suffering, miserable people better than anyone else. When the still-vengeful Epenow decided it was only fair to take Dermer captive to atone for the fate of himself and his kinsfolk, Squanto rushed to Dermer's defense and helped end the quarrel. He joined forces with another savvy translator, the Eastern Abenaki sagamore named Samoset, who was himself a former captive. Both offered their services as English speakers to the new village of Plymouth. The Plymouth leadership, duly frightened by the hostile reception they received from Nausets on Cape Cod, would soon come to prize Squanto's skills as a negotiator.

More than any colonist could, the Patuxet man secured Plymouth. He helped the invaders form a simple treaty with Massasoit; he reduced tensions between them and the Nausets; he offered the colonists valuable advice in planting and fishing; and his diplomatic legwork brought about an important ceremonial feast in the fall of 1621 that we misremember today as the First Thanksgiving. The feasting was meant to celebrate the shared harvest and alliance; it was not a proper Christian Thanksgiving at all. We think of it that way thanks to late nineteenth-century writers who rediscovered the long-obscure feast and reinterpreted it as a providential moment of cross-cultural cooperation. Moreover, the menu almost certainly featured more seafood and venison than poultry. As a diplomatic event it served English needs by checking the rising power of the Narragansetts and ensuring comity with their nearest Wampanoag neighbors. As the historian Daniel Richter points out, "It was less a reflection of godly Pilgrims making peace with Indians than of a hard-headed, divide-and-rule strategy of which any conquistador would have approved."[30]

As he became aware of his indispensable nature, being the only person fluent in both Wampanoag and English, Squanto began to toy with the flow of information. He spread dubious rumors that frightened both Wampanoags and colonists, as it appeared that Squanto hoped to topple Massasoit and take his place. In 1623, in the midst of this controversy, as the Wampanoag leadership began to agitate for his execution, Squanto died a sudden, mysterious death that may have been caused by disease or perhaps poison. Bradford summed up his interpreter's career with the blunt assessment that "Squanto sought his own ends and played his own game, by putting the Indians in fear and drawing gifts from them to enrich himself, making them believe he could stir up war against whom he would, and make peace with whom he would." Bradford and Massasoit alike were learning, like a lot of sea captains before them, that having once been denied their freedom, former captives were eager to seize power as soon as they had the chance. Still, Squanto's legacy would endure. The Plymouth–Wampanoag alliance set a precedent of English leaders seeking out Native translators and attempting to engage with Indian rules of diplomacy. Sheer chance and unintended consequences also played an outsized role here. The partnership was possible only as a response to the sudden population losses and could be put into place thanks only to a decade-long cycle of captive taking that just happened to create a small cohort of translators.[31]

Looking west toward Manhattan, where the Dutch West India Company enticed several Walloon families to make their homes a few years later, one uncovers a rather different story. Whereas Plymouth colonists embraced the complex business of forming an alliance with the Wampanoags, Dutch officials dealt with their neighbors at arm's length. Compared to English sources where proper tribal and personal names were frequent, generic *wilden* (wild men) abound in Dutch accounts. New Netherlanders were far less attentive to all particulars of Native culture; they consistently depicted their neighbors as shadowy, inscrutable figures. Reverend Jonas Michaëlius, the first formally trained minister in New Netherland, would complain soon after his arrival in the late 1620s that Indians were being deliberately opaque. The minister alleged that no Dutch colonist had actually achieved fluency in a Native tongue, and no Indian was willing to be a true interpreter. It seemed to him that the locals "design to conceal their language from us," letting the foreigners learn only a simple version, "a made-up, childish language" consisting of "signs with the thumb and fingers," "half sentences, shortened words," and purposely vague terms. "Even those [Dutch colonists] who can best of all speak with the savages, and get along well in trade," he observed, "are nevertheless wholly in the dark and bewildered when they hear the savages talking among themselves."[32]

The Dutch, it seems, were seldom speaking actual Munsee dialects but instead a simplified "trade pidgin," a functional but incomplete "contact language" suited only for commerce, not full communication. The linguist Ives Goddard conducted a study of word lists compiled by colonists throughout the Northeast who claimed to know Native languages. He concluded that total colonial fluency was rare. The Munsees and New Netherlanders had one of the most enduring trade pidgins, but Goddard finds evidence that such contact languages prevailed among New Englanders as well. Sailors would use this basic, halting vocabulary when dealing with Natives across the shore, showing little regard for local shifts in dialects. Since Indians could usually understand cognates from neighboring tongues, the movements of colonists muddled languages together into functional pidgins. Hence the Narragansett *netomp* or *netop* ("my friend") would drift further west with Dutch sailors who would introduce the word into Munsee usage. Similarly, English mariners would carry Eastern Abenaki terms *sagamore* ("chief") and *wigwam* ("house") southward and conflate them with the Massachusett and Wampanoag terms *sachem* and *wetu*.[33]

The few colonists who were truly conversant were those who immersed themselves in indigenous villages for long periods, that is, mostly English preachers concerned with the fate of Natives' souls. Still, Puritans had better translators than Dutchmen from the start, as there was little doubt that after living in London Squanto grasped English quite fluently. In the coming decades Indians' forced education in English continued in colonists' missionary overtures and through their more frequent use of Natives as domestic servants. The English thus gained a robust population of truly bilingual colonists and Indians. Men who were similarly adept in the full Munsee and Dutch languages remained rare among the company leadership. New Netherland's lack of devout, university-educated colonists who were willing to mingle with Natives hindered Dutch comprehension. Writing in the early 1650s, the Leiden-trained lawman Adriaen van der Donck observed that a few veteran Dutch traders "can understand and say everything" in local Munsee, Mahican, and Mohawk dialects. "Not being learned men, however, they are unable to teach others or set out the principles of the language."[34]

Munsees' "design to conceal their language" suggests that these pidgins were not simply a product of Dutch indifference but a carefully crafted mystique. Local sachems' preference for brief dealings with the newcomers on Manhattan fit well in the diffuse political landscape on this side of the coast. These sachems had plenty of good reasons for wanting only narrow channels of communication. This allowed Natives to size up newcomers without allowing them to intervene in local disputes and upset the delicate web of alliances and partnerships between villages. Furthermore, Munsees as a whole were spared major depopulation until the 1630s. Unlike the Wampanoags, they had no immediate need for a powerful new ally to guard against aggressive Native powers looking to find them in a vulnerable moment. And since Rodrigues had disappeared from the records by 1625 and presumably died, there was no figure like Squanto, no individual with the necessary experience or motives to hammer out a partnership. Nor was there a man like Massasoit, no single sachem who could, at least in theory, speak for several thousand people. Any Dutch envoy looking to forge a stronger relationship with the Indians nearer to Manhattan would have to manage the opinions and feelings of over a dozen leaders, a task even more difficult than the feats of diplomacy that guaranteed the mutual survival of Plymouth and Massasoit's sachemship.

For their part, the Dutch, too, were hesitant to make binding alliances beyond the level of simple trading partnerships. The secretary of the colony Isaac de Rasières summed up the official policy in a letter of 1626 in which he outlined a general strategy of seeking *vrientschap* ("friendship") with all nearby nations, treating "each according to their condition and humors," all the while remembering that Natives were "much like children" seeking affection and gifts. "One must be familiar with them and lead them to believe that one trusts them a great deal," he advised, while always staying "on one's guard, or else things are apt to go wrong." The Dutch definition of friendship may have been standoffish and condescending, yet early relations could be mutually beneficial. Manhattan colonists' neutrality in Native affairs kept them from trying to adjudicate local disputes and becoming ensnared in conflicts, as had happened to the upriver traders at Fort Orange (present-day Albany), who unwisely became entangled in a

Mohawk–Mahican dispute in the mid-1620s. In its move toward permanent settlement, the West India Company preferred to purchase Indian land, seeing payments in trade goods as an easy way to avoid conflicts and maintain clear boundaries. This policy was seldom as fair as the Dutch claimed, but it represented a far greater acknowledgment of Indian property rights than the English allowed. And while Dutch colonists were slower than the English when it came to partnering with politicians, they would be the first to discover a convenient medium for linking economies. Their discovery would transform the region's simple barter system into a more complex currency-based market.[35]

The Wampum Trade

The economic transformation began, as many things did in this region, with sailors taking Indians captive. A key actor was the Dutchman Jacob Eelkens, a man with the typical cutthroat character of early colonial traders and thus no stranger to shipboard confrontations. He had been a crewman aboard the *Fortuyn* during the scuffle with Rodrigues in 1614, and he was also supercargo aboard the eighty-ton vessel *Witte Duyf* (white dove) on a trade mission off Long Island in 1620. On the latter trip, the skipper, Willem Hontom, had become wary of a group of Natives who complained about the merchandise and seemed to be looking a little too eagerly at a chest of knives, so he drove most of them from his deck, keeping four men hostage. But curiously, the Native traders returned to the *Witte Duyf* with long strings of beads as gifts to redeem their kinsmen, an act the skipper read correctly as a gesture of goodwill.[36]

This scene replayed itself in 1622 when Eelkens, now commanding his own small yacht, met a party of Pequots near the mouth of the Connecticut River. This was another routine meeting to swap furs and wares, but, for reasons long obscure, the offshore meeting became hostile. Eelkens seized the Pequot sachem Tatobem "in his yacht and obliged him to pay a heavy ransom, or else he would cut off his head." The Pequots responded the same way the Long Islanders had two years earlier: they redeemed their countryman with strings of "small beads they manufacture themselves, and which they prize as jewels." Eelkens accepted the 140 fathoms of beaded strings, a ransom so massive that if those strings were laid end to end they would have stretched more than a tenth of a mile. Dutch traders soon discovered that the powerful value Natives attached to these beads could be twisted to serve colonial interests.[37]

Foreigners would become familiar with two kinds of beads. The most common were white or ivory colored and the more rare ones were called black, though they were truly a deep shade of purple with streaks of white. White beads came from the common whelk, which resembles a small conch with a spiral structure and an inner column. After the rest of the shell was carefully cracked away, the column served as a smooth cylinder that could then be fashioned into beads. Dark beads came from the hard-shelled clam, or quahog. Mature quahogs have a lustrous aubergine growth spot just inside the hinge of their shells that Narragansetts called the *suckauaskee-saquash*, or "the black eyes." Bead makers broke these black eyes into long blanks, which were then rounded into columns, bored through, and divided into individual beads.[38]

Coming from the intersection of land and sea, these shiny purple-and-ivory beads made a durable, beautiful gift from the world of spirits. Woven into necklaces, belts, and bracelets, then worn conspicuously, shell ornaments marked the wearer's high birth or influence. In the words of an English colonist, the beads were "a rare kinde of decking." Indians also gave the beads in marriage dowries, buried them with the dead, exchanged them to cement allegiances, offered them as symbols of condolence, and used them as bounty payments to redeem captives. Colonists called this shell jewelry by several names, though none was precise. The preferred Dutch term, *zeewan* or *seawan*, meant "scattered" and referred only to loose beads. The common English name *wampum* was an abbreviation of *wampumpeag*, which meant "white strings."[39]

Archaeological digs have shown that sacred shell ornaments were part of coastal Algonquian culture for centuries. Well before Eelkens's fateful kidnappings, observant visitors took note of them. In 1602 John Brereton described Wampanoag men wearing long sashes of the beads and copper "about their bodies like bandelieres" and remarked that Indians "offered

Painting of Native American sachem, ca. 1700; photography by Erik Gould, courtesy of the Museum of Art, Rhode Island School of Design, Providence. Note his wampum headpiece, earrings, and necklace.

their fairest collars or chaines, for a knife or such like trifle." Champlain would notice "little shell beads" along the fringe of a headpiece worn by a Nauset girl in 1605. An account of Hudson's voyage in 1609 mentioned river people decked in "stropes of Beades." Still, it never occurred to any of these sailors that they could use this local jewelry to serve their own ends.[40]

Soon after Eelkens accepted the heavy strings as a ransom for the second time, his countryman Pieter Barentsen returned to Pequot country to form a conciliatory alliance with Tatobem, the sachem who had been kidnapped. Barentsen seemingly shared the improvisational smarts of men like Epenow, Rodrigues, Orson, Samoset, and Squanto. Apt with trade pidgins, Barentsen claimed he "can understand all the tribes thereabouts," ranging from the inland Mohawks to the easterly Wampanoags, and his yacht was a familiar visitor in Native harbors throughout the Dutch claims. While the sources do not specify who exactly came up with the novel idea that this surplus of beads could be recycled in future trades with other Indians, the likely innovator was Barentsen, as he forged the partnership with Pequots that allowed both to prosper.[41]

Over the next couple of years Dutch sailors would start carrying the beads with them on their yachts to serve as a kind of pidgin currency. From their perch at the tip of Manhattan they could make a short trip in yachts and shallops to the wampum-producing coastal areas to barter cloth, tools, and pots. Traders could then travel lightly up the Hudson or Connecticut with the portable beads to trade them for furs from inland peoples, especially the Mohawks and Mahicans, who lived near their new outpost Fort Orange. Ships laden with beaver, mink, deer, fox, bear, raccoon, marten, rabbit, and squirrel skins weighed anchor off Manhattan and arrived in Amsterdam several weeks later, where sales of their precious cargo would be tallied up carefully by clerks of the West India Company. Buyers in Europe would then outfit American-bound ships with the goods prized by Indian consumers. The cargo would then be shuttled back across the sea and parceled out in trading yachts headed for wampum-making towns, completing the cycle that would make local Algonquian economies part of the emerging global one.[42]

Wampum would change Europeans' relations with each other, too. As the Dutch began to prosper in their shell-based traffic, De Rasières stopped in Plymouth in October 1627. There, he told English colonists about the Dutch discovery of "Wampampeake" as part of a strategy to prevent a potential trade war. After selling them fifty fathoms of wampum, he politely suggested that the English could trade the beads with Indians to the north and east, away from the Dutch presence on the Hudson and Connecticut rivers. Up to this point, competition between Christian neighbors had been minimal. The Dutch West India Company centered its fur-trading operations on the Hudson, while Plymouth traders generally stayed near Cape Cod and points north. But De Rasières miscalculated in hoping that his gentle discouragements would keep the English away from the obvious center of the wampum trade. Soon after the visit Plymouth traders began flocking to the shores of Long Island Sound and Narragansett Bay, the most productive sites for bead making.[43]

As zeewan became the standard coin of this saltwater frontier, Natives in the region made a series of changes to their village economies that were so sweeping that one historian called it a revolution. Though coastal folks had long trafficked with their inland neighbors, the higher volume and transoceanic reach of trade with colonists was unprecedented. They began taking on new kinds of labor to engage with nearby and distant Christian consumers. Men began hunting animals with an eye for the quality of their pelts rather than their meat; women began expanding their cornfields to provide surplus harvests to sell to colonists. And all would find that becoming the clients of European traders changed the texture of daily life.[44]

As consumers, Indians often looked to satisfy practical concerns, valuing some trade items (metal tools, above all) for their time-saving capabilities and potential as weapons. But Natives also shopped with an eye for the beauty and spiritual status the objects carried with them. Thus local customers would respond to foreign goods in ways that would surprise the vendors. Instead of using new kettles for cooking, Indians might see better use for the copper as raw material for earrings, bracelets, knives, fishing lures, and arrowheads. Male hunters sometimes adorned the guns they bought more to their liking, and they sought out drab, dark cloth to camou-flage themselves from their prey. Commerce between cultures was an ongoing cultural dialogue, as determining the worth of a trade item revealed local and foreign sets of values and needs.[45]

Stores of shellfish became self-replenishing mints that financed this booming commerce in foreign goods. But turning mollusks' skeletons into beads was a tough, labor-intensive business from start to finish. Both the common whelk and the hard-shelled quahog clam were abundant along the shore, but they lived in distinct settings. Whelks cling to nearshore rocks in the summer, while quahogs and their empty shells can be found on sandy and muddy surfaces below the high-tide line; live ones also burrow in protected salt bays and brackish estuaries up to forty-five feet deep. Ecologists believe that the colonial-era rocky intertidal zone was greener and more slippery than it is today. The introduction of the common European periwinkle in the nineteenth century limited seasonal algae growth, leaving a barer, drier modern shore.[46]

For women and children, the traditional shell fishers, harvesting these two vital species meant they had to forage for whelks along slimy rocks and dig through muddy clambanks or sometimes dive into deeper water to comb the sandy bottom for the largest clams with the biggest "black eyes." Men were more often responsible for fashioning shells into beads, while women typically had the job of stringing beads into necklaces, bracelets, and "girdles." Both tasks of working with the tiny beads were painstaking and tedious. Still, the craft of minting was so prized that some bead makers took it with them to their afterlives in the Southwest. Excavations of indigenous graves on Jamestown Island on Narragansett Bay found men buried with beads, shell blanks, and drills.[47]

Indians originally made the beads with stone awls, but European metal tools turned the bead-making process from an idiosyncratic art into a standardized craft. Beads became more uniform, shifting from irregular, fatter shapes into a tubular, smaller form. In fact, small purple wampum beads probably did not exist until Indians had the lathes and drills needed to make them. A single bead was typically less than a centimeter in length and one-third of a centimeter in diameter. The average whelk shell had raw material for about half a dozen beads, while a common quahog yielded even fewer, just 3 or 4. Units were never perfectly standard, as *fathom* was often a loose stand-in for an *arm's-length* and thus could range from five to six feet and contain anywhere from 180 to 300 beads. Early exchanges typically numbered dozens of fathoms at a time. Therefore, a fairly small trade of 20 fathoms of white beads would require at least 3,600 beads, made from at least 600 individual whelks. Large diplomatic exchanges and any exchange involving black beads required even more work. One tribute payment in New England in 1657 consisted of over 1 million beads and was worth roughly seven hundred English pounds.[48]

When Indian men traded the beads they followed strict standards for finish, shape, and uniformity, considering shoddily made wampum worthless. They needed standardization to validate the craft of wampum makers, prevent careless overproduction, and discourage counterfeits. Despite the attempts of colonists to pass off cheaper fakes, "the Salvages have found a great difference to be in the one and the other; and have knowne the counterfett beads from those of their owne making." Roger Williams admired Native merchants' eye for forgeries, remarking, "I never knew any of them much deceived." Accounts of the early trade indicate that Indians retained a powerful sense of wampum's symbolic value: wampum kept its status as fine jewelry and became more important only in diplomatic and kinship rituals even as it became more abundant. Yet Natives had little trouble seeing the beads as discrete units of exchange, much like currency. Indian dealers negotiated prices on the understanding that each bead had a quantifiable value, while they offered and accepted promises of future zeewan as credit for furs and other goods. Williams found that the most opportunistic Native merchants "beate all markets and try all places, and runne twenty thirty, yea forty mile, and more, and lodge in the Woods, to save six pence." Another colonist alleged that opportunistic Indians were reselling English goods in order to "make a double profit, by selling them to more remote *Indians*, who are ignorant at what cheape rates they obtaine them . . . so making their neighbours ignorance their enrichment."[49]

Algonquian traders seemingly had the same enterprising spirit as their European partners, but they were responsible to a rather different body of shareholders, as their births into long lineages and their loyalties to their sachems were more lasting bonds than the temporary contractual obligations that ship captains had to their metropolitan backers. And while most English and Dutch investors saw the effects of the trade as numbers in account books, this traffic obviously had a more profound impact on the lives of its Native sponsors. Combining wampum's new purchasing power with its older symbolic heft, Native leaders who commanded the flow of beads would be able to exercise authority over their neighbors.

Not surprisingly, access to clam banks became a major factor in regional politics. The Pequots, who lived in what is now the southeastern corner of Connecticut and had established strong ties with Dutch sailors, were the single greatest beneficiaries of the growing wampum industry. Tatobem took the opportunity to expand his regional web of tributary sachemships, which included groups from the northern shore of Long Island and several of the smaller groups near the Connecticut River. Tatobem's easterly neighbors, the Narragansett co-sachems Canonicus and his nephew Miantonomi, also strengthened their rule by demanding wampum tributes from their neighbors on Narragansett Bay and Block Island. The once-shaky Wampanoag sachemship similarly expanded its reach by providing wampum to its closest colonial partners. Bradford marveled at how "strange it was to see the great alteration it made in a few years among the Indians them selves," noting that, as Massasoit's realm rebounded from its nadir in the early 1620s, "it makes the Indians of these parts rich and powerful and also proud therby." The Siwanoys, who lived in present-day Bronx County, and Shinnecocks, who lived on eastern Long Island, became well known as industrious, profitable wampum makers, though no such great sachems or composite powers emerged on the western side of the shore.[50]

The lure of wampum redirected the European presence on the coast. Shallops bound from Plymouth challenged their Christian competitors on Manhattan as they pursued a greater market share from the bead-making villages south of Cape Cod. These beads—and the frontier economy they helped create—were at the center of a localized imperial rivalry that would run hot and cold over the next half century. The competition of seafaring powers would ensnare Native peoples, who sometimes found themselves, and sometimes placed themselves, in the middle. Just as canoes laden with shells transformed the region in the 1620s, at the beginning of the next decade the shore would change again with the arrival of ships loaded with people.

English Migration

In the spring of 1630 a Puritan armada set sail from England. Eleven ships headed for Massachusetts Bay on a direct but dangerous route across the North Atlantic, their hulls crowded with 240 cows, 60 horses, and 700 passengers. The soon-to-be governor, John Winthrop, traveled aboard the flagship *Arbella*, a vessel "manned with fifty-two seamen and twenty-eight pieces of ordnance" and a 350-ton hold, meaning it had nearly twice the capacity of the *Mayflower* and ten times the capacity of many smaller Dutch vessels. As this passenger-heavy fleet left Cowes on the Isle of Wight, several "small ships" were also weighing anchor "bound for Newfoundland." Soon thereafter the flotilla met a handful of other English and French ships headed to the fur-trading outposts and fishing banks of Canada as well as a Dutch "man of warre" escorting another ship, "a pri[z]e he had taken laden with sugar and Tobacko." The *Arbella* and her fleet were the aberration here: the North Atlantic was still very much the sphere of fishermen, merchants, and warriors, a place where civilian passengers were rare and women and children rarer still.[51]

Those 700 colonists who sailed in the Winthrop Fleet were the first of 14,000 to come, the so-called Great Migration of colonists to New England from 1630 to 1642. This exodus was a fluke, a rush of religious families across the Atlantic that ended quickly. As mass migrations go, this one was peculiar. English Atlantic migrants were predominately young, unmarried, and male; New England's newest migrants had a demographic profile different from that of most other colonial populations. Compared to ships headed to other settlements, the Boston-bound vessels of the 1630s contained more old people, more children, more women, and more whole families. Nearly 75 percent of the migrants traveled as nuclear families, "that is, groups composed of husbands and wives, with or without children." While sizable, New England migrants were far fewer in number than the 100,000 English who sailed for what became the Chesapeake and Carolina colonies, and a downright piddling group compared to the 250,000 of their countrymen who left for Caribbean islands. Puritans sailed for New England as a temporary reaction to the injustices of Charles I's personal rule. They stopped coming as soon as war broke out between parliament and the king, and it seemed their twin goals of humbling the king and creating a more godly nation would soon be realized.[52]

In his plan of 1629 for colonizing, Winthrop noted that this newly providential and respectable colony would thrive only because of the crisis between the king and parliament. There were already "diverse plantations of the Dutch and English being settled in severall parts of those countries," but "the ill condicions of the tymes being likely to furnish those plantacions with better members then usually have undertaken that worke in former

tymes." In England the middling sorts did not look kindly on the first genera-
ation of New Englanders and Virginians, those who came over before 1630.
Robert Ryece, one of Winthrop's fellow ministers, implored him not to go
to America on the grounds that (at forty-two) he was too elderly, too religious, and too educated to become a colonist. "Plantations ar for yonge
men, that can enduer all paines and hungere," Ryece warned his friend.
"The church and common[wealth] heere at home, hathe more neede of
your beste abillitie in these dangerous times, then any remote plantation,
which may be performed by persons of lesser woorthe and apprehension."
Ryece openly fretted about how Winthrop would fare in this rough world
dominated by sailors and Indians. "How harde will it bee for one browght
up amonge boockes and learned men to live in a barbarous place where is
no learninge and lesse civillitie[?]" Ryece wondered. Perhaps "if in your
yewthe you had bin acquainted with navigation, you mighte have promised
your selfe more hope in this longe vyadge."[53]

Winthrop largely agreed with his friend's characterization of the colonies, though he had more faith that these outposts could be turned into
learned and Christian places. Looking at the initial phase of colonization
that had been undertaken by seaborne merchant-adventurers and financed
by fur peddlers and fishermen, he was quick to differentiate his planned
settlements from the coarse, improvised plantations that had preceded
them. "Ther were great and fundamentall errors in the other [colonies]
which are likly to be avoyded in" Massachusetts Bay, Winthrop argued.
Colonies such as the failed Popham venture at Sagadahoc (now Maine)
were filled with "a multitude of rude and misgoverned persons the very
scumme of the land," their backers "aimed cheefly at profitt and not the
propagation of religion," and their leaders "did not establiysh a right forme
of gover[n]ment." Part of the critique of the early colonies was that their
economic activities—trading for pelts, logging pines for masts—were too
extractive and not productive. A biblical commonwealth would therefore
be built on a foundation of farms. Perhaps the best summation of this new
colonial ethos can be found in Thomas Tillam's poem "Uppon the first
sight of New-England" (1638), which opened with the couplet, "Hayle holy-
land wherin our holy lord / hath planted his most true and holy word."[54]

This new wave of settlers chose the area near Massachusetts Bay precisely because it was where "Plague" had fallen "on the Indians with such a mortall stroake that they died on heapes," leaving behind a nightmare landscape of desolate villages scattered with "bones and skulls" and "but a small number of Salvages" to contest their arrival. In justifying their claims to a country that the historian Francis Jennings famously labeled a "widowed land," not a "virgin" one, the English often made seemingly contradictory statements that they had asked for permission to take something for free. Plymouth settlers simultaneously claimed in the same sentence that Native land was "a common land or unused and undressed country" and that "we have it by common consent, composition and agreement" with Massasoit. Winthrop seemed at times to dismiss the surviving Natives' property rights, scoffing that "these savage people ramble over much land without title or property," but he went on to insist that even if Indians had claims there were not enough surviving Indians to contest them as "god hathe consumed these nations in a myraculous plauge wherby a great parte of their country is left voyd without inhabitants: we shall com in with good leave of these nations." Ultimately, the land was simply too ample for this issue to matter: "Ther is more then enough for them and us."[55]

An anecdote from Winthrop's journal aptly demonstrated the complex reality undermining the Puritans' assurances that they had arrived in a "waste" or "wilderness." When the governor "walked out after supper" from "his farm house at Mistick" one October night in 1631, carrying a gun and "supposing he might see a wolf," the governor "mistook his path" in the dark about a half mile from his fields. Thankfully, Winthrop "came to a little house of Sagamore John which stood empty" and "so spent the night, sometimes walking by the fire, sometime singing psalms, sometimes getting wood, but could not sleep." After dawn "there came thither an Indian squaw," but Winthrop "barred her out; yet she stayed there a great while essaying to get in, and at last she went away, and he returned safe home." The little house, it seems, was no random structure but a building with a very specific purpose. Menstruating Algonquian women typically isolated themselves in small wigwams for four to six days. Likely Winthrop had inadvertently broken a major taboo by occupying an exclusively female space.

To whom did this land belong? To the woman furious at the man violating her monthly ritual of solitude and rest? Or to the armed man who had barricaded himself in a stranger's edifice and was so nervous he could not sleep through the night? Which fact was more precious: that Winthrop's unexpected adventure happened less than a mile from his own backyard? Or that he actually called himself governor of this domain with a straight face?[56]

The English claim to Massachusetts Bay was riddled with inconsistencies. On the one hand, colonists claimed they had arrived in a land that belonged to no one, a land where there was no government, and therefore it did not need to be purchased because the supposed first discovery of John Cabot in 1497 conferred the authority of the English king over the land. Their evidence was the lack of a recognizably European style of cultivation—Puritans refused to see portable villages, burned hunting grounds, and lumpy cornfields as comparable to a patchwork of pastures and furrowed fields, complaining that Natives failed to follow the command in Genesis 1:28 to "replenish the earth, and subdue it." Abandoned, postepidemic villages gave the accounts of vacancy a degree of truth. Yet on the other hand, in seeking Natives' "common consent" and "good leave," the English were tacitly acknowledging some kind of Indian claims. Puritans soon went back on their assertion that land could not be purchased: in 1642 Winthrop himself bought a plot of over one thousand acres from Indians along the Concord River. Such purchases were not common in the early decades of the Bay Colony, but they further illustrate the ambiguity of colonists' claims that American land was free for the taking.[57]

There was a crucial distinction that allowed for the disparity between Puritan words and Puritan actions: when colonists asked Natives for permission to settle, they were seemingly only recognizing Indian sachemships as physical threats and not as sovereign bodies with valid territorial claims. By that same logic Winthrop could be governor of a place in which he was so easily lost and terrified. Furthermore, Puritans' legal claims had little bearing on real-world dealings with Indian leaders, as the colonial leaders hardly expected that a sachem would challenge them on the basis of international law. Contesting possession with Indians would come down to complex cultural negotiations rather than to a declarative legal writ; the claims that God handed officials this land were intended to allow the colonial government to assert the superiority of its territorial rights over its subjects' rights. Massachusetts banished the Salem preacher Roger Williams in 1636 in part for his belief that Indian land should be purchased. His argument was troubling not just because it claimed that Indians had sovereign rights, but also because it could empower ordinary colonists to challenge the Bay colony's tight control over land transfers.[58]

The ambiguity of establishing landownership in New England was a reflection of the overall ambiguity of property itself in western Europe. In the seventeenth century landownership was still undergoing a vast legal and economic transformation, as the last remnants of a feudal legal structure gave way to emerging capitalist notions of land use and commodities. Because the legal right to own land was still intimately tied to the person and authority of the monarch, each colony needed a royal charter before being parceled into towns by founding proprietors, who slowly transferred the land from common to private ownership. By contrast, Dutch colonists' methods of securing land on the west side of the coast would look somewhat different, in no small part because the ratio of Indians to Europeans was considerably higher.[59]

Dutch Stagnation

The Dutch were slowly building a colony with a bare minimum of colonists. By 1625 they made their first earnest go at colonial settlement. To sustain their new outpost on Manhattan the company attempted to recruit colonists by setting up a system of semimanorial colonies-within-the-colonies called *patroonships* to sustain the New Amsterdam settlement year-round. Their principal aim was to attract enterprising Dutch colonists, though French-speaking Walloons, French Huguenots, and English settlers ended up becoming a sizable minority population. The Dutch also brought a small but not negligible number of African and African-Caribbean slaves to their Manhattan settlement. Yet even with immigrants coming from beyond the Low Countries, the colony grew slowly, accumulating people in the 1630s at a rate of fewer than one hundred a year. Of the seventy-three ships the company outfitted for trade in 1626, only two were bound for New Netherland. That same year, out of the total company expenditures of ƒ7,304,000, only ƒ120,000 — 2 percent of the budget — was earmarked for New Netherland.[60]

Rather than being an intentional choice, the scarcity of migrants was a symptom of the lack of recruits in the thriving Dutch fatherland and an indicator of New Netherland's marginal place within Holland's larger scheme of empire. One faction within the early company, led by one of its chief organizers, Willem Usselincx, saw the Hudson territory as a potential laboratory of Calvinist principles, while the majority of backers saw the company as an instrument of trade and war to be wielded against the Spanish. To them, New Netherland was only primarily interesting as a source of profits and a convenient port, not as the ground in which a new society would be planted. Recruiting migrants for their North American colony remained a low priority, seeing as the company remained preoccupied with the far more glamorous and rewarding business of capturing Iberian galleons laden with silver and smuggling goods between Caribbean islands. The focus for the next decade would be less about working land than about filling their outgoing ships with furs.[61]

The methods the Dutch used for claiming land were distinct from those of their English neighbors. While both made similar claims of first discovery and both parceled up their larger claims in vaguely similar ways (with the corporate body taking first ownership, then reselling land to *patroons* and private owners), the Dutch were much more likely to offer Indians payment for land. And Netherlandic notions of territorial authority were linked not just to the perceived improvement of land through agriculture, but also to the control of commerce within a region, meaning they saw possession as being intimately linked to trading as well as to farming. In their lengthy war of independence from Spain, the seven provinces of the Republic were untethered from the authority of a single Hapsburg emperor. Land was governed by local jurisdictions that had already established considerable control over property before the revolt. Sovereignty in the fatherland was thus locally strong and nationally weak; the real power brokers of the Netherlands were found in the burgher elites of provincial market towns. There was a similar architecture to the colonial power structure. While the

States General was the sovereign body underwriting all claims, landowner-ship was managed by the merchants of the West India Company, and their sovereignty was demonstrated by their local monopoly of all trade.[62]

To establish the bounds of their trading zone Dutch colonists affixed "the Arms of the States General" in prominent places along the coast. Soon these shield-shaped plates of metal adorned spots from Cape Cod to the current site of Philadelphia. The historian Patricia Seed points out that since the Middle Ages Dutch market towns used "municipal arms as equiva-lent to modern 'No Trespassing' signs." Posted around the outskirts of town, they allowed a city to assert "its freedom from the local lord, warning revenue, judicial, and military officers to 'keep out' for the town administered these functions." These metal plaques served as warnings that any violation of Dutch commercial territory would be answered with force. Amsterdam's emblem, adorned with three diagonal crosses in a kind of triple-X shape, is the most famous of these medieval seals.[63]

The exact appearance of the States Arms is unknown, but most were likely fashioned from copper, and they almost certainly featured *De Nederlandse leeuw* (Dutch lion) holding seven arrows in its right paw, repre-senting the seven provinces united against Spanish tyranny. As the historian Simon Schama points out, this heraldic climbing *leeuw* was a ubiquitous symbol in seventeenth-century Dutch visual culture. Lions appeared in relief on silver coins, pressed into sealing wax, etched in woodcuts, and traced on maps that arranged the seven provinces into the form of the iconic leeuw, while the animal itself was shown holding raised swords, bounding from the sea or surrounded by a stockade wall in defiance of Spanish sieges. Perhaps a few centuries-old leonine images are still scattered somewhere deep in the soil near Manhattan; in 1972 an excavation at the footprint of Fort Amsterdam unearthed a finely made clay pipe dating to the 1660s with a maker's mark on the heel featuring the triumphant great cat.[64]

The copper lions the West India Company affixed to trees were subject to frequent vandalism. "Mischievous savages" from the Delaware Bay had pilfered one of these arms near the Swanendael settlement in 1631, possibly as a protest against an act they recognized as staking out territory or perhaps to reuse the valuable copper. The furious Swanendael colonists demanded that the Indians bring them the head of the thief. The Natives obliged the request, but the Dutch remained suspicious: a colonist later assumed the incident was the cause of the eventual destruction of the settlement by Indians. Colonial competitors were likewise known to have defaced the arms on multiple occasions.[65]

The West India Company's belief that marking their trading zones with metal seals would reify the borders of New Netherland was just as compromised and self-serving a ploy as the opportunistic claims of *vacuum domicilium* by the English. There was a basic ideological chasm between the rivals on the topic of possession. The Dutch tended to believe that trafficking where Indians were still present would grant them ownership and authority over the territory, while the English gained a purchase on the mainland by opportunistically repopulating and replanting the ruins of a devastated Native

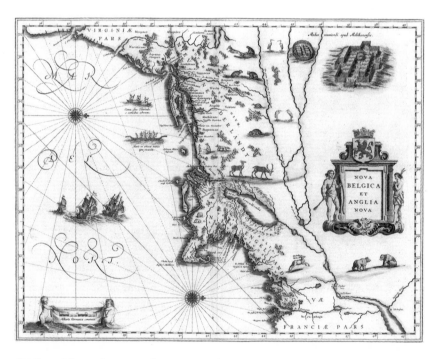

Willem Blaeu, "Nova Belgica et Anglia Nova" (1635); courtesy of the John Carter Brown Library at Brown University. The Dutch mapmaker gave New Netherland a generous swath of the coast.

landscape. To put it in the most simple terms, the Dutch leadership presumed that American territory could be theirs through commerce, while the English liked to think their chosen corner of the continent was a gift given by God.

Claims to the Sea

The two foreign nations differed not only in their practices of claiming land but also over whether the ocean could be claimed at all. The Dutch Republic's merchants and lawmakers were avid backers of the theory of *mare liberum*, or freedom of the seas. The nation's preeminent jurist Hugo de Groot (better known by his Latin title Grotius) described the principle as a kind of theological and geographic common sense, declaring "do[es] not the ocean, navigable in every direction with which God has encompassed all the earth . . . offer sufficient proof that Nature has given to all peoples a right of access to all other peoples?" Since "the sea is common to all . . . it cannot become a possession of any one, and because it is adapted for the use of all." The theory fit nicely with Dutch goals. Unrestricted naval traffic would be central to ensuring the growth of a nimble seaborne empire made up of more ports than plantations.[66]

By contrast, many in the English kingdom would favor the theory of *mare clausum*, or closed seas. In laying out the legal basis for maritime possession, their countryman John Selden rejected De Groot's theory that the sea was outside the rule of man. Selden contended that biblical covenants granted man ownership of both land and sea, while fortunately the new mapping technologies made bounding waters a perfectly feasible task. Waterways, shorelines, and fisheries could be claimed by a seaborne empire willing to defend its bounds with robust tariffs and duties, abundant forts, and well-armed naval and merchant fleets. Despite their differences, De Groot and Selden agreed that the central question was whether sovereignty over the ocean and its margins would belong to discrete European nations or be shared by all Christians; neither seriously considered indigenous coastal powers as major factors in their emerging debate over international law.[67]

This lofty discussion of maritime possession would come to life as the English and Dutch contested their claims to American shores. King Charles

I's charter for Massachusetts Bay explicitly gave the colony right "to have and to hould, possesse, and enjoy all" American territory from N 40° to 48°, including "seas, waters, fishings, with all and all manner their commodities, royalties, liberties, prehemyences, and profits." The Dutch West India Company made a far more modest claim of N 39° to 41°, bounds that, by their imprecise instruments, gave them the rights to the continent from Cape Cod to Delaware Bay. The company's claims to the Hudson River were based in rights of *De Halve Maen*'s first discovery and later purchase from Natives. The English would try to discredit both assertions, scoffing at the notion of Indians' dominion and maintaining that Hudson's English birth somehow lent rights of discovery to them, ignoring the fact that he sailed on an East India Company ship. The Dutch further argued that the original claims of the London and Plymouth companies left a hundred-mile coastal gap between Virginia and New England, a gap that New Netherland now filled. In correspondence that truly tested these ideals in practice, the West India Company laid out the case for a mare liberum on American shores, reminding Charles I that they had "from all time, in coming and going, freely enjoyed your Majesty's ports and harbors without any objection."[68]

Whatever their ideological leanings, neither colonial power adhered to a foolish consistency in North America. Dutch colonists had threatened to fire on English ships sailing in their supposedly free waters, while English colonists who dismissed Dutch purchases of Indian land would also soon seek out deeds from their Native neighbors. And despite its paltry number of colonists, the Dutch West India Company appeared positioned to dominate all trade south of Cape Cod. Thus when New England traders attempted to grasp a larger share of trade, they signaled a looming challenge to the status quo. The English were openly jealous of the Dutch. "Glance your eye upon Hodsons river," the colonist John Underhill wrote in 1637, "a place exceeding all yet named" in "the garden of New England." Around the same time, the trader Thomas Morton enviously estimated that New Netherland's "great trade of Beaver" on the Hudson reaped them some "20000 pound a yeare." Morton was entranced by tales of "a very spacious Lake" that fed the Hudson and was "the principal part of all New Canaan for plantation, and not elsewhere to be paralleled in all the knowne world." "It would be adjudged an irreparable oversight," he warned, to "suffer the Dutch (who are but intruders upon his Majesties most hopefull Country of New England) to possesse themselves of that so plesant and commodious Country."[69]

Fanciful dreams of the Hudson's path to a bountiful inland sea and more verifiable reports of wampum-rich villages on Long Island would lure English ships to the New Netherlanders' favorite harbors. As early as 1626 New Amsterdam colonists were sending alarmist letters back to Holland griping about Plymouth colony traders who "come near our places to get wampum in exchange" and "threaten to drive away" the small colonial population on the Hudson. With "two or three large sloops more," the Dutch were determined to hold their waters, "either [by] force or by spoiling their trade by outbidding them." New Netherland traders also "request[ed] the aid of forty Soldiers for their defence" from the States General, though the West India Company's governing board preferred to have the matter settled "by friendly alliance."[70]

Fights over the uncertain maritime boundary surfaced on both sides of the ocean. In the spring of 1632 officials in Plymouth, England, seized the *Eendracht*, a Dutch ship laden with "over five thousand beaver skins" headed from New Amsterdam to the old one. They held the foreign vessel, "first, on pretence that the cargo of the ship was procured in the English Colonies; next, that the Company had appropriated some countries belonging to the English." The seizure triggered a minor diplomatic crisis between the Netherlands and England, as the envoys from the Low Countries, in a series of increasingly exasperated letters, petitioned Charles I to release the ship to the point that the Stuart king granted the Dutch ambassador a private audience to discuss the matter. The *Eendracht* and its passengers languished for weeks in Plymouth before being released with no official penalty, though the delay cost the West India Company untold guilders in lost revenue, as some of the crew illegally off-loaded pelts in England.[71]

Two years later a London-based ship named *William* sailed to the mouth of the Hudson in search of fur-trading partners, triggering another "quarrel with the Dutch about the possession of New Netherland." The gunners at

Fort Amsterdam actually trained their cannon on the intruding ship, which eventually sailed away empty-handed. Jacob Eelkens, the man who kidnapped the sachem Tatobem and helped spark the wampum trade, was on board the *William*, having defected to serve the English. Likely he was there to serve as an envoy to the Hudson River peoples he had traded with many times before. These English attempts to undermine Dutch claims in North America were part of the ongoing ideological conflict over mare clausum and mare liberum between the rival empires. And while the English spoke most covetously about the Hudson, it was the more easterly water highways—Long Island Sound and the Connecticut—that became the first flash points.[72]

In the 1630s the English went from playing a secondary role south of the Cape to eclipsing both the West India Company and the Pequots as the region's greatest power. This was hardly the most likely development. There were a number of restraints on potential English settlement in the area: not only the competing Dutch claims to Long Island Sound but also the robust Indian population, which had yet to experience the devastating pandemics that had emptied so many Native villages near Massachusetts Bay. Even when smallpox swept through the area in 1633, deadly as it was, it did not clear the entire area for easy settlement. And as sizable as the English Great Migration was compared to Dutch stagnation in the 1630s, it consisted only of fourteen thousand people, a small flood by the standards of most mass Atlantic migrations and deemed great only by later nationalistic mythmakers.

New England's southward creep was not quite the logical, preordained result of an unstoppable Puritan flood or an inherent Dutch coyness about colonization. Rather, it took a series of chance events and fateful choices by sachems, captains, governors, and directors to allow the English to move down the coast. Though cartographers' pens created the supposed borders of New England and New Netherland, the colonies' bounds were truly drawn with bullets, swords, and fire.

FOUR

Blood in the Water, 1634–1646

The attack began in darkness, on a hill that overlooked the Mystic River and Long Island Sound. Before dawn on a May morning in 1637 ninety English soldiers accompanied by some two hundred Native allies crept silently up the hill's slopes. Fanning out, the men surrounded the fortified Pequot town that sat at the summit. A dog picked up the scents or sounds of the approaching men as they crept outside the wall and began to bark. Then a Pequot voice called out, "Owanux! Owanux!" (Englishmen! Englishmen!). The English fired a volley of gunshots between the gaps in the Pequots' stockade wall. Bullets tore through the sides of wigwams and hit still-slumbering bodies. The shock of this horrific awakening "bred in them . . . a terror" that caused the villagers to "brake forth into a most dolefull cry."[1]

As the soldiers charged inside the walls, Pequot men rushed to grab their weapons. Their arrows and bullets ricocheted off the invaders' metal helmets, snagged in the soldiers' heavy coats, and pierced over twenty colonists' flesh, "some through the shoulders, some in the face, some in the head, some in the legs." A frustrated captain called out, "WE MUST BURN THEM; and immediately stepping into the wigwam where he had been before, brought out a Fire-Brand," which he used to kindle the roofs of nearby houses. Once the English had torched the Pequots' buildings they retreated outside the town's walls where their Indian partners were waiting, and they shot at any villagers trying to escape. A holocaust swiftly consumed the dense cluster of wooden buildings and "blazed most terribly, and burnt all in the space of halfe an houre." In those thirty minutes three to four hundred people perished, most of them women, children, and elders. Soon "so many soules [lay] gasping on the ground so thicke in some places, that you could hardly passe along."[2]

Six years later another assault began in a similar moment of calm. On a snowy February night in 1643 Dutch boats packed with armed men closed in on two hushed Native settlements near the long, hilly mass of Manhattan. One gathering of houses sat on the island's bulging lower east side, just up the East River from the colonial capital of New Amsterdam. The other stood on the west banks of the Hudson, fires glowing in plain view of the colonists' main fort. Around midnight, as the soldiers began charging the Hudson settlement, their initial shots caused "a great shrieking" so piercing that it could be heard a mile across the river. The most detailed source on the events of this night alleged that the Dutch men committed atrocities, including the slaughter and drowning of small children, with no mercy given to their horrified parents. Meanwhile, on the banks of the East River another "forty Indians were in the same manner attacked in their sleep" by Christian soldiers bearing firearms and swords.[3]

The next morning the bodies of at least eighty Munsee people lay scattered near where they had bedded down the night before. The townsfolk in New Amsterdam witnessed a shocking parade of their maimed neighbors desperately seeking help, "some with their legs cut off, and some holding their entrails in their arms, and others had such horrible cuts and gashes." The soldiers believed "they had done a deed of Roman valor," and Director Kieft "thanked them by taking them by the hand and congratulating them." The author of the most lurid account of the event, a longtime critic of the director, concluded that the atrocities were "indeed a disgrace to our nation."[4]

Two Wars, One Shore

These two dark moments are part of a single chapter of bloodshed. Over one decade nearly two thousand coastal Algonquians, many of them young, elderly, or female, would die at the hands of Europeans. Natives would slay over one hundred colonists and wound scores more, though most of their victims were adult men. These bursts of terrifying violence started on the eastern side of the shore in the late 1630s and reignited on the west side in the mid-1640s. Traditionally, historians who wrote about these incidents of bloodshed divided them into two unrelated events. The eastern, English-led campaign of 1636–38, known as the Pequot War, is one of the most well studied and infamous episodes of the New England past, while the western, Dutch-led conflict of 1642–45, known as Kieft's War, is a far less famous but more brutal moment from the history of New Netherland.[5]

Neither war was truly confined within the bounds of one colony. The English skirmishes with Pequots raged within thirty miles of Manhattan, and fleeing Pequots would show up further westward along the shores of Long Island Sound and up the Hudson Valley. Six years later Dutch soldiers ventured well beyond New Haven's limits in pursuit of their Native enemies. Not only did these two wars share a stage, but they featured some of the same actors. The most famous was the man known on the eastern side of the coast as John Underhill and on the western as Jan Onderhill, an English-born, Dutch-trained mercenary Puritan soldier who commanded massacres of Indian civilians in both the Pequot War and Kieft's War. When he fought the second time several veterans of his first campaign marched alongside him. And other colonists who witnessed parts of the first war would become participants and victims in the second one, including numerous Dutch traders who sailed through the midst of the Pequot War, the sea captain Isaac Allerton, the colonial governor Roger Williams, the banished heretic Anne Hutchinson, and other English colonists who left Narragansett Bay and the Connecticut Valley to settle under the Dutch.

The illusory Anglo–Dutch boundaries were even more meaningless to Indians, who carried older, more complicated maps of the shore in their heads. In these years of war many Native people would range widely across the coast's ancient boundaries as both refugees and fighters. Some people might have even been dislocated twice: likely a few of the surviving Pequots who fled the English forces to shelter among Hudson River peoples would find themselves fleeing Dutch soldiers just a few years later. And no doubt some Indians living near Manhattan who had sheltered, captured, or killed runaway Pequots were then the targets and partners of Dutch campaigns.

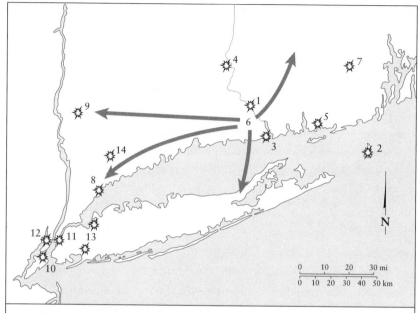

1 Murder of John Stone, January 1634
2 Murder of John Oldham, July 1636, English Attack on Manisses, August 1636
3 Pequot Attacks on Saybrook Fort, September 1636-March 1637
4 Pequot Attack on Wethersfield, April 1637
5 English Attack on Mystic Fort, May 1637
6 Paths of Pequot Refugees, Summer 1637 (indicated by arrows)
7 Pequot Battle with Nipmucks and Narragansetts, July 1637
8 English Attack on Pequot Refugees, August 1637
9 Murder of Pequot Sachem Sassacus, August 1637
10 Raritan and Dutch Attacks and Counter-attacks, 1640-1641
11 Dutch Attacks on Pavonia and Corlear's Hook, February 1643
12 Munsee Attacks on New Amsterdam area, February-March 1643, August- December 1643
13 Dutch-English Attacks on Long Island Natives, Winter-Spring 1644
14 Dutch-English Attack on Tankitekes, March 1644

Major events in the Pequot War and Kieft's War.

No Native leader was more prominent in both wars than the Narragansett sachem Miantonomi, who was an ally of the English colonial aggressors in the Pequot War but an early advocate of Native resistance to the Dutch in Kieft's War. Examining connections between the two conflicts, one finds it difficult to think about one without considering the other.[6]

Viewed from a colonial perspective, the conflicts were the first hot moments of a longer Anglo–Dutch cold war. By slaughtering and subjugating

Indians, Europeans were also fighting each other in proxy, as their aggressive moves were attempts to claim much of the same shoreline. Both hoped this coast would become a profitable and strategic node in their emerging Atlantic empires, making it a small theater of a global rivalry. Colonists' geopolitical goals coincided with their desire to overcome logistical problems of geography: both wars were fights over spaces that were far too fluid for the colonists' liking. The Pequot War began with a chain of vicious attacks that were a continuation of the decades-old phenomenon of seaborne squabbles between traders and Indians. Naval attacks also contributed to the outbreak of Kieft's War, a conflict that was similarly amphibious. During the fighting the Dutch would soon find that their haphazard coastal settlement pattern among the many Munsee villages would make them highly vulnerable to canoe-borne raids.[7]

These wars allowed New England and New Netherland to end their initial tentative, maritime-based stage of colonization and begin a more invasive, territorial-based stage in which the foreigners openly tried to subjugate their Native neighbors. Yet even in these wars of domination, diplomacy was essential. English governors' attention to—and sometimes deliberate manipulation of—Algonquian rules of alliance was in sharp contrast to the Dutch leadership's indifference to Native peacemaking protocols. The English, who killed far fewer of their enemies than the Dutch, would end up claiming more territory and more Indian partners, while the grueling Dutch war with their Munsee neighbors ended with the colonists in the same position as when they began.

These killing years would remake the Native political world. Colonists' destructive ways of war would cause some Indian leaders to argue that all the original peoples of the shore should forgive old wrongs between them and unite as one. Others would decide that forming strategic partnerships with newcomers was the best path forward. To the east, where supposedly monarchical sachems maintained tributary webs of allies, the decade of war would realign all villagers toward becoming clients of the English, whether through choice or coercion. The English advance would also cause great turmoil among the noble-born elites of these larger coastal sachemships. In the immediate power vacuum created by the death of many Pequot elites, the bold, opportunistic Mohegan sachem Uncas built a new composite sachem-ship that largely replicated the former Pequot realm. The Narragansetts as well would undergo a crisis of authority in the years following, as the younger sachem Miantonomi rejected the accommodating strategies of his uncle Canonicus and cause a split in the Narragansett leadership.[8]

For the more independent Munsee-speaking democracies to the west, war with colonists led first to a sense of solidarity between sachems, but that cohesion faded the longer the war dragged on. Some powers, particularly the Raritans and Esopus, were defiant throughout the conflict and remained dismissive of Dutch authority in the years following. Other powers that had long sought peaceful dealings with New Amsterdam—the Wiechquaesgecks, Hackensacks, Tappens, Tankitekes, and Canarsies—were at first frustrated at the Dutch director's incompetence in diplomacy and then became enraged at his provocation. Still, most slowly and begrudgingly reconciled themselves to a peace. In the years after the fighting, trends that began in the landless stage of colonization would continue even as colonists became more grounded. Western sachems as a whole continued to have looser, more ambivalent alliances with their Dutch allies than the eastern leaders, who formed closer and more conspiratorial relationships with their English partners.

Seen at a village level, the outside factors driving this decade of death were not obvious. Christians living along the muddy lanes of Manhattan would see things quite differently from those on the Connecticut, while Natives whose cornfields faced the Hudson had a distinct perspective from those on Narragansett Bay. And yet as one charts the course of the two wars, it becomes clear that across this saltwater frontier, politics were never entirely local. Whether they knew it or not, the fates of all these peoples were bound together by regional waters and the larger Atlantic.

The Naval Origins of the Pequot War

A convoluted chain of waterborne murders would turn the Connecticut River and Long Island Sound into the center of the imperial rivalry. Tensions over the region began to rise in 1632, when Dutch traders bought a plot near modern Hartford and raised a small compound with the cheery name Huys de Goede Hoop (house of good hope). Plymouth traders founded a rival outpost a couple of miles upriver soon after to intercept southbound Natives carrying furs. The next Dutch attempt to leapfrog the English, however, coincided with a catastrophe for the locals. Setting their sights on a powerful, fortified upriver village well north of the Plymouth traders, "three or four Dutchmen went up in the beginning of winter to live with them, to get their trade, and prevent them for bringing it to the English." As William Bradford recalled, however, "Their enterprise failed, for it pleased God to visit these Indians with a great sickness, and such a mortality that of a thousand, nine and a half hundred of them died." As smallpox killed off their hosts with horrifying swiftness, "the Dutch men almost starved before they could get away" on account of "ice and snow," leaving behind many corpses that "did rot above ground for want of burial."[9]

This was the beginning of a smallpox epidemic that would sweep across the Northeast. Perhaps the most lethal outbreak hit the farming villages that lined the banks of the Connecticut. By the winter of 1634 the shores that were once home to some of the densest towns and richest cornfields in the region suddenly stood empty. To colonists in Massachusetts Bay, where the Great Migration of thousands of farming families from England was causing their numbers to swell, news of the sudden depopulation of "a place of a very good soyle, good meadow, divers sorts of good wood" piqued their interest in the area; the first attempts at English settlement would begin just months later. As one colonist remarked, "The fear of [those Connecticut tribes] was an obstacle unto them before," but with the locals "being now taken away, they began now to prosecute it with great eagerness."[10]

Looking to maintain order in the devastated region, the ever hopeful Dutch West India Company tried to create a kind of free trade zone in the region. While maintaining their primary partnership with the Pequot sachem Tatobem, they insisted that he allow his competitors to have safe passage to do business at the Dutch post on the Connecticut. But in the midst of the desperate, uncertain months of the smallpox epidemic, Pequots killed a group of Narragansetts on their way to the Dutch trading house. Angry at this blatant breach of their agreement, the Dutch responded by taking Tatobem hostage aboard a trading yacht and "demanded of [the Pequots] a bushell of Wampam-Peke." It was a disturbing restaging of the very acts that had awakened the Dutch to the idea of using wampum as a trade currency. But this time the resolution of the hostage situation was destructive rather than creative. The distraught Pequots dispatched a canoe with the massive ransom, but the Dutchmen nevertheless murdered their hostage, apparently out of spite. A Pequot elder later reported that this sense-less act "much exasperated our spirits, and made us vow a revenge."[11]

Just months later, as the Pequots were still grieving the death of Tatobem, a hard-drinking Virginia trader named John Stone came sailing through Long Island Sound with mischief on his mind. His meeting with a group of Pequot men at the mouth of the Connecticut took a fraught turn when Stone took two hostages, "bound them, and made them show him the way up the river." That night parties of Pequots and Niantics snuck aboard Stone's ship to free the captives. In the commotion they killed Stone but accidentally lit his store of gunpowder ablaze: his pinnace "suddenly blew up into the air." Most of the Indians escaped the blast, then swam back onboard the flaming vessel and "killed such as remained, and burned the pinnace." Later English inquiries revealed that the attackers had multiple motives: while the primary mission was rescue, some had apparently mistaken the captain for a Dutchman and thought that slaying him and destroying his vessel was just recompense. When officials in Boston demanded justice for Stone's killing, their interest could not be explained by sympathy for the deceased. After all, Stone was persona non grata in the Bay: his last visit to the colony was soured by his drunken attempt to bed a married woman, for which he paid a hefty one-hundred-pound fine and was ordered "upon pain of death to come here no more." The motives of the English would become ever more transparent two years later, when yet another naval attack would once again inspire them to claim authority over the region.[12]

The third and most fateful slaying came on a July day in 1636. Guided by a Native pilot, the trader John Oldham sailed his small pinnace toward Block Island to barter with the local Manisses villagers, who were subordi-nate partners of the powerful mainland Narragansetts. For two years the Narragansett sachems had carefully cultivated an amicable economic relationship with Oldham, but there were no friends among the islanders that came to greet Oldham in a great canoe. Led by a sachem named Audsah, the party of at least fourteen Manisses men boarded the Englishman's vessel, killed him with a tomahawk blow to his head that "cleft to the brains," off-loaded his cargo into their vessel, and took his Native crew hostage. They were in the middle of ritually removing Oldham's hands and feet when a small bark helmed by one John Gallop happened upon the scene.[13]

A brief naval battle broke out between Gallop's craft and the captured pinnace, as the Manisses pirates "set up sail" and "drove towards the main," standing on the deck "ready armed with guns, pikes and swords." In the melee that followed, Gallop killed ten Indians and rescued Oldham's crew. But the English avengers ultimately had to give Oldham a burial at sea and abandon his craft to the remaining raiders who were barricaded in its small cabin. The conspirators kept the stolen pinnace for a month before the "vessel was strangely recovered from the Indians by another that belong[ed] to the Bay of Massachusetts." Acting in open defiance of their mainland sachems, the islanders were animated by a false rumor that Oldham was dealing with their Pequot enemies; they also seemed eager to keep the pinnace and its cargo, implying that simple piracy was also a motive.[14]

Seen together, the murders of Tatobem, Stone, and Oldham fit the familiar patterns of offshore violence that had been going on for thirty years. Two of these incidents were sparked by the Europeans seizing Algonquian captives aboard their vessels, and the latter two likewise involved Natives raiding foreign craft for plunder and revenge; all of these types of assaults were common acts on this saltwater frontier. The difference this time was the colonial reaction or, rather, overreaction to the blood in the water. Weeks after Oldham's murder, Massachusetts organized a punitive raid led by two English veterans of the Dutch Revolt, John Endecott and Underhill. With orders to capture the killers of Stone and Oldham, a Puritan flotilla of pinnaces and shallops headed first to the Manisses villages on Block Island, then to a Pequot village located near the present site of New London, Connecticut.

Both encounters turned into amphibious attacks on property rather than on people. After the Block Islanders fired a few arrows at the approaching colonial vessels, they fled, leaving the frustrated colonists to burn their houses and cornfields and scuttle several canoes. The ensuing visit to the Pequots began with a lengthy shipboard parlay in which a Pequot "Ambassadour," described as "portly, cariage grave, and majesticall in his expressions," attempted to smooth over the matter of Stone's murder. Maddened to find that the Pequots were not immediately submissive, the English stormed their main town, spoiling their fields and raiding their houses "for bootie." This attack, along with the murder of a Pequot man by a Narragansett shortly thereafter, marked the beginning of the war for the Pequots, who up to that point had earnestly attempted to resolve Stone's murder with traditional gifts of wampum, symbolizing condolence and regret.[15]

Massachusetts Bay's interest in avenging the slayings was in part to protect a vital sea passage that was holding the expanding but fragile collection of English plantations together. Cracking down on these naval attacks would secure a kind of local mare clausum well into Long Island Sound and maintain a crucial link between the Bay colony and its new satellites. No matter all the perils of the sea voyage to the Connecticut, colonists still preferred it over land routes. Furthermore, these offshore murders demonstrated how colonists were hopelessly vulnerable in the absence of major territorial holdings: both Stone and Oldham were reliant on Indian pilots to find their way through local waters. However, the Pequots would be vigorously prosecuted for their role in slaying Stone, while the Narragansetts, who were just as culpable for Oldham's murder, would be spared the blunt of colonial wrath. This result was partly owing to the fact that the Narragansett leadership was more responsive to the Puritans' calls for justice. Shortly after the Oldham murder the younger sachem Miantonomi led his own punitive expedition of "seventeen canoes and two hundred men" to Block Island "to take revenge," and soon he would execute the plot's ringleader, Audsah.[16]

Still, the English chose to go to war with the Pequots, just as they could have chosen to go to war with the Narragansetts. Just a few years later colonists would openly admit that the conquest was elective. "When we undertooke a warre against the Pequots," Winthrop recalled, there was "no necessity" driving their push for war, "only in point of Conscience ([the Pequots] had done us no injury) on others behalf." It helped that the Pequots were both the largest and most unstable Native power in the region. Shortly after Tatobem's less revered son Sassacus came to power in 1636, his closest ally, Uncas, cut his ties with his old friends and kin and began to position the Mohegans as allies of the English. Meanwhile, several Pequot tributaries chose this moment to defect and ally themselves with the Narragansetts. As the Pequot elites realized the true danger posed by these new alliances, they sought to reconcile their differences with their historic enemies. But the Narragansetts were eager to humble their old foes, refusing the proposal and quickly relaying news of it to the English.[17]

War with the isolated, friendless Pequots would help the English extinguish the Dutch West India Company's easterly claims in a way that inciting war with the Narragansetts would not. The Pequots sat in a more strategic location, straddling Long Island Sound and the mouth of the Connecticut, and attacking them would strengthen English relations with both the Mohegans and Narragansetts, drawing them out of the Dutch orbit and bringing two reliable wampum producers into the English sphere. The mutual English and Indian decision to marginalize the Pequots represented a calculated compromise between the colonists' desire for secure passages and their Native allies' desire for protected trade. To pull off this cynical conquest, Massachusetts Puritans willingly forgot the true details of their friend Oldham's murder while feigning anger over the death of the hated drunkard Stone.[18]

The war began as a series of estuarine battles between pinnaces, canoes, and shoreside snipers. After the first raids on their territory in 1636 the Pequots began a standard Algonquian-style war consisting of small raids for captives and trophies. Even before Oldham died, one Connecticut colonist reported a rumor that Pequots had made plans for "cutting off of our Plymouth Barke" but were foiled, "for as soone as those bloody executioners arose out of Ambush with their canoes, the[y] deserned her under sayle with a fayre winde returning Home." A watery defense would remain a key strategy as the war escalated. "The Pequts heare of your preparations etc.," Williams informed Winthrop, but they "comfort them selves in this that a witch amongst them will sinck the pinnaces by diving under water and making holes." A notorious slaying came shortly thereafter when "one Master Tillie master of a Vessell, being brought to an ankor in Conetticot River, went ashore, not suspecting the bloody-mindednesse of those persons, who fell upon him, and a man with him, whom they wickedly and barbarously slew." Soon just passing up the river was too perilous for the English, as "the Indians are many hundred of both sides the river and shoote at our Pinaces as they goe up and downe." When Pequot raiders took two teenage girls captive from Wethersfield, the English were at a loss to stop them as they sailed past Fort Saybrook at the mouth of the Connecticut, for though they "made a Shot at them with a Piece of Ordnance, which beat off the Beak Head of one of their Canoes . . . it was at a very great distance." Soon the Pequot war party "drew their Canoes over a narrow Beach with all speed and so got away."[19]

Ultimately the English were finding that they could not best their Indian opponents as long as the fighting stayed off land. Traveling with Native allies only further demonstrated that dugouts were much better suited to combat in shallow waters. As a Mohegan flotilla went "sailing down the River of Connecticut" together with a group of colonial allies in sailboats, the English "fell several times a ground, the water being very low," while the Mohegans, "not being wonted to such Things with their small canoes," soon became "impatient of Delays." Miantonomi was similarly exasperated with the ineffectiveness of the English forces. He suggested they lend him their largest pinnace, load it with fifty or so of his men and a small colonial crew, so he could personally "direct the Pinnace" to the main Pequot village under the cover of night. His men would then go ashore, kill their enemies, raze their cornfields, and "despoile them of their Canowes." The whole attack would be done "without landing an English man." The Narragansett sachem surely valued the English pinnace for its carrying capacity, but he did not seem to trust his partners with an amphibious attack.[20]

The Native guerrilla-style, irregular maritime defense could hold only so long. As colonists realized that on the immediate coast and rivers *they* were actually the inferior naval power, they formed a new strategy. Their shift toward a land assault led to the most notorious moment of the war, the devastating burning of the Pequots' second-largest village on May 27, 1637, the massacre that secured the eventual English victory. The colonial war party played on the Pequots' assumption that they were in the midst of a strictly coastal war when they first sailed by the village in plain sight, "deluding the Pequeants thereby" to "surprize them unaware." The day before the massacre, spies reported the Pequots "were secure, having been fishing with many Canooes at Sea." That night the four hundred townsfolk had been "exulting and Rejoycing with Songs and Dances" under a moonlit sky, for they assumed the English "were affraid of them and durst not come near them." The Pequots, so accustomed to facing seaward to deal with colonists, never saw the English soldiers coming.[21]

Heads Changing Hands

There were other unexpected outcomes from the meeting of Native and English military and diplomatic cultures, especially when it came to dealing with enemies' bodies. Throughout the war Mohegans, Narragansetts, and other Native peoples gave parts of slain Pequots to their English partners. Most secondary accounts of the war mention trophies only in passing, seeing them as just another grisly aspect of this notoriously violent conflict. But these incidents were more than a macabre footnote. A close look at the exchange of war trophies helps explain how the English won the war and how they became a legitimate regional power in the eyes of their Native partners. By attempting a military conquest at a moment when they could not yet assert cultural hegemony, English colonists dealt with Indians in ways that were at once aggressive and accommodating.[22]

All early modern Europeans had a robust tradition of butchering disobedient subjects and foreign foes that superficially resembled Native practices. Drawing and quartering was the Christians' most elaborate ritual: a criminal would be hanged, disemboweled, emasculated, and decapitated, and the remainder of his corpse would be divided into quarters. While English nobles typically had only elites of the realm beheaded, soldiers sometimes beheaded foreigners in a more indiscriminate fashion. In a notorious incident in 1569 during the Tudor reconquest of Ireland, Sir Humphrey Gilbert unleashed a total war against the defiant people of Munster. Declaring that "the stiffe necked must be made to stoupe," Gilbert decapitated the bodies of slain rebels and created a "lane of heddes" leading to his tent so that approaching villagers would have to pass "the heddes of their dedde fathers, brothers, children, kinsfolke, and freendes." Noting the prevalence of dismemberment in the Bible, the English jurist Sir Edward Coke, a mentor to Roger Williams, legitimized these sorts of actions as "godly butchery." Inspired by their holy texts and by the daily realities of early modern England, colonists used dismemberment to assert their authority over a foreign land.[23]

The Pequot War would bring the differences between English dismemberment and Indian trophy taking into sharp relief. To colonists, detached heads were always more important than any other body part because only heads conjured up the awesome authority of the English monarch and the even greater authority of the English god. Severed heads were most potent while at rest and on display in a prominent location, suggesting the futility of resistance, advertising the price of betrayal, and projecting the permanency of God's people in a new promised land. A displayed head functioned conclusively, like a period marking the end of a declarative sentence, bringing the episode of rebellion to a close. To Indians, bodily trophies made sense only within a system of warfare that centered on taking captives and torturing them. Native peoples did not exclusively favor heads, seeing scalps, hands, and sometimes even feet as similarly meaningful objects. And though Indians displayed trophies, human pieces had more political import while in motion and being passed from sachem to sachem because traveling trophies could bind the grievances of many into one. Indians saw heads and hands as connective, less like periods and more like semicolons in the middle of complex sentences linking past violent actions to conditional future actions. The intersection of these diverse meanings shaped Indian and English relationships during the war. Using human pieces as punctuation, Natives and newcomers created shared idioms of power.[24]

When Uncas pledged to help the colonists, the English demanded a test of his loyalty. Uncas responded by delivering "five Pequeats heads" to Fort Saybrook. "This mightily incouraged the hearts of all," Captain Underhill remarked, "and wee tooke this as a pledge of their further fidelity." By means of this act Uncas demonstrated that he was agreeing to a pact of mutual defense and obligation. But once the heads were in English hands, they were translated from tokens of allegiance into props of dominance. Lion Gardiner, the English commander at Fort Saybrook, "set all their heads upon the fort," just as a king would display the heads of traitors. Objects that the Mohegans offered to cement promises between themselves and the English now carried an additional layer of meaning.[25]

When receiving such trophies, colonists made a habit of responding with another gift. Soon after Uncas delivered his heads, a party of Narragansetts came to Boston "with forty fathom of wampom and a Pequod's hand," and the English governor gave them four coats in exchange. Williams, who had learned the Narragansett tongue while founding his new colony of Providence, would rightfully take much of the credit for winning over Native support against the Pequots. Later he boasted that he broke "to pieces the Pequts negociation and Designe" of an anti-English alliance and performed most of the diplomatic legwork to create "the English Leauge with the Nahiggonsiks and Monhiggins." Williams not only performed much of the face-to-face negotiation with Indians but also wrote letters instructing his fellow colonists on how to meet Native expectations of reciprocity and even counseled them on appropriate gifts for specific men. Though many Puritan leaders grasped the importance of giving back to Indians, they never quite perfected or standardized the practice.[26]

In 1636 the English-led alliance became even stronger when a single Indian began circulating a trophy. Cutshamakin, a Massachusett warrior and guide to the English, "crept into a swamp and killed a Pequot, and having flayed off the skin of his head, he sent it to [the elder Narragansett sachem] Canonicus, who presently sent it to all the sachems about him." Once the scalp finally reached English hands, they rewarded the assassin with "four fathom of wampom." Cutshamakin's gift was not simply an example of an Indian offering a token of loyalty to his supposed overlords; crucially, the scalp had passed through a series of Indian villages before it got to Boston. Gardiner demonstrated a general understanding of the scalping's meaning in galvanizing the anti-Pequot alliance when he declared that the single scalping "began the war between the Indians and us in these parts."[27]

After the massacre at Mystic, colonists and their Native partners spent the summer chasing hundreds of Pequots as they scattered to Long Island and the Hudson River Valley while the sachem Sassacus tried in vain to reassemble his people and fight back. The specter of Mystic undoubtedly helped colonists recruit former Pequot tributaries to join the coalition. When the Long Island sachem Wyandanch came to Saybrook "to know if [the English] were angry with all Indians," the fort's commander, Gardiner, replied, "No, but only with such as had killed Englishmen." Wyandanch then asked if his people could resume trade. Yes, Gardiner said, but with the following conditions: "If you will kill all the Pequits that come to you, and send me their heads," then "you shall have trade with us." Gardiner also insinuated that Indians who refused to bring heads and wampum would be assumed to be harboring Pequots and could be held responsible for any belligerent actions. The Indians who had avoided the war now had only two choices: they were either with the English or against them.[28]

The English enticed and bullied Indians from all around Long Island Sound and the interior into bringing them body parts. In the case of the Mohegans, Narragansetts, and Niantics, trophies were insurance against the return of Pequot warriors. For other, previously neutral groups, such as the Montauks and Quinnipiacs, heads and hands were the price of admission into an English protection and trade racket that superficially resembled the structure of an Indian sachemship. The triumphant John Mason explained the effect of the demand for body parts: "The Pequots now became a Prey to all Indians. Happy were they that could bring in their Heads to the English: Of which there came almost almost daily to Winsor, or Hartford." The delivery of parts became such a common occurrence in the summer of 1637 that Governor Winthrop seemed to lose track of the specifics, at one point making a casual remark about the "still many Pequods' heads and hands [coming] from Long Island and other places."[29]

The English were both celebratory and wary when Mohawk Indians arrived in Connecticut in the fall of 1637 with "part of the skin and lock of hair of [chief sachem] Sasacus and his brother and five other Pequod sachems." According to Bradford, whether the Mohawks' delivery was "to satisfie the English, or rather the Narigansets, (who, as I have since heard, hired them to doe it,) or for their owne advantage, I well know not; but thus this warr tooke end." After Connecticut colonists presented the scalp to Winthrop in the fall of 1637, he immediately summoned his soldiers home. Though Winthrop and Bradford chose to see Sassacus's scalp as punctuation marking the end of the war, the conflict came to an official close a year later, when the English, Mohegans, and Narragansetts met in Hartford. The Treaty of Hartford in 1638 gave the colonists and their closest allies a chance to divvy up the material and human rewards of the war, a process they actually began the previous summer, when Indians and English split the Pequots' corn harvest. Additionally, the treaty formalized the existing practice of area Indians offering wampum tribute to colonial governors. The English could recirculate the tributes in the fur trade, using the spoils of conquest as subsidies for further colonial growth.[30]

The treaty also settled the fate of the surviving Pequots. With most of the refugees now taken captive, the English, Mohegans, and Narragansetts each wanted their share of the defeated population. The two major Indian sachemships had already been incorporating captured Pequots into their lineages for more than a year, but the colonists declared all Pequots theirs by right of conquest, saying that the Indians would have to purchase the captives they had already taken. The English demanded a fathom of wampum beads for every adult Pequot and half as much for each child. The English also confiscated several dozen Pequots for themselves. Some of these were "branded on the shoulder" and became slaves within colonial households; others found themselves sent to work on distant plantations in Bermuda and Providence Island. An additional clause in the treaty stipulated that the Indians "shall as soon as they can possibly take off [the] heads" of any remaining Pequot fugitives. The Treaty of Hartford codified head exchange and slavery and intimately linked the two as the colonists took possession of the living bodies and the lifeless parts of their enemies.[31]

The English won the war not just by slaughtering Pequots but also by usurping them as the greatest power on the shore and emulating their methods of rule. Indians certainly saw resemblances. On hearing of the English demand for wampum and heads, Wyandanch immediately drew a parallel to the old regime, saying, "We will give you tribute, as we did the

Pequits." A Quinnipiac sachem echoed this feeling, telling the English that "as Long Iland had payd tribute to [the Pequot sachem] Sasacas hee would procure it to us." Yet these acts of cultural impersonation were never fully convincing because the Indians' and colonists' most talented brokers—men such as Williams, Uncas, and Miantonomi—could not reconcile the disparities between each other's beliefs. More important, the English had no reason to resolve the situation: these garbled translations worked to their advantage. Though the English imitation of Native reciprocal practices may have made the new alliances seem familiar to the eastern sachems, the differences soon became evident.[32]

Narragansetts and Mohegans had to come to terms with a conquest that was as creative as it was violent. They had not entered the war with the intention of submitting to their new partners; they fought to defeat a declining but still dangerous enemy and to secure a steady source of European trade goods. Yet what began as a military partnership quickly became a relationship between unequals, as Puritans demanded deference to their authority. By the 1640s English governors had accomplished what Tatobem had tried to create in the 1620s: a network of tributaries stretching across much of Long Island Sound. There was no simple top-down imposition of the invaders' order; rather, the English seized power by both intimidating Natives and reinterpreting their symbolic gifts. And for the people who delivered trophies to the English, these actions had an ironic consequence: for every Pequot head they cut off, an English one grew back in its place.

The Atlantic Origins of Kieft's War

The Netherlanders living near the Hudson would soon hear news of the massacre at Mystic and the English triumph. But no Dutchman witnessed the many gestures of diplomacy, the trading of wampum, trophies, coats, and captives, the lengthy meetings between Native and colonial leaders, all those crucial acts before and after the Mystic attack that made the English conquest successful. This would constitute a dangerous blind spot, above all for the new director, Willem Kieft, who arrived on Manhattan just as the Pequot War was winding down. Kieft and his supporters would remain carelessly indifferent to Native customs around making war and peace, thinking that their neighbors understood only blunt force. Indeed, so many Dutch actions in the years to come were gross miscalculations stemming from colonial officials' ignorance and from the West India Company's nagging fear that their colonial project had fundamental flaws in its design.

At first, the Dutch were more concerned with where the war took place than with how it was won. From their perspective the entire English campaign against the Pequots happened within New Netherland, in familiar waters they had claimed, mapped, and trafficked in for the past decade. As the conflict heated up, the Dutch showed little sympathy toward their fellow Christians, perhaps sensing that an overwhelming English victory was not in their interest. Some Dutch traders even bartered with Indians for goods that had been lifted off the bodies of the slain English traders Stone and Oldham. Even when Dutch sailors redeemed two captive English girls from the Pequots, their actions were baldly self-interested: they agreed to the task only in return for continued rights to trade with Pequots and demanded a payment of ten pounds for their troubles.[33]

Puritans remained wary of Hollanders throughout the war. Shortly before the attack on Mystic, the English dispatched twenty men to their stronghold at the mouth of the Connecticut, "to keep the fort, both in respect of the Indians, and especially of the Dutch, who, by their speeches and supplies out of Holland, gave cause of suspicion, that they had some design upon it." The rivalry would also inform English expansion after the war. A commander chasing fugitive Pequots westward noted key locations like the "so excellent a country at [Quinnipiac] river, and so all along the coast we travelled, as I am confident we have not the like in English possession as yet"; he urged his fellow colonists to flock to the area because "the Dutch will seaze it if the English do not." Perhaps New Netherland's administrators later regretted that they had not intervened directly in the fighting. They soon realized that while the Pequots lost the war, the Dutch were losing the Connecticut coast.[34]

When the Amsterdam chamber of the Dutch West India Company first heard a full account of New England's westward creep in 1638, the company demanded to know "by what right and under what pretext" the English had usurped their claims. "The right," their colonial informant replied, "is that of the strongest." Even before this frank discussion, Dutch lawmakers had noted that if their colony's weak growth was "not seasonally attended to," New Netherland's English neighbors "will at once entirely overrun it." Facing a more populous and land-hungry rival nearby, the company would have to start rethinking its strategy of possession, as it no longer seemed like the mere act of trading was a viable means of securing territory. From its formation the West India Company debated the value of colonists. Most investors saw colonization as a slow, difficult business, preferring the quick returns that came from looting the riches of the Spanish empire and trading items with higher profit margins like sugar, slaves, and dyewoods. In the first two decades of New Netherland's existence, the small population of several hundred migrants often flouted the company's trade restrictions, and the flourishing illegal traffic in pelts and wampum was nearly impossible to police. It is easy to see how many backers concluded that parasitic colonists were hardly worth the trouble.[35]

However, by the late 1630s the long Dutch war of independence from Hapsburg Spain was winding down. This was unwelcome news for the company, which had thrived over the past two decades by preying on Iberian ships and colonies. By the time they learned that New England was swallowing whole chunks of New Netherland, the Heren XIX, or ruling council of Nineteen Men, was already concerned about the company's fate after the eventual peace with Spain. At the same time, a bubble of speculative trading in flower bulbs had suddenly burst. The aftermath of "tulipmania" was a minor economic crisis but a major crisis of confidence in the emerging Dutch capitalistic system. The bubble had vividly demonstrated the inherent anxieties and problems of trust created by a market economy, leading some Dutch investors to seek out more stable sources of income to cushion the ups and downs. Building up their American settlements would allow the company to maintain a friendly harbor in the North Atlantic and reap a steady supply of grain, timber, tobacco, and furs. While New Netherland would never be a major part of the West India Company's grand scheme, by 1638 a series of confluent events—the coming peace with Spain, tulipmania, and the ascendance of the English as an imperial rival both on the

Connecticut and in the Caribbean—made it more strategically important than ever before.[36]

Officials in Amsterdam began drawing up plans to lure more Europeans across the Atlantic. Colonists who brought five or more people with them were guaranteed ample land and the labor of company slaves to start their farmsteads. The company also allowed more local autonomy for town governments, opened up the fur trade to more ordinary settlers, and invited more lay ministers, called *ziekentroosters* (comforters of the sick), to the Hudson colony. In order to recover lost profits from loosened trade laws, the company simultaneously slapped tariffs on all goods coming from and going to the colony, a policy that became a point of contention between the new and old Amsterdams. This was an ambitious slate of economic and social reforms for a chronically underperforming colony. The men who dreamed up these plans knew that their success or failure rested on an untested new leader.[37]

The outgoing director of the colony, Wouter van Twiller, had been found wanting as an executive. The nephew of a wealthy colonial backer, Van Twiller had seemingly done little to improve the struggling colony of only a few hundred people. Some colonists accused him of encouraging "unruliness" among company men, and he was known for becoming so tipsy that "he could scarce speak a right word." Though some colonists found Van Twiller embarrassing, many Natives found him charming. His fondness for entertaining won them over. At one point he established a regular ritual whereby "the Indians came with ten, twenty, and thirty persons at the same time" to his house in the company fort, where he feasted with them. After a brief dustup with the Raritans in 1634, Van Twiller had negotiated a satisfactory peace, which undoubtedly involved the exchange of gifts. His reputation for honoring the local peoples' principles of generosity and reciprocity was strong enough that years later, after the new director, Kieft, had squandered whatever goodwill Natives were willing to grant him, crowds of Munsees gathered outside Fort Amsterdam and demanded his return by chanting, "Woter, Woter—meaning Wouter van Twiller."[38]

The incoming director shared his predecessor's wellborn pedigree but none of his gregariousness. The son of a prominent Amsterdam merchant family with experience in the grain and wine trades, Kieft was thirty-five years old at the time of his appointment. Likely he saw the post as a stepping-stone to a more lucrative career in trafficking Atlantic riches. Although New Netherland was not a notably profitable colony, running it was a good way to get the attention of its overseers in Amsterdam. One of Kieft's first letters back home, written shortly after his arrival on Manhattan in March 1638, was fairly upbeat about the colony's potential. Relieved to be done with the "long and tediouse journey," he was in awe of the richness of "so brave a Country, which is fitt for all that is to be wished for, and would in no way be inferior to Italie or France if but peopled." But he also was sad to see "the Companies buysinesse in a poore case," in no small part because "the English doe sucke this Land of all its strength & profits."[39]

While looking to recruit more Christian farmers to counterbalance the English, Kieft would soon find that New Netherland was not a coherent, bounded territory at all but a loose collection of multilingual peoples scattered across the many kills, rivers, and bays at the mouth of the Hudson. Manhattan sat in the center of an expanding archipelago of small colonial homesteads, which in turn were interspersed with the mobile farming and fishing communities of Munsee-speaking peoples. By the early 1640s news of the cheap land and open fur trade in the Dutch colony had spread through an international circuit of like-minded protestants, drawing migrants from French, German, and Scandinavian kingdoms and from both England and New England. Looking for good soil and easy access to waterways and Indian villages with which to trade, the hundreds of new colonists scattered. They began plowing fields and building houses in the areas that are now Newark Bay, Jersey City, Hoboken, Staten Island, Queens, Brooklyn, and the Bronx. Though artisans, merchants, and tavern keepers settled in the dense village of New Amsterdam, most newly arrived planters did not stay on Manhattan, which had mediocre land and was largely reserved for the company. It did not help that these newcomers spoke several languages and were competing with each other to trade with the same Indians. As one anonymous colonist—whose account was sympathetic to Kieft—later complained, all the division and dispersal were "contrary to their High Mightinesses' [i.e., the States General] motto": *Eendracht maakt macht*, or "unity makes strength."[40]

The growing number of colonial houses only heightened tensions with Natives sharing the shore. A writer sympathetic to Kieft would later assert that while "the liberty to trade with the Indians" helped the colony grow, it was also "the cause of its ruin." Kieft's secretary, Cornelius van Tienhoven, worried that "too much familiarity with the Indians" would bring "forth contempt, usually the father of hate." He scolded settlers for inviting Natives to dine in their houses, asserting that the locals would become entitled. And he cautioned against hiring Munsees for day work, warning that some of the Indians "stole much more than the amount of their wages." Another source of tension was the settlers' free-roaming pigs, cows, and goats, which feasted on colonial and Native crops and "against which fences and rails are of no avail." While Munsees welcomed the growing market in foreign wares, there was no telling how long they would keep their patience with these sprawling, intrusive colonists. Kieft's initial Indian policy was to try to cause as little offense as possible. In his first two years he occasionally met with Munsee sachems to hear their grievances over loose livestock, although it is not clear if he entertained them as well as Van Twiller had. The director also set minimum fair prices for Indian trade, outlawed the sale of "guns, powder, and lead" to Indians, and repeatedly urged the colonists to strengthen their fences to keep animals out of Munsee cornfields.[41]

Mediating between the overlapping populations of Christian and Indian farmers was difficult enough, but the real source of trouble lay in the fact that New Amsterdam was an important garrison and homeward-bound waypoint for the Atlantic fleet of the Dutch West India Company. Indeed, the director's first antagonists were the low-paid, heavy-drinking sailors and soldiers from the colony's pool of transients. Perhaps his indignation flowed from his austere dislike of disorder — Winthrop would later describe Kieft as being sober, discreet, and prudent. This temperate impression was borne out just two months into his term, when he announced strict regulations to stop the free-flowing casks of wine, citing the "evil and mischief" caused "by immoderate drinking." Kieft looked to reverse the lax order of his predecessor by requiring all visiting sailors to return to their vessels by sundown and by forbidding soldiers to leave Manhattan without permission; essentially he meant to use ships and the island itself as containing cells to prevent rowdy crews from wreaking havoc among colonists and Indians. Kieft also soon decreed that all "must refrain from fighting; from adulterous intercourse with heathens, blacks, and other persons; from mutiny, theft, false testimony, slanderous language and other irregularities."[42]

Company employees swiftly set about breaking every single one of these laws, sometimes just days after they were written. From 1638 to 1641 the enlisted men of New Netherland were convicted in two cases of manslaughter, half a dozen knife fights, and many more counts of slander, theft, fraud, and seeking sex with slaves and Indians. One soldier had to pay a fine of fifty stivers for snatching an Indian's wampum and cloth and shoving his victim off his boat. When the sailor Jan Dondey and his cabin boy Claes roughed up a Munsee woman and "cut loose with a knife and took away the seawan which [the] squaw carried around her waist," the director's advisory council had Claes whipped and sentenced Dondey to surrender two months' wages and "ride the wooden horse," that is, to sit astride an elevated pole with weights tied to his feet for several hours.[43]

Disorderly, drunken acts by company men bothered the colony's leadership—the ban on casks of wine came just two days after one intoxicated soldier murdered another. But the offenses that troubled Kieft most were undoubtedly the ones that bordered on outright mutiny, such as when nine soldiers openly defied his orders to repair the derelict structure of Fort Amsterdam in the late summer of 1639. Perhaps it was no coincidence that Kieft and his council made a dramatic shift in his Indian policy just weeks after the soldiers' defiant protest. Noting the "great expense both in building fortifications and in supporting soldiers and sailors," they "resolved to demand from the Indians who dwell around here and whom heretofore we have protected against their enemies, some contributions in the form of skins, maize, and seawan." In essence, the colony was demanding that Indians bow down before the unproven military superiority of the Dutch and cough up payment for protection they had neither asked for nor received.[44]

The timing of the order, coming so close after the near mutiny, strongly hints that it was Kieft's own initiative to impose order on an unruly landscape and population. The ill-considered tax on Indians was the beginning of a series of increasingly aggressive moves that pushed the colony toward open war. As a Tappan man later remarked to the colonist David de Vries, Kieft "must be a very mean fellow to come to live in this country without being invited by them, and now wish to compel them to give him their corn for nothing." To Natives whose political culture was centered on the ideals of obligation, reciprocity, and emotive declarations of feelings, few actions could be more offensive than brusquely demanding one thing without offering anything in return.[45]

As Kieft was attempting to secure the immediate environs of Manhattan through tone-deaf demands, the English advances down Long Island Sound continued apace. Just weeks after he ordered new seals with the Lion of Union affixed to trees along Long Island's north shore, Indians reported that English colonists had arrived at Manhasset Bay. The copper arms of the States General had been "torn off and . . . on the tree to which they had been nailed a fool's head was carved in the stead of said arms." The fool's head was a mocking icon of folly and greed, associated with speculative deals gone bad. The graphic itself was usually a grotesquely smiling face or sometimes just a bicorned jester's hat. Dutch prints lampooning the tulipmania used the fool's cap as a form of "graphic satire." The appearance of a fool's head was a universal insult throughout northern Europe at the time—it had even appeared as a punch line in a scene in Shakespeare's *The Merchant of Venice*. Whoever took a knife to that tree was calling the whole colony a joke, and the director was not a man renowned for his sense of humor. Kieft sent his secretary Van Tienhoven to Long Island with twenty-five soldiers to surprise the English at daybreak and "make a strong protest" but cautioned the secretary to "above all things, avoid bloodshed." This show of force successfully intimidated the "eight men, one woman, and a little child" at the fledgling homestead; they soon decamped for Long Island's eastern forks. But no sooner had Kieft fended off intruders from one side of the watery reaches of New Netherland than trouble appeared on another shore in yet another offshore scuffle.[46]

It began on a company yacht, perhaps too optimistically named *De Vreede* (peace). The vessel was on an annual trade mission to the Raritans' villages southwest of Staten Island that spring. The skipper, Cors Pietersen, likely had a bad reputation among Indians throughout the region. He was the same sailor who once faced charges of robbing a Munsee man and pushing him off his boat. Though court records described his victim only as a generic Indian, perhaps that man had ties to the Raritans. That might explain why "instead of showing the customary friendship and disposition to trade with our people," the Raritans who boarded *De Vreede* "began to scoff" and slapped Pietersen across the face with some squirrel skins. Soon Native men began to flood the deck of the sloop "in large numbers, all armed with tomahawks, rapier blades, and other weapons," while another party of Indians in canoes, "all lusty fellows," wedged their heavy dugouts against *De Vreede* "at each side of the yacht and wanted to tow us back" into a shallow inlet. Finally, as the colonists appeared ready to shoot their guns, the Raritan pirates relented but not without first stealing the Dutchmen's canoe from the yacht's deck. Before the attack could resume again, a sudden heavy thunderstorm swept in, allowing *De Vreede* to sail off without any further losses.[47]

This episode marked yet another floating fight, much like dozens of incidents that had happened before on these waters and likely the product of an old grudge. But this kind of bullying was all new to the director on Manhattan, who saw darker motives behind the Indians' actions. Kieft's council would soon accuse the Raritans of killing several pigs and plundering a "negro's house," though other colonists would attribute that mischief to company men. Acting with far less mercy than he showed his English neighbors, Kieft gave "orders to attack [the Raritans], to cut down their corn and to make as many prisoners as they can, unless they willingly come to an agreement and make reparation." When Kieft's right-hand man Van Tienhoven arrived with seventy soldiers in Raritan territory, "the troop wished to kill and plunder." Van Tienhoven at first refused, citing his orders, but eventually, "on account of the pertinacity of the troop," he allowed the near-rebellious men to range freely. Once out of his sight, "the troop killed several of the savages and brought the brother of the chief a prisoner." Van Tienhoven insisted they spare the sachem's kinsman, not out of mercy but because the man owed him a large trading debt. On the passage back to Manhattan, one of the soldiers "standing at the mast, had tortured the chief's brother in his private parts with a piece of split wood." As De Vries dryly remarked, by "such acts of tyranny" these soldiers "were far from making friends with the inhabitants."[48]

The Raritans' simmering dispute with the colony continued into the late summer of 1641, when they attacked a colonial plantation on Staten Island and killed four servants before burning down two houses. To counter the escalating Raritan threat, Director Kieft attempted to "induce the Indians, our allies hereabout, to take up arms." Perhaps he was reluctant to dispatch soldiers again, remembering how the men had usurped Van Tienhoven's command and turned what was supposed to be a measured punitive mission into a nasty bout of murder and torture. To solicit allies, the director's council promised to pay friendly warriors for producing a Raritan head. Kieft's proposed market for heads never quite materialized. In November 1641 a Tankiteke sachem named Pachem made the only documented response. He arrived in the Dutch settlement "in a great triumph, bringing a dead hand hanging on a stick, and saying that it was the hand of the chief who had killed or shot with arrows our men on Staten Island, and that he had taken revenge for our sake, because he loved the Swannekens (as they call the Dutch), who were his best friends." Pachem's actions looked like those of a leader seeking to form an alliance, not of a mercenary seeking a bounty—he failed even to bring the requested body part. This one offer from Pachem aside, Kieft's attempts to form a larger regional alliance largely failed. When the Raritans came to Fort Amsterdam to try to settle the matter, the negotiations "came to a standstill."[49]

In just two years Kieft's Indian policy had shifted dramatically from his early stance of maintaining clear boundaries and defending Indians against colonial offenses. Reacting to a few isolated but troubling moments of Native aggression, the colonial leadership had developed a habit of making demands, but they had nothing to show for their domineering. Even as the number of colonists was multiplying, the realm of New Netherland remained as fragile and porous as ever. Another disturbing attack would only further harden Kieft's feelings about Indians. During that summer of 1641 a Wiechquaesgeck man coming from territory north of Manhattan murdered an elderly, harmless Dutch wheelwright named Claes Smits. Though the Wiechquaesgeck knew Smits well, he apparently decided to ambush and behead the colonist as revenge for his uncle, "who, it was alleged, had been slain by the Dutch twenty-one years before."[50]

As previous diplomatic overtures had seemingly failed, Kieft now felt certain that Indians would defy his authority. Asking Wiechquaesgecks to bring Smits's murderer to justice, he grumbled, was "like knocking on a deaf man's door." Stronger, more terrifying measures were needed. Summoning his council of twelve male heads of households in New Amsterdam, Kieft proposed "to ruin the entire village to which [the murderer] belongs." Most of the "Twelve Men" agreed to the plan but proposed waiting a few months to "lull the Indians to sleep" and to allow another supply "ship to come from the fatherland."[51]

Only one colonist, Frederick Lubbertsen, openly voiced doubts, as reported in the council minutes. "The war cannot be carried out successfully," he predicted, remembering that "the undertaking against the R[aritans]s" had failed. Lubbertsen may have been more sympathetic to Munsees than most. A wealthy landowner, he had regular contact with his Native neighbors. During the trial of Cors Pietersen, the squirrel-slapped skipper found guilty of assaulting a Munsee man in 1638, Lubbertsen testified that "he well knew the Indian and received from him a half fathom of seawan to procure from the defendant the return of the cloth which was taken from him." Not only had he befriended Natives but at least one of those friends trusted him enough to seek his help in a crisis. Lubbertsen rightfully suspected that his fellow colonists were underestimating the Munsees. De Vries, another member of the Twelve Men, also contended after the fact that he privately warned Kieft that "no profit was to be derived from a war with the savages." But the other ten men chose not to dwell on the mediocre Dutch record of dealing with Natives, believing instead that a single surprise attack would secure their colony. One cannot say for sure if their arrogance was based on an oversimplified understanding of how the English had triumphed over the Pequots, but no doubt the example of Mystic crossed the minds of a few. What was even more striking was how swiftly and carelessly they abandoned the idea of negotiating with sachems or at the very least trying to recruit local allies before punishing the neighbors they saw as enemies.[52]

Over the next few months, as winter fell, Kieft and his backers kept their plan a secret, encouraging their fellow colonists to continue their daily traffic with Indians while betraying no hint of the looming attack. During the dark, long hours in his house within the fort, while his slaves tended to the fire, Kieft had time to imagine the consequences of the coming assault. No doubt he hoped the fearsome demonstration of European firepower and armor would finally cure the stubborn savages of their insolence and complaints. And maybe the chance to shed a little blood might do the same for the soldiers, another constant annoyance. Indeed, if Kieft's plan succeeded, he would command the respect even of the English. With the local Indians pacified and paying regular tributes to Fort Amsterdam, the colony's Christian rivals would no longer feel free to disparage the legality of the Dutch presence on these shores. Perhaps Kieft even dreamed of a day when his term was over, when he would stride up Haarlemmerstraat to the West India Company's headquarters in Amsterdam to be greeted warmly by the weightiest burghers in Holland and feted as the savior of New Netherland.

Miantonomi's War

Kieft was not the only leader on these shores to wonder if a few terrifying, bold acts could remake the coast's political terrain and elevate his own fortunes. Over the same years that Kieft was beginning his first term, Miantonomi, the younger sachem of the Narragansetts, faced a number of dispiriting trends. Governing with his uncle Canonicus, Miantonomi was an adept politician. He had been a frequent visitor to Williams's home when the banished Englishman first moved to the edge of the Narrangansett realm. During the Pequot War he had been a confidant of Williams, passing along intelligence, suggesting battle tactics, and garnering gifts of cloth, sugar, and munitions that he redistributed among his people. As the most vocal representative of a collection of villages, the younger sachem could reasonably claim at the war's end that his acts of diplomacy and valor helped bring peace and prosperity to his people.[53]

But the aftermath of the war was dispiriting, and Miantonomi's actions may have soon seemed foolish to his constituents. Before the conflict the Narragansett homelands had a near ideal position between Plymouth colony and the Dutch traders, allowing them to trade with both. It was fast becoming evident that this new world without the Pequots and with fewer Dutch traders was not a better one. While Munsees to the west had seen just one thousand Dutch colonists ebb into their territory in the past decade, Narragansetts had witnessed approximately six thousand English settlers come flooding onto nearby shores and rivers in the same period. The Narragansetts' Mohegan rival Uncas was now the favorite of Puritan governors, lessening the influence of coastal peoples and their access to colonial traders. Miantonomi soon was making his displeasure known, at one point grumbling to Williams: "*Chenock eiuse wetompatimucks?* that is, Did ever friends deal so with friends?" Though the English had been respectful and solicitous before the war, now that there were more of them they had become indifferent to Native claims and dismissive of Native leaders.[54]

Speaking to a gathering of Long Island Indians, Miantonomi reflected on the changes he had seen since his youth, voicing sentiments that no doubt were common across the coast. He remembered vividly the days when "our fathers had plenty of deer and skins, our plains were full of deer, as also our woods, and of turkies, and our coves full of fish and fowl." But in just the few years since the conquest of the Pequots "these English having gotten our land, they with scythes cut down the grass, and with axes fell the trees; their cows and horses eat the grass, and their hogs spoil our clam banks, and we shall all be starved." As Miantonomi saw it, "The [E]nglish did gett possession of all the best place[s] in the countrey & did drive the Indians away & were likely to take awaye the countrey from them."[55]

Miantonomi argued that Indian ideas about sovereignty were the only legitimate ones. He pointed out that Puritan governors "are no Sachems, nor none of their children shall be in their place if they die; and they have no tribute given to them; there is but one king in England, who is over them all, and if you would send him 100,000 fathom of wampum, he would not give you a knife for it, nor thank you." Miantonomi wanted to shatter the illusion that an elected governor could ever be the equal of a sachem. Even if the English tried to impersonate sachems' methods of rule, their actions were ultimately unconvincing because their notions of power were so foreign. They belonged to a far larger polity, one that did not function through recognizable rituals of reciprocity or structures of kinship, one that invested earthly power in a distant sovereign and spiritual power in a single, even more remote god. Any gifts given or received by them were rendered useless by their ingratitude and insincerity.[56]

The Narragansett proposed a vast exchange of wampum to form an alliance between "all the Sachems upon the maine from the Dutche to the [Narragansett] Bay & all the Indian Sachems from the Eastward." One day soon this alliance would rise up and expel the English and Dutch intruders. On that day Miantonomi "would kill an Englishman & send his heade & handes to Longe Iland & they should send it abroade amonge the Indians" stretching all the way to Manhattan. Those Indians should do the same to all their neighbors, then "send the heade & the handes to them [to] Naragancetts & they would send [them] to the Indians abroade & this would be a meanes to knitt them togeather." These exchanges were in keeping with the Algonquian tradition of offering trophies to establish alliances. The Narragansett sachem dreamed of a sudden, swift massacre that would clear the land of European "men, women, and children"—though he would spare their livestock, "for they will serve to eat till our deer be increased again." If it actually came together, Miantonomi's grand alliance would be larger than any network Tatobem ever had and indeed much larger than any de facto territorial possessions of the Dutch and English. More than one colonist had already accused the Narragansetts of wanting to be "the only lords of the Indians," while Miantonomi expressed some admiration for the English success at conquest, which he believed came from their unity as a people. "We [are] all Indians as the English are," he told the gathered sachems. "So we must be one as they are, otherwise we shall be all gone shortly." Some sachems protested, saying "the English were too stronge for them." The Narragansett replied, "It is true if they did not all joine they should be too weake but if all joine then they should be stronge enough." The Dutch were not the only regional power to take stark lessons about English might from the Pequot War, nor were they the only ones to rally around the idea that "unity makes strength."[57]

In the spring of 1642, as Miantonomi was articulating the idea of an Indian uprising against all colonists, Wiechquaesgeck and Raritan sachems were still attempting to restore peaceful relations with the Dutch. Kieft's first attempt to intimidate them had failed: that winter, under the woefully inept command of Ensign Hendrick van Dyck, a war party headed north to surprise the Wiechquaesgecks, but they got lost—not once, but twice. After finding the tracks of Dutch soldiers near their villages, a party of Wiechquaesgeck ambassadors petitioned for peace, an offer which, the Dutch announced, they would consider only if the Natives surrendered Smits's killer. Weeks later, a young Hackensack warrior, drunk on brandy and cursing the "villainous Swannekens [colonists]" killed a Dutchman who was thatching a roof near Newark Bay. Hackensack sachems were quick to disavow the actions of this errant arrow; they offered the thatcher's widow a generous gift of wampum and then proposed banning liquor sales to their young men.[58]

That summer Miantonomi and his entourage of a hundred men began paying visits to Munsee villages all along the Hudson and East rivers in his fleet of great canoes. The Narragansett sachem began "soliciting them to a general war against both the English and the Dutch," probably making speeches similar to the one he had made to Montauketts a year earlier. A colonial source related that shortly after Miantonomi sailed home "some of the neighboring Indians attempted to set our powder on fire and to poison the Director or to inchant him by their devilry." But no general war ensued after this visit, and it was not hard to see why: Narragansett problems differed from Munsee ones. As annoying as the Dutch and their livestock could be to Munsees, their comparatively small numbers made them more of a nuisance than an overwhelming threat and hence local sachems stuck to traditional diplomatic routes in resolving disputes. Despite Kieft's efforts at bullying, Munsees still did not have to pay him tribute, and his attempts at terror had thus far fizzled out. Just months later, however, the words of the Narragansett sachem may have seemed less alarmist and more prophetic.[59]

Schools of War

In a peculiar echo of Miantonomi's visit, another advice-filled visitor from Narragansett Bay happened to be stopping in the area in the snowy days of late February 1643, just as Kieft was about to launch the twin nighttime attacks. Roger Williams was on his way back to England to secure a charter for his colony when he met with Kieft and his advisers, relating his vast experience with Indian negotiation. But he found the director was dead set on attacking the Hackensacks and Wiechquaesgecks who had just raised their wigwams nearby along the Hudson and East rivers. Williams "offered to mediate" with the Indians in "the Name of Peace," but that was "foolish and odious to them." Confident that Indians could be easily cowed, "they questioned not to finish it in a few dayes." The Dutch were so convinced of their strength and so sure of the Indians' weakness that they ignored the primary architect of the English success in the Pequot War.[60]

The next morning, as news of the carnage along the rivers spread, Miantonomi's earlier warnings of European treachery and his plea for Indian solidarity must have no longer seemed like debatable propositions. Enraged at the attack on their friends and brothers, the area sachems banded together and retaliated. The next day and for the next two months a confederated force of eleven local Indian sachemships launched constant raids on the Dutch settlements, killing colonists as they labored in their fields, slaughtering cows, and lighting houses ablaze. As Williams sailed off to England, he witnessed "that first breaking forth of the Indian War . . . their Bowries were in Flames, Dutch and English were slaine." Watching from the deck of the ship, he "saw their flames at their Townes end and the Flights and Hurries of Men, Women, and Children." Williams lamented that his counsel had been ignored, while the warmongers were baffled that their strategy had failed. When De Vries came to Manhattan shortly after the Indian attacks, Kieft "wondered that no Indians came to the fort" to submit to his authority. De Vries retorted, "Why should the Indians come here when you have so treated them?"[61]

Still, after several weeks of attacks, some sachems broke away from the Munsee alliance and attempted to rein in their warriors and restore the peace. With De Vries's encouragement, parties of Rockaways and Hackensacks came to Fort Amsterdam that April hoping for a ritual exchange of gifts to wash away the enmity and create a firm alliance. But the director's gifts were far too meager, and his attitude was haughty rather than conciliatory. An Indian commented that he "could have made it, by his presents, that as long as he lived the massacre would never again be spoken of; but now it might fall out that the infant upon the small board would remember it." Again, the locals could not understand why the Dutch so consistently failed to meet their expectations of condolence. Thinking of politics as a family matter, they felt Kieft had failed not just them but their smallest children.[62]

The following summer of 1643 was an uneasy one for all people crossing the contested waters between Dutch and Munsee villages. Several elder sachems reported to colonists that "many of the Indian youths ... were constantly wishing for a war" to avenge the murders of their kin. Kieft, upon hearing of this, again tried to use bounties to buy allies—this time offering a handsome wampum payment to a sachem to compel him to "kill these young madcaps." Once again the governor failed to grasp the nature of a sachem's authority. On hearing of Kieft's offer, De Vries said he "laughed within myself," scoffing at the notion that an "Indian should kill his friends for two hundred fathoms of zeewan—that is eight hundred guilders—to gratify us." Kieft's ineptitude in peacemaking enraged even Indians who had once solic- ited his friendship. Pachem, the Tankiteke sachem who once offered the director a Raritan hand as a token of alliance, now followed Miantonomi's example and "ran through all the villages urging the Indians to a general massacre." Perhaps Pachem cited the Narragansett and made a similar case about Native unity and colonial duplicity.[63]

Whatever their contents, Pachem's speeches were galvanizing. That fall the Munsee alliance reformed and renewed their attacks with vigor. Soon outlying Dutch farmers on Newark Bay and the Haarlem River again reported the alarming sight of fire-tipped arrows, glowing blue, whistling out of the darkness toward their houses. Frightened colonists began abandoning their many far-flung settlements, hurriedly piling possessions into canoes, and seeking refuge within Fort Amsterdam. Munsee fighters to the east began to direct attacks toward the Dutch-controlled English settlements on the mainland and Long Island, where "many complaints are heard daily of thefts, robberies, shooting of hogs and goats and other depredations." Two months after a stand of colonial homes along Newark Bay burned to the ground, colonists were reluctant to venture far off Manhattan, as they were still deathly afraid of "the great number of Indians, who burn and kill every- thing they can lay hold of in the woods, on water, or elsewhere."[64]

As the conflict again spiraled out of control Kieft and his council looked to one of the veterans of the Pequot War who happened to have a tobacco farm on Long Island: the man known as John Underhill or Jan Onderhill. Hiring him as the commander of a mixed Dutch and English force of 150 men mustered in towns from Manhattan to Stamford, Kieft's council disbursed the staggering sum of twenty-five thousand guilders. This was not the first time some of those men bore arms in exchange for Dutch coins. Underhill's earliest experience of war was in the Netherlands' revolt against Hapsburg Spain, when he was a soldier in the standing army of the Prince of Orange and stationed in the besieged city of Breda in the province of North Brabant. Plenty of his fellow New Englanders also fought as mercenaries in this conflict, including Miles Standish, John Mason, Israel Stoughton, Daniel Patrick, and Lion Gardiner. Many became fluent in Dutch during their tours of duty, and some, like Underhill and Patrick, married Dutch women. The Netherlands' seemingly unending revolt served as a training ground for thousands of soldiers across Europe and the Atlantic, leading some vets to call it, with a note of battle-earned cynicism, "the school of war." As they again donned armor to face not Spaniards but Indians, these grizzled fighters no doubt shared memories of their previous service. In one moment in his account of the Pequot War, Gardiner chummily referred to himself, Mason, and Underhill as "we old soldiers."[65]

This seasoned mercenary force fought Indians with fiery siege craft. Both times Underhill campaigned on American shores he used the tactics of traveling at night, employing Native guides, and using the element of surprise. He and his hired army spent the fall 1643 and the winter of 1643–44 waging destructive raids on Indian villages on western Long Island and the mainland, killing hundreds. In February 1644 Underhill learned of an Indian village recently raised in the hills north of Stamford. Most of the wigwams housed Tankiteke families, but several belonged to Wappingers, who had "gathered to celebrate one of their festivals in their manner"—probably the winter feast that many colonists compared to Christmas. The moon was full "and threw a strong light against the winter hills," so the approaching Europeans had a clear vantage of the Native town nestled behind a ridge, its houses lined up tightly along three parallel streets. Just as he and Mason had done seven years earlier against the Pequots, Underhill used the Tankitekes' compact settlement as a means to trap them. Once again he incinerated an entire village of men, women, and children in an hour's time. It was the deadliest day in the whole decade of war. Native losses neared seven hundred, while only a handful of colonists perished. The massacre of the Tankitekes did not immediately end the Indian attacks, but these unrelenting assaults demoralized the opposition.[66]

The already shaky Munsee alliance soon collapsed. Within weeks a party of mainland sachems met with Underhill near Stamford. Suing for peace, they promised "they will not come on the island of Manhatans as long as we Netherlanders are at war with other heathen, except in a canoe before Fort Amsterdam." In the last few months of the war a Long Island sachem volunteered forty-seven armed men to "embark in one of the sloops of the Company where he is to put ashore his spies to discover the enemy." Both sides formed a formal and lasting peace within a year. Williams saw the final treaty as a European defeat. "After vast expenses, and mutual slaughters of Dutch, English, and Indians," he wrote, "the Dutch were forced, to save their plantation from ruin, to make up a most unworthy and dishonorable peace with the Indians." Most dishonored of all was Kieft. The war had been an utter disaster: all told over a thousand Munsees perished, scores of colonists died, and hundreds more Christians fled back to Europe.[67]

The campaigns of slaughter that won the war apparently took a toll on the perpetrators as well as the victims. Reports surfaced that painted the soldiers as heavy drinkers who were quick to anger, perhaps suffering posttraumatic stress. As New Netherland's army stalked fleeing Munsees near Greenwich in the late fall of 1643, a frustrated soldier accused the Englishman Daniel Patrick of treason for continuing to trade with Indians. Patrick, a hardened graduate of the school of war who had killed more Pequots than almost any other colonist, did not take this accusation kindly. Patrick "spet in the Dutch mans face," to which the Dutchman responded by drawing his pistol and shooting Patrick in the head, killing him instantly. Another telling incident came when Underhill and several fellow soldiers were drinking wine in a Manhattan tavern in the spring of 1644. A separate party of guests politely asked that the men yield some space in one of the rooms, but the request triggered a sudden rampage.

"Onderhill and his companions with drawn swords knocked to pieces all but three of the mugs which hung from the shelf in the tavern" and then burst back into the room they had just left. Drawing his sword partway from its sheath so its blade could plainly be seen, Underhill growled at the shocked tavern-goers, "Clear out of here, or I shall strike at random." Brutal acts, it seems, bred brutal men.[68]

Wartime horrors lingered in Natives' minds as well. Colonial sources contain little direct evidence of the aftermath of widespread psychological trauma that surely followed the Pequot War and Kieft's War. But there are glimpses of Indians witnessing unspeakable sights and grieving the absence of so many loved ones who had been shot, beheaded, and burned alive. There was the party of Pequots who came upon the smoking remains of the Mystic massacre "and beholding what was done, stamped and tore the Hair from their Heads" and soon began firing arrows wildly at English soldiers in a blind rage. A more resigned group of Pequots later told Underhill, "wee are a people bereaved of courage, our hearts are sadded with the death of so many of our deare friends." And perhaps De Vries was referring to the widows of Kieft's War when he spoke of frequently seeing wives of dead Natives "come daily to the grave, weeping and crying," pacing mournfully around the small hills that marked the burial plots of their husbands.[69]

Archaeological finds also speak to the bitter lessons that Algonquian communities learned from their unwilling enrollment in the European school of war. Excavated sites of Native forts from around the region reveal a striking shift that can be clearly read as a reaction to colonial aggression. Before the fighting escalated Natives built castles called *aumánsk* or *waukaunòsint* in Narragansett, intended "to shelter their wives and children from an assault, in case they have enemies so near by they could be fallen upon by small parties." Since men were targets for killing, torture, and trophy taking, while women and children were prized as captives, built defenses served as a physical manifestation of the indigenous rules of war. At the moment of attack adult men stood outside the refuge or at its immediate periphery, while women, children, and the elderly hid deep within. The buildings themselves were usually circular and located on "a high or steep hill near water or on a riverbank" on a rise that was "difficult to climb and often accessible on one side only" or else near wetlands that served as natural moats.[70]

A Dutchman observed that Indians "think highly of their forts and castles." This was certainly true of the Native fighters who warned the English in 1637 that the Pequots' two main aumánsk were "almost impregnable." But colonists offered more withering assessments, dismissing Indian builders, for "they do not as yet have any knowledge of properly equipping such a work with curtains, bastions, and flanking walls, etc.," while another caricatured their sieges as crude affairs involving "naked assailants" who lacked "butting Rammes and battering Ordinances." The Indians' palisaded towns, colonists agreed, were "of little consequence and cause them more harm than good in a war with the Christians." Bluntly put, European attacks with guns and fire turned fortified villages into death traps.[71]

More than a dozen excavated sites around Long Island Sound served as tacit acknowledgment that Natives' previous methods of building were deadly and outmoded. The degree of European influence on Indian forts varied across the shore. Some had irregular shapes that seemed to be the work of indigenous architects, while others had exacting square sides and precise dimensions that could have been made only with colonial tools that no local had yet learned to use. A few of these forts were apparently raised by Natives following European examples, while others were unmistakably built by colonists, then occupied by Indians. The key new features of these postwar structures were bastions, protruding structures at the corners that allowed men in the fort clear sight lines for any attack with firearms. A few of the forts were also ringed with simple dry moats and ramparts. In the most brazen attempt to match colonial defenses, a sachem living on the Hudson requested that his Dutch allies supply him with "a small Cannon for his Castle."[72]

Though these strongholds mostly perched on prime spots close to water, none of the sites were suited to house whole villages. Most showed little evidence of permanent occupation, having few fire pits or refuse heaps within their footprints. This shifting architecture implies that Indians were abandoning old notions of small-scale bow-and-arrow wars fought for captives and trophies. They now assumed that fire was the greatest threat and firearms were the best defensive weapons, building unfortified, easily dispersed villages as an acknowledgment that colonists considered women and children fair targets. Indians' selective mimicry of colonial designs and their repurposing of the work of foreign engineers might be read as visible concessions to Europeans' rules of engagement. Yet these forts can also be seen as distinctly Native places that served Native needs first. Hybrid structures, built with past conflicts in mind, could become a means of asserting Indian autonomy during a future war. Forts, much like guns and sailboats, were potent technologies. And colonists always had to worry that tools they shared with Indians might some day be used against them.

Of the two European powers, the Dutch had most cause for concern. The past decade had not gone as planned. New Netherland's attempt at conquest had backfired when compared to New England's. The English decisively vanquished the Pequots and took thousands of acres of land as their spoils, while the Dutch accomplished only a drawn-out, ambiguous victory over their Munsee opponents. In the Pequot War colonists carefully inserted themselves on one side of an ongoing conflict between sachemships and escalated it with terrifying violence, while in Kieft's War colonists' sudden, unprovoked attacks inspired a ring of local sachemships to form a robust anti-Dutch alliance. The English built effective alliances with Indian partners before the fighting with Pequots began; the Dutch first attacked their neighbors without the aid of a solid Native ally and only slowly gained begrudging partners during the course of their war.

Perhaps many Dutch and Native people across the region hoped for a fresh start, counting on a new generation of leaders to secure their futures. After all, two of the most belligerent voices in this decade of war were gone. Miantonomi had come to a grim end. His plot was revealed by Long Island Indians who had decided that partnering with the English led to a surer future than following the Narragansett. In unraveling this conspiracy, Uncas, a longtime rival of the Narragansetts, used his friendship with colonials to empower his people over the other Native sachemships in the region. He played a major role in the discovery and repression of the Narragansett plot, and his brother executed Miantonomi in 1643 with a blow to the head. It was an undoing that demonstrated anew the effectiveness of English–Native alliance building and information sharing.[73]

Kieft also faced an unhappy ending, though in his case mere chance was to blame. He remained director for another two years after the peace but continued to be deeply unpopular. Holing up in his house for days on end, he made no secret of his general contempt for most of the people of New Netherland, Native and Christian alike. After the Dutch West India Company relieved him of his command in 1647 and he set off for home, the vessel carrying him wrecked off the coast of Wales. Kieft drowned along with the other eighty-five people aboard. Had he lived, the disgraced director likely would have faced a reckoning: a later series of inquests in New Amsterdam condemned him and his lieutenants for their conduct.[74]

The idea that either the Dutch colony or any one indigenous sachemship could once again become a dominant power that stretched across the coast now looked unlikely. Kieft's and Miantonomi's respective dreams had been deferred, if not totally defeated, in a war that seemed to have no winners.

FIVE

Acts of Navigation, 1647–1674

In the years after the Pequot War and Kieft's War villages started rising across the shoreline, in some places exactly where Indian towns had been recently destroyed. Before the fighting started almost a hundred miles separated the nearest English and Dutch communities; by 1650 they stood as close as ten miles apart. The Dutch-controlled settlements of Oostdorp, Vlissingen, Heemstede, and Nieu Tuyn sat near the fully English towns of Stamford, Stratford, Fairfield, and New Haven. As colonists drew closer on land, they kept their eyes on the water. People in these villages could spot sails coming and going, while many rival settlements could be reached by dugout in just a few hours. In some spots imperial competitors were practically close enough to smell the smoke from their respective chimneys or hear each other singing psalms on Sundays: up to the 1650s Dutch trading houses on the Connecticut River and Narragansett Bay stood just a few thousand feet from English towns. It was harder now for passing canoes to spy inside towns, as many hid behind lines of sharpened tree trunks. Much like their Native neighbors, colonists raised dozens of new stockades, blockhouses, and forts in the 1640s, 1650s, and 1660s. The most famous of these structures was the long, reinforced wooden stockade that girded New Amsterdam and lives on in the American lexicon within the place and metonym Wall Street.[1]

The overseeing bodies of these overlapping colonies, the United Colonies of New England and the Dutch West India Company, regularly bickered over boundaries. But until the 1650s they had preferred to keep their disputes on paper, only rarely making direct threats over small trespasses. The generally civil tone of Anglo–Dutch relations in the first half of the century was, as an English diplomat put it, "grounded upon the union of Religion," or Protestant solidarity against Papist rivals. And on a more practical and local level, colonists' fear of Indians helped keep the peace. These sentiments of shared perils would surface even at the late date of 1663, when the Connecticut governor John Winthrop Jr. hoped for "friendly peace and union" and the New Netherland's director general Petrus Stuyvesant wished for "neighbourhood betweene Christians in these wildernes, under soo great multitude off barbarians Indians lievinge."[2]

The Dutch Republic and English Commonwealth went to war for the first time in 1652, and soon the global conflict threatened their distant villages' détente. Adding to colonial concerns that neighbors would become conquerors, New Englanders and New Netherlanders could not forget the previous decade and a half, when both had attempted conquests of Natives. Some must have recalled the vital role of Indian scouts and assassins in the Pequot War. Others simply wanted to prevent their European foes from recruiting Indian allies, as Natives' ability to inflict carnage and terror had been amply demonstrated in Kieft's War. Colonists continued to be anxious about indigenous enemies who "would be glad to see us att variance heere in these parts that thereby they might have occasion and opportunitie to work mischeif to either," in which case, "neither nation will be able to resist them." While colonists to the west fretted about the perilous state of New Netherland, threatened "on the one side [by] the war with the savages and on the other side [by] the approach of the English," Puritans to the east imagined the day they would be attacked "by the duch from theire ships and the Indians by land."[3]

The shared nightmare that a global war might flare up at the same time as a local one was all too plausible. Indians were more than bystanders to Anglo–Dutch disputes. When Natives came to English towns telling stories of a rumored alliance between Manhattan and a powerful sachem in 1652, the news carried all the way to London and Amsterdam. Seeing this threat of a simultaneous Native and European attack as an egregious offense

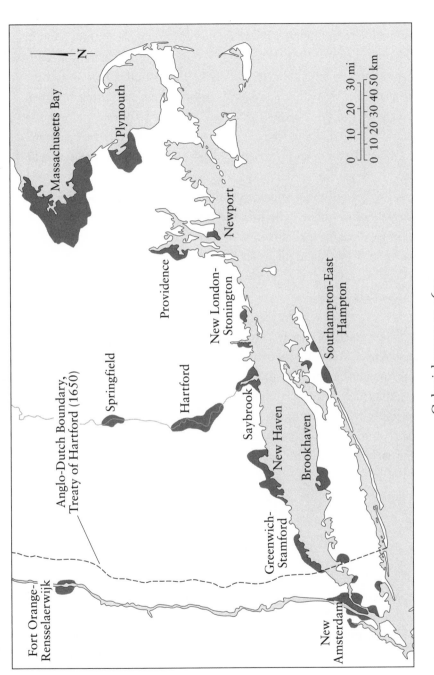

Colonial presence, 1650.

meriting a strong response, Lord Protector Oliver Cromwell planned an invasion of New Netherland. It was aborted at the very last minute. And in 1663, months before a fleet sent by the restored English monarchy actually did capture the Dutch colony peacefully for the first time, Raritan Indians nearly sparked a premature naval battle in the waters off Manhattan when they invited English colonists to Newark Bay. Had either of these tense moments escalated, a few Native sachems living at the very fringes of the Western world would have inserted themselves dramatically into a struggle between Europe's two ascendant naval powers.

Looking beyond these tantalizing what-if moments, one can discern a subtler pattern of Indian actions in the Anglo–Dutch wars emerging. The threat of violence from all directions only made cross-cultural partnerships all the more vital. Algonquians sought colonists to serve as their scribes, arms dealers, and engineers, while Europeans continued to hire Natives as spies, couriers, pilots, and translators. Indians were finding that the foreigners' suspicions could be put to use in winning campaigns against their Native neighbors, as these local conflicts concerned them more than colonial affairs. When they waded into this Atlantic conflict, sachems were seldom looking far beyond their own horizons. By trading in ominous secrets, they plotted tricky courses between the two empires and through a dense fog of rumors. But as wars between England and the Netherlands began to wane, wampum gradually lost its value as currency. Only when the tangled webs of commerce and alliance fell apart did Indians across the coast begin to wonder once again if all indigenes should look beyond their old differences and unite against the invaders.

Uncas and Ninigret

A recently wed young Puritan couple named Antipas and Elizabeth Newman were sailing from New Haven to Boston when they happened upon a gruesome sight. As they passed by the tiny mass of Gull Island just east of Long Island on a July day in 1660 they spied a party of Narragansetts on the islet's rocky shores who "had taken a canooe of the Long-Iland Indians" and "were beheading of them closse by the way as wee came."

Antipas described the spectacle to his father-in-law, John Winthrop Jr., as "so dreadful to my wife that she had much adoe to get over it," though he reassured him she "was very well againe before the evening." The seaside attack was part of a complex, ongoing set of feuds between the Montauketts and other peoples from eastern Long Island and the Niantics and Narragansetts. These fights were a continuation of mainland sachems' long-standing practice of bullying outlying folks for wampum and other tributes. Puritan authorities would later declare the beheadings a "barbarouse and inhumaine acte," a phrase that conveniently ignored the many times they requested and received severed heads in the Pequot War. Massachusetts officials would use this act of violence as a pretense to extract a new punitive wampum tribute from the Narragansetts. The surprising scene that sickened Elizabeth Newman illustrates how at the same time colonists were engaged in an Atlantic contest with each other, they sailed in the midst of multiple coastal battles they only partially understood.[4]

Roger Williams gave a terse summary of the region's "Indian affairs" in 1647 that pithily summed up the next two decades: "Lyes are frequent; Private interests, both with Indians and English, are many." Historians' understanding of the conflicts among Indians is also somewhat vague and incomplete—it is easy to share the sentiments of the colonial governor who sighed, "I understand not their quarells." These fights defy any easy organization, as they involved many permutations of hostile actions between the Mohegan, Pequot, Niantic, Narragansett, Wampanoag, Quiripi, Pocumtuck, Montaukett, Corchaug, Shinnecock, Unkechaug, and Massapequa peoples. However, these skirmishes had a few features in common. They all involved raids along and across the shore and movements of men in large war canoes between the mainland and outlands. The first scholar to study these conflicts in any depth described them as "Naval Campaigns." Furthermore, nearly every one of these seemingly desultory actions can be linked to one of the two most powerful Indians in the region, Uncas and Ninigret.[5]

Uncas was chief sachem of the Mohegans; Ninigret was head of the Eastern Niantics and Narragansetts. Both were deft leaders who had hybrid forts near the mouth of Long Island Sound where they could easily greet passing English and Dutch pinnaces. Each lived in a stately house that dwarfed all others, had multiple wives, commanded fleets of dozens of canoes, collected regular tributes of wampum from the villages of their friendly neighbors, and, on occasion, took captives and heads from enemies. The two were also distant relatives. The ruling class of coastal Algonquians regularly married into each other's families, and both sachems had direct ties to the elite Pequot dynasty. They paid close attention to the flow of past and future bloodlines—Uncas went so far as to dictate a detailed genealogy to a colonist before he died. Indeed, their male heirs would ape European titles by styling themselves as Uncas II and Ninigret II, while men in subsequent generations would convert the titles into last names. The two men shared an aversion to Christianity. The Puritan missionary John Eliot griped about the mutual stubbornness of "Unkas and Nenecrot," the "two great Sachems in the Countrey that are opened and professed enemies against praying to God." Given the symmetry in their ambition and character, perhaps it is no surprise that Uncas and Ninigret loathed each other.[6]

Bad blood between Mohegans and Narragansetts ran deep, but the bitter animosity between the two leaders truly began in the Pequot War and its aftermath. Ninigret could not forgive Uncas for the murder of his close ally Miantonomi, but Uncas showed neither signs of remorse nor any interest in reconciliation. More than a decade after the division of the powerful Pequot sachemship, the rival sachems were still fighting over who could claim the most surviving Pequots' loyalties and lineages. Uncas had consolidated power by taking multiple wellborn Pequot women as his wives; as colonists saw it, "He hath drawn all the scattered Pequots to himself" and "plotteth universall monarky betweene [Indians] and Duch and Long Iland and laies strong foundations for the future greatnesse of his family [in] one boy by [a] Pequot squar." Ninigret, too, tried, with somewhat less success, to keep the highest-ranking Pequot refugees within his realm. When the Pequot Tausaquonawhut, who "was a child when the Pequt wars were," married one of his daughters around 1650 Ninigret noted to Williams, perhaps with some glee, that the Pequot suitor had first rejected one of Uncas's daughters as a wife "because of her sore eyes." Ninigret was so fond of his discerning, well-pedigreed son-in-law that he "desires they might live neere together" and protested vigorously when some English tried to deport

Tausaquonawhut to Long Island because they were suspicious of his Pequot blood.[7]

These feuds troubled the English colonists, who were wary of "setting up new monarkes of the treacherous hethen." It disturbed them most when these small wars came to their very doors. Robert Lay, a farmer raising a herd of cattle on an island in the Connecticut River, described a terrifying day in 1659 when Narragansetts came looking for one of his cowhands, a Mohegan named Cheshanamp. The attacking men spent three days in hiding on the far side of the island, finally making their move when Lay summoned Cheshanamp to help him move a fallen animal. Sneaking "doune from the backline of the hill with their gunes ready presented," the raiders took aim at their Mohegan target "and shot him doune." Lay was relieved they did not hit his sons and daughter, all of whom were under the age of ten and standing nearby. The children burst into tears as Cheshanamp drew his final breaths. Lay's wife, Sarah, came running out of the house upon "hearing the children shreakeing," and, seeing armed murderers and a dying man, "was taken in such a fear that when she will out grow it I cannot tell." The raiding party carried off two more men as captives, including Lay's African slave, whom he referred to as a "negar." Recalling previous moments when warring Indians had crossed his island, Lay would complain, "Now this is the third time that they have ben at my house and have dun murder."[8]

Though people of color were the main victims of this fighting, white colonists wondered if the bloodshed was really somehow all about them. "I feare the Indeans may have some deepe plott against the Inglish in killing the Indians in severall howses of the Inglishe," wrote one Thomas Welles to Governor Winthrop. "Such Insolent cariag, in, or neere our English houses, is not to be borne," fretted another Connecticut man. John Mason, a veteran of the Pequot War, was similarly alarmed by the constant scuffles between Uncas and Ninigret, as he claimed their raiding parties "contynually ly sculkinge" on the Connecticut shore. "Truly Sir," he wrote to Winthrop, "I looke at it as a matter unreasonable as also very unsafe to suffer Indians to mannage and manetene a seat of warr at and in our very bowels." And yet even in this moment of distress and distrust, colonial elites and sachems

were becoming wholly dependent on each other for the delivery of information. Even in the mid-seventeenth century a delicate network of Indian foot-
paths and canoe routes was a major part of the infrastructure holding the
imagined territory of New England together.[9]

Indians did not just carry folded papers covered with looping lines of ink;
recognizing the power of the medium, they soon began commissioning
letters on their own behalf. The Niantic sachem was particularly assertive
when hiring Englishmen as scribes. Ninigret "now with me importunes me
to write this to you," began Williams's letter to Winthrop in 1650 concerning
Ninigret's new son-in-law. "I could [get] no quiet with Nyngret till I did put
pen to paper to write," a colonist in Stonington, Connecticut, related in a
letter to Winthrop in 1665, adding, "though his patience be little worth."
The Niantic headman was hardly the only Native who hovered by colonists'
desks as they wrote. "I am Importuned by som Indians to write to your
worship" began a letter from a colonist to Governor Winthrop in 1661 on
behalf of some Pequots. In 1665 a Brookhaven colonist on Long Island
started a note to Winthrop with a desperate plea on behalf of an Unkechaug
leader besieged by Narragansett, Mohegan, and Montaukett raids, writing
in a rushed script, "Your friend unchcage shacim deed desyer me to
acquaint your worthy that he is In greatt danger of his Life." Many more
letters that did not lead with an acknowledgment of an Indian coauthor
were filled with news of Natives requesting action on their behalf, like the
Connecticut colonist that reported, "Indains comme yesterday to our
Governor and magistrats to Complaine of Injurys donne to them by
Uncus."[10]

The coastal contests of the Mohegan and Niantic chiefs were the single
greatest factor in originating this communicative codependence. Letters
could support and undermine these dueling sachemships that expanded
over the Sound's waters, and yet in relying on them for deliveries of mail,
colonists were occasionally subject to the power of these "new monarkes,"
each attempting "to augment their own Kingdom." Sachems also were wary
of becoming too reliant on colonial pens—as early as the 1660s they started
employing some of the first literate Christian Indians to write English letters
on their behalf. At least one Englishman would opine that what with

colonists "not knowing the ground and reason of the Indians so preceding" perhaps "the less wee meddle with these Indian quarrills, the better."[11]

Natives and the Dutch

Dutch sources lack the same kinds of detailed discussions between colonists and Indians that run through New England's papers. The reasons for this absence are myriad. Though they too hired Indians as letter carriers, the Dutch seldom named the men who delivered their epistles. Nor did colonists to the west act as scribes on their behalf like those to the east did. Tellingly, the main evidence that Dutchmen used indigenous postmen comes from their account books, which listed the payments given, which were usually in gunpowder. The English also could rely more on Native couriers because their expanding constellation of colonial villages fit nicely with the existing indigenous routes across Long Island Sound. This was not always so for the Dutch. Willem Beekman, a colonist stationed along the Delaware in the late 1650s and early 1660s, apologized in his letters that "I could not induce a Savage to go on this journey" and "the Savages disappointed me again."[12]

Nonetheless, just because reconstructing vivid Munsee–Dutch dialogues is difficult does not mean they did not happen. Many of New Netherland's traders and farmers had sizable vocabularies of Munsee words, leading some English to think of their colonial neighbors as masters of Native tongues, like the ship's carpenter who boasted in 1653 that he could comprehend Algonquian dialects "as well as most Duch men." This was not true of all New Netherlanders. Aeltie Sybrants, a woman briefly taken captive by Munsees, never came close to fluency, commenting that their language sounded to her like *kinterhaye*, or "children's prattle." A few talented go-betweens did emerge. The careful detective work of the historian Susanah Shaw Romney uncovered the extraordinary case of Sara Kierstede, a *huysvrouw*, or "housewife," who lived right by the shoreside market in New Amsterdam where Indians and colonists met every Saturday. Week by week over two decades she picked up Munsee vocabulary and grammar while haggling over groceries and firewood. By July 1663 her skills were so well known she was called to translate at peace negotiations between the colony and several Hudson River sachems. (Romney points out that the thirty-six-year-old Kierstede was pregnant with her tenth child at the time.) She did such a fine job that "she was besought and bidden" by the sachems when they returned for a meeting that November.[13]

Although Dutch colonists' desire to do business led many of them to pick up snatches of local dialects, their quest to win souls had no such urgency. The clergy of the Dutch reformed faith in America were reluctant when it came to seeking Indian converts and thus creating potential translators. The leading minister in the colony complained that his one convert had pawned his Bible for brandy and declared that their language was impossible to learn. Perhaps an Indian youth heard some of the gospel in Dutch in 1660 when colonial leaders told a visiting party of Munsees that it would be "good and needful" for an Indian to be fluent and literate in the invaders' tongue, and proposed "they allow some of their children to be raised by us." The delegation agreed to leave one child and maybe send more, though no record of this child's fate survives. Such lackadaisical efforts were a far cry from the work of zealous Puritan preachers on the other side of the coast. By the 1660s they had published a dictionary, several prayer books, and a whole Bible in Native languages, ministered to hundreds of Indians in their own tongues, and were starting to teach their new congregants to read and write English. Though scholars who try to estimate which colonial populations achieved more fluency in Indian languages are largely at a loss, concluding that few got beyond a basic level of speaking, this region was a uniquely complicated linguistic space. Adding to the babel of confusion in meetings between sachems and company men, two of the best Native interpreters living by the multilingual villages of New Netherland, the Wiechquaesgeck Joseph and the Massapequa Adam, spoke only English, not Dutch.[14]

Even if true mutual fluency was rare, by midcentury relations between the Dutch and Munsees had advanced far beyond the initial stage of awkward *vrientschap*, or "friendship." As they had since the days when Kieft was director, company authorities tried to discourage any excess familiarity, warning colonists not to invite Indians to do chores or eat in their houses. Yet most frontier neighbors ignored this advice, instead leading thoroughly intertwined daily lives. Trading not just furs and beads, Indians shared freshly slain turkeys and fish while colonial bakers offered cookies, cakes, and pretzels, and all were apt to enjoy countless glasses of brandy and beer. Officials fretted that the trade in spirits led to fighting, and even more troubling was the trade in guns, which both English and Dutch tried to ban, though by the 1650s the company all but gave up on policing arms dealing.[15]

Still others were swapping genetic material. The male-heavy population of Dutch sailors and traders discovered that unmarried Native women were free to have sex with any man they felt like. One Indian sachem commented during Kieft's War that upon first meeting Dutch traders his men "have given them their daughters to sleep with, by whom they had begotten children, and there roved many an Indian who was begotten by a Swannekan [Dutchman]." By the 1630s authorities regularly hauled sailors and soldiers into Thursday court sessions to answer for the Native women found in their quarters. These women who slept with colonists expected small presents—in fact, they were insulted if their lover gave them nothing. Dutchmen, always unclear on the concept of a gift-centered society, called local women *hoeren*, or "whores." "The women are exceedingly addicted to whoring," wrote one, while another marveled that mature Native women would boast about having affairs with various powerful men "as if it were praiseworthy and glorious." Sharing beds and dining tables appeared to be a far more common practice among the Dutch than the English, hinting that on a strictly physical level relations had become more intimate on the western side of the coast. Still, as one historian notes, Europeans' assumption that their Indian bedmates were merely *hoeren* driven by profit "ensured that sex between Native women and colonial men divided people more than it brought them together."[16]

Food and fornication did not forge better alliances between elite men either. Instead, it was matters of violence—the acts of resolving it, planning for it, and redirecting it—that formed one of the strongest relationships the Dutch colony had with Indians, its partnership with the people of western Long Island, headed by the Massapequas. The life story of their chief sachem, Tackapousha, uncovers the pressures and perils that Massapequas and their allies faced. Compared to exhaustively documented figures like

Uncas and Ninigret, who made their marks on many deeds and treaties and were quoted and discussed in hundreds of primary texts, Tackapousha was elusive and reticent, appearing in far fewer records despite the fact that he lived to a ripe age, dying in 1699. Still, like Uncas and Ninigret, he was part of an old ruling dynasty, thus he shared their interest in bloodlines and legacies. Tackapousha was the heir of the partially blinded Canarsie sachem Penhawitz, known to Dutchmen as One Eye, while his brother Chopeycannows would become the lead sachem of the Secatogues. Often using the English-speaking Native Adam as his chief emissary and as a translator, Tackapousha dealt with both Dutch and English colonists over his long life. He relied even on the aforementioned Sara Kierstede as a translator at least once. In the turmoil of Kieft's War the sachem began his career as a frontier diplomat by stepping into Penhawitz's office of "Chief Sachem [of] all the Indian Sachems from Marsepege, Seacataug, Meracock, Rockaway and Canarse," a realm that stretched over much of modern Queens, Kings, and Nassau country.[17]

Tackapousha's rise was unlike the calculating ascent of the Mohegan and Narragansett sachems who had eagerly partnered with the English at the outset of their war against the Pequots. The Massapequas had joined the anti-Dutch alliance during Kieft's War, and they paid a terrible price for their opposition. A traveler visiting their homelands five years after the war wrote that the shores that were home to "great numbers of Indian Plantations" a few years earlier "now lie waste and vacant." Facing the pressures of land forfeiture, declining trade, diminishing populations, and vanishing game, Tackapousha seemingly arrived at the same conclusion that many other sachems near the Sound did: fighting older enemies was a safer route to holding power than challenging the true cause of their problems, the colonists. In an address delivered by his spokesman in 1655 the Massapequa lamented that in the decade since Kieft's War he had continued to feud with Indian foes, but his people had "done no harm to the Dutch Nation, not even to the value of a dog."[18]

The Massapequa headman's realm was never quite as expansive as those of Uncas and Ninigret. Instead he served as more of a figurehead for connected groups of peoples of western Long Island, less a chief sachem than a chief spokesman. He became a regular guest at Fort Amsterdam from the 1640s onward, even as his rival for control of Native Long Island, the Montaukett sachem Wyandanch, forged a closer relationship with the English at the eastern forks. The eastern Montaukett sometimes styled himself as the unrivaled chief sachem of all Long Island, a title Tackapousha also professed to hold from time to time. More than once Wyandanch, much to Tackapousha's annoyance, tried to sell tracts on the western side of the island to Puritan colonists. The Massapequa also kept a wary eye on Ninigret, who occasionally sent canoes to his villages to extract wampum tributes. It is possible that observing the examples set by his powerful English-allied foes encouraged Tackapousha to treat the Dutch director more like his fellow sachems dealt with Puritans, even if Stuyvesant never became as adept at sharing information as the English governors Williams and Winthrop the younger. In the final months of Kieft's War, Tackapousha volunteered to fight on behalf of the Dutch, taking up arms against holdout groups of Indians on the lower Hudson. He repeatedly offered tidbits of military intelligence as well and would raise dozens of his own men to fight alongside Dutch forces in the colonists' several wars against Hudson Valley Indians in the 1650s and early 1660s, while also becoming one of the company's leading suppliers of wampum. Though the Massapequa–Dutch relationship began as one of begrudging submission, in time it began to yield mutual rewards.[19]

Soon after the close of Kieft's War in 1645 the most powerful Indian leaders from all sides of the coast were crafting negotiated relationships with both sets of colonists, though their bids for power and control often came at the expense of weaker Indians. The Dutch fought a series of small wars in the 1650s and 1660s with Esopus and Susquehannock people from the mid-Hudson and the Delaware, while eastern Natives and English showed admirable restraint in keeping their suspicions from turning into a direct confrontation until the fateful year of 1675. To be sure, those intervening decades were jittery ones, the Puritans becoming alarmed at any hint that nearby Indians were dealing with either the Dutch or Mohawks: they saw the Dutch, correctly, as the main supplier of firearms and gunpowder in the Northeast and the Mohawks as their biggest Native customers. In fact, the

English tended to minimize the potential threat posed by the Indians who lived nearest to them—they almost always imagined that if their neighbors were to attack them en masse some day, they would do so only with the encouragement and support of other European or Indian agitators. Maybe it was too upsetting to believe the men with whom they regularly shared letters might decide without any outside reason to slaughter them.[20]

When the next Dutch director, Petrus Stuyvesant, arrived in 1647 to replace the disgraced Kieft he unwittingly got tangled in the webs of communication that stretched across the region. Within a few years his English and Native neighbors would accuse him of provoking a conflict that threatened to consume every village in the region. "There bee a sperit of war in the minds and mouths of peopell heare," wrote one frightened colonist. He was agonizing about a possible conflict that could, in one alarmist view, engulf "the whole world." Likely the director's reputation as a possible warmonger started taking shape as soon as he took his first clip-clopping steps on the streets of New Amsterdam. He was obviously a seasoned military man with the wooden leg to prove it.[21]

The First Anglo–Dutch War

This new leader of New Netherland was not just battle-hardened but also university-educated; thus he preferred to go by the Latin Petrus rather than the vernacular Pieter. This pompous flourish was a hint that Stuyvesant could match his predecessor in arrogance, but colonists would find that he surpassed Kieft in both competence and luck. Stuyvesant had been an agent of the West India Company since 1630, starting his career in the final tropical act of the Dutch Revolt, when the Netherlands' war of independence had morphed into an overseas war between the Dutch and Spanish empires. Stuyvesant worked on the South American mainland and several Caribbean islands before he led a thousand men in a daring assault on Spanish-occupied St. Martin in 1644, where a cannonball shattered his right leg. Once he had fully recuperated, the company offered him a generous salary of three thousand guilders a year to replace Kieft. Stuyvesant left Europe at a rare moment of peace. After seven years of halting negotiations, the Hapsburgs and the Dutch States General agreed in the Treaty of Münster in January 1648 to cease hostilities, bringing the exhausting eighty-year revolt to a close.[22]

American shores, though, were never quite calm. Correspondence between New Amsterdam and the United Colonies had taken on a bickering, petulant tone. When Kieft objected to English traders' attempts "to fasten [their] foote near Mauritius River," a Dutch name for the Hudson, the United Colonies Commissioners sarcastically wrote back, "We know noe such River, nor can conceive what River you intend by that name unlesse it be that which the English have longe and still do call, Hudsons River." Puritan governors chided the Dutch for making "various and unsertaine" claims "sometimes upon one ground and otherwhiles upon an other which leaves us in the dark and unsatisfied." An especially snippy exchange flared up when a Connecticut magistrate allegedly quipped, "The English were fooles to suffer the Dutch to live" near Manhattan. Stuyvesant similarly tweaked the English by insinuating that a Puritan conference in Hartford was, owing to the nearby presence of a Dutch fort, actually held "in New Netherland."[23]

Trading jibes was easy, but it was becoming tiresome. The commissioners attempted to start their relationship with Stuyvesant on a pleasant note, writing with warm congratulations and the hope that the English "shall enjoy within your limits all the fruites of a neighbourly and friendly correspondency." But the English once again begged Dutch traders not to sell guns, powder, and shot to Indians, and the Dutch further raised their ire by seizing the English ship *St. Beninjo* in New Haven harbor in 1648. Stuyvesant soon realized that resolving that matter was a convenient pretense for settling the larger boundary question. The death of John Winthrop Sr. in 1649 also opened up an opportunity for reconciliation, as many New Netherlanders had a sincere respect for the elder Winthrop. "I doe reallie Condole with you," Stuyvesant wrote to the New Haven governor Theophilus Eaton, "we being all of us in these partes participants in the sad losse." Eaton was touched and agreed to a meeting. The resulting Treaty of Hartford, signed in September 1650, gave the western third of Long Island and the mainland west from Greenwich to the Dutch. The document was provisional at best, as it failed to settle all lingering points of contention regarding the Delaware Valley and arms trade. But it was a real diplomatic achievement all the same.[24]

Stuyvesant had other reasons to clear the air: by his second year as director he faced serious political challenges from multiple directions. Many colonists saw him as a tone-deaf, haughty authoritarian just like Kieft. A movement was underfoot, led by the young lawman Adriaen van der Donck, to transfer the colony's administration from the private hands of the West India Company to public control under the States General, a move that would relieve Stuyvesant of his office. Meanwhile, to the east on Long Island Stuyvesant continued the practice, started under Kieft, of welcoming English migrants to form towns under Dutch protection. Though he appreciated the new population, these foreigners with uncertain loyalties were inherent security risks. Stuyvesant chafed over the colony's southern boundaries, where Pieter Minuit, a former director, had taken command of the New Sweden colony in the Delaware Valley and was looking to edge in on Dutch trade with the Lenni Lenape and Susquehannocks. Equally vexing to him, English traders from Virginia and New England began to send ships to the region. Wary of the many mistakes of his predecessor, Stuyvesant knew any one of these conflicts could sink his directorship.[25]

Though New England and New Netherland now had a clear boundary stretching across land and sea, on the larger Atlantic this moment of tense peace was short-lived. In England a devastating civil war between king and parliament and simultaneous violent uprisings in Scotland and Ireland made for a solid decade of bloodshed. The uprising against the crown reached a dramatic climax with the trial and beheading of Charles I in 1649 and ended with the triumph of parliament over Charles II in the Battle of Worcester in 1651. The slaying of the king would end up having notable relevance to people on these shores a decade later, as several of the judges who convicted Charles I fled to the Puritan stronghold of New Haven to hide from his vengeful son.[26]

With the English Civil War over or at least paused for a decade, parliament's victorious general, Oliver Cromwell, assumed control of a kingless Commonwealth. Soon the self-titled lord protector laid out ambitious plans to conquer rebellious Scots and Irish provinces and seize as much Atlantic trade and territory from European rivals as he possibly could. The legal blueprint of his imperial dreams was the Navigation Acts of 1651, passed just weeks after the final victory at Worcester. Intended to buoy merchant interests by requiring English-owned hulls and mostly English crews to ferry the country's import and export cargo, the Navigation Acts decreed that any domestic ship carrying goods between foreign nations must pass through English ports. These laws put the central ideas behind mare clausum into action, creating an exclusive English Atlantic in which all the spokes of overseas trade led to the ports of Cromwell's Commonwealth.

The acts heightened English competition with the Netherlands. There, a faction that supported the Prince of Orange was shocked at the execution of Charles I, genuinely concerned about the collapse of hereditary authority and the terrifying future of military dictatorships represented by Cromwell. The Republic's stadholder Willem II died in 1650, days before the birth of his namesake and sole heir. Lacking a genuine monarchical structure that would have allowed for a formal regency during Willem III's youth, the Republic entered its first stadholder-less period. The mayor of Amsterdam, Cornelis de Graeff, and his nephew Johan de Witt quickly moved to run a commonwealth of their own through the States General. De Graeff appointed De Witt as grand pensionary of Holland, all the while seeking to extinguish the young Prince of Orange's future claim to the office of stadholder. De Graeff and De Witt shared Cromwell's antimonarchical views but little else: in the Netherlands royalists were Calvinists (more akin to English Puritans) while parliamentarians were Arminians (not unlike High Church Anglicans), the exact opposite of England.

The Dutch Republic without a stadholder was therefore a kind of a funhouse-mirror reflection of the kingless Puritan Commonwealth across the North Sea. Having no great sympathy for the deposed House of Stuart, De Graeff and De Witt and their pro–States General faction were just as eager to challenge Cromwell for economic gain and national valor, having correctly read the Navigation Acts as a direct challenge to Dutch maritime supremacy. The North Sea neighbors' long-standing feud over the freedom of the seas began to move out of the realm of minor diplomatic spats and toward a full-on war. Their respective classes of politically radicalized urban merchants were now helming their foreign affairs, and the two nations were set to face off on the high seas. A battle between two freshly decapitated states, the First Anglo–Dutch War (1652–54) featured awkward spasms of nation building and lurching attempts at imperial expansion.

Ultimately, this naval war and the two Anglo–Dutch wars that followed (in 1665–67 and 1672–74) were cynical, expensive, propaganda-fueled affairs that risked the lives of many for the interests of few. In 1653 alone it cost the English parliament £2.16 million to fight the Dutch, and Cromwell would ultimately spend more on the first Anglo–Dutch war than on all his campaigns in Scotland and Ireland combined. Pamphleteers in London churned out satiric poems that called the Netherlands the "ingested Vomit of the Sea" and mocked the Dutch governors as Hogs—a play on the title *hoog*, or "high"—and vowed to make "their Sea-sick Courage puke." Dutch publishers favored derogatory prints: one popular cartoon depicted the Spanish and French monarchs, who, unlike the States General, swiftly recognized the Commonwealth, rushing to kiss Cromwell's bare buttocks.[27]

As wartime fever hit its pitch the English attempted to inflame anger toward Holland by swearing to avenge the Amboyna Massacre, a nasty dispute between their respective East India Companies in the Spice Islands in which the Dutch killed twenty English men. But they were waving a rather faded bloody shirt, considering that the murders occurred in 1623, thirty years earlier. These transparent strategies of mockery and manufactured outrage had a real human toll: approximately five thousand combatants perished in the first Anglo–Dutch War, twelve thousand in the second, and four thousand in the third. Spurred on by each nation's powerful merchant interests and brittle sense of national pride, the Anglo–Dutch wars were sadly typical of the cycle of warfare in seventeenth-century Europe. Once peaceful fields became hastily dug graveyards, while the bodies of slain sailors washed up on North Sea beaches.[28]

From both states' perspective the affairs of several thousand of their respective countrymen on a distant stretch of coastline were a minor and peripheral matter. At first, no one in Amsterdam or London thought of their overlapping villages on Long Island Sound as a key arena of war. And no colonial governor in the region wanted to be responsible for triggering a bloody incident like Amboyna that could heighten the international conflict. Yet that very possibility remained. By the spring of 1652 the company's Amsterdam bureau warned Stuyvesant to "be on guard there. It is feared that the English of New England might pick a quarrel with us." By that winter, though the war was in full swing in Europe, company officials told Stuyvesant they were "pleased to learn that your honor has not experienced any disharmony with the English over there," urging him "to cultivate commerce with one another, esp[e]cially with Virginia."[29]

The director had written to the Massachusetts governor John Endicott lamenting "the sad newes of differences . . . betwixt the states of our Native countries." War was a luxury that could not be afforded in "a vast wilderness." After another rumor of a pending English attack in March 1653, Stuyvesant declared, "Fort Amsterdam cannot hold all the inhabitants nor defend all the houses and dwellings in the City," and stockades could not surround every village on the mainland and Long Island, "where the people live at great distances from each other." The colony agreed to set up a new system of alarms and peripheral defenses, with the general goal of concentrating the population in Manhattan in the event of an attack. And thus began the wall that later gave Wall Street its name.[30]

Meanwhile, New Englanders heard their own set of worrisome rumors. "Att a meeting extraordinary" on April 1, 1653, the United Colonies investigated the "Rumors of the Duch engageing of severall Indians to cutt of the English" and forming "so hiddius a plot." This was a new allegation. The English had long accused Dutch and French traders who sold guns of indirectly "strengthening and animating the Indians against them," but to accuse the weapons dealers of being in league with their customers was a far more serious charge. The rumors told a straightforward tale of one sachem's betrayal and a looming bloodbath. Native spies reported that Ninigret had visited Manhattan the previous winter and had supposedly exchanged wampum for guns, the first step in forming an alliance. An Indian woman told a Connecticut colonist that "the Duch and Indians generally were confeaderated against the English Treacherously to cut them of[f]" on "the day of election of Majestrates in the severall colonies because then it is apprehended the plantations wilbee left naked." A Dutch fleet would seize their ports in Long Island Sound, and parties of Indians would torch their outlying villages. Styling herself a Cassandra, the Indian informant reminded the English that she had previously warned them of Pequot treachery and been ignored.[31]

The United Colonies Commissioners staged an interview with Ninigret, his brother Pessicus, and Canonicus's heir Meeksam, "three of the chiefest Narragansett Sachems," to "acquaint us with what hath passed betwixt the Duch and you." In their responses, probably translated by Thomas Stanton, whom Ninigret knew from their service together in the Pequot War, the sachems were both articulate and indignant. Ninigret openly volunteered that he had indeed been in Manhattan that winter, but "he went thether to take Phisicke," "hearing there was a frenchman there that could cure him." He never specified the illness that troubled him. Ninigret was unambiguous in his denial of the plot, soon becoming exasperated by having to "answare these things over and over againe." As for the rumors of gift exchange, he admitted he "carried with him thirty fathome of wampume," but every last bead could be accounted for. Ten fathoms went to the French doctor, fifteen went to Stuyvesant, who gave him "sleeved coates" in return "but not one gun." His last five fathoms of wampum had been spent buying guns from Indians, not Dutchmen. Though he had one brief audience with Stuyvesant, Ninigret alleged that his reception was frosty. "I found noe such entertainment from the Duch Gov[erno]r," he told his interrogators. "I stood a great part of a winter day knocking att the Gov[erno]rs dore and he would neither open it nor suffer others to open it to lett me in."[32]

After accounting for his own dealings Ninigret began to question the entire logic of the supposed Dutch–Narragansett conspiracy. "What doe the English thinke[?]" he asked incredulously. "That I think they bee asleep and suffer me to doe them wronge[?]" The charges may have seemed laughable to the Narragansetts and Niantics, as they all remembered the Puritan aggression in the Pequot War. "Doe not wee know the English are not a sleepy people[?] . . . doe they thinke wee are madd to sell our lives and the lives of our wives and children and all our kin[d]red and to have [our] countrey destroyed for a few guns powder shott and swords[?]" "If these things were soe," the accused Indians wanted to know, "how can [we] expect to bee preserved . . . by a few Duch men whoe are soe Remote when wee doe live by the dore of the English[?]" Why, indeed, would Ninigret choose a more distant and weaker ally over his demonstrably more populous and dangerous neighbors? The rumors were further undermined by the fact that many Indian informants were connected to Uncas, a sworn foe of the eastern Niantics and Narragansetts. Echoing his actions during the Pequot War and his campaign against the Narragansett sachem Miantonomi, Uncas was once again seizing on English suspicions of other Indians to keep the Mohegans in a privileged place.[33]

Increasingly, Natives who were far out of Uncas's orbit began coming forward. Munsees from near Manhattan swore that the Dutch were ranging "up and downe amongst the Indians." Coco, a mainland chief whose homelands abutted Stamford, presented himself and gave a detailed account of a meeting held with the company secretary, Cornelius van Tienhoven. The sachem claimed he rebuffed the invitation to join a limited strike against Stamford. Even the Niantics, who denied that any plot was under way, reported that the Indians from the west side of the Hudson "said there was a ship arived att the M[anhattan] and shee brought guns powder &c And that more shipps were a cominge to fight with the English here." Yet that news alone was hardly proof of a coming sneak attack. Of course the Dutch were preparing for a possible conflict with the English—it would have been foolish not to.[34]

The supposed meeting with Secretary Tienhoven was the most credible report in its specificity. But there is no evidence in Dutch sources to suggest the widespread conspiracy described by Natives was true. In the period that the supposed plot was being hatched, most of the company's attention was directed toward reinforcing New Amsterdam's walls and fort. It seems possible that a few Dutch agents were offering guns and powder to Indians as part of their strategy of creating a system of alarms should "we be visited by our neighbors." But the idea that the Dutch officials bumblingly tried to make a grand secret alliance with Natives that was immediately exposed, yet at the same time perfectly concealed all mention of this plot from their private papers, seems unlikely. If they happened at all, it seems probable the Dutch overtures were more simple than sinister, a combination of off-the-books dealing in firearms combined with some halfhearted attempts to win more friends among their Native neighbors.[35]

Company officials were troubled to learn that Indians along the coast appeared to fear and respect the English more and saw them as the likely victors in a showdown. Just in passing along rumors of the Dutch governor's overtures, they were siding with the English. Sachems like Tackapousha who genuinely profited from an alliance with the Dutch and actually seemed fond of the men at Fort Amsterdam were rare. Kieft had poisoned any chance that Stuyvesant may have had of swaying the bulk of Indians to join the Dutch camp. As a sachem near Stamford supposedly put it in rejecting the advances of Van Tienhoven, "Why should wee kill the English that have donn us noe wronge but you have killed many of our people wrongfully[?]"[36]

Seizing on their neighbors' weakness, Puritans cranked up their outrage to a higher level. A hawkish publisher in London made the irate letters from New England the basis of a short pamphlet with the fair and balanced title *The Second Part of the Amboyna Tragedy; or a Faithful Account of a Bloody, Treacherous, and Cruel Plot of the Dutch in America, purporting the total Ruin and Murder of All the English Colonists in New England* (1653). The printed account curiously traced the origins of the plot to Indians, painting the Hollanders as merely greedy mercenaries "stirred by presents and promises" from "four of the principal heathen sagamores, great princes" all, "fell, blood-thirsty men" who, in this version, planned not to attack on election day but on "a Sunday, when the English would be altogether in their meeting houses." (In Cromwellian England it was no stretch to imagine that Hollanders could always be lured by money and carelessly profaned the Sabbath.) A copy soon arrived at the West India Company's Amsterdam headquarters near the IJ, the city's main waterway, where officials would describe it as "frivolous and false charges" invented "to cover their evil intentions," making it "the most shameless lying libel which the devil in hell could not have produced." They sent a translated version back to Stuyvesant and his council so "that your Honors might see what stratagems that Nation employs, not only to irritate the populace, but the whole world, if possible, and to stir it up against us."[37]

"The whole world" may not have been watching the shores near Long
Island Sound that closely, but at least one man, the then-current occupant
of Whitehall Palace, found the pamphlet compelling. In response to the
propaganda and pleading of those distant fellow Puritans, Cromwell hired
Major Robert Sedgwick and Captain John Leverett to sail four ships toward
"the Manhattos," where they "shall by way of surprize open force or otherwise" and "Endeavour to take in that place in the Name of his Highnes the
Lord Protector of the Commonwealth of England Scotland and Ireland."
Cromwell's orders made no direct mention of using Indians, but English
colonists in New Haven looking to respond to Sedgwick's and Leverett's
repeated pleas for "some means of a constant intelligence" of "how things
are at the Manhatos" in all probability would have spoken to indigenous
spies.[38]

Cromwell's men had actually left Boston in June 1654 "with their vessels
and soldiers upon the sea" on a course to Manhattan when colonists urgently
interrupted them with "news of the peace" between the Low Countries and
England. Not looking to waste their efforts, they set a new course to capture
French forts in Acadia (present-day Nova Scotia) instead. Looking back to
the origins of this affair, it seems a single Indian sachem's winter canoe trip
across Long Island Sound would alarm a series of Christians from the
Quinnipiac to the Charles to the Thames to the IJ and could well have
tripped off another phase of naval war. In reality the attack was not truly
avoided but merely redirected toward French colonists who undoubtedly
had no clue their attackers had been summoned thanks to Indians dabbling
in Atlantic geopolitics. And if Uncas was the source of the rumor, for a brief
moment antimonarchists in London and Amsterdam were being swayed by
the propaganda of a Native man's "universall monarky."[39]

Dutch visions of a hostile fleet appearing off Manhattan came true in just
a couple years, only the vessels came in from the Hudson estuary, not the
Atlantic. "At a very early hour of the morning" on September 15, 1655, a fleet
of sixty-four canoes bearing several hundred Indians came gliding down the
Hudson, "almost before anyone had risen from bed." At first the visit looked
like a mere incident of harassment and robbery, as Indians loudly looted
colonial homes. But by nightfall it escalated into a shooting war. Over the

next three days Natives killed fifty colonists, razed dozens of farms, rustled or slaughtered more than five hundred head of cattle, and carried off dozens of colonists as captives for ransom. Colonists estimated the property damage alone totaled over two hundred thousand guilders. Historians used to call these events the Peach War, as some of the Dutch believed the entire incident was due to Munsees avenging a colonist's murder of an indigenous woman who had been caught stealing his peaches. Scholars now see the raid as the work of both inland Susquehannas and coastal Munsees, responding not only to the murder but also to the Dutch takeover of the New Sweden colony on the Delaware. In the uneasy months afterward, Natives resumed offshore raids that were reminiscent of the saltwater attacks from the colony's early days. In October Indians surprised a vessel on a "pleasure excursion" in New York harbor, leaving the body of one of their victims in a canoe while taking the women captive. When a company yacht called *De Eendracht* (union) grounded in the shoals off Sandy Hook in January 1656 its helpless crew was "robbed under threats" by a party of thirty Indian pirates.[40]

New Netherland's constant anxiety at the approach of any unfamiliar ship or canoe would present an opportunity for the Natives of western Long Island. In 1656, just as the nastiness of the Peach War had passed, English-speaking settlers of Heemstede drew up a detailed and generous treaty with Tackapousha. Noting that the Treaty of Hartford of 1650 nearly split Long Island at the place where his realm ended, Tackapousha promised his peoples' loyalty to the Dutch over the English, a move that would fend off both land-hungry colonists and his Montaukett rivals at the eastern forks, who looked to profit by selling Massapequa land to Englishmen. In addition, the treaty served to defend him from Ninigret. Soon after signing the agreement, Tackapousha lobbied Stuyvesant for protection on hearing of a Narragansett plot to cross Long Island Sound and raid his villages. The pact between the sachem and the director secured the Massapequas' role as the West India Company's most steadfast Indian ally and leading local supplier of wampum. They maintained two busy trading posts on the north and south sides of modern Nassau County. This was never quite a partnership of equals, however. During an annual renewal of the alliance in 1660

Tackapousha reminded the director that "he & his Indians are a small number," while the Narragansetts remained a potent foe. Bearing a generous gift of wampum, the Massapequa affirmed that the leaders of the West India Company were his only true allies, declaring that if "his Indians Should be Molested, they require assistance having no other friends but us."[41]

There is tactile evidence of this Dutch–Massapequa partnership. One of the articles of agreement from 1656 committed the company to "build a house or a forte" which "shall be furnished with Indian trade or commodities." The site was later uncovered by archaeologists on a peninsula known as Fort Neck, where the fort's blocky body was still visible as lines in the soil. The structure had the unmistakable fingerprints of a colonial designer. It had all the new features Indians appreciated: bastions, a dry moat, and a small interior rampart on the most exposed corner. A massive pile of cracked shells sitting just outside the south wall confirms that the "house" was a hub for manufacturing wampum. Indeed, the Indians probably chose the site for just that reason, as the nearby shoreline was an ideal habitat for hard-shelled clams and whelks.

The freshly minted beads were likely traded soon thereafter on the premises. Modern digs found ample evidence of European commerce at the fort: clay pipes with Dutch and English makers' seals, an antler-handled knife with an iron blade, green and clear glass bottles, white ceramic plates, glass beads, mirrors, a metal needle, a heavy iron spike, a brass mouth harp. Imported wares and wampum debris point to how important trade had become to the Massapequas and, moreover, how vital wampum was to the nearby colonists. Yet the site also confirmed that everyday activities in nearby villages—farming, hunting, cooking, sewing, fishing—were still largely conducted with traditional tools. From scattered artifacts we can piece together a picture of a community that had close economic and diplomatic ties to the Dutch through shell beads yet maintained a fair degree of material independence. While this site speaks to the specific history of the Massapequas, one can see patterns here that could be found across the region. Numerous other indigenous communities balanced everyday innovations and traditions and weighed the merits of alliance versus defiance, all the while staying close to the shore for survival.[42]

The Second Anglo–Dutch War

The first sounds of the English invasion of New Netherland were hoofbeats. On a July day in 1663 a pack of "16 or 18 Men on horseback" came charging into "the village called Oostdorp," now part of the Bronx, where they loudly demanded the town's English majority renounce their oaths of loyalty to the States General. A similar scene played out a few weeks later in Gravesend on Long Island, where a posse of "150 English of Hoorse & foote" led by one John Schott swarmed around the house of the most prominent English ally of the Dutch "demanding him dead or alive, breaking open his house & using all manner of Violence" to force his surrender. With similar gusto and "sounding trumpet, beaten drum, flying colors, great noise and uproar," the band of Puritan conquerors seized the blockhouses of Anglo–Dutch towns on Long Island that same night. When seizing these towns in the name of Charles II, the invaders gave lengthy "harangues in the English tongue," listing their spurious legal grounds to "the silly and common people" with "a strange, unblushing shamelessness." In a mildly threatening letter written to the Connecticut governor, Stuyvesant pointedly reminded his neighbors that his overseers in Amsterdam were constantly encouraging him "to recover al the trackt of land between Greenwich and the fresh River." Though he believed this move within his rights, he personally demurred, as "great Murther & Bludsheade might be the result."[43]

These aggressive moves to erode New Netherland's eastern flank angered the Dutch in Amsterdams new and old, but some Munsees looked on with delight. The sachems of the Raritans, who lived south of Newark Bay, had nursed numerous grudges against the company for the past thirty years. Their attack on a Dutch trading sloop in 1640 had led to Kieft's attempting to hire other Indians to kill them. Raritans' feelings about the Dutch had been further soured by the actions of the Staten Island patroon Cornelis Melijn, whom they considered "a sorcerer," declaring that "he has poisoned them, that he has sold bad powder and guns." At some point in the fall of 1663 Raritans got in touch with the leading families of several English towns on Long Island, inviting them "to purchase their Land." The colonists, "being straitned for Land" gladly "accept[ed] their motion." This little real estate venture would give the Raritans a steady source of trade and a hedge against their Indian enemies, who presumably included the Dutch-empowered Massapequas. The new coastal property would also allow the English to crowd even further on Dutch claims.[44]

The closing, however, did not go smoothly. As the English buyers set sail for Newark Bay, "the Governour of the manadoes [meaning Stuyvesant] sent forth a man of warre to take us." With some deft tacking the English got "the wether gage of them," leaving the downwind Dutch ship to retreat back to Manhattan and allow the English to go ahead with the sale. But "the next morning they made after us agayne, but runing the[ir] vessell aground, they landed the[ir] soldiers, & marched to us by land, so when they came to us, they called us many base names." This clumsy naval engagement ended when the English retreated to Long Island and the Raritans "promised to maintaine our purchase." In the report of the event that made its way to Winthrop, the English included a dire rumor that their rivals were recruiting Indians. "If we had bin taken," the colonists asserted, "the Indians tould our Interpreter, the Dutchmen persuaded them to kill us, & bury us in the sand."[45]

The Dutch were right to anticipate an invasion. But they myopically assumed that their future conquerors were standing sharply in front of them and not far over the horizon. Company officials despaired at their competitors' seemingly unstoppable growth, wondering if "the English, reinforced from places round about . . . would, like the heads of the Serpent Hydra, have grown more numerous the more they were lopped off." It was fitting to liken New England to a beast with many heads, as its several colonies ultimately lacked the unity, motivation, and finances to raise a full invading force. Back in England, though, the newly restored House of Stuart had all the means at their fingertips. Since reclaiming the throne in 1660, Charles II looked to continue England's maritime expansion, a goal shared by his ambitious younger brother James of York, later King James II. Upon hearing news of the ongoing conflicts between New England and New Netherland, York and his circle of like-minded advisers planned a daring invasion of the Dutch colony. Removing the Dutch West India Company from the Hudson and Delaware would create a vast, uninterrupted English realm in North

America, affording the Stuarts a wider foundation for rebuilding their scattered and unruly Atlantic empire.[46]

Once he received his brother's approval in March 1664 York used his own purse to hire Colonel Richard Nicolls and a force of two thousand men to sail in four frigates. Nicolls arrived in the last week of August. First, the fleet anchored off Long Island and sent parties to seize the Breukelen ferry landing and the garrison on Staten Island before sailing into plain view of Fort Amsterdam. Both the besieged Dutch governor and the attacking English colonel looked to emerge from the standoff with their hands clean and honor intact. Though Nicolls could have quickly seized the colony with force, he offered generous terms of surrender, which Stuyvesant mulled over for several days. Finally, on September 8, 1664, in a calm ceremony marked by martial pomp and a bittersweet tone of resignation, Stuyvesant capitulated to Nicolls. In honor of his royal sponsor, the new governor changed the fort's name to James and rechristened the town and colony New York.[47]

Months later the Second Anglo–Dutch War (1665–67) officially began. The slosh of powers and peoples across Long Island Sound did not cease with Nicoll's arrival: the Dutch would briefly hold the colony for fifteen months from 1673 to 1674. But the English takeover in 1664 marked a tidal shift in the region's frontier relations, a series of far-reaching changes that no one could yet understand on that late summer's day when the Dutch West India Company's orange and blue colors were set and the crimson Cross of St. George first fluttered over Manhattan. And although the English enjoyed greater popularity among the majority of local Indians, not every sachem was glad to hear the news. As one careful historian notes, in the months after the English arrived in 1664 Tackapousha "was among the few sachems who did not formerly welcome Nicolls," perhaps still hoping, as many colonists were, that the grizzled man with the wooden leg would return to his fort.[48]

This confusing period of alliance building and rumor mongering may have seemed like preparation for an American war that was never actually fought. The Puritan chronicler William Hubbard's summary of the "molestations" of the first Anglo–Dutch war conclude that "though they never produced any violent effects by war, or the like," these foreign wars "yet did provoke and exasperate all that side of the country." But Hubbard was mistaken when he assumed that overlapping Indian and Anglo–Dutch intrigues "never produced any violent effects by war." Certainly in the case of the Dutch, overreactions to the threat of English conquest and their resulting aggression toward New Sweden would only inflame their disputes with local groups like the Susquehannocks and Esopus. Stuyvesant accurately diagnosed that the colony was fatally crippled by its constant low-level wars with Indians. The Dutch worst-case scenario had come true: they were indeed undermined "on the one side [by] the war with the savages and on the other side [by] the approach of the English."[49]

Williams got closer to the essence of these overlapping conflicts when summarizing the recent hostilities in a letter of 1654 to the assembly of Massachusetts Bay. In his view the Pequot War, Kieft's War, and the First Anglo–Dutch War were all unnecessary tragedies. He took a darker view of the North Sea fighting, mourning "the loss of many thousand seamen" and bemoaning the rivalry's staggering cost. He determined that England "had better have born loans, ship money, &c, than run upon such rocks." Williams, always more of a walk-the-talk Christian than many of his countrymen, genuinely thought that New England could be secured through peaceful measures. "Although we are apt to play with this plague of war," he wrote portentously, "I beseech you to consider how the present events of all wars that ever have been in the world have been wonderful fickle" and often led to "future calamities and revolutions." "Future calamaties" were indeed on the horizon. In this murky mix of coastal and global conflicts one can faintly see the origins of King Phi p's War, a bloody orgy of "Massacres, barbarous inhumane outrages" that would so disgust Hubbard that he would later declare that it did not "deserve the Name of a War."[50]

"Masters of the Whole Country Right or Wrong"

In moments of peace, when colonists bought land from Indians, plots along the coast and rivers were always the first to go. Natives had been signing real estate papers as early as the 1620s in New Netherland and started in earnest in the 1640s in New England once the plague-swept lands had all been claimed. Sharing the shore led to trespasses. Indians voiced constant grievances about free-ranging livestock that hungrily tore their way through cornfields and clam banks, while colonists who crowded the coast had their own quibbles about Indians who had little regard for the outlandish colonial notion that live animals could be property. These conflicts were so widespread that one exasperated colonist begged his countrymen to stop "fighting with Indians about horse and hogs," as these were "matters too low to shed blood."[51]

When Niantics living near Stonington, Connecticut, slaughtered a small herd of their neighbors' hogs in 1650 their methods looked more like those of hunters than butchers. A man named Pametoraknit led the attack on "a great blacspottd sow, and 5 great pigs." While he corralled the beasts "into the water," a young man named Amadridge "shott with arrowes," picking off the squealing prey, and eight "squaes" worked together to capture and kill another pig. The plundered beasts "were all great fatt swine," and the Niantics chopped off their ears, then "boyled the hogges by the water side, and put the bones in the mudde." The poachers sold the rendered lard, or pummy, to their Mohegan neighbors. This was only one such incident of many, leading both indigenous and colonial farmers across the coast to build wooden and stone fences around their crops and creatures. These barriers were tiresome to maintain and easily breached. Indians also had to accept a new dividing line in their heads, as they came to terms with foreigners' funny distinction between wild beasts and livestock.[52]

Both water and fences helped make better neighbors. The ragged, glacially formed shore was "drowned coastline," as the irregular edges of the region's moraines created many jutting peninsulas and scattered islands. These features offered convenient natural divisions between Christian and Native spaces. In coastal land transfers colonists sought out islands to let their herds range freely, while Indians held tight to necks of land that could be more easily bounded, keeping their cornfields secure. (Pigs and other grazers often swam far from their home pastures and slowly began to poison local fisheries with their copious amounts of dung.) The whole business of land sales was a notoriously tricky process. Indians would remark again and again that colonists had been lying to them about the contents of the deeds they signed. Colonists, too, would tire of the locals' insistence on relitigating what they thought were settled matters. Some places required multiple deeds—Staten Island, for instance, was sold three times. Still, even in the official records Natives arranged joint-use agreements that allowed them continued coastal access. When the Narragansett sachem Coginaquam signed over a bayside plot in 1659 he explicitly reserved "the priviledge of fishing and gathering Clamms and other shell fish." A Pequot land cessation in 1661 granted them "free libertie to pas and Repas to the usuall places to the River and sea without molestation." A deed from Long Island specifically gave Indians the ongoing right to fell trees on the property for dugouts.[53]

Thickening foreign farms along the water made it harder for Algonquians to continue burning woodlands. In 1667 a group of Western Niantics who had been allies with Uncas expressed great discontent to Connecticut officials that being stuck between the strong-arming Mohegan sachem and settlers crowding the shore threatened their whole livelihood. Uncas had restricted them "to hunt by the seaside," but the Niantics were "afraid to do for if we should fire the wods so neare to the ingli[sh] we should wrong theyr cattell and horses." But if they dared hunt inland in Uncas's grounds "he will tack away our guns there fore we desire to be under the inglish and not under uncus." Asking the colony to "let us have land to live upon," the Niantics promised that "we will be radey to help the inglish when they shall ever stand in need of us." Having less reliable access to both their bays and forests, coastal Natives started to borrow the ways of newcomers, raising their own pigs as a convenient protein substitute for wild catches and kills. Those Niantics asking to live "under the inglish" were typical of an ominous trend beginning in the 1650s and continuing through the 1670s: selling property became linked to surrendering sovereignty. This process was accelerated for smaller groups like those Niantics, who had to choose between Native bullies and colonial ones. All those decades of low-level feuds between chiefs long troubled the English, but the Puritans were finding that the longer these quarrels dragged on the more easily they could step in and twist the disputes to their advantage.[54]

Under intense colonial pressure, the three composite coastal monarchies were breaking into pieces. Years before they officially made themselves subordinate allies of Connecticut, Niantics and other River Indians had already turned to the colony's leadership for help in mediating conflicts provoked by Uncas and his son Joshua. Rhode Islanders reported that nearby "Coweset and Nipmucks have long since forsaken the Narragansett sachems, and subjected themselves to the Massachusetts." This fracturing was the deliberate action of colonists' inviting dissatisfied Natives into new alliances and then pressuring them to sell their land. Massachusetts led the way in picking apart the major sachemships bit by bit, using their agreements with lesser sachems to snatch away lands also contended by Rhode Island and Connecticut. A Rhode Islander eventually alerted the newly restored Charles II to this double-dealing and malfeasance, grumbling that "theese men have inlarged their terrotories, by drawinge away pettie Sachims from their alegience and Relations from the grand Sachims to whom they were ingaged."[55]

The English were nakedly aiming to become, as the Dutch so aptly put it, "Masters of the Whole Country right or Wrong." Each colony's officials looked to best not only Natives but each other. The first conquest of the Dutch only hastened this land rush. Soon after Nicolls, a proxy of the Duke of York, arrived on Manhattan in 1664 he added eastern Long Island, Martha's Vineyard, and Nantucket to the duke's dominion, swiping these island tracts away from Connecticut and Plymouth. At the same time, Connecticut swallowed its neighboring colony of New Haven, then started looking hungrily at a large coastal tract also claimed by Rhode Island. English infighting over boundaries after the Dutch departure was such a mess that ultimately agents of King Charles II had to step in. Many of these colonial borders remained bones of contention up to the American Revolution.[56]

The redrawing of the region's map had more immediate repercussions for Natives. Following their conquest of the Dutch in 1664 the English tried to create a much simpler world in which all Native people now had only a few allied governors to bargain with, and beyond them just one king. (Owing to his proper ascension to office through birth, however, the king was a figure Natives always held in higher regard than they did his nearby appointed and elected proxies.) English attempts to harden their rule and cement their regional supremacy seemed nearly complete with the final conquest of New Netherland in 1674. But the rise of the renascent Stuart empire in the Northeast was achieved not just by warships but also through processes far beyond London's control.[57]

Wampum, Guns, and Rumors

While colonists were dreading the rumble of cannon fire off their coasts during the Anglo–Dutch wars, a quieter battle of currencies was under way. Since the late 1620s, when shell beads became acceptable tender for colonial debts, the English, Dutch, and Natives were, in essence, members of a shared currency zone. But this zone had no central bank, no overseers of its mints to control circulation. Coastal Natives produced most of the specie, while the Dutch circulated much of it to inland Natives. Thus the two most wampum-dependent populations in the region also happened to be its declining, vulnerable powers. Algonquians were facing ongoing population losses from disease, while the Dutch colony, though attracting more migrants than ever in the 1650s and 1660s, could not catch up with the booming birth rate of neighboring Puritans.[58]

In the absence of ample hard specie flowing back from the fatherland, Dutch colonists, more than their English neighbors, used zeewan in everyday transactions, making it "in a manner, the currency of the country." Pegged to pounds and guilders, shell beads could buy "everything one needs," liquor, food, sex, clothing, furs, slaves, boats, animals, land. Larger purchases among colonists often combined metal and shell currencies, though early on, Massachusetts Bay tried to limit transactions in shell to small exchanges. But wampum's use was so widespread that even Harvard College held a hefty pile of the beads as part of its early endowment. Stores of zeewan were an especially common item in Dutch household inventories, listed alongside gold and silver European coins. One of the richest men on Manhattan "was said to have whole Hogsheads of Indian Money or *Wampam*" socked away as his children's inheritance. Yet New Netherlanders worried that "the payment in Wampum, which is the currency here, has never been placed on a sure footing."[59]

The problem was that wampum's value was also pegged to a wholly unregulated nonrenewable commodity: furs. The link between beads and pelts was so obviously vital to New Netherland's existence that the seal of the colony featured a beaver encircled by a string of zeewan. With the founding of Massachusetts Bay's first mint in 1652 wealthy English households had silver specie in the form of the so-called pine tree shilling, named for the crudely drawn conifer on its face. These Puritan coins appeared just as populations of beaver and other furry mammals across the greater Northeast were crashing from decades of overhunting. As the Dutch upriver trade in furs began to slow, colonists trading with nearby Algonquians found themselves flooded with surplus beads.[60]

By 1658 authorities in New Amsterdam upped the Native–Dutch exchange rate from six white beads a *stiver* (one-twentieth of a guilder) to eight. Fearing sudden further inflation of zeewan and an ensuing currency crisis, they further decreed "payment in wampum in sums above ƒ20 shall not be held valid in law," lest colonists start to offload all their shell at once on expensive items. These precautions did not help: within a few years wampum had inflated by 300 percent and was trading at twenty-four beads per stiver. Some scholars see an English pattern of dumping their wampum in New Netherland as a deliberate plan to weaken the Dutch colony in advance of their conquest in 1664, though even some English were surprised at the speed with which the beads' worth cratered. Thomas Willet bewailed in a missive to Winthrop in 1663 that his stores of "wampon falenge moar and moar in vallo," for though he thought "et war a betar comodetey, bute et stell fell." Wampum's runaway inflation played no small part in the colony's end by creating a fiscal crisis just as the international conflict between the two home nations came to a head. Though Stuyvesant petitioned the West India Company to help the colony set up its own mint in 1659, the remote Amsterdam overseers failed to grasp the gravity of the problem. Indians' sense of wampum's value was always separate from its commercial functions; nonetheless, its dropping monetary worth hurt them too, as it drastically shrank their purchasing power with colonial merchants.[61]

Crashes in the economies and ecology of the Northeast sent aftershocks across the continent. While the intense demand for furs had decimated the stocks of beaver for hundreds of miles around, the Dutch still wanted pelts from their prime partners, the Iroquois Five Nations. Composed of the Mohawks, Oneidas, Onondagas, Cayugas, and Senecas, this mighty league of allied peoples called themselves Haudenosaunee, or People of the Longhouse. To keep the easternmost Mohawks coming to their upriver outpost, the Dutch turned to a potentially hazardous trade good: flintlock muskets. The company had previously banned the selling of weapons to Natives, with little success. By 1650, desperate to keep their edge in the fur trade, company agents simply gave in to Indians' demand for guns, making their upper Hudson outpost the hub of a wide-reaching firearms market that would transform a vast swath of the continent. Over the next twenty years Haudenosaunee fighters began undertaking expeditions further and further westward through the Great Lakes, reaching the present-day lakeshores of Manitoba, Minnesota, and Wisconsin by the 1660s. These so-called Beaver Wars were complex events. From the Dutch perspective, the far-ranging Iroquois raids were worth encouraging for the pelts they garnered to fill up the holds of homebound ships. To Haudenosaunee communities, on the other hand, the raids were "mourning wars," that is, captive-seeking campaigns intended to replace their dead and keep their nations flourishing. Plying their favorite partners with more guns, powder, shot, and excess wampum than ever, the men at Fort Orange kept the cycle of warfare rolling.[62]

While Dutch-provided guns fired shots that rang out over a thousand miles away, they also echoed back in New England and New Netherland. Though company traders wanted their guns to flow only to Native hands that would then return fur, the market was never so easily controlled. Soon Mohawk dealers were peddling guns eastward and southward from Fort Orange through webs of alliance and commerce formed with inland and coastal Indians between the Hudson and Massachusetts Bay. English colonists likewise were getting in on the arms trade illegally. A group of Heemstede colonists predicted that these newly armed "Indians will, in a short time, be the destruction both of the Dutch and English." By 1656 the effects of the company's arms trade were so obvious that Williams bemoaned, "The barbarians all the land over, are filled with artillery and ammunition from the Dutch, openly and horridly, and from all the English over the country (by stealth)." Thinking of Kieft's War and the more recent Peach War, he dreaded that Natives "threaten to render us slaves, as they long since (and now most horribly) have made the Dutch."[63]

Williams's prediction was not exactly wrong. The Dutch left a deadly legacy for their soon-to-be conquerors. Much of the gunfire aimed at the English in King Philip's War came from firearms, shot, and powder that were originally the merchandise of the Dutch West India Company. In the midst of the war colonists in Newport, Rhode Island, were apoplectic when they discovered "a ship from Holland riding in our Harbor" and carrying "armes and ammunition" as its cargo was almost certainly bound "to traiders at Yorke or Albany" and "may soone be found in the enemies hands." They swiftly embargoed the ship. Connecticut's governor was similarly outraged when his spies relayed that "the enemie do boast of great supply from those parts about Albany, whether it be directly or indirectly by Indians there inhabiting." He saw the traders' actions as a flaw of national character, blaming "the Dutch people, who you know are soe much bent upon theire profit."[64]

Dutchmen contributed to the war's beginnings not just as salesmen but as specters. Back in 1667, when the English hold on New York was still tenuous, Plymouth colonists heard that a local sachem had signaled his peoples' "readiness to comply with French or Dutch against the English, and so not only to recover their lands sold to the English but enrich themselves with their goods." The sachem was the Wampanoag named Metacom, the man the English called King Philip. The Plymouth took this rumor seriously, fearing that Philip was using old contacts with Dutch traders to help them reconquer their Hudson colonies, a goal Netherlanders would eventually accomplish briefly six years later without any Indian help. This account merits a skeptical reading: Metacom dismissed it as "a meer plot of Ninnegrett . . . his professed enimie," the chief the English once saw as the most treacherous Indian in the region and suspected of allying with the Dutch in 1653. Just two years later Ninigret faced charges that he was cooking up the exact same conspiracy.[65]

Slanderous, sensational, and cyclical rumors seemed to gain currency with colonists just as wampum was losing its value. Tales of dark geopolitical conspiracies, whether coming from indigenous or colonial informants, never failed to get English governors' attention. It helped that colonists remained haunted by visions of warships flying orange and blue colors. In the midst of the supposed Wampanoag–Franco–Dutch plot of 1667, Rhode Islanders made plans "for the erecting of beacons in the most convenient places along the coast from east to west throughout the whole Collony." They would again wonder about "the danger wee are in" upon hearing news of the Dutch return to Manhattan in 1673. A familiar scary story made the rounds, as "men from Rye" reported an ominous summit of "very Stout and Surely" Indians who said that "the Dutch offer unto them Coates and powder [to] helpe them, and that there would be 500 of them ready to helpe the Dutch against the English." Plymouth colonists referred to the reconquest as an absolute emergency caused by "the present insolency of the Dutch."[66]

Though true "insolency" lay closer to home. Well before the Dutch capitulated for the last time, Indians closer to the English were growing increasingly disgruntled, perhaps even disgusted at the sight of colonists. The colonial population was thriving, trade was vanishing, cycles of debt and land forfeiture were gaining speed. As a Connecticut man put it in 1665, the English were "in hazard of stinking in the nostrels of the hethen." In 1668 Narragansetts harassed parties of passing colonists "as they rode about their Occasions, by throwing many stones at them and their horses, and beating their horses as they rode upon them with Clubs and Staves using many treating Speeches to their Persons." Soon colonial attention began to focus more and more on Metacom. In 1671, in the midst of a series of rumors that he was plotting against his neighbors, colonists complained he had become "very high and insolent, and provocking in his speeches and carrages towards us."[67]

With New Netherland turning into a memory, colonial officials were slowly cured of their nightmares of Natives assisting conquering ships. Some were inclined to crack down harder on Indian plots. In 1671 John Eliot urged Plymouth to disarm the Wampanoags "with speede and vigor untill they stoop and quake." The missionary scoffed at his fellow Christians, who, unlike him, did not live surrounded by Natives, for being "more afraide of them and their guns, that indeed we are, or have cause to be." Thus when whispers swirled once more around Metacom in 1675, this time suggesting that he was planning an all-Native alliance, Plymouth officials assertively moved to isolate and punish Philip and his men. After all, there had been plenty of homicides committed by Indians in New England before the suspicious death of the Christian Indian John Sassamon that triggered the war. The difference was in Plymouth's gusto in prosecuting the crime. The trial and hanging of three Wampanoag men for Sassamon's murder were intended to shatter the remaining brittle autonomy Metacom still had. It was no coincidence that the English felt secure in making such a bold move just months after the last Dutch governor stepped down. The war began not long after the executions. Over the summer of 1675 Philip's alliances grew into the largest Native campaign ever against colonists in the region. "King Philip's War" is something of a misnomer, as the Native actions were never fully under his control, and within the war that colonists saw as one were actually numerous inter-Indian conflicts. Still, the Wampanoag sachem's leadership was not a trivial factor in building the Native force that temporarily wiped much of New England off the map. Metacom had been making passionate critiques of colonial conduct for years, not unlike Miantonomi had thirty years earlier.[68]

The differences between the Wampanoag sachem's warring alliance and the Narragansetts' unrealized one seem telling. When Miantonomi had attempted to rally Niantics, Munsees, Montauketts, and others to rise against the English and Dutch in 1642, he failed in part because he was trying to unify a multipolar political landscape, one in which colonists were still confined in a few clumps, the flow of beavers, beads, and trade goods was steady, and guns were expensive and rare. It proved difficult to build an alliance of peoples who had a genuine economic stake in the status quo, mixed feelings about colonists, and inferior weapons. When Metacom started making a similar case for Indian unity in 1675, he was speaking to an impoverished, marginalized indigenous population whose homelands were now studded with thousands of foreign homes, under the sway of a single king, and awash in firearms. Courting allies in great dances held on hilltops under starry skies, Philip no doubt sounded a lot like Miantonomi. But this time audiences were ready to listen.

SIX

Sea Changes, 1675–1750

In the opening days of King Philip's War saltwater quite literally became a *frontier* in the oldest sense of the word, meaning a regulated boundary between peoples. By late June 1675 Plymouth started policing its southern coast with "a smalle bote we hath fitted up for the purpose." Its mission: to capture "any Indeans that may be found passing over" Narragansett Bay or headed to the outlying glacial islands. Weeks later New York outlawed canoe travel across Long Island Sound. After announcing that he had closed the maritime perimeter in early September, Governor Edmund Andros sailed his own pinnace through the Sound's choppy waters, looking for rogue dugouts. He made a standing order for "an armed Sloope to ply" the passage in the coming weeks, "so no ill Indyans may have opportunityes to Cross it at their pleasure."[1]

Soon New York ordered all Natives on Long Island to surrender their guns and dugouts, as both were obviously tools of war. In a further attempt "to prevent any intercourse" between islanders and "the Indyans on the Maine," the colony's high court decreed "all Canooes whatsoever, belonging to Christians or Indyans, on the North side of Long Island, to the East of Hell-Gate" were to be delivered "into the Constables Custody, to be Laid up and secured by them, neare the Block-House." After their deadline, "whatsoever Canooe shall be found upon the sound after that time [shall] bee destroyed." The ban on indigenous boats stayed in place for almost a year. Later that fall Rhode Island expanded its patrols to the Narragansett and

Niantic homeland, sending a fleet of three sloops to destroy "all the Indians Cannoos from Providence on the Coast as they can [find] to Paucatuck River." Summing up New York's role in the war years later, Governor Andros boasted, "Wee kept good continued guards by land and water."²

These attempts to close the shoreline are a reminder that the Northeast's most infamous Indian–colonial war and its long aftermath could be seen as a sequence of maritime events. Viewing the years from 1675 onward from a coastal perspective certainly revises a famous cliché about the conflict. Witnessing Indian fighters celebrate a victory in early spring of 1676, the captive Mary Rowlandson heard them declare "they would knock all the Rogues in the head, or drive them into the Sea, or make them flie the Country." The phrase "drive them into the Sea" has become a standard description of Metacom's goal, regurgitated in countless textbooks. But the quotation obscures the irony that Natives actually suffered the fate they wished on the English: they were the ones driven into the deep. As fighting wound down, close to a thousand Indians, most of whom were women and children, were carried away as slaves to live in far-off lands. The thousands of Natives who remained would find themselves more dependent on the sea than ever before. Indians' postwar voyages further into the Atlantic were often ruthlessly exploitative, both of their bodies and of the sea itself. Nonetheless, some of these journeys helped ensure their survival.³

The saltwater frontier did not close after Metacom's defeat in 1676, but it did change dramatically. Continuing trends that began before the conflict, the generation of Indians who came of age after the colonists' arrival learned to navigate within the new boundaries that now engulfed them. But the encounter between cultures had not ended, and neither had the frontier's characteristic cycles of boom and bust. Exchanges between maritime cultures continued for decades, as did conflicts over coastal resources. Whale oil replaced wampum as the key commodity that linked communities, while the expanding institution of slavery and the spread of the Christian faith further transformed Algonquians' lives. The shore ceased being an active military front by the late seventeenth century, but it remained a fluid, contested space.⁴

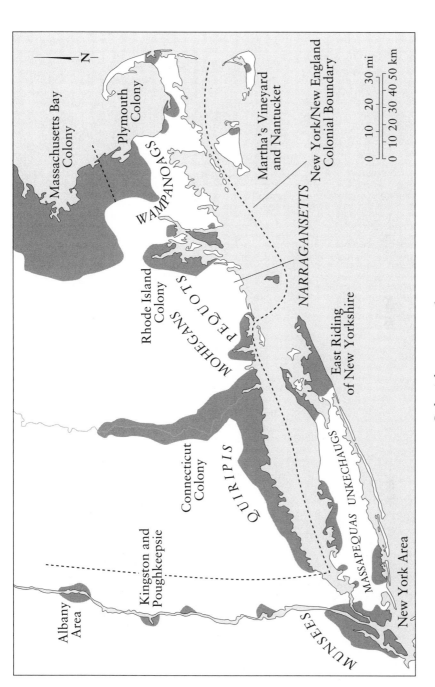

Colonial presence, 1675.

"Hunting Philop from All Sea Shors"

After weeks of hostilities between Indians and English, "a most violent Storm of Wind and Rain, the Like was never known before" came surging up the coast on August 29, 1675. In Boston "it blew up many Ships together," "broke down many Wharffs," "blew down some Houses," and tossed "severall Vessells on shoare." Few saw the arrival of a "Hirocane" during the outbreak of war as a mere coincidence. Colonial and Native elders may have been reminded of the tropical system that ripped across the shore just months before the Pequot War, another extraordinary tempest that bore ill omens. On Barbados, where the whites had just put down a brewing slave uprising, a hurricane hit at almost the same time as the one in New England, flattening nine churches. It seemed clear that some greater malicious power was at work, targeting the scattered clusters of English Christians across the western Atlantic.[5]

Likening human insurgencies to the sea's fury, one Barbadian observed that these two satellites of England had "tasted of the same Cup." The next year, when a nor'easter soaked Puritan troops, one preacher described it as a "cold Euroclidon," using the biblical name for a system with northern winds and musing that "the Lord . . . seemed to fight against them by the storm." A Quaker writer despaired that "there seems to be a thick Cloud between the Lord and our Prayers." Some of their Indian foes also saw divine wrath in the weather. Wampanoags attributed the tropical system of 1675 to an unnamed shaman, or "Pawwaw." Claiming he had summoned the great cyclone as an ominous force, the holy man turned the familiar metaphoric phrase of the "storm of war" into a prophecy. His followers boasted that "as many Englishmen shall die, as the Trees have by this Wind been blown down in the Woods."[6]

Unlike those preachers and pawwaws, historians seldom make connections between King Philip's War and the sea. Many accounts focus on the conflict's most terrestrial phase from the late summer of 1675 to the late spring of 1676, when fighters and refugees chased each other across the hilly homelands of the Pocumtucks and Nipmucks. Inland peoples formed the bulk of Metacom's supporters; coastal peoples west of Philip were fragmented by a solid four decades of Dutch and English divide-and-rule strategies that had undermined sachems and expanded colonial jurisdictions, while those toward Cape Cod and its outlying islands were coping with a smaller foreign incursion. The one major seaside group that joined Philip, the Narragansetts, were deeply ambivalent. They had a long-standing enmity with the Wampanoags dating back to before the days of Squanto and Massasoit. They were drawn into the war only through a series of bullying provocations—at first they seemed to trust the colonists, who told "them, if they kept by the watersides and did not meddle, that the English would do them no harm."[7]

Though much of the fighting in King Philip's War took place in woods that were over a day's travel from the ocean, hostilities began and ended on the same two headlands at the north end of Narragansett Bay. One peninsula, known as Pokanoket, was home to Metacom's chief village of Sowams. This "gallant Neck of Land" featured a stubby hill that served as Metacom's lookout and primary rallying point, a hill the English named Mount Hope. On a neck to the east sat Swansea, an outlying village of Plymouth colony that had been Sowams's nearest neighbor for some forty years. Only a couple of marshy tidal rivers separated the respective villages of bark-sided and clapboard houses, though colonists underscored the boundary by raising "a very substantial fence quite cross that great Neck between the English and Indians." Brackish and wooden boundaries divided indigenous cornfields and colonial pastures and split the realm of King Philip from that of King Charles II. Those inlets were Atlantic spaces as well, sites where the geopolitics of the ocean could be seen and felt on a human scale. The Dutch decline and defeat were palpable events: they slowed the flow of shell beads between Sowams and Swansea while concurrently increasing the number of guns held on the Native neck. And as the victorious English began to take bolder stances in calling for Philip's submission, their actions radicalized the villagers on the western peninsula. After the hanging of three Wampanoags in the spring of 1675, the waters between Sowams and Swansea roiled. As a Rhode Islander put it, "The English wear afraid and Philop was afraid and both incresed in arems," though some felt sure the unease would pass, as "for 40 years time reports and jelosys of war had bine veri frequent" and come to nothing.[8]

Though always wary, neighbors must have had a general pragmatic acceptance of their differences during those forty years of peace. But by June 1675 that last little bit of mutual tolerance evaporated. With all standing "in a posture of war," it took only a handful of brash boys and men, some of whom had grown up just miles apart, to turn posture into action. On June 23 three Indians crossed onto the English peninsula, where they mischievously poked around an empty house. An older colonist and youth spotted them fleeing the premises, and the boy shot one of the suspected burglars dead. Stunned, the other two Wampanoags came to the garrison demanding "why thay shot the indian." The first response they got was from an "English lad" who cruelly "saied it was no mater." The adults, embarrassed at such teenage callousness, tried to apologize for "an idell lads words but the indians in hast went away and did not harken to them." The next day Metacom's men returned to kill the young shooter, his father, and five more Swansea men, while other parties attacked the nearby settlements of Rehoboth and Fall River. And "so the war begun with philop." Soon "this fire which in June was but a little spark, in three months time [was] become a great flame."9

As Plymouth and Philip each took up arms, it was clear that Narragansett Bay would be a central theater. Some lessons seem to have been learned from the past few decades, as this time the English were determined to seize the upper hand on the water. Colonists had long witnessed the far-reaching "naval campaigns" of coastal sachems—in fact, just as the war was breaking out, a canoe of Niantics capsized deep in Buzzards' Bay, a good fifty miles from their home harbors. The English knew all too well that if hostile Indians kept their boats they would have a much wider striking range. In addition to banning canoes and establishing shore patrols, colonial soldiers targeted every enemy craft they saw, stripping Philip's forces of their nearshore navy. In an early campaign a former pirate known to the English as Cornelius the Dutchman surprised sixty of Metacom's men near Mount Hope while they were hauling "their Cannoues a-shore." It seems he had discovered the bulk of Philip's fleet, some forty watercraft in total, likely a mix of birchbark boats and dugouts. After killing several Natives and chasing the rest away the Dutchman returned to the beach littered with watercraft and "burnt all those Cannoues." Meanwhile, a separate party "hunt[ing] Philop from all sea shors" crossed the beaches of Weetamoo, a Pocasset squaw sachem, or female chief, where they "seased sum Cannos on hir side" of Mount Hope Bay, "suposing they wear Philops." Plymouth's governor reassured his counterpart in Massachusetts: "We have taken the best care we can to Cutt off the Canoose att mount hope" and elsewhere along the bay.[10]

From the colonial perspective these moves seemed wise. If Indians had kept their boats and the colonists had not watched the coast so closely, it seems quite plausible that a much larger portion of the region would have been drawn into the conflict. Certainly that is what Governor Andros dreaded. The same day New York outlawed the use of canoes on Long Island Sound he wrote a letter to Governor William Leete of Connecticut sharing the dire rumor that "there is an extraordinary confederacy between all ye neighboring Indyans & Eastward, (in which your pretended to be included) & designed this light moone to attack Hartford itself, & some other place this way, as farr as Greenwich." While reeling from the early land-based attacks, colonists could reasonably claim that the region's waters, if not the actual shore, fully belonged to them, not to Indians. In this early estuarine fighting Roger Williams went so far as to compare Metacom's cause to a capsized dugout lost at sea. Calling the Wampanoag "deafe to all Advice and now overset," the colonist confidently declared that Metacom "shall never get ashoare." When he spoke these words in the fall of 1675 Williams was actually riding in his own large canoe with a handful of Native partners, traveling close by Sowams. Those Indian allies were no doubt grateful for Williams's company, as it protected them from being arrested and having their boats taken. The colony of Rhode Island had recently declared that all Indians traveling in the island-strewn waters of Narragansett Bay needed to have a colonial escort with them. Months later, when Narragansetts finally joined Philip's side, the colony's three sloops carefully bided their time cruising along the coast, waiting for the perfect moment "when the blow shall be stricken and the Indians so alarumed" that they could sneak ashore and perform "that service of Destroying all their Cannoes."[11]

Colonists' efforts to scuttle all Native craft often left their opposition without any boats at hand, so Indians improvised simpler vessels. In an early fight near Dartmouth, Plymouth soldiers believed they could corner Philip's forces by backing him "on owre narrow neck of land or on sume of the Ilands, from whence he cannot Easily make his escape." But as would happen so many times, Native warriors were more nimble than the English. No sooner had the colonists tried to push them toward the coast than Metacom's men "got over and thay could not find him." Deep in the interior in 1676 English fighters almost caught Philip's forces at the banks of Bacquaug (now Miller's) River. But the Native men "quickly fell to cutting dry trees, to make rafts," conveying their families over the icy waters. It was an ingenious move, as when the pursuing soldiers arrived at the same shore just hours later "this River put a stop to them." King Philip pulled off a similar escape as soldiers closed in on him north of Mount Hope Bay in the spring of 1676. His forces crossed the three-mile-wide estuary "on two Rafts, in which passage they lost several Guns, and wet much of their Ammunition" but nonetheless foiled their pursuers. These haphazard craft came with risks. Weetamoo, the Pocasset sachem who was one of Metacom's closest allies, "furnished Philip with Canooes for his men" in a later escape but neglected to save one for herself. As she crossed an inlet of Narragansett Bay in a makeshift raft it fell to pieces and she drowned.[12]

Natives tried to find boatless colonists in vulnerable moments. And like the Pequots before them they sometimes became shoreside snipers. In that initial summer of fighting, the Plymouth officer Benjamin Church found himself and twenty soldiers cornered on Punkatees Neck on the easternmost passage of Narragansett Bay as three hundred hostile Pocassets and Sakonnets descended a slope toward them. As he dictated his memories to his son decades later, he recalled "the hill seemed to move, being covered over with Indians, with their bright guns glittering in the sun." Church drily commented that the sight "put him upon thinking what was become of the boats that were ordered to attend him." Some men were watching from Aquidneck Island a mile away and tried to send a boat over, only to be scared off by volleys of enemy fire. Finally, as night fell with "numerous enemies" still making "the woods ring with their constant yelling and shouting," Church spotted a sloop heading south. His savior, one Captain Golding, bravely dropped anchor, coming to the rescue of the besieged colonists. Paddling through whistling bullets, his sailors had to make multiple trips in a tiny canoe that could hold only a couple of men at a time. For Golding's troubles "the enemy gave him such a warm salute that his sails, color, and stern were full of bullet holes."[13]

Staying near the coast, where colonists knew the terrain well and could easily mass their forces and supplies, seldom ended well for Philip's allies. And some found out the hard way that European-style fortresses were not fail-safe. By late fall 1675, despite a split in the top sachems, the bulk of the Narragansetts were drawn into the escalating conflict. (In a rare moment of agreement that spoke to their mirroring sensibilities, both Ninigret and Uncas sided with colonists.) The anti-English Narragansett faction retreated to a new refuge in the vast, marshy wetlands west of the bay, a region the colonists called the Great Swamp. Working with an Indian mason known as Stonewall John, they had built the most ambitious hybrid fort yet in the region, a sprawling compound standing on "a Kind of Island of five or six Acres of rising Land in the midst of a Swamp." Composed of multiple "Sconces [a defensive work] and fortified places," this indigenous stronghold housed a forge for melting down new bullets. Its perimeter was ringed with a wooden palisade and a thick "Hedge" of brambles "through which there was no passing." When colonists surprised the fort on December 19, 1675, the struc-ture at first utterly bewildered them. "It seems that there was but one Entrance," William Hubbard wrote in his account of the siege, yet "the Enemy found many Ways to come out" and "neither the English nor their Guide well knew on which Side the Entrance lay." Unfortunately for the besieged, "they had not quite finished the said Work," and though the Narragansetts' defenses held for hours, the fort ultimately became a self-made trap. The thousand-man-strong attacking force, made up of colonists and Indians, eventually breached the redoubt. In the ensuing melee, later known as the Great Swamp Massacre, they killed and enslaved hundreds of people who had been hiding within the structure's labyrinthine walls.[14]

Those who escaped fled northward. The bulk of refugees joined Metacom, who was waging a guerilla war on English towns from the woodlands between the Connecticut River Valley and Massachusetts Bay. Meanwhile, Puritan forces at the coast emptied their enemies' winter cellars in an attempt to starve them into submission. By February 1676, when Narragansetts took

Mary Rowlandson from her home northwest of Boston, their desperation was obvious. She remembered her wartime rations in stomach-turning detail, as her captors improvised broth out of horses' hooves and by cleaning off rotting bones "full of worms and magots" and ate meals of "Horses guts and ears," even "the very Barks of Trees." Narragansetts missed the taste of shellfish and corn grits as much as Rowlandson missed beef and bread. One young woman headed out on a dangerous three-week journey back to some hidden storage pits just to return with "a peck and a half of Corn." Weeks after Rowlandson was redeemed, three hundred of these famished exiles abandoned their inland camps and were spotted heading to an inlet near Mount Hope "to eat clams (other provisions being very scarce with them)." Canochet, Miantonomi's son, was caught, tortured, and killed by Mohegans when he ventured near home seeking provisions from another secret food store. "As a Token of their Love and Fidelity," his executioners "presented his Head to the Council at Hartford." It was a gesture reminiscent of the Pequot War, though this time there was no question that it symbolized the submission of both their indigenous foes and friends. The gruesome dismembering of the Narragansett brought his peoples' resistance to an end.[15]

Meanwhile, Church, the officer who survived the early peninsula battle, started recruiting new partners to end Philip's withering campaign for good. Church had spent part of the winter of 1675–76 nursing gunshot wounds sustained at the Great Swamp, and as he returned to the fight he leaned heavily on Indian mariners and translators to form his counterinsurgency. His diplomatic forays began with a moment of chance. When Church found himself without a boat on the Elizabeth Islands west of Cape Cod in the spring of 1676, he "was forced to hire two of the friend-Indians to paddle him home in a canoe." His escorts, who were Christian Indians from Martha's Vineyard or Cape Cod, started off on the twenty-mile sea voyage to Aquidneck Island. Their passage brought them past the craggy headlands of Sakonnet country. Now enemy territory, the shores were quite familiar to Church; he had started a colonial settlement along this coast years earlier (now Little Compton, Rhode Island) that stood abandoned. While rounding "Sogkonate-point" he spotted some of his former neighbors fishing. Sensing an opportunity, he asked his pilots to take him in close. A brief standoff ensued, with the "friend-Indians" trying to shout out reassuring greetings to the fishermen, but the men on shore complained that "the surf made such a noise against the rocks, they could not hear anything they said." But Church was in luck, as one of the men turned out to be a good acquaintance of his whom he had nicknamed Honest George. Once Church was finally ashore and satisfied that "the coasts were clear," he and George arranged a conference with the Sakonnet sachem Awashonks.[16]

Awashonks, a partner considered crucial for winning the war, was a squaw sachem. While highborn women long held sway within Algonquian communities, they seldom appeared in diplomatic roles in early colonial accounts. By the 1660s they had become more common, which led some scholars to infer that these women stepped into foreign relations after decades of epidemics and wars had thinned the ranks of eligible male heirs. Awashonks's nearest neighbor was the Pocasset Weetamoo, a close relative of Philip and the same woman who later died after falling from her faulty raft. On the opposite side of the bay the "Old Queen" Quaiapen was a prominent Narragansett who perished in the fighting as well. Though poorly documented when compared to their male counterparts, this cohort of leading women can be glimpsed in English accounts leading communal dances, greeting visiting colonists, signing land papers, and fashioning wampum belts. By the 1670s they also fell under the same general cloud of suspicion that hung over male sachems.[17]

A few moments of explicit gender differences surfaced as these women dealt with colonial men. When Awashonks was late to respond to a colonial summons in 1671, she explained she "hath a young Child that it was the Reson that shee ded not Come down to the Cort." It was an excuse no male sachem had ever given. Still, female sachems had more household help than ordinary Indian women, as they were attended to by personal maids and could rely on the assistance of captives during war. In 1683, when Awashonks was old enough to be a grandmother, she faced allegations that she helped her daughter commit infanticide. The charges were ultimately dropped, but the incident spoke to female sachems' plummeting postwar status in the eyes of colonial law. Perhaps King Philip's War itself marked an early peak of female political power across the region, as in the conflict

Native women definitely were not disqualified from making military decisions. Quaiapen even commissioned her own hybrid fort after joining Philip's coalition. Situated among glacially deposited boulders, the site had likely been a wartime refuge for centuries. As war broke out in 1675 Quaiapen's band reinforced the stronghold with new stone bastions, a renovation that was almost certainly the design of Stonewall John. Tucked away in the woods, her fort remained hidden from soldiers during the war, and the foundations of its walls still stand today.[18]

Elite Algonquian women awed colonists with regalia that appeared far more elaborate than men's. During her captivity Rowlandson was an attendant to Weetamoo. She described her mistress as "a severe and proud Dame," as meticulously dressed as "any of the Gentry of the land." When getting ready for a spiritual dance Weetamoo wore "a Kersey [heavy wool] Coat," and wrapped "Girdles of Wampom" around her body, while "her Arms, from her elbows to her Hands, were covered with Bracelets; there were handfuls of Neck-laces about her Neck, and several sorts of Jewels in her Ears: She had fine red Stockings and white Shoes, her Hair powdered, and her face painted Red, that was always before Black." This elaborate costume of European and indigenous finery came apart over the long day of singing and dancing, as Weetamoo and her husband shed their many "Girdles of Wampom" by tossing them "to the standers-by." These women were no more queens than the male sachems were kings. Trappings that may have looked haughty and aristocratic to outsiders were in fact evidence both of each elite woman's personal labor in sewing the shell belts and of the obligations she had to her followers.[19]

Church's summit with Awashonks in 1676 was consequential both for its effect on the war's outcome and as a rarely seen moment of direct political negotiations between a male colonist and a female Native. While Weetamoo sided firmly with her close kinsman Philip, Awashonks was always more skeptical of his chances. Her old neighbor Church was well aware of her mixed feelings when he first tried to court her support in the initial days of the war. Though she rebuffed him then, she evidently considered him trustworthy. Two days after the surfside encounter Church and his translators headed across Narragansett Bay's westernmost passage in two canoes, bound

for Sakonnet country. Landing at a rocky beach, they trudged to a prominent boulder that stood near a deserted farmhouse. Negotiations got off to an
uneasy start. Awashonks's men had taken advantage of overgrown pastures to
wait unseen. Church was startled when her entourage, "all armed with guns,
spears, hatchets, etc., with their hair trimmed and faces painted," silently
arose all at once from the tall grasses. It seemed to be a purposefully discom-
fiting welcome, one meant to keep the meeting on Sakonnet terms.[20]

Presumably dressed in her best clothing and wearing many pieces of shell
jewelry, Awashonks calmly presided over the talks. When Church offered to
share some rum and a roll of tobacco, the sachem ordered him to drink from
his bottle first to prove it was not poisoned. Then, after taking "a good hearty
dram" herself, she passed a shell filled with rum around her party. The gathered group then filled and lit their pipes. An awkward three-way negotiation
began, the two Christian Indians in the middle carefully relaying every utter-
ance in either Wampanoag or English. The meeting almost took a dark turn
when one of the Native men realized that Church had killed his brother at
Punkatees Neck the previous year and began making vengeful threats. But
Awashonks's chief lieutenant swiftly shut him down. The discussion ended
with solemn vows. Church swore to be "theirs and their children's fast
friend," and Awashonks and her men promised to take "Philip's head before
the Indian corn be ripe." After several weeks of back-and-forth in boats and
canoes to allow the female sachem to sign a formal treaty of submission with
Plymouth, the two erstwhile neighbors reaffirmed their alliance at the
chief's seaside summer homestead. Awashonks invited Church to share a
sunset feast of bass, flounder, eels, and shellfish—since war had cleaned out
their cellars, neither grits nor cornbread were served. After dinner the
Englishman stood awkwardly at the edge of a great circle of onlookers,
watching a solemn war dance around a bonfire on the beach. The squaw
sachem's leading men lit and danced with dry sticks of pine, each flaming
torch representing the leading fighters in the enemy coalition.[21]

Awashonks's and Church's canoe-borne diplomacy helped seal Philip's
fate. The Sakonnet sachem's son Peter and her man known as Lightfoot were
easily Church's best spies. Constantly crossing the bay's passages in a leaky,
beat-up canoe, these men served as translators, recruited more defectors, and

passed along the latest news of Philip's whereabouts. They were the English's ears and eyes in Wampanoag and Narragansett country just as hunger pushed refugees home. Though Philip's lengthy series of lethal raids on Massachusetts farmsteads in the spring of 1676 had killed hundreds of colonists, these attacks were the last hard strikes of a sputtering insurgency that was running out of munitions, food, and allies. To the west, Governor Andros solicited the Mohawks' friendship as part of a canny regional strategy to ensure his government's supremacy in the Northeast. When the Mohawks sided with New York, Metacom lost his best source of arms and powder as well as the only potential ally with the necessary might to change the course of the war. By August Church's platoon of mostly indigenous men stalked the fleeing remnants of Philip's coalition back to where the war began: the marshy inlets at the northeastern corner of Narragansett Bay. It was then that Weetamoo met her watery end—when her pursuers found her body washed ashore they took her head. Finally, in a brief anticlimactic skirmish in "mirey swamp" on Pokanoket Neck, an Indian marksman shot Philip in the chest. The sachem "fell upon his face in the mud and water." His killers dragged his nearly naked, dirt-smeared body to nearby Mount Hope, where they quartered and decapitated it, so "in that very place where he first contrived and began his mischief, was he taken and destroyed."[22]

New England was not quite at peace, though. The conflict upset a far-reaching set of regional alliances and sparked hostilities along the shoreline well north of Boston. Members of the Wabanaki confederacy went to war against Massachusetts Bay just as Church was seeking out the last few Wampanoag war parties. Some chroniclers include these northern battles as part of King Philip's War, but in truth the Wabanaki war of 1676–77 against the English was a tangential offshoot, much like Kieft's War was to the Pequot War. Like the previous set of tandem wars, these two conflicts were more connected at their roots. The Wabanakis, like Wampanoags, were empowered by the flow of firearms and worried about the expanding English presence. It helped that the war-weary Puritans looked vulnerable. The fighting to the northeast also had a decidedly naval dimension. In a pattern that continued for a century, the Wabanakis turned to piracy to loot passing vessels. In the summer of 1677 they started an offensive on English fishing boats in the Gulf of Maine. Over twenty vessels in total were taken by roving crews of Indian sea raiders. At one point, these indigenous buccaneers built up a fleet five vessels strong and manned by captive sailors, whom they forced to hail fellow English vessels in attempts to make their flotilla even larger.[23]

The Wabanaki attacks were a potent example of the kind of naval war that could have easily happened in the south had the English not grounded Native fleets. And even so, the shore in King Philip's War was a kind of magnetic space that drew the warring parties together. Although colonists attempted to clear the coast of enemies and control its passages, the exiled Natives were inevitably pulled back to the continent's margin, drawn by its food sources and marshy hideaways. But those clam banks and swamps, the final stores and refuges of people at war, had become bait in a colonial trap. Still, the English were never quite in full control of the shore. For though Philip's forces never launched any pirate attacks, colonial sailors still dreaded the possibility. When Ephraim How wrecked his ketch on a barren island off Cape Cod in 1676 he spent weeks desperately trying to get the attention of passing fishing vessels. But "none came to him, being afraid; for they supposed him to be one of those Indians who were then in hostility against the English." It seems hard to believe that seven decades had passed since English and Dutch ships first sailed these waters ever so gingerly. Here were ships manned mostly by men born on the American continent, and they were just as wary of the Native coast as their fathers had been.[24]

Sailing to Slavery

The actual Indians on the shore were haunted by another old fear: that ships were coming to steal them away. Well before Philip's War, in September 1650, Pequots came to John Winthrop Jr. "expressing themselves to be afraide," as they had just heard "some of the English threten to send them away to the Sugar Country, and that they shall not live no where in the Pequot Country." Winthrop reassured the Pequots that the colonists had just been cruelly taunting them, but these Natives' fears were completely valid. From the moment they arrived Europeans had sought to seize control not only of the shore but also of Indians' very bodies. Men like Epenow, Orson, and Squanto were among the first to get a taste of European captivity, but subsequent generations encountered confinement that was more deliberate and permanent.[25]

War first became a mechanism of enslavement when Puritans seized around three hundred Pequots as their property during the war of 1637–38. These slaves, mostly female, suffered many fates: 1 went to England, 17 to Bermuda, and the remaining 280 ended up as servants in the Massachusetts Bay colony, "disposed aboute the townes." The elder Winthrop, who had accepted one of the sachem's wives as his property, found her to be "a womon of a very modest countenance and behavior." Hearing of her leniency toward the English captive girls during the conflict, he honored her request "that her children might not be taken from her" and within two years set her free. Most of the other enslaved Pequots are hard to trace in records. Some evidently returned to their home country, like the "Indean mayde sarvant" who ran away from the colonist Richard Morris. Another Pequot woman was so often "beaten with firesticks" in a Boston household that she too tried to flee. Undoubtedly some of these enslaved Pequots died young, being suddenly immersed in a foreign population rife with pathogens. And surely all of the captured women shared the most immediate concern of the wellborn Pequot lady, whose "first request was that the English would not abuse her body."[26]

The Dutch, too, took enemies as permanent captives in their wars with Munsees. Judging from their fragmentary records, it seems they captured more men than women. In 1644 a *wilde Indiaen* named Jacques" was sent back to the Netherlands, where two company soldiers planned to display him as a wonder, much as Epenow had been in London thirty years earlier. Several more Munsees became the servants of Dutch fighters, and an unspecified number were sent "to the Bermudas as a present to the English governor." In April 1660, during a war against the Esopus of the mid-Hudson, Petrus Stuyvesant got ahold of fourteen enemy men, including a sachem, and vowed "to send them to the Indyes and to prosecute that nation to their extirpation." Those Esopus men went to Curaçao, the island off Venezuela that was also under Stuyvesant's command. Tracing the existence of Indian slaves within the Dutch colony is difficult. Sources are ambiguous, like the estate inventory of Willem Quick, who died in 1641. The document included the usual list of household items — napkins, aprons, bowls, spoons, a pillow, a pewter chamber pot—but concluded surprisingly with "1 Indian child." Still, though evidence of indigenous slavery in New Netherland is murky, the evidence for Africans is more robust: when the English seized the colony in 1664 it was home to nearly six hundred black people living either in bondage or in an ambiguous state of "half-freedom." Those six hundred were the beginnings of a deeply rooted population: New York City continued to host the largest concentration of enslaved people north of the Chesapeake until slavery finally ended in the Empire State in the nineteenth century.[27]

All across the shore, from Manhattan to Boston, colonists and Indians engaged in a broad spectrum of labor practices that varied in degrees from willing to coerced. From the 1620s onward Natives regularly volunteered to help their neighbors with tasks in exchange for wages and gifts. These working relationships often led to deeper entanglements: if Indian hands took loans or damaged colonial property, their service became punitive. A study of frontier labor in Warwick, Rhode Island, found that colonists whipped, sued, and fined their Indian servants and threatened chronic Native debtors that they could be "sould as a slave." This practice of "judicial enslavement" continued for a century. Indentured servitude was another option for Indians, though few of these servants really had a choice in the matter. In 1658 the United Colonies made an official policy of "Incurragement" to Natives "willing to putt theire Children apprentices for convenient time proportionable to theire age to any Godly English." Parents who lent out their children would receive "one coate" a year plus "meate drinke and clothing Convenient for theire children." The few of these boys and girls who appear in the sources were obviously miserable. In 1669 Thomas Ferry on Block Island "hath had six Indyans servants run away from him," fleeing twenty miles in an unknown vessel to seek protection from Ninigret, who sheltered them even though they were not his people. Perhaps news of the Niantic sachem's hospitality spread among runaways. Just a couple of weeks later he hid two more escaped teenagers from their pursuing master, Samuel Cheesebrough. In the midst of Philip's campaigns some colonists held their young Indian help as hostages in their homes. Rhode Island decreed that all Native servants over the age of twelve needed strict supervision and had to obey a nighttime curfew.[28]

King Philip's War prompted the English to start imprisoning and enslaving Indians on a scale never seen before. The first Natives to lose their freedom in the war were people who had actually disavowed Philip. In the summer of 1675, 150 Wampanoags voluntarily surrendered at Plymouth Plantation. Expecting shelter, they walked into a trap. Officials "sold all but about six of them for slaves, to be carried out of the country." When the missionary John Eliot heard news of this episode, he wrote a searing letter, blasting his countrymen for "the terror of selling away such Indians, unto the Ilands for perpetual slaves." Eliot was sure that the targeting of Natives who were willfully surrendering would only backfire, resulting in "an effectual prolongation of the warre and such an exasperation of them, as may produce, we know not what evil consequences, upon all the land." Massachusetts Bay as well ordered hundreds of Christians living in the clusters of "Praying Towns" at the fringes of their colony to move to internment camps on Deer Island and Long Island in Boston Harbor. "It was intended they should plant corn upon the Islands," but life there turned out to be a desperate experience, as "the Islands were bleak and cold with the sea winds in spring time, and the place afforded little fuel, and their wigwams were mean." When given a choice, many of the men elected to serve as soldiers and risk death in battle rather than remain on these offshore prisons. For those still stranded, the winter of 1675–76 was catastrophic. More than half died from hunger, disease, and exposure.[29]

As the war dragged on, some English came to see enslavement as the most expeditious means of disposing of their enemies. Soldiers regularly rounded up fighters and their families during the war's battles, the single biggest haul coming from the Great Swamp Massacre in December 1675. Selling these captives became a profitable side business: the average value of a single Indian neared three pounds sterling. Governors, soldiers, and even a few Native allies engaged in a short-lived regional slave trade. The captured Indians became so valuable that some human poachers started stealing away prisoners from the internment camps on Boston Harbor and kidnapping servants from colonial homes. In the summer of 1676 merchants in Boston collected 180 Natives aboard a vessel with an uncannily familiar-sounding name: *Seaflower.* It was one of several hulls that weighed anchor from New

England during the war bearing humans as cargo. Even in this moment of near total powerlessness the refugees turned out to have some agency: their solidarity ultimately ruined their value on the global market. The captives, who all spoke similar dialects and were united by their common trials and well-earned hatred of the English, made bad merchandise. Soon their reputation for insubordination and violence spread across the Atlantic. Planters in Jamaica and Barbados passed laws forbidding New Englanders to send more Algonquians, declaring them to be "too subtle, bloody and dangerous" to be good plantation workers. Barbados in particular was loathe to increase their population of disgruntled slaves, having just put down an uprising months earlier. One of the last Englishmen to sail with one hundred Indians in his hold discovered he could not sell them in any Caribbean ports, so he instead tried to off-load them in France and Spain.[30]

Many of the hundreds of Natives taken by colonists in New Netherland and New England lived out their days as refugees or slaves in the far corners of the ocean. They passed through places as varied as Bermuda, Jamaica, Barbados, Curaçao, Cádiz, Málaga, Calais, London, and Amsterdam. Their forced exile offers a glimpse of the region's connections to the larger Atlantic world as it existed in the 1670s, demonstrating how an incredibly varied collection of islands and ports could all be bound together by the commerce in human bodies. Most remarkably, in 1680 Eliot heard news of Algonquian captives who were miserably stranded in Tangier at the northern tip of Africa and tried to help them obtain passage back to Boston or at least London. These Indians who went from America to Africa were neither the first nor the last to undergo a "reverse middle passage." Historians estimate that across the Americas two to four million Natives were enslaved, and six hundred thousand endured a medium-range or oceanic "blue water transhipment." The majority of Indians who sailed into slavery came from the South and Central American mainlands and headed to the West Indies or mainland Spain. But the English empire was no stranger to this traffic, as the early Carolina colony thrived on exporting mainland Native slaves by the thousands.[31]

While slave exportation from the Northeast became rare again after the war, no doubt memories of the deportations lasted for decades. Fighters on both sides of the conflict had attempted to utterly terrify and demoralize their opposition, but only the English truly succeeded. Slaving was never as profitable as they hoped it would be, though perhaps the true value of the practice was political. The confinement, commodification, and destruction of Indians' bodies during the war sent a clear message that the new colonial order was going to be unforgiving and often brutal. The once patchwork-like region of alternating foreign and indigenous necks was transforming into an incontestably English-dominated landscape in which Indians were pushed to tiny enclaves at the literal margins.

The Destruction of the Right Whale

Like those who sailed aboard the *Seaflower* and other vessels, the Algonquians remaining in their ancestral territories after the war had arrived in a strange and foreign land. While in 1600 some ninety thousand Indians lived along the coast, by 1750 their numbers hovered near five thousand—most died of foreign diseases, though if no Natives had been killed or enslaved in wars, the surviving population easily would have numbered several thousand more. And while the colonists' advance was temporarily paused by Philip's War, the earth was in a poor state. Decades of free-foraging livestock and rampant deforestation made once bountiful forests seem bare. As they were pushed onto some of the first reservations Algonquians had no choice but to rely more than ever on coastal resources. Fisheries, which largely eluded colonial control, helped Indians find a way into the dominant economy, as they were no longer just seeking sustenance but also profits to buy all the things they could no longer count on the land to provide. In the fall of 1676 Pequots who had loyally fought for Connecticut petitioned the colony to lend them "connews" or other boats that could "help us to work or fish." An English visitor to New York around 1680 noticed Indians making their way through Hellgate and the East River in small bark canoes, carrying "Oysters and other fish for the Market."[32]

Accounts of passing travelers from succeeding decades revealed the strong connection between Indians and the water. When Sarah Kemble Knight traveled from Boston to New Haven in 1704 she found a coast with surviving pockets of its older past. Tippy "canoos" were still common ferries, cornbread and oysters were everyday staples, and "there was every where in the Towns as I passed, a Number of Indians the Natives of the Country." In his tour of the colonies four decades later the Scots doctor Alexander Hamilton witnessed ten "stark naked" Munsees "fishing for oysters" in the Bronx, passed the small village of Western Niantics by the mouth of the Connecticut, and took note of the Montauketts living at the south fork of Long Island. Colonial mapmakers even suggested a general continuity in a certain line of work. While an oft-copied Dutch map from 1635 placed illustrations of indigenous *mishoon* just off Long Island, an updated English map from 1685 featured a similar image on nearly the same spot, only the vessels were now whaleboats, not canoes.[33]

More than any other maritime industry whaling shaped coastal Natives' postwar world. The industry just happened to take off in the 1670s, the same decade that both the Dutch and Philip were defeated. The map from 1680 did not indicate the boatmen's ethnicity, but it did hint at the species of their prey: the forked spout was a characteristic of the North Atlantic right whale. Slow and friendly creatures, right whales grew to an average size of forty-five feet and were once the most plentiful large whale found off New England and New York. Unlike other species that dive to feed, right whales are skimmers: they eat at the surface, their enormous mouths open to the air, filtering clouds of small marine critters through curtains of baleen. These distinctive top-feeders were most populous in the late fall and winter on their migrations between Canadian waters and southerly calving grounds off Georgia and South Carolina. Their poky habits and tendency to float when dead made them exceedingly attractive to whalers, hence the folk etymology that they were the "right" whale to hunt. And their patterns of feeding along the shore meant their bodies frequently drifted up on beaches, especially after storms.[34]

Native traditions explained that when whales, or *pótop-pauog*, washed ashore they were gifts from the coastal giants. Their bodies were certainly packed with treasures. The flexible baleen "whalebone" in their mouths made excellent material for crafts, jewelry, and belts. Their ample blubber made an all-purpose grease for tanning, cooking, and wearing, while the

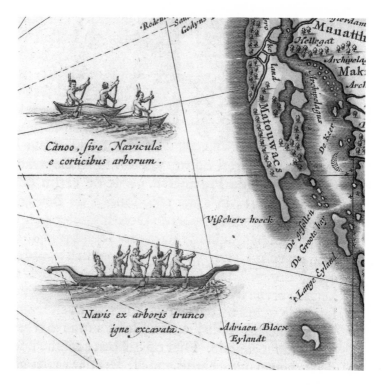

Detail of canoes in map by Willem Blaeu, "Nova Belgica et Anglia Nova" (1635). Courtesy of the John Carter Brown Library at Brown University.

dense, fatty meat in their fins and tails was a fine delicacy. Williams observed that after Algonquians butchered the bodies of stranded cetaceans, they sent choice cuts "farre and neere for an acceptable present." The harvesting of whales had long been such a common practice that one of the first things *Mayflower* passengers witnessed was Nausets "cutting up a great fish," probably a pilot whale, on a Cape Cod beach. Whales swam through many sacred stories, where they were common companions and prey of giants. Their shapes surfaced on a wide range of Indian artifacts. Algonquians made pendants in the form of whale tails and carved outlines of their bodies and flippers on pictographic tablets. A Connecticut sachem known as Misquis alias Weekoshawen even made his mark on a land deed from 1641 in the shape of a dolphin, or *tatackommmàuog*.[35]

Detail of whaleboats in map by Richard Daniel, "A map of ye English empire in ye continent of America viz Virginia, Maryland, Carolina, New York, New Iarsey, New England, Pennsilvania" (1685). Courtesy of the John Carter Brown Library at Brown University.

Colonists also coveted these gifts from the sea. They did not relish the gamey whale meat, instead seeing the mammals as giant stores of commodities. Whalebone could be manufactured into corsets, buttons, and sail stays, while blubber could be melted into lucrative oil used to light lamps and manufacture soap. Massachusetts and Southampton colonists were among the first to start processing drift whales regularly; Southampton paid scouts to search beaches for stranded animals after storms. Processing whales into marketable products was messy work, and it took practice. When a disoriented, "fairly big" whale "beached itself not far from the great Cohoes Falls, forty-three miles from the sea" on the Hudson estuary in 1647, an enterprising group of Dutch colonists set about rendering its fat. Not having much experience, they did a rather sloppy job, as "the whole river, though flowing strongly, remained oily and covered with grease for up to three weeks afterwards," while the stench of the rotting carcass was so pungent it could be smelled two miles away.[36]

Beached beasts were yet another source of contention between coastal neighbors. Especially at first, when colonists were thinly scattered, the rule seemed to be finders keepers. Some settlements even explicitly favored indigenous claims. The English on Nantucket were generous enough to declare "all the whal fish and Other drift fish belong to the Indian sachems," while Southampton residents agreed to reserve "only the fins and tayles" for Indians. But many other colonists asserted that their charters gave them exclusive ownership of all leviathans found ashore. When large baleen whales "cast upon a parcel of Beach" owned by John Cooper on Long Island they sparked a minor dispute between Cooper and the local Unkechaugs who "have taken and carried away the Whale-Bone." Even when colonists acknowledged Natives' rights to harvest drift whales, they twisted those allowances to their advantage. Scholars suspect the Nantucket law granting drift whales to Indians was actually a legal ploy that allowed merchants to evade royal taxes and export the oil duty-free.[37]

Settlers long schemed to start a genuine shore fishery, meaning they would actively hunt whales rather than wait for them to wash up. Yet for decades all their attempts failed. John Smith considered a venture in the Gulf of Maine in 1614 but soon abandoned it upon realizing the local finbacks were not a commercially viable species. Dutch sailors were the first to try hunting in earnest, setting up a whaling station in Delaware Bay in 1634. Over four months they managed to strike seventeen whales with their harpoons—which would have been a credible start, if not for the fact that ten of the whales managed to swim away. The first English ventures were even more clueless. There are records of colonists in Connecticut and Long Island boldly declaring their intent to kill whales offshore in 1647 and 1650, but no evidence they ever produced a single barrel of oil. Another "joynte partner-ship" formed in Boston in 1659 to hunt out "Spermesitte" whales also came to naught. Finally, in the late 1660s whalers on the east end of Long Island actually started filling barrels with oil. The sudden birth of the fishery was the subject of a letter from New York to King Charles II in 1672. Although "they had endeavored above these twenty years" to capture passing cetaceans "in the adjacent seas," Long Islanders "could not bring it to any perfection till within these 2 or 3 years past." What changed three years earlier that made "perfection" possible? Colonial whalers started working with Indians.[38]

A nagging question of cultural origins surrounds the history of whaling in early America. Noting that both England and the Netherlands had emerging whaling industries at this time and that the only accounts of Indians whaling offshore were from distant spots on the coast, historians are rightly skeptical of the spurious claim that Algonquians instructed colonists on how to hunt the leviathan. Scholars instead describe the use of Indian whalers as a symptom of the grand truism of early America, namely, that "no one was willing to serve as a common laborer." A recent sweeping survey of American whaling declared outright that Natives were employed "not as teachers but because they were cheap labor . . . skilled and strong enough to perform the more menial tasks they were almost always assigned." The general point is correct: the initiative and technologies that started shore whaling were entirely European. The Dutch and English came equipped with iron harpoons and wide, plank-built boats with effective oars as well as the knowledge of how to refine blubber for export, while Indians were the most obvious and available source of muscle. Yet after Europeans spent forty years trying to catch these creatures in vain, the sudden jump-start of the industry after the inclusion of Indians cannot be explained away as the mere addition of "cheap labor" to do "menial tasks."[39]

Just thinking about the work involved makes it obvious that Natives provided more than inexpensive brute strength. After all, the sea hunt required knowledge of right whales' migration patterns and their favored feeding spots, things Native fishermen who revered the animals and prized their meat surely knew. Whale hunters had to rapidly launch a small boat loaded with a half dozen men directly into surf without tipping over. At sea, if the whale dove away, crews needed the patience and awareness of seasoned hunters while waiting for the prey to surface. As the harpooned, dying catch towed them in its death throes, whalemen needed to be confident swimmers should their craft be overturned in frigid waters. Given that they were in small boats without navigational tools, the crews needed to know the basic tricks of finding land should they end up far at sea or caught in fog. And all needed to be seasoned at long-distance rowing, both to chase the prey and to achieve the backbreaking task of hauling the massive floating carcass to a nearby beach. Every one of these challenges matched the traditional strengths of Native seafarers, just as every one was a point of comparative weakness for European mariners.[40]

American shore whaling, in short, was not a purely colonial invention but the joint creation of two overlapping maritime societies. While the invaders probably would have started a whale fishery eventually, the presence of skilled, inexpensive Native labor was central to the industry's early and fast evolution. The Dutch presence also played a role. A crucial actor in creating the fishery was Jacobus, or James, Loper, a recent immigrant with knowledge of the Netherlands' lucrative Arctic bowhead fishery. Loper suggested that "the Indyans on those parts may bee very instrumental unto them," and soon his neighbors followed suit. In 1669 John Laughton of Southampton requested a license to "sell some small quantity of liquors and powder" to nearby Shinnecocks and Montauketts to entice them to work for him. As whaling rather quickly turned profitable, colonists from elsewhere in New York and New England began flocking to the Hamptons to join the season and hire Natives as crew. Locals would complain about the opportunism of these "Strangers coming a whaling." Soon colonists were competing for Native labor, sometimes even getting into bidding wars. John Cooper, who boasted of being "one of the first that brought the Indians to be serviceable" to work in shore whaling, wrote to Governor Andros grumbling that his Shinnecock and Montaukett employees kept breaking their agreements with him and taking their talents to other beaches.[41]

New York authorities stepped in to regulate the burgeoning industry, as they worried it could cause rifts in the island's delicate social fabric, especially when war broke out to the north. The colony passed laws compelling Native men to honor their contracts, and they only slowly allowed more English to hire Indians, reducing competition in the labor market. Noticing a correlation between excessive drinking, "powwaw" religious dances, and incidents of violence among Natives, town officials in the Hamptons also cracked down. They attempted to ban the dances and control sales of liquor, fretting that Native whalers being paid in alcohol could only fuel this disorder. By 1672 East Hampton ordered its colonists to compensate indigenous sailors only with trade cloth and whale meat, not spirits. Given that the fishery was contained in New York and on the south side of the island, it was largely uninterrupted by King Philip's War. Still, at the opening of the winter whaling season of 1675–76 some Long Islanders getting a colonial approval were sure to emphasize that their whalemen were "of Civill Deportment."[42]

Soon the arrangements between whaling companies and their employees started to resemble the exploitative patterns formed decades earlier in domestic and farm labor. Whaling interests did not pay Indians until the end of the season, the whalers' pay being dependent on the amount of oil produced. Colonists held Indians responsible for any lost or damaged equipment while inviting them to spend their shares liberally at company stores. The goods the stores sold were some of the same wares once peddled by traders. A Long Island whaler's account book dating from 1691 to 1721 offers a glimpse at what his indigenous employees bought on credit. The most commonly purchased items were ammunition, corn, liquor, and warm, colonial-style clothing, including mittens, stockings, shoes, and coats. Those garments were surely most useful during the time the whalers spent at sea in the fall and winter, though they also serve as a reminder that deer and furry mammals were now far too rare to serve as a reliable source of clothing. This rigged system of debt peonage left whalemen contractually obligated to return to the hunt the next year and work for the same backers. And for the Long Islanders who began the practice, it also was a convenient solution to the problem of Native free agency. Legally it fell short of slavery, but in practice it could look much the same. By 1690, as rival entrepreneurs formed "Whaling Designs" on Cape Cod, Martha's Vineyard, and Nantucket, they replicated the same accounting practices that undervalued indigenous labor while protecting colonial profits.[43]

As tall, lookout masts started popping up along the region's dunes, underpaid Natives occasionally made vocal protests. Even in the fishery's early days a few Natives tried to start their own whaling design. In the spring of 1676, at the close of the season, a party of Unkechaugs arrived to see Governor Andros in Manhattan, first to "give thankes for their peace," handing him wampum strings, out of gratitude that "they may live, eate and sleepe quiet, without feare on the Island." But there was something else on their minds. Noting that they were "free borne on the said Island," they asked "to have a whale boate with all the other materiells to fish and dispose of what they shall take, as and to whom they like best." The governor mulled it over for a day and decided to given them permission to kill whales, but he turned down their request for a boat and equipment. The historian John Strong suggests that the Unkechaugs' petition led to contracts that gave the whalemen a small share of the profits, though shares always were meager enough to keep Indians in the red and colonists in the black. Tensions over labor and land ran high on Nantucket in 1738, when colonists became alarmed at rumors of a Native conspiracy to murder all the colonists on a set night. It soon appeared that the rumor was utterly false. Still, the mere fact that the master class took the threat seriously spoke to the plantation-like relationship between whaling companies and their hired hands. Open labor disputes had been a fact of island life since the 1720s, when whalemen first started to issue formal complaints about being cheated of their rightful pay. The Nantucket Indian Paul Quabb petitioned the Massachusetts legislature in 1747 to express his exasperation that no matter how hard he and his fellow whalers worked, their debts would follow them to their graves, and the "English will leave nothing for Indians wife and children and so they become poor."[44]

Though colonists refused to fully pay their workers, much less let those Unkechaugs seize the means of production, they did allow them daily autonomy. Contracts indicate that backers let their Native men operate their vessels unsupervised for much of the season. A contract from 1673 between Dutch and English sponsors and six Native men in Southampton was fairly typical. The Indians pledged "to use and Improve our best skill, and strength, and utmost endeavor for killing whales" and promised "to preserve the boat and craft committed to our management." Six Indians signed the document, two names (presumably those of the steersman and harpooner) appearing above the rest (the oarsmen). Whaling crews faced long stretches of tedium punctuated by bursts of terror and toil. A visitor's account from 1680 indicated that the actual moment of harpooning could be as lethal to Indians as it was to whales. "As soon as [the whale] is wounded, he makes all foam, with his rapid violent Course, so that if they be not very quick" to let the towline attached to the harpoon run out, "its a hundred to one he over-sets the Boat." Working in winter meant risking an almost instant death in frigid seas. When a thrashing whale damaged an East Hampton boat in February 1719 four oarsmen died within minutes, as they were too stunned by hypothermia to climb back in their boat. Even once safely ashore with their catch, whalemen faced the unenviable task of melting blubber into oil in shoreside "try houses," a smoky, foul-smelling industrial process that no doubt took years off their lives. Colonists tsk-tsked the drinking habits of Native whalemen, but their thirst for relaxing, anesthetizing beverages seems like a predictable response to the stresses of the job.[45]

There were good reasons to endure the freezing water and noxious fumes. Despite the high prices they paid, Native whalemen kept a steady flow of colonial-made goods moving back into their communities. And they no doubt picked up other marketable skills from their regular interactions with colonists, as dealing with these employers encouraged them to learn English faster than nonwhaling Natives and allowed some to dabble in other maritime industries in the off-season. The work may have particularly appealed to Native men, because it allowed them to continue regular fishing rather than take up farming, which many derided as women's work. It also created male-dominated social spaces at the literal margins of the colonial realm. Archaeologists uncovered the site of a forgotten tavern on a barrier island off Cape Cod where the early whalemen passed their days waiting for spouts. Its foundations held broken dishes, bottles, pipe stems, cutlery, a broken harpoon iron, and a giant whale vertebra that served as a chopping block. On many a winter day the tavern air must have been thick with cooking smells, tobacco smoke, and sea stories told in both English and Wampanoag. The presence of Native men in the whale fishery generation after generation implies that the job's unique trials and fraternities held a continuing allure.[46]

The initial coastal whale fishery was short-lived. Marine biologists estimate that the initial unexploited population of right whales in the eastern North Atlantic was only seven thousand strong. At their peak, crews of indigenous whalers across the coast were culling hundreds of individuals a year. In distant waters where the western Atlantic met the Arctic Ocean, Dutch and Basque whalers were fishing right whales and bowheads, and their activity could have further disturbed oceanwide stocks. Adding to the unsustainability of the hunt, harpooners had no qualms about targeting young animals before they hit their reproductive prime. The killing itself was also wasteful, as whalemen did not always collect their prey. The bodies of wounded animals sometimes appeared days later in surprising places, like the pair of harpooned right whales that washed up on the beaches of Delaware Bay in 1742, two hundred miles from the nearest whaling grounds.[47]

As early as 1708 colonists observed that the annual harvest was wildly unpredictable. "Some years they have much more fish than others," wrote a New York official, marveling that Long Island's coastal stations could produce four thousand barrels of oil one year, while the next season yielded only six hundred. A petition from American whalers to the London Board of Trade in 1716 complained they were grossly overtaxed, noting, "[The] fishery at present is in so uncertain a condition." The letter confirmed that the labor force was still mostly made up of "the native Indians," who "go on the high seas to kill, bring on shoar, and convert the whale fish." In asking for tax relief, the whaling companies disingenuously appealed to the trials of their indigenous employees, who "undergo the hardship of waiting at sea many months, and the difficulty of bringing into New York the fish and at last paying so great a share of their profit." The unpredictability of the catch did not discourage either Indians or colonists from manning their boats; as one writer remarked, "If the Whale fishing be decay'd it is not for want of numbers of fishers." Shore whalers were largely mystified at the sudden drops in the catch. Long Island's company owners speculated in 1716 that any "decay" in the fishery was a fiction or else could be fixed. Maybe other whalers along the coast smuggled out their oil duty-free, they speculated, hence the plummeting numbers of recorded barrels. Or else, perhaps repeating an Indian theory, they conjectured that wounded whales "[fright] away the rest" from the shore. The idea that the mammals themselves were finite did not seem to cross their minds, but soon that fact would become obvious. By the 1720s the annual catch was in a free fall, and by 1740 colonists declared the nearshore stocks of whales "fished out."[48]

Within a generation shore whaling became a faint memory. From Long Island to Nantucket the towering lookout masts, the humble taverns with whale-skeleton furniture, and the smelly try houses were torn down or abandoned. On a trip to Cape Cod in 1762 the Connecticut theologian Ezra Stiles kept hearing stories of a staggering hunt now long gone. Provincetown whalers complained that they "last year catched but Two Whales," but the local Nauset Indians vividly remembered when they and their fathers "catch'd 70 & 100 Whales a season." A writer in 1793 repeated stories he had heard of smaller pilot whales who schooled so thickly off Wellfleet they could be "as easily driven to the shore as cattle or sheep are driven on land." Stiles met another elderly sea captain who recalled seeing two thousand of the mammals at one time. The enormous pod massed in the shallow waters inside the peninsula's curving uppermost hook, where the thick herd of surfacing shiny backs stretched almost to the horizon. He estimated this creature could "have made a Bridge from the End of the Cape to Truro Shore; which is seven Miles across." Perhaps the old man was recalling the winter of 1699–1700, when whales were so plentiful inside the hook that "all the boates round the bay killed twenty nine whales in one day."[49]

Though the majority of whales taken off New York and New England from the 1660s to the 1740s were killed by Indians, the blame for their near-extinction falls wholly on the shoulders of colonists. After all, Indian whalemen joined the industry out of necessity. Their land was disappearing beneath their feet, and they were trapped in a deepening cycle of debt and material dependence. They were simply trading on the most valuable skills they had to supply their communities with food, clothing, and a modest selection of foreign goods, while their consumption of whale meat held sacred significance. Colonists' interest in whales was primarily commercial, driven not by any urgent need but by their desire for greater profit and comfort. If given the chance, Indians could have prospered from whaling too, but colonists rather quickly made that impossible by using lopsided accounting to guarantee that Natives' work rarely provided more than basic sustenance.

This is a familiar frontier story. When colonists combined their technology with indigenous labor to target a sought-after mammal that produced desired commodities for a global market, the combination of Indian needs and colonial wants led to rapid overhunting. A dramatic near-extinction predictably followed. But this narrative is usually told about beavers and bison, seldom about whales — even though the existence of Indian whalemen is well known to scholars. Indeed, it was hardly an obscure fact to Herman Melville; in *Moby-Dick, or the Whale* (1851), Melville named his doomed whaleship *The Pequod* and gave the job of harpooner on *The Pequod's* second watch to Mr. Tashtego, an "unmixed Indian" from Martha's Vineyard. Even though these facts have been bare for centuries, historians have overlooked the ecological pressure that exploited Native communities put on the ocean, simply because most assume that Indian history stops at the water's edge.[50]

Thesis

Pointing out the role of Natives in depleting coastal whaling grounds is also more than an inclusionary "they were there too" footnote. Indigenous sea hunters' skills and economic desperation were the single biggest factors in American whaling's rapid half-century transformation "from an idea into a major force in colonial life." And the swift destruction of the right whale was a watershed event in American economic history, as it transformed the Yankee whale fishery from a local one to a global one. Much like the traders and Indian hunters that kept ranging deeper inland in search of unexploited stocks of furs and hides, captains and Native whalers kept chasing whales further offshore. Journeys of forty to fifty miles in large vessels became common by the 1730s. The industry was revolutionized when Nantucket shipbuilders invented onboard furnaces called tryworks in the 1750s that allowed crews to process whale oil without coming ashore. This innovation, born out of the necessity of the region's depleted fishery, soon made New Englanders and New Yorkers the most enterprising and far-ranging whalers in the world. American crews repeated the cycle of overfishing right whales and sperm whales in Arctic and South Atlantic feeding grounds in the eighteenth century and sailed all the way to the Pacific and Indian Oceans by the nineteenth. Just as nimble fur traders served as the vanguard for wagon trains, New England's whaling ships were a pioneering presence, establishing connections and routes across the Pacific, where many more American hulls would soon follow.[51]

Generations of Algonquian fathers and sons continued to staff whale-boats and deck crews, spending whole years of their lives lodged in ships' cramped forward cabins. Over the eighteenth century those berths slowly became integrated. The classic revolutionary-era narrative of J. Hector St. John de Crèvecoeur took special notice of Natives' continuing presence in the now-global whaling business based on Martha's Vineyard and Nantucket, averring that "five of the thirteen" in the crew "are always Indians" and remembering that until recently "whale vessels were manned by none but the Indians and master." The majority of the men serving alongside Natives were white, although enslaved and free black sailors joined their ranks. Both African Americans and Indians would find sources of strength and security in mastering this meanly paid but specialized labor. Their increased presence in the region's port towns would further connect the fates of both populations later in the colonial period and after the American Revolution.[52]

The Devil and the Deep Blue Sea

As whales vanished from nearshore waters, fishers of men worked the coast. The Mohegan Samson Occom recalled hearing news of "Extraordinary Ministers Preaching from Place to Place" in the year 1739, when he was sixteen years old. Initially drawn by the preachers' impressive oratory, then driven by his desire to learn to write, Occom made a full "discovery of the way of Salvation through Jesus" a year later. To be sure, these were hardly the first missionaries in Indian country. English colonists had made two concerted efforts to form so-called praying communities among Natives: the first wave was led by John Eliot in the 1650s and 1660s, and a second wave came in the 1710s and 1720s. This third push to bring Christianity into the region's wigwams peaked in the 1750s and 1760s and was distinguished by the Native ministers who led the way. Occom became the most famous of these apostles, though he was joined by dozens of others, including his fellow Mohegans Samuel Ashpo and Joseph Johnson, both of whom were whalers before becoming ministers. The historian Linford Fisher calls this tide of religious fervor that swept Algonquian villages in the mid-eighteenth century "the Indians' Great Awakening," deliberately linking these stirrings of faith to the more famous mass revival that touched all of colonial society at the same time.[53]

Coastal Algonquians' spiritual journeys were diverse. Some merely attended meetings and sermons given by passing Indian and white preachers, while others became official members of established churches. Whether professing to be Quakers, Anglicans, Presbyterians, Congregationalists, Methodists, or Baptists, a few Indians took a rigidly orthodox approach to their faith, worshipping in colonial clothes in colonial buildings and essentially blending in with their neighbors on Sundays. But most retained a flexible faith, joining Native congregations that first worshipped in large wigwams. The fusing of Christian and Native beliefs could be striking, as in the instance of the Pequot family who included a page from a King James Bible along with a bear paw in the medicine bundle they buried with their daughter. Other believers were more subtle, like the Nantucket Presbyterians who closed their otherwise conventional and mostly English-language services by passing lit pipes around the congregation, handing over the tobacco with a blessing of "'*tawpoot*,' which is, 'I thank ye.'" As part of the wave of Native-led evangelism, Indians created an offshoot denomination of Christian Indian Separatism. This "thriving, largely underground" movement, led by unlicensed Native preachers, was marked by creative combinations of new and old tenets. These independent believers reworked ancient practices with new ideas: they turned rain dances into rain prayers, discovered the figure of Jesus in their interpretations of dreams, and continued to celebrate the holidays of their old corn-centered calendar while adopting new Christian ones.[54]

None of these converts thought that accepting foreign ideas about the fate of their souls represented an abandonment of their indigenous identity. If there was a single idea shared by all these believers, no matter their denomination, it was that becoming Christian was the best way to remain Indian. Occom was fond of sharing a parable of an oft-repaired knife shared by a father and son that "had had half a dozen blades, and as many handles, but still it was all the time the same knife." Joining a church could serve other social and political purposes beyond personal salvation. For some, like the "more ambitious" Mashpee Wampanoags who bought up all the front pews in their local church, joining the Congregationalists helped establish rank within their community. And yet for maritime peoples, churches helped form a standing safety net; those same status-conscious Mashpees also established poor relief for the widows of whalers lost at sea. Some of the earliest indigenous converts became their communities' primary teachers, establishing schoolhouses across the coast to teach Native children to read and write. Most also cited their religion as a basis for being afforded the same legal and political rights that their white neighbors already enjoyed. Scholars argue that the widespread move toward Christianity in the eighteenth century helped erase old indigenous borders by making shared faith rather than tribal affiliation a badge of belonging. The foreigners' faith offered community-strengthening bonds through its shared ceremonies and strong prohibitions against violence and drinking, while tendering as well the tools of language and literacy—allowing figures like Occom to petition the colonial and imperial governments in defense of Mohegan land claims and to write forceful essays that questioned the colonists' racial hierarchy. The accepting of Christianity worked almost like an inoculation that strengthened Indians' defenses against the more virulent aspects of colonialism.[55] *p. 323*

For some communities, awakenings coincided with migrations. For Munsees near the Hudson the years after King Philip's War marked a slow pivot toward the interior as they formed closer links with their fellow Lenape speakers along the Delaware Valley and forged a protective alliance with the inland Haudenosaunee. As Indians in smaller villages banded together and moved to tracts further away from colonists, they slowly stopped identifying as Wappinger, Esopus, Raritan, Nyack, and Hackensack and began to see themselves as a common people. Colonists would call this larger emerging ethnic group *Delaware*, although that term was a broad one that obscured many complex divisions. In the Hudson area, for example, peoples identified both by their clan and by the generic term *Munsee*, a corruption of the old group name *Minisink*. Though some of these migrants joined missionary communities of Moravians in Bethlehem, Pennsylvania, and Congregationalists in Stockbridge, Massachusetts, many more joined traditional revivals. Two of the leading Native prophets in the Northeast, Papoonan and Neolin, were both Delaware. Though their visions were explicitly *not* Christian, their preaching imparted similar messages, as they encouraged their Native congregants to resist alcohol and devote themselves to a single Creator god.[56]

In 1762 Stiles described the Delawares as being "mixt with all nations," after many were "driven off their Lands by the sea side." Some forty years later another account confirmed their westward progress past the Ohio River, noting Delawares who once "inhabited the Atlantic shores, but by gradual retirement had now reached the fertile banks of the Miami." Yet this same description from 1808 intriguingly intimated that not every Munsee had yet gone inland, reporting that a "band of these River Indians returned to Long Island" and were still living near New York City, where most men worked as fishermen. Some of these Munsees, especially those from western Long Island, moved east to join the Unkechaugs on the Poospatuck reservation near Mastic, New York. Hundreds of New England Algonquians also moved to the interior, joining the Stockbridge and Brothertown communities in western Massachusetts and upstate New York. While the bulk of Hudson peoples became inland-bound migrants, most of the indigenous population of New England stayed rooted in place.[57]

Sources ranging from the eighteenth century to the nineteenth include scenes of the many coastal Native communities who remained fixed on the map thanks to their local maritime resources and global maritime jobs. Alexander Hamilton, the Scottish tourist in 1744, dined with the "Indian King named George," a descendant of Ninigret who lived outside Stonington in a fine house and prosperous farm. While King George was raising cattle, many of his countrymen were no doubt working aboard ships leaving from the nearby port at Stonington. In 1761 a visitor to the Pequot town of Mashantucket a few miles away similarly noted "the Indian Familys Which Seem to be Flourishing their houses and Wigwams fill'd with Children and Youth." These peoples' decisions to stay close to rich fisheries were deliberate and explicit. A group of Montauketts told a missionary in 1789 that they were reluctant to move to Brothertown because "they would suffer and come to poverty if they should move as a body into this part of the world, where there were no oysters and Clams." Narragansetts rejected an invitation to resettle in the West in 1820, asserting that they already had farms and "gain the salt water, own Boats for [f]ishing etc." A nineteenth-century Mohegan similarly insisted his people "live well enough" near New London, where they had "land enough — and good fishing!"[58]

Life by the sea still held ample dangers, especially for men who became deepwater sailors. There is no single census of losses at sea, but scattered records indicate that the job had high rates of mortality and injury. A scholar looking at Nantucket records estimated that well over a hundred Indians from the island perished in no fewer than thirty-eight shipwrecks from 1750 to 1779. For some the mortal threat came from foreign diseases, like the two Mohegans who succumbed to smallpox they caught in Ireland in 1732. For others it was common accidents, like that suffered by the Narragansett named Primus Thompson, who was crippled in a mishap on a Jamestown wharf in 1775. Still others died of a lack of caution, like the Indian sailor who came to a grim end on the deck of a sloop in New London in 1744 after attempting to show off his skills at the top of the mast. Small wonder, then, that even the greenest Native sailors saw the sea as a powerful supernatural space. When the young Pequot William Apess first shipped aboard a brig in Hartford in 1813, the captain soon deduced that he was both a runaway servant and an Indian. To get the delinquent to confess, the captain resorted to a scare story that seemed to evoke both Weetucks and Satan, no doubt resonating with the teenager's Pequot and Christian upbringing. When the ship neared Hellgate he told Apess "the devil would come on board in a stone canoe, with an iron paddle, and make a terrible noise, and that [the captain] intended to give us to him." Terrified at the "devil's" approach, young Apess immediately confessed that he was a fugitive.[59]

Some whites argued that oceangoing men contributed to the erosion of their communities. The eighteenth-century white missionary Gideon Hawley saw seafaring as a scourge among the Mashpee Wampanoags on Cape Cod. "The long whaling voyages of my Indians injures their morals," he wrote. "When they come home there is little else but drinking whoring fighting etc etc. I generally rejoice with almost all my neighbors when they are gone again." Hawley was particularly troubled when the Mashpee woman Hannah Babcock turned her wigwam into a makeshift brothel and tavern for passing Native and white sailors in the 1760s. Writers who described Indian whalemen often mentioned their fondness for liquor, though there was a racial tinge to accounts that characterized tavern going as rampant among Indians, for alcoholic revelry was rife throughout colonial America. Many Indian ministers agreed that becoming a sailor could imperil one's soul, but the devil did not spring from some inherent flaw in the indigenous character.

After all, no Native village was nearly as licentious and rum-soaked as port towns. Occom was aghast at the flagrant sin on display in 1761 New York City. He recalled a Manhattan Sunday disturbed by noisy drunkards whom he described "Realing and Stagaring in the Streets, others tumbling off their Horses," while "their Mouths were full of Cursing." To men like Occom, it was these "English Heathen" that were the greatest threat to the morals of Native men. When eulogizing the convicted murderer Moses Paul, Occom blamed the Indian man's service as a sailor and soldier for "confirm[ing] those evil Habits": his time in the port of New Haven left him "living in a very unsteady Way," drinking, fighting, and frequenting brothels before he took another man's life in a drunken rage. There was plenty of sympathy in Occom's censures, for he too could take to sinful ways. He confessed in a contrite letter of 1769 to his fellow missionaries that during the recent boozy Christmas season "I have been Shamefully over taken with Strong Drink, by Which I have greatly wounded the Cause of God." The Mohegan Christian Ashpo had a similar struggle with sobriety, as a reunion with fellow whalers in the 1750s led, first, to a relapse and then to a strength-ening of his religious fervor. While the sailing life could spread the disease of addiction, one should take care not to adopt these preachers' view that every time an Indian walked into a tavern he was necessarily taking a step down the road to damnation. Not every indigenous sailor who drank was drowned in the bottle.[60]

Seafaring had the side effect of bringing new people into Native commu-nities. With so many indigenous men regularly absent on long whaling voyages or lost at sea, women frequently sought out non-Native partners. A study of Martha's Vineyard found that Wampanoag families sometimes took on an international character over the eighteenth century, as Indian women married Dutch, Portuguese, and Cape Verdean sailors. By far the most common outsiders to marry into indigenous villages were black men, who, like Indians, found an economic niche in maritime trades. By the 1750s mixed Native–African children, called mustees, mulattos, and, later, people of color by colonists, were common across the coast from Manhattan to Boston. The trend toward biracial babies got a further boost when the new independent northern states started abolishing slavery in the 1780s and 1790s, and freed blacks flooded port towns looking for work. This creole population had a knack for making cameos in some of the early moments of the American Revolution. Crispus Attucks, the lanky mariner and rabble-rouser who fell to a British bullet on King's Street in Boston on March 5, 1770, was the child of Indian and African parents. (His last name meant "deer" in most coastal dialects.) Though not much is known about Attucks, he was more colorful than the sanitized martyr that appears in textbooks. Onlookers at the Boston Massacre maintained that in the minutes before he died Attucks gave out a piercing "war whoop" and vowed to eat the claws of one of the redcoated "Lobsters." Another, more obscure "Negro-Indian" waterman named Aaron Briggs was a key witness to Rhode Island colonists' attack on the grounded British schooner *Gaspée* in 1772.[61]

Native peoples' attitudes toward mixed-race marriages and the children produced from them were complex. In many places biracial couples seemed fully accepted into indigenous communities, with little friction visible to outside colonial observers, though stories of Indians rejecting those who married outsiders also surfaced. Some historians believe the work ethic of sailors created a shared antiracist sentiment among Indians and blacks, while others credit these communities' shift toward the egalitarian Baptist and Methodist denominations in fostering common cause among people of color. Yet other scholars find that as skin color became a qualifying characteristic for citizenship in the United States, some Natives rejected their kin with African ancestry. Questions of race, belonging, and the ever-shifting color line in Native communities were never easy or simple, though in time most Algonquian peoples across the coast came to accept the ambiguous label of "people of color" and embrace the shared legacies of their combined North American and African heritage. For many whites, however, this cultural mixing had an obscuring effect. The numerous shades of faces in Indians' communities, they declared, meant that Natives were actually extinct and thus no longer had a right to their ancestors' lands and tribal status.[62]

The idea that seafaring, with its customary bad habits and tendency to introduce racial mixing, had a devastating impact upon Indian communities remained a common sentiment in the nineteenth century. In a letter to his fellow ex-president Thomas Jefferson in 1812, John Adams reminisced fondly about a Native family who were his neighbors when he was a boy in Massachusetts. "But the Girls went out to Service and the Boys to Sea, till not a Soul is left," he wrote, adding, "We scarcely see an Indian in a year." The Massachusetts official John Milton Earle lamented in 1861 that Indians kept disappearing because those "near the seaboard, in the immediate vicinity of our fishing and commercial ports, [find] the temptation to a race naturally inclined to a roving and unsettled life, are too great to be resisted, and nearly all the males, first or last, engage in seafaring as an occupation." Assuredly there were real destructive elements in maritime life, yet true stories of Indian sailors never quite conformed to outsiders' stereotypical narratives of decline and degradation. As Adams and Earle gave their elegiac farewells to Native mariners, the real men were quite busy manning the boats in the final boom of American whaling, as ships flying the Stars and Stripes chased sperm whales and right whales across the Pacific. The historian Nancy Shoemaker points out that after a century in the profession, indigenous men were finally starting to make real social gains. A small number became officers and even captains.[63]

There was ample evidence that many Indian sailors actually enjoyed their work, despite—and perhaps because of—its many perils. A visitor to Martha's Vineyard remarked that the local Wampanoags considered whaling "their favourite employ" and that sea captains openly solicited the best harpooners and oarsmen for their crews. Shipping off could be a happy, if bittersweet, moment. Enthusiasm and homesickness alike were evident in the letter of a young Wampanoag, Malchizedick Howwoswe. Writing in Vineyard Haven just before he began a voyage with Captain Henry Luce to "Verginny" in 1807, he said to his parents, "I embrace this oppertunity To inform you that I am well" but asked that they send a letter in four weeks "to meat with me when I arive at Boston." Another teenaged Algonquian, Paul Cuffe Jr., remembered his first time shipping out in 1808 with giddy anticipation, writing, "This was new business to me, and with the novelty of attending a sea voyage I was highly pleased." Even for women who were excluded from maritime jobs there was a romance in the deep. The Abenaki Betsey

Chamberlain remembered a former sailor named Old Bill who did odd jobs around her small New Hampshire town when she was a child in the early nineteenth century. The old salt regularly filled her head with "queer stories" and "marvellous tales of Spaniards, Frenchmen, Indians, and Negroes." No matter how exploitative maritime labor could be, some took pride in their difficult jobs and relished the chance to broaden their horizons.[64]

The thoughts of the Mohegan Joseph Johnson are a fitting response to those premature eulogies that assumed seafaring only caused harm. After returning from a difficult voyage in 1772, the whaler and missionary wrote in his diary, "Altho I have been whire dangers were and great dangers too" and witnessed "the rage of the great whales who obey His Voice," he had been kept safe by "thou only living and True God." Johnson himself did not take to the sailing life. But his experiences are a reminder that most Native mariners did in fact come home, again and again. While taking to the sea changed their worlds, fishermen and whalers from Long Island Sound to Cape Cod Bay knew that their engagement with a larger ocean could help keep their communities intact. Johnson spoke for many of his fellow Algonquians when summing up his salvation at sea: "I have been Preserved on the mighty Waters."[65]

"What Need Is There to Speak of the Past?"

At a gathering held a thousand miles away from the glacial shores featured in this book, a visiting speaker may have used the distant region to teach a little lesson in American history. The setting was the Mississippi Delta, the year was 1811, and the speaker's name was Tecumseh. A Shawnee chief, Tecumseh was also the head of a Native spiritual and military movement that opposed the flow of whites that been surging westward since the Revolution. The United States and Britain were once again headed to war, and his coalition of Indians from near the Great Lakes saw a rare chance to stop the American advance. Tecumseh left his home on the Wabash River to recruit warriors from the Chickasaws and Choctaws along the lower Mississippi, where he allegedly gave his famous speech, often titled the "Sleep No More" speech. All we know of what he said came from an account written decades later. It is, at best, a loose summary of his talk.[1]

By joining his campaign, Tecumseh supposedly argued, Choctaws and Chickasaws could change the course of history. The past two centuries of colonization told a dispiriting, repetitive tale, as the same story that happened in New England and New York happened over and over again, with only one lesson to offer for the present moment: "But what need is there to speak of the past? It speaks for itself and asks, 'Where to-day is the Pequod? Where are the Narragansetts, the Mohawks, Pocanokets, and many other once powerful tribes of our race?' They have vanished before the avarice and oppression of the white men, as snow before a summer sun. In the vain hope of alone defending their ancient possession, they have fallen in the wars with the white man."[2] This speech has an aura of doom—the usual telltale of a white writer ventriloquizing an Indian—yet it nonetheless regularly appears in anthologies of Indian speeches. But even if these were not Tecumseh's words, the passage does capture some very real fears that many Natives in the 1810s held about the booming republic to the east. The speech was correct in claiming that "avarice and oppression" had stripped these nations of much of their lands and languages. And the urgings about the "vain hope" of acting alone spoke to an ongoing challenge that had once vexed both Miantonomi and Metacom: the quest for indigenous unity.

Despite the larger truths contained in this oft-quoted passage, its summary of the Northeast's frontier past was mostly wrong. While members of some smaller Algonquian ethnic groups joined larger composite tribes, all the named peoples were living nations then and still are today. Tellingly, Tecumseh could not have included Munsees among the vanished, for the simple reason that he knew too many of them. Many of his neighbors and some of his supporters were the children and grandchildren of folks who grew up paddling canoes through New York Harbor and up the Hudson. One of their largest western settlements, now the site of Muncie, Indiana, was a few days' journey from Tecumseh's home at Prophetstown. And many Pequots, Narragansetts, Mohegans, and Wampanoags also were well aware of Tecumseh's campaign.[3]

This apocryphal speech demonstrates some common problems with describing the long arc of Native American history since 1492. On the one hand, we cannot ignore the human and cultural toll of colonialism. But accounts that center only on losses have a shrinking quality. The Native social world becomes a kind of disappearing miniature, set on postage-stamp reservations where an always dwindling population holds on to a small repertoire of sacred stories and a tiny vocabulary in the ancient tongue. Implicit in these grounded narratives is the idea that the essence of indigenous culture rests in genes or in the soil, and thus vanishes with every "full blood" elder who dies or with every acre of earth that is ceded. Therein lies the flaw in likening Native dispossession to snow melting: the metaphor assumes that true Indian cultures exist in a pure and frozen state and thus that there was no way to be culturally fluid and still be Indian. Taken to their logical endpoints, these diminishing accounts either insist that Native people can reside only in the past or imply that their modern existence is a microscopic matter that can be safely ignored by everyone else.[4]

The truth is, in 1811 Algonquians' world was getting bigger, not smaller. It was a process that had been under way ever since Epenow, Tisquantum, Orson, Uncas, Miantonomi, Ninigret, Tackapousha, Metacom, Weetamoo, Awashonks, and thousands more navigated between canoes and ships, between the English and Dutch empires, between their maritime past and their maritime future. Even after the wampum trade and New Netherland disappeared, these Natives never stopped engaging with the economy and politics of the larger planet, despite being shoved to the very margins of colonial society. Drawing on seafaring traditions that long predated the arrival of the *Mayflower*, they helped build the region's most profitable and global industry (for better or for worse); they were vocal participants in the colonies' revolution against Britain (for better or for worse); their societies became increasingly multiracial, multidenominational, and mobile. These processes were seldom pleasant or easy. Any saga of these coastal peoples is dominated by the themes of inescapable oppression, racism, poverty, and loss. But pointing out the cultural buoyancy in their history reveals how even compact reservations could be dynamic, intellectually rich communities that were open to concepts and people from across the globe. Likewise, gatherings of Algonquian seamen in whaleboats bobbing deep in the Pacific or in the smoky grog shops of London could temporarily turn these far corners of the earth into profoundly indigenous places.

Ultimately, that is the value of seeing Indians as historical players who ranged far beyond their home continent and outside the contained, grounded field of American borderlands. Telling the stories of saltwater frontiers can uncover the many unexpected ways in which Native history could be both global and modern. For Algonquians' expansive strategies of engagement were not exactly rare. In pointing out the vital parts Indians played in shaping and opposing the movements of people, things, ideas, and empires across the ocean, the scholar Jace Weaver argues convincingly that there was a "Red Atlantic," just as there was a black one, an English one, and a Dutch one. For that matter, the experience of being "Preserved on the mighty Waters" was shared by many traditional maritime peoples across the world living within colonial and state societies. Natives have also long realized that even after losing on the battlefield or treaty ground, they could fight on in the pages of history books. Indeed, at the moment Tecumseh reportedly declared their nations gone, this is exactly what a few veteran Native seamen were starting to do. Brief glances at their lives afford a satisfying answer to that dismissive rhetorical question, What need is there to speak of the past? Was it really just the same grim story repeating itself?[5]

One Pequot man in particular, the sailor and historian William Apess, shared much of Tecumseh's defiant spirit. Apess pointed out that Natives were "doubly wronged by the white man—first, driven from their native soil by the sword of the invader, then darkly slandered by the pen of the historian." As the Shawnees and the United States went to war in 1811, Apess was just starting to face his own battles. Born to desperately poor parents who were heavy drinkers, Apess spent much of his childhood as an indentured servant in eastern Connecticut. He remembered his early visits to the bustling port of New London as a moment of awakening: "I saw, as I thought, everything was wonderful: Thither I determined to bend my course, as I expect that on reaching the town I should be metamorphosed into a person of consequence." After several attempts, in 1813 he finally ran away to become a sailor—it was on his very first voyage that a captain convinced him that the devil rode a stone canoe through the rapids of Hellgate.[6]

Perhaps Satan was indeed lurking in those waters. Although Apess soon enlisted and served a brief stint on a sweetwater patrol during the final days of the War of 1812, he quickly became disillusioned with the lure of port towns. Rather than turn him into a "person of consequence," the mariner's life was making him a drunk. Moving around the coast from New York to Ontario, Apess worked for stints at sea and on land, sometimes slipping into long alcoholic benders or pausing for tearful moments of sober piety. In his later writing Apess repeatedly used the sea as a powerful metaphor for eternity and the vastness of God's salvation, describing himself in early torments as "a tempest-tossed mariner who expects every minute to be washed from the wreck to which he fondly clings." As he committed to being a good

Methodist, Apess generally stopped chasing mean wages and cheap rum, with only a couple of painful relapses. He became an itinerant minister who preached the gospel to Algonquian communities across the Hudson Valley, Long Island, and Cape Cod.[7]

As his fame grew among whites as well as Indians, he published an autobiography, A Son of the Forest (1829), which included a summary of New England's indigenous history. Apess continued to research Native cultures from across the continent and published several passionate essays pillorying the rank racism he found in most white writers' work. (His half brother Elisha Apess, also a sailor, shared his dislike of authority: in 1838 Elisha led a mutiny on the vessel Ajax off New Zealand, where he soon settled and married a Maori woman.) By the mid-1830s, as President Andrew Jackson enacted his national policy of ethnic cleansing, euphemistically titled Indian Removal, Apess became even more political. His series of provocative defenses of the rights of the Mashpee Wampanoags played off the recent debates over federal authority in Washington. In his most celebrated work, a eulogy to King Philip, Apess imagined Philip's rhetoric to be so animating that "every Indian heart had been lighted up at the council fires, at Philip's speech, and that the forest was literally alive with this injured race." The Pequot preacher made no secret of his admiration for Philip. He, too, wanted his words to electrify Indian country.[8]

As a thinker, Apess seems both ancient and modern. Viewed from the seventeenth century, he looks like the descendant of the many sachems who criticized colonists with sticks or wampum in their hands and dictated letters to prominent Puritans who served as their scribes. Viewed from the present, he also looks like the forebear of a long line of Native scholars and activists who draw from traditional indigenous thought and global anticolonial movements to criticize old and new injustices. But it would be a mistake to depict Apess as the sole godfather of Native intellectuals and to forget that he was also a Christian thinker. Following in the long tradition of Samson Occom and other indigenous ministers, he combined the intimate language of grievance and condolence from Indian orations with a distinctly Protestant rhetoric of sin, redemption, and self-improvement. In the years after the release of A Son of the Forest an increasing number of Natives started publishing autobiographies and fiction. In New England alone there was a whole cohort of Indian literary voices, including Olivia Ward Bush-Banks (Montaukett), Joseph Nicolar (Penobscot), Betsey Chamberlain (Abenaki), Elleanor Eldridge (African–Narragansett), Ann Plato (African–Native), and Paul Cuffe Jr. (African–Wampanoag–Pequot). Cuffe was the son of an even more famous mariner, Paul Cuffe Sr., a figure whose papers offer some of the most compelling evidence of how complex and large the nineteenth-century Algonquian world had become.[9]

Of the hundreds of indigenous men who became salts, the elder Cuffe stood out. He was born on the small island of Cuttyhunk in 1758 to an African-born Akan father and a Wampanoag mother. His father, Cuffe Slocum, had been brought into the Quaker fold by his masters, and he raised his ten children in the same denomination. Paul Cuffe's faith may also have been strengthened by a turn toward spirituality in his young adulthood. After a daring and hard-drinking stint as a blockade-running sailor during the Revolution, Cuffe quit the bottle and rededicated himself to the Holy Spirit. As he began raising a family with his Pequot wife, Alice, he grew closer to prominent Quakers in the area. Through his friendships with weighty Friends from Boston to Philadelphia he became a leading voice among the nascent antislavery movement. Though historians often identify Cuffe as being African American, he referred to himself as black, Indian, and mustee interchangeably, while his extended family had mostly Native heritage. His son Paul preferred to identify as a Pequot, perhaps with an understanding that *Pequot* was already a multiracial label.[10]

By 1811, the same year his larger family was supposedly written off for dead, Cuffe had a good claim to be the early republic's wealthiest black man or, alternately, one of its richest Indians. He made his home in Westport, Massachusetts, a handsome mainland village of saltbox houses and stone-walled pastures where he and Alice lived for thirty years. Hiring mainly "peopel of Colour" as his shipbuilders and sailors, he built his own fleet of ships and put them to every possible use: American coastal trading, Grand Banks fishing, Arctic whaling, and African colonization. His fortune became so renowned that one wily con man tried to make a career out of impersonating his son. Throngs of Englishmen gathered at the docks of Liverpool in

1811 just to catch a glimpse of his ship. Some were there as fellow abolition-ists, others just to gawk at his entirely indigenous and black crew. What really made Cuffe's fleet noteworthy was not the skin hues of the ordinary sailors—racially diverse crews were common—but the fact that nonwhite men were in command of the quarterdeck. Some of Cuffe's favorite captains and mates were his brother-in-law, his sons, and his nephews, all of whom actually had more Algonquian ancestry than African. Though he often worked with white investors, Cuffe had a 50 percent or greater ownership share of almost all his vessels. And his ships had self-confident American names with a spirit of daring enterprise: *Ranger, Traveller, Hero, Alpha.*[11]

The year 1811 was also when Cuffe made his first journey to Sierra Leone. Technically a possession of Great Britain, Sierra Leone was the project of abolitionists experimenting with repatriating freed Caribbean and American slaves to Africa. The colony had attracted a lot of enthusiasm among American antislavery activists, including Cuffe and his Quaker brethren. The black Wampanoag captain did not personally want to emigrate, but he saw the colony as ripe ground for saving souls. And he believed that his ships could foster vibrant trade links between West Africa and New England. His brig *Traveller* first dropped anchor in Freetown harbor that spring. In his initial visit Cuffe was most heartened by his encounters with groups of mariners he called the Cruemen, today known as the Krumen or Kru people. Their ethnic name actually may have derived from their seafaring, for the men from these highly maritime societies came from "Severall hundred miles Distance" in canoes just to serve as crewmen aboard ships leaving Freetown. Most of the Krumen Cuffe met were followers of Islam, or, as he put it, "Professors of Mahomet" who "Ware very Exspart in righting Arabeck."[12]

There was no small amount of condescension in Cuffe's descriptions of Sierra Leone. "People of the Colony are Very fond of Spiritual Liquor," he wrote, adding "there is not So much industry as Would be best for them" and "their farmes are too much neglected." He blamed this in part on seafaring, as the "young men are too fond of Leaveing the Colony and become Seamen for other people." Cuffe's scolding of African sailors was not quite as hypocritical as it might first appear. The real problem he diag-nosed was not that the locals took to the sea; it was that they did so "for other people." If Americans and Britons would invest in Sierra Leone and if freed black entrepreneurs created a critical mass of Freetown-based merchants, he could "see no Reason why they may not become a Nation to be Numbered among the historians nations of the World." He even had a strong leaning toward one trade in particular to make the colony prosper, writing, "Some Sober famileys may find their Way to Sierra Leone more Espcialy if the Whale fishery Can be Established in the Colony." And no doubt he saw a glimpse of himself in the "Sober young" Krumen sailor he invited to serve aboard the *Traveller* "to instruct him in the useful art of Navigation hopeing he may become a Servisable Subject among them."[13]

The *Traveller*'s journey to Africa in 1811 conjures up some uneasily familiar images. Cuffe's account had unmistakable echoes of the scenes of English and Dutch ships approaching American shores and carrying indigenous mariners away. Only this time the past was being bizarrely reenacted on the opposite side of the ocean two hundred years later with Indians playing the part of visiting Christians. The comparison does not quite hold up when we remember that those Krumens' ancestors had been dealing with European ships for a century longer than Algonquians had. And no doubt Cuffe would reject the parallels, as he truly believed he was there to give things to the locals, not to take things from them. Though a strong streak of Yankee Protestant evangelism inspired Cuffe's prescriptions for the Krumen Muslims, one aspect of his mission seemed more pure at heart. For Cuffe saw his fine ship full of "people of Colour" as a testament to what "the useful art of Navigation" could bring. The most precious cargo he could share was his own biography.

To Paul Cuffe and William Apess there was no question of "What need is there to speak of the past?" Their personal stories spoke so clearly to their belief that the region's Natives had both a past *and* a future. Bush-Banks put it best in her poem "Driftwood" (1898), which likened the work of recovering her heritage to combing a beach after a catastrophic shipwreck. No matter how painful and fragmented this shoreline's history was, collecting its pieces could still provide "a gleam of light, / After the fury of the blighting storm."[14]

AAS American Antiquarian Society, Worcester, Massachusetts.

AP Peter A. Christoph and Florence Christoph, eds., Charles A. Ghering, trans., *The Andros Papers, 1674–1677*. 2 volumes. Syracuse: Syracuse University Press, 1990.

AHR *The American Historical Review.*

BNA British National Archives, Kew Gardens, London.

CCR J. Hammond Trumbull and Charles J. Hoadley, eds., *The Public Records of the Colony of Connecticut, 1636–1776*. 15 volumes. Hartford: Brown and Parsons, 1850–90.

DRCHNY Edmund B. O'Callaghan, Berthold Fernow, and John R. Broadhead, eds., *Documents Relating to the Colonial History of the State of New York*. 15 volumes. Albany: Weed Parsons, 1853–87.

DRNN Arnold J. F. Van Lear, ed. and trans., *Documents Relating to New Netherland, 1624–1626*. San Mateo, Calif.: Henry E. Huntington Library, 1924.

EAS *Early American Studies: An Interdisciplinary Journal.*

JAH *The Journal of American History.*

JCBL John Carter Brown Library, Brown University, Providence.

JHL John Hay Library, Brown University, Providence.

MCR Nathaniel Shurtleff, ed., *Records of the Governor and Company of the Massachusetts Bay in New England*. 5 volumes. Boston: William White, 1853–54.

MHS Massachusetts Historical Society, Boston.

MHSC Charles Hudson et al., eds., *Collections of the Massachusetts Historical Society*. 90 volumes. Boston: Massachusetts Historical Society, 1795–2006.

N-YHS Patricia D. Klingenstein Library, New-York Historical Society Museum and Library, New York.

NEHGR	*New England Historical Genealogical Register.*
NEQ	*New England Quarterly.*
NHCR	Charles J. Hoadley, ed., *Records of the Colony of New Haven, 1638 to 1664.* 2 volumes.
NNCM	Charles T. Gehring, trans. and ed., *New Netherland Documents Series: Council Minutes.* 2 volumes. Syracuse: Syracuse University Press, 2000.
NNC	Charles T. Gehring, trans. and ed., *New Netherland Documents Series: Correspondence.* Syracuse: Syracuse University Press, 2000.
NNN	J. Franklin Jameson, ed. *Narratives of New Netherland.* Original Narratives of Early American History, volume 9. New York: Scribner's, 1909.
NYCA	Peter A. Christoph and Florence Christoph, eds., *New York Historical Manuscripts: Court of Assizes, 1665–1682.* Baltimore: Genealogical Publishing, 1983.
NYCM	Arnold J. F. Van Lear and Charles A. Ghering, eds. and trans., *New York Historical Manuscripts: Council Minutes, 1638–1656.* 3 volumes. Baltimore: Genealogical Publishing, 1974–83.
NYGE	Peter A. Christoph and Florence Christoph, eds., *New York Historical Manuscripts: General Entries, 1664–1682.* 2 volumes. Syracuse: Syracuse University Press, 1982.
NYRPS	Arnold J. F. Van Lear, ed. and trans., *New York Historical Manuscripts: Registrar of the Provincial Secretary,* 2 volumes. Baltimore: Genealogical Publishing, 1974.
PCR	Nathaniel Shurtleff and David Pulsipher, eds., *Records of the Colony of New Plymouth in New England.* 12 volumes. Boston: William White, 1859–61.
RICR	John Russell Bartlett, ed., *Records of the Colony of Rhode Island and Providence Plantations, 1636–1776.* 7 volumes. Providence: A. C. Greene and Brothers, 1857–62.
RNA	Berthold Fernow and Edmund Bailey O'Callaghan, eds., *Records of New Amsterdam from 1653–1674.* 7 volumes. New York: Knickerbocker Press, 1897.
RTEH	Joseph Osborne et al., eds., *Records of the Town of East Hampton, Long Island, Suffolk Co., N.Y.* 5 volumes. Sag Harbor, N.Y.: John H. Hunt, 1887–1905.
RTH	Benjamin D. Hicks, ed. *Records of the Towns of North and South Hempstead, Long Island, New York.* 8 volumes. Jamaica, N.Y.: Long Island Farmer Print, 1896.
RTS	William S. Pelletreau et al., eds., *Records of the Town of Southampton with other Ancient Documents of Historic Value.* 8 volumes. Sag Harbor, N.Y.: James H. Hunt, 1874–1930.

RWC   Glenn W. LaFantasie, ed. *The Correspondence of Roger Williams.* 2
     volumes. Providence: Brown University Press, 1988.
WMQ   *The William and Mary Quarterly: A Magazine of Early American History*
     and Culture. Third Series.
WP   Allyn B. Forbes et al., eds. *The Winthrop Papers, 1498–1654.* 6 volumes.
     Boston: Massachusetts Historical Society, 1929–92.
YIPP   Paul Grant-Costa et al., eds., Yale Indian Papers Project, Yale University.

NOTES

Introduction

1. On the complex relationship between Natives, land, and history in the Northeast, see William Cronon, *Changes in the Land: Indians, Colonists, and the Ecology of New England* (New York: Hill and Wang, 1983); Jean M. O'Brien, *Dispossession by Degrees: Indian Land and Identity in Natick, Massachusetts, 1650–1790* (Cambridge: Cambridge University Press, 1997); David Jaffee, *People of the Wachusett: Greater New England in History and Memory, 1630–1860* (Ithaca: Cornell University Press, 1999); Lisa Brooks, *The Common Pot: The Recovery of Native Space in the Northeast* (Minneapolis: University of Minnesota Press, 2008); O'Brien, *Firsting and Lasting: Writing Indians Out of Existence in New England* (Minneapolis: University of Minnesota Press, 2011); Christine DeLucia, "The Memory Frontier: Uncommon Pursuit of Past and Place in the Northeast After King Philip's War," *JAH* 98.4 (2012): 975–97.

2. On ground-taking myths and images created about Plymouth and New Amsterdam, see John Seelye, *Memory's Nation: The Place of Plymouth Rock* (Chapel Hill: University of North Carolina Press, 1998), esp. 6–22; Edwin G. Burrows and Mike Wallace, *Gotham: A History of New York City to 1898* (New York: Oxford University Press, 1999), xiv–xv; James Deetz and Patricia Scott Deetz, *The Times of Their Lives: Life, Love, and Death in Plymouth Colony* (New York: Anchor Books, 2000), 12–13; Joseph A. Conforti, *Imagining New England: Explorations of Regional Identity from the Pilgrims to the Mid-Twentieth Century* (Chapel Hill: University of North Carolina Press, 2001) 1–34, 203–62.

3. This is not the first book to look at the maritime dimensions of North American Native–colonial encounters, though such analyses have been sparse until recently. See Horace P. Beck, *The American Indian as a Sea-Fighter in Colonial Times* (Mystic, Conn.: Greenwood Press, 1959); Daniel Vickers, "The First

Whalemen of Nantucket," *WMQ* 40.4 (1983): 560–83; Barry M. Gough, *Gunboat Frontier: British Maritime Authority and Northwest Coast Indians, 1846–1890* (Vancouver: University of British Columbia Press, 1984); T. H. Breen, *Imagining the Past: East Hampton Histories* (Reading, Mass.: Addison-Wesley, 1989), 147–205; Mark A. Nicholas, "Mashpee Wampanoags of Cape Cod, the Whalefishery, and Seafaring's Impact on Community Development," *American Indian Quarterly* 26.2 (2002): 165–95. In the past few years, several like-minded scholars have asked similar questions about Indians and maritime spaces in early America. See Donna Merwick, *The Shame and the Sorrow: Dutch–Amerindian Encounters in New Netherland* (Philadelphia: University of Pennsylvania Press, 2006); Joshua Leonard Reid, " 'The Sea Is My Country': The Maritime World of the Makah, an Indigenous Borderlands People" (Ph.D. diss., University of California, Davis, 2009); John R. Gillis, *The Human Shore: Seacoasts in History* (Chicago: University of Chicago Press, 2012), esp. 68–127; Matthew Bahar, " 'The Sea of Trouble We Are Swimming In': People of the Dawnland and the Enduring Pursuit of an Atlantic World" (Ph.D. diss., University of Oklahoma, 2012); James L. Hill, " 'Bring them what they lack': Spanish–Creek Exchange and Alliance Making in a Maritime Borderland, 1763–1783," *EAS* 12.1 (2014): 36–67; Kelly K. Chaves, "Before the First Whalemen: The Emergence and Loss of Indigenous Maritime Authority in New England, 1672–1740," *NEQ* 87.1 (2014): 46–71; "The Indian Mariners Project," an online digital mapping and archiving initiative led by Jason Mancini along with the staff of the Mashantucket Pequot Museum and Research Center: http://indianmarinersproject.com/.

4. Scholars have noted this critical zone of Anglo–Dutch overlap for a while, though there has been no book-length study of the entire region's entangled process of colonization. See Lynn Ceci, "The Effect of European Contact and Trade on the Settlement Pattern of Indians in Coastal New York, 1524–1665: The Archeological and Documentary Evidence" (Ph.D. diss., City University of New York, 1977); Joshua W. Lane, ed., *The Impact of New Netherlands upon the Colonial Long Island Basin: Report of a Yale–Smithsonian Seminar held at Yale University, New Haven, Connecticut, May 3–5, 1990* (New Haven: Yale–Smithsonian, 1993); Benjamin Schmidt, "Mapping an Empire: Cartographic and Colonial Rivalry in Seventeenth-Century Dutch and English North America," *WMQ* 54.3 (July 1997): 549–78; Faren R. Siminoff, *Crossing the Sound: The Rise of Atlantic American Communities in Seventeenth-Century Eastern Long Island* (New York: New York University Press, 2004); Cynthia Van Zandt, *Brothers Among Nations: The Pursuit of Intercultural Alliances in Early America, 1580–1660* (Oxford: Oxford University Press, 2008); the special issue of *Early American Studies* edited by Ned Landsman and Andrew Newman titled "The Worlds of Lion Gardiner, c. 1599–1663: Crossings and Boundaries," *EAS* 9.2 (2011).

On the need for better syntheses of early America and this region in particular that incorporate both Netherlanders and Natives, see Karen Ordahl Kupperman, "Early American History with the Dutch Put In," *Reviews in American History* 21.2 (June, 1993): 195–201; William A. Starna, "Assessing American Indian–Dutch Studies: Missed and Missing Opportunities," *New York History* 84.1 (2003): 4–31; William Voorhees, "Tying the Loose Ends Together: Putting New Netherland Studies on a Par with the Studies of Other Regions," in *Revisiting New Netherland: Perspectives on Early Dutch America*, ed. Joyce D. Goodfriend (Leiden: Brill, 2005), 309–28; Lauric Henneton, "La Nouvelle-Angleterre: une exclave anglaise en Amérique du Nord," *Outre-Terre* 38.1 (2014): 382–91.

5. Historians have long emphasized violence as a central feature of the region's colonization, though they almost always see the bloodshed as contained within separate English and Dutch colonial spheres. See Francis Jennings, *The Invasion of America: Indians, Colonialism, and the Cant of Conquest* (New York: W. W. Norton, 1975); Neal Salisbury, *Manitou and Providence: Indians, Europeans, and the Making of New England, 1500–1643* (New York: Oxford University Press, 1982); Alfred Cave, *The Pequot War* (Amherst: University of Massachusetts Press, 1996); Jill Lepore, *The Name of War: King Philip's War and the Origins of American Identity* (New York: Vintage, 1998); James D. Drake, *King Philip's War: Civil War in New England, 1675–1676* (Amherst: University of Massachusetts Press, 1999); Evan Haefeli, "Kieft's War and the Cultures of Violence in Colonial America," in *Lethal Imagination: Violence and Brutality in American History*, ed. Michael A. Bellesiles (New York: New York University Press, 1999), 17–40; Merwick, *The Shame and the Sorrow*; Bernard Bailyn, *The Barbarous Years: The Peopling of British North America: The Conflict of Civilizations, 1600–1675* (New York: Alfred A. Knopf, 2012).

6. John Underhill, *Newes from America; or, A New and Experimentall Discoverie of New England . . .* (London, 1638; repr., Lincoln, Nebraska, 2007), 31 ("more men"); Williams to John Winthrop, August 25, 1636, RWC 1:54 ("Ocean"); Roger Williams, *A Key Into the Language of America; Or, An help to the Language of the Natives in that part of America called New-England . . .* (London, 1643; repr., Bedford, Mass., Applewood Books, 1997), 183 ("*Chépewess & Mishittâshin*," "Northerne storm of war"), 85 (*Chepewessin*), 87 (*Mishittâshin*).

7. Frederick Jackson Turner, *The Frontier in American History* (New York: Henry Holt, 1921), 1–38, 3–4 (quotations).

8. For particularly clear summaries of Turner's thesis, its exceptionalism, and its assumptions about continents and oceans, see Patricia Nelson Limerick, *The Legacy of Conquest: The Unbroken Past of the American West* (New York: W. W. Norton, 1987), 17–32; Martin Ridge, "The Life of an Idea: The Significance of Frederick Jackson Turner's Frontier Thesis," *Montana: The Magazine of Western History* 41.1 (1991): 2–13; François Furstenberg, "The Significance of the Trans-Appalachian Frontier in Atlantic History," *AHR* 113.3 (2008): 647–77.

9. Limerick, *The Legacy of Conquest*, 17–32; Patricia Nelson Limerick, *Something in the Soil: Legacies and Reckonings in the New West* (New York: W. W. Norton, 2000), 74–92, 141–65; David J. Weber, "Turner, the Boltonians, and the Borderlands," *AHR* 91 (February 1986): 66–81; Albert L. Hurtado, *Herbert Eugene Bolton: Historian of American Borderlands* (Berkeley: University of California Press, 2012), 5–6 (pioneer childhood). Hurtado speculates that the term *borderlands* was provided by Allen Johnson, Bolton's series editor at Yale University Press, the publisher of his first book on Spanish North America. See Hurtado, "Bolton and Turner: The Borderlands and American Exceptionalism," *Western Historical Quarterly* 44.1 (Spring 2013): 10–11.

10. Limerick, *The Legacy of Conquest*, 17–32; Limerick, *Something in the Soil*, 74–92, 141–65. On new definitions of *frontier*, see Leonard Thompson and Howard Lamar, "Comparative Frontier History," in Thompson and Lamar, eds., *The Frontier in History: North America and Southern Africa Compared* (New Haven: Yale University Press, 1981), 7; James H. Merrell, " 'The Customes of Our Countrey': Indians and Colonists in Early America," in Bernard Bailyn and Philip D. Morgan, eds., *Strangers Within the Realm: Cultural Margins of the First British Empire* (Chapel Hill: University of North Carolina Press, 1991); Kerwin Lee Klein, "Reclaiming the 'F' Word, or Being and Becoming Postwestern," *Pacific Historical Review* 65 (May 1996): 179–215. On the complex and never openly confrontational relationship between mentor and student, see Hurtado, "Bolton and Turner," 4–20. And for an overview of what the word *frontier* meant to Anglo-American colonists, see Patrick Kehoe Spero, "Creating Pennsylvania: The Politics of the Frontier and the State" (Ph.D. diss., University of Pennsylvania, 2009), esp. 25–44. The shift toward using the continent as a frame for work on Indians and Euro-Americans was largely initiated by Richard White's *The Middle Ground: Indians, Empires, and Republics in the Great Lakes Region, 1650–1815* (Cambridge: Cambridge University Press, 1991). For critical assessments of how White's work changed the field (and how it hasn't), see Jeremy Adelman and Stephen Aron, "From Borderlands to Borders: Empires, Nation-States, and the Peoples in Between in North American History," *AHR* 104.3 (1999): 814–41; Nancy Shoemaker, "Categories," in *Clearing a Path: Theorizing the Past in Native American Studies*, ed. Nancy Shoemaker (New York: Routledge, 2002), 51–69; "Forum: The Middle Ground Revisited," *WMQ* 63.1 (2006): 3–96; Claudio Saunt, "Go West: Mapping Early American Historiography," *WMQ* 68.4 (2008): 748–78. Influential borderlands/frontier studies that creatively use land as their central frame include James H. Merrell, *Into the American Woods: Negotiators on the Pennsylvania Frontier* (New York: W. W. Norton, 1999); Colin Calloway, *One Vast Winter Count: The Native American West Before Lewis and Clark* (Lincoln: University of Nebraska Press, 2003); Kathleen DuVal, *The Native Ground: Indians and Colonists in the Heart of the Continent* (Philadelphia: University of

Pennsylvania Press, 2006); Alan Taylor, *The Divided Ground: Indians, Settlers, and the Northern Borderland of the American Revolution* (New York: Alfred A. Knopf, 2006); Ned Blackhawk, *Violence Over the Land: Indians and Empires in the Early American West* (Cambridge: Harvard University Press, 2006); David Chang, *The Color of the Land: Race, Nation, and the Politics of Landownership in Oklahoma, 1832–1929* (Chapel Hill: University of North Carolina Press, 2010).

11. Bernard Bailyn, *Atlantic History: Concepts and Contours* (Cambridge: Harvard University Press, 2005), 1–56.

12. For a broad overview of the field's origins, methods, and potential, see Bailyn, *Atlantic History*; David Armitage, "Three Concepts of Atlantic History," in *The British Atlantic World, 1500–1800*, ed. David Armitage and Michael J. Braddick (New York: Palgrave Macmillan, 2002), 11–27; Marcus Rediker, "Toward a People's History of the Sea," in *Maritime Empires: British Imperial Maritime Trade in the Nineteenth Century*, ed. David Killingray et al. (London: Boydell Press, 2004), 195–206; Alison Games, "AHR Forum: Atlantic History: Definitions, Challenges, and Opportunities," *AHR* 111.3 (June 2006): 741–57. For more critical takes on Atlantic history's shortcomings, see Peter A. Coclanis, "Atlantic World or Atlantic/ World?," *WMQ* 63.4 (October 2006): 725–42; W. Jeffrey Bolster, "Putting the Ocean in Atlantic History: Maritime Communities and Marine Ecology in the Northwest Atlantic, 1500–1800," *AHR* 113.1 (2008): 19–47. Paul Cohen argues that the exclusion of Natives from Atlantic studies reflects the limits of a Eurocentric concept, while Jace Weaver argues that it is really a lack of research that excludes Indians from transoceanic narratives. See Cohen, "Was There an Amerindian Atlantic?: Reflections on the Limits of a Historiographical Concept," *History of European Ideas* 34.4 (December 2008): 388–410; Weaver, *The Red Atlantic: American Indigenes and the Making of the Modern World, 1000–1927* (Chapel Hill: University of North Carolina Press, 2014), esp. 10–31.

13. The "surf and turf" approach is exemplified by Daniel K. Richter, *Facing East from Indian Country* (Cambridge: Harvard University Press, 2001); Alan Gallay, *The Indian Slave Trade: The Rise of the English Empire in the American South, 1670–1717* (New Haven: Yale University Press, 2002); April Lee Hatfield, *Atlantic Virginia: Intercolonial Relations in the Seventeenth Century* (Philadelphia: University of Pennsylvania Press, 2004); Furstenberg, "The Significance of the Trans-Appalachian Frontier," 647–77; Paul Timothy Conrad, "Captive Fates: Displaced American Indians in the Southwest Borderlands, Mexico, and Cuba, 1500–1800" (Ph.D. diss., University of Texas, Austin, 2011); Brett Rushforth, *Bonds of Alliance: Indigenous and Atlantic Slaveries in New France* (Chapel Hill: University of North Carolina Press, 2012); Catherine Cangany, *Frontier Seaport: Detroit's Transformation into an Atlantic Entrepôt* (Chicago: University of Chicago Press, 2014).

Scholars are paying more and more attention to the Atlantic journeys of Native people, with several looking specifically at coastal Algonquians from this region. See Alden Vaughan, *Transatlantic Encounters: American Indians in Britain, 1500–1776* (Cambridge: Cambridge University Press, 2006); Jenny Hale Pulsipher, "Playing John White: John Wompas and Racial Identity in the Seventeenth-Century Atlantic World," in *Native Acts: Indian Performance, 1603–1832,* ed. Josh David Bellin and Laura Mielke (Lincoln: University of Nebraska Press, 2011), 195–220; Coll Thrush, " 'Meere Strangers': Indigenous and Urban Performances in Algonquian London," in *Urban Identity and the Atlantic World,* ed. Elizabeth Fay and Leonard Von Morzé (New York: Palgrave Macmillan, 2013), 195–213; Weaver, *The Red Atlantic.*
On the central role of islands and peripheries, see Peter E. Pope, *Fish Into Wine: The Newfoundland Plantation in the Seventeenth Century* (Chapel Hill: University of North Carolina Press, 2003); John Gillis, *Islands of the Mind: How the Human Imagination Created the Atlantic* World (New York: Palgrave Macmillan, 2004); Michael Jarvis, *In the Eye of All Trade: Bermuda, Bermudians, and the Maritime Atlantic World, 1680–1783* (Chapel Hill: University of North Carolina Press, 2010); W. Jeffery Bolster, *The Mortal Sea: Fishing the Atlantic in the Age of Sail* (Cambridge: Harvard University Press, 2013); Gillis, *The Human Shore.*

14. On the fluorescence of Native writing in the nineteenth century and its role in opposing historical erasure, detribalization, and cultural genocide, see Maureen Konkel, *Writing Indian Nations: Native Intellectuals and the Politics of Historiography, 1827–1863* (Chapel Hill: University of North Carolina Press, 2004); Robert Warrior, *The People and the Word: Reading Native Nonfiction* (Minneapolis: University of Minnesota Press, 2005); Arnold Krupat, *"That the People Might Live": Loss and Renewal in Native American Elegy* (Ithaca: Cornell University Press, 2012), 108–33; Brooks, *The Common Pot,* 198–218, 249–52; O'Brien, *Firsting and Lasting,* 145–99. On Bush-Banks, see "Introduction," in *The Collected Works of Olivia Ward Bush-Banks,* ed. Bernice F. Guillaume (New York: Oxford University Press, 1991), 3–7; Nathan L. Grant, "Olivia Ward Bush-Banks," in *Harlem Renaissance Lives,* ed. Henry Louis Gates and Evelyn Brooks Higginbotham (New York: Oxford University Press), 93–95.

15. Olivia Ward Bush-Banks, "Driftwood," in Guillaume, ed., *Collected Works,* 51–53.

16. For further discussion of the clichéd formulation that "Indians are the rock, European peoples are the sea," see White, *The Middle Ground,* ix. Bush-Banks would return to the imagery of seashores and seafaring throughout her work, as can be seen in her larger anthology of poems, also called *Driftwood* (1914), her essay "On the Long Island Indian" (1916), her short play *Indian Trails; or, A Trail of the Montauk* (c. 1920), and her unpublished memoir, "The Lure of the Distances" (c. 1935–44), in Guillaume, ed., *Collected Works,* 45–130, 188–94, 269–314.

17. My thinking about objects draws from many sources, including Arjun Appadurai, ed., *The Social Life of Things: Commodities in Cultural Perspective* (Cambridge: Cambridge University Press, 1986), esp. the introduction; Christopher L. Miller and George R. Hamell, "A New Perspective on Indian–White Contact: Cultural Symbols and Colonial Trade," *JAH* 73.2 (1986): 311–28; Nicholas Thomas, *Entangled Objects: Exchange, Material Culture, and Colonialism in the Pacific* (Cambridge: Harvard University Press, 1991); Annette Weiner, *Inalienable Possessions: The Paradox of Keeping-While-Giving* (Berkeley: University of California Press, 1992); Patricia Seed, *Ceremonies of Possession in Europe's Conquest of the New World, 1492–1640* (Cambridge: Cambridge University Press, 1995); James Deetz, *In Small Things Forgotten: An Archeology of Early American Life*, 2d ed. (New York: Anchor Books, 1996); Laurier Turgeon, "The Tale of the Kettle: Odyssey of an Intercultural Object," *Ethnohistory* 44.1 (1997): 1–29; Robert Blair St. George, *Conversing by Signs: Poetics of Implication in Colonial New England Culture* (Chapel Hill: University of North Carolina Press, 1998); Merrell, *Into the American Woods*; Fred R. Myers, ed., *The Empire of Things: Regimes of Value and Material Culture* (Santa Fe: SAR Press, 2001); Daniel Miller, ed., *Materiality* (Durham: Duke University Press, 2005); David Preston, *The Texture of Contact: European and Indian Settler Communities on the Frontiers of Iroquoia, 1667–1783* (Lincoln: University of Nebraska Press, 2009).

18. Patricia E. Rubertone offers an extended critique of streaming methods in general and how they apply to this region and one vital source in particular, Williams's *Key*. Rubertone makes a necessary point that scholars have a tendency to read Williams uncritically and authoritatively and that sources like his represent the narrow perspective of the elite European men who wrote them. Still, for all of Williams's faults, there is not a single seventeenth-century source on Algonquian life that is as rich or descriptive. See *Grave Undertakings: An Archaeology of Roger Williams and the Narragansett Indians* (Washington: Smithsonian Institution Press, 2001), esp. 69–114. Books that serve as particularly instructive methodological models include Patricia Galloway, *Choctaw Genesis, 1500–1700* (Lincoln: University of Nebraska Press, 1996), which represents a conservative use of up- and side-streaming, focusing on what colonial sources cannot tell us as much as on what they can, pointing out how European cultural assumptions infused their texts and maps; Richter, *Facing East from Indian Country*, lays out cautious examples of how to use archaeology and anthropology to reconstruct Native viewpoints from both colonial and Native-authored sources; Pekka Hämäläinen, *The Comanche Empire* (New Haven: Yale University Press, 2008), presents a bold model of using archaeology, environmental history, and world-systems theory to synthesize observations from sources.

19. *Biographies*: Robert S. Grumet, ed., *Northeastern Indian Lives, 1632–1816* (Amherst: University of Massachusetts Press, 1996); Michael Leroy Oberg, *Uncas*:

The First of the Mohegans (Ithaca: Cornell University Press, 2003); Walter
W. Woodward, *Prospero's America: John Winthrop, Jr., Alchemy, and the Creation
of New England Culture, 1606–1676* (Chapel Hill: University of North Carolina
Press, 2011); John M. Barry, *Roger Williams and the Creation of the American Soul*
(New York: Viking, 2012); Donna Merwick, *Stuyvesant Bound: An Essay on Loss
Across Time* (Philadelphia: University of Pennsylvania Press, 2013); Julie A. Fisher
and David J. Silverman, *Ninigret, Sachem of the Niantic and Narragansetts*
(Ithaca: Cornell University Press, 2014).
Tribal/Native Studies: Kathleen J. Bragdon, *Native People of Southern New
England, 1500–1650* (Norman: University of Oklahoma Press, 1996); O'Brien,
Dispossession by Degrees; John A. Strong, *The Montaukett Indians of Eastern Long
Island* (Syracuse: Syracuse University Press, 2001); Grumet, *The Munsee Indians, A
History* (Norman: University of Oklahoma Press, 2009); Strong, *The Unkechaug
Indians of Eastern Long Island* (Norman: University of Oklahoma Press, 2011).
Colonial Studies: Oliver Rink, *Holland on the Hudson: An Economic and Social
History of Dutch New York* (Ithaca: Cornell University Press, 1986); Russell Shorto,
*The Island at the Center of the World: The Epic Story of Dutch Manhattan and the
Forgotten Colony That Shaped America* (New York: Doubleday, 2004); Nathaniel
Philbrick, *Mayflower: A Story of Courage, Community, and War* (New York:
Penguin Books, 2006); James E. McWilliams, *Building the Bay Colony: Local
Economy and Culture in Early Massachusetts* (Charlottesville: University of
Virginia Press, 2007); Jaap Jacobs, *The Colony of New Netherland: A Dutch
Settlement in Seventeenth-Century America* (Ithaca: Cornell University Press,
2009).
Gender: Ann Marie Plane, *Colonial Intimacies: Indian Marriage in Early New
England* (Philadelphia: University of Pennsylvania Press, 2000); Ann M. Little,
Abraham in Arms: War and Gender in Colonial New England (Philadelphia:
University of Pennsylvania Press, 2006); Gunlög Fur, *A Nation of Women: Gender
and Colonial Encounters Among the Delaware Indians* (Philadelphia: University of
Pennsylvania Press, 2009); R. Todd Romero, *Making War and Minting Christians:
Masculinity, Religion, and Colonialism in Early New England* (Amherst:
University of Massachusetts Press, 2011).
Slavery/Captivity: Michael L. Fickes, " 'They Could Not Endure That Yoke': The
Captivity of Pequot Women and Children after the War of 1637," *NEQ* 73.1
(March 2000): 58–81; Margaret Ellen Newell, "The Changing Nature of Indian
Slavery in New England, 1670–1720," in *Reinterpreting New England Indians and
the Colonial Experience*, ed. Colin G. Calloway and Neal Salisbury (Boston:
Colonial Society of Massachusetts, 2003), 106–36; Thelma Wills Foote, *Black and
White Manhattan: The History of Racial Formation in New York City* (New York:
Oxford University Press, 2004), 3–52; Wendy Anne Warren, " 'The Cause of Her
Grief': The Rape of a Slave in Early New England," *JAH* 93.4 (2007): 1031–49;

Andrea Robertson Cremer, "Possession: Indian Bodies, Cultural Control, and Colonialism in the Pequot War," *EAS* 6.2 (2008): 295–345; Mac Griswold, *The Manor: Three Centuries at a Slave Plantation on Long Island* (New York: Farrar, Straus, and Giroux, 2013); Katherine Howlett Hayes, *Slavery Before Race: Europeans, Africans, and Indians at Long Island's Sylvester Manor Plantation, 1651–1884* (New York: New York University Press, 2013).

Religion/Conversion: David Silverman, *Faith and Boundaries: Colonists, Christianity, and Community Among the Wampanoag Indians of Martha's Vineyard, 1600–1871* (Cambridge: Cambridge University Press, 2005); Jessica R. Stern, "A Key into the Bloudy Tenent of Persecution: Roger Williams, the Pequot War, and the Origins of Toleration in America," *EAS* 9.3 (2011): 576–616; Sarah Rivett, *The Science of the Soul in Colonial New England* (Chapel Hill: University of North Carolina Press, 2011); Linford Fisher, *The Indian Great Awakening: Religion and the Shaping of Native Cultures in Early America* (New York: Oxford University Press, 2012); Evan Haefeli, *New Netherland: The Dutch Origins of American Religious Liberty* (Philadelphia: University of Pennsylvania Press, 2012); Edward E. Andrews, *Native Apostles: Black and Indian Missionaries in the British Atlantic World* (Cambridge: Harvard University Press, 2013).

Communication/Diplomacy: Allen W. Trelease, *Indian Affairs in Colonial New York: The Seventeenth Century* (Ithaca: Cornell University Press, 1960); Lois M. Feister, "Linguistic Communication Between the Dutch and Indians in New Netherland, 1609–1664," *Ethnohistory*, 20 (Winter 1973): 25–38; Van Zandt, *Brothers Among Nations*; Tom Arne Midtrød, *The Memory of All Ancient Customs: Native American Diplomacy in the Colonial Hudson Valley* (Ithaca: Cornell University Press, 2012); Katherine Grandjean, *American Passage: The Communications Frontier in Early New England* (Cambridge: Harvard University Press, 2015).

Trade/Networks: David Murray, *Indian Giving: Economies of Power in Indian–White Exchanges* (Amherst: University of Massachusetts Press, 2000); Alison Games, *The Web of Empire: English Cosmopolitans in an Age of Expansion* (New York: Oxford University Press, 2008); Christian Koot, *Empire at the Periphery: British Colonists, Anglo–Dutch Trade, and the Development of the English Atlantic, 1621–1713* (New York: New York University Press, 2011); Susanah Shaw Romney, *New Netherland Connections: Intimate Networks and Atlantic Ties in Seventeenth-Century America* (Chapel Hill: University of North Carolina Press, 2014).

Ecology/Environment: Cronon, *Changes in the Land*; Virginia DeJohn Anderson, *Creatures of Empire: How Domestic Animals Transformed Early America* (New York: Oxford University Press, 2004); Tom Andersen, *This Fine Piece of Water: An Environmental History of Long Island Sound* (New Haven: Yale University Press, 2002); Eric W. Sanderson, *Mannahatta: A Natural History of New York City*

(New York: Harry N. Abrams, 2009); Strother E. Roberts, "The Commodities of the Country: An Environmental Biography of the Colonial Connecticut Valley" (Ph.D. diss., Northwestern University, 2010); Christopher L. Pastore, *Between Land and Sea: The Atlantic Coast and the Transformation of New England* (Cambridge: Harvard University Press, 2014); Katherine A. Grandjean, "New World Tempests: Environment, Scarcity, and the Coming of the Pequot War," *WMQ* 68.1 (2011): 75–100.

20. William Wallace Tooker, *Indian Place Names on Long Island and Islands Adjacent With Their Probable Significance* (New York: J. Putnam's Sons, 1911), 49 (Connecticut), 232–33 (Sewanhacky).

21. On Dutch names, see Jacobs, *New Netherland*, 2–3. On the peculiar case of defining Narragansett Bay, see Pastore, *Between Land and Sea*, 82–129.

Chapter 1. The Giants' Shore

1. William S. Simmons, *Spirit of the New England Tribes: Indian History and Folklore* (Hanover, N.H.: University Press of New England, 1986), 172–234 (whale diet, pipe smoke and ash, Cape Cod and islands); anonymous letter, c. 1705, Curwen Family Papers, AAS (Hudson River). The latter source was correspondence regarding the recent discovery of the "Claverack Giant" in the Hudson Valley. See Amy Morris, "Geomythology on the Colonial Frontier: Edward Taylor, Cotton Mather, and the Claverack Giant," *WMQ* 70.4 (October 2013): 701–24.

2. Frank G. Speck, "Geographic Names and Legends at Mohegan," in *Languages and Lore of the Long Island Indians*, ed. Gaynell Stone Levine (Stony Brook, N.Y.: Suffolk County Archaeological Association, 1980), 249 (devil's footprint); Egbert Benson, *Memoir Read Before the Historical Society of the State of New-York* (Jamaica, N.Y.: Historical Society of the State of New-York, 1826), 71, 121–22 (stepping-stones, footprints); Gabriel Furman, *Antiquities of Long Island* [1824–28] (New York, 1878), 56–57 (stepping-stones, footprints); Simmons, *Spirit of the New England Tribes*, 172–234 (names); anonymous letter, c. 1680–1700, Curwen Family Papers, AAS ("Maughkampoe"); Simmons, "The Mystic Voice: Pequot Folklore from the Seventeenth Century to the Present," in *The Pequots in Southern New England: The Fall and Rise of an American Indian Nation*, ed. Laurence M. Hauptman and James D. Wherry (Norman, University of Oklahoma Press, 1990), 144; Roger Williams, *A Key Into the Language of America; Or, An help to the Language of the Natives in that part of America called New-England* (London, 1643; repr., Bedford, Mass.: Applewood Books, 1997), foreword, vii ("many strange," "Sonne of God"). This cultural hero may also have links to the "Wach que ow" figure that Munsee speakers mentioned in Charles Wolley, *A Two Years' Journal in New York: And Part of Its Territories in America* (1701), 36.

3. On the concept of manitou, see Neal Salisbury, *Manitou and Providence: Indians, Europeans, and the Making of New England, 1500–1643* (New York: Oxford University Press, 1982), 37–39; Kathleen J. Bragdon, *Native People of Southern New England, 1500–1650* (Norman: University of Oklahoma Press, 1996), 184–87; David J. Silverman, *Faith and Boundaries: Colonists, Christianity, and Community among the Wampanoag Indians of Martha's Vineyard, 1600–1871* (Cambridge: Cambridge University Press, 2005), 26–30; Julie A. Fisher and David J. Silverman, *Ninigret, Sachem of the Niantic and Narragansetts* (Ithaca: Cornell University Press, 2014), esp. 15 ("the threshold to the underworld"); Elizabeth Alden Little and J. Clinton Andrews, "Drift Whales at Nantucket: The Kindness of Moshup," in *Nantucket and Other Native Places: The Legacy of Elizabeth Alden Little*, ed. Elizabeth S. Chilton and Mary Lynne Rainey (repr. of 1982 article; Albany: State University of New York Press, 2010), 63–77.

4. Dorothy Sterling, *Outer Lands: A Natural History Guide to Cape Cod, Martha's Vineyard, Nantucket, Block Island, and Long Island* (New York: W. W. Norton, 1978), 9–20; Robert N. Oldale, "How Cape Cod and the Islands Were Formed," Greg O'Brien, "The Forces of Erosion," Donald J. Zinn, "The Seashore," in *A Guide to Nature on Cape Cod and the Islands*, ed. Greg O'Brien (New York: Viking Penguin, 1990), 15–34, 73–90, 29 (Nantucket lifespan); Andersen, *This Fine Piece of Water*, 16–22.

5. Sterling, *Outer Lands*, 9–20. In a recent overview of the history of vegetation in the region, Glenn Motzkin and David R. Foster see this moraine region as "characterized by a common geological and human history, environment, soils and biota" and cite eight other scientific studies that make the same assumption. Motzkin and Foster, "Grasslands, Heathlands and Shrublands in Coastal New England: Historical Interpretations and Approaches to Conservation," *Journal of Biogeography* 29 (October 2002): 1570.

6. William Wood, *Wood's New England's Prospect* (London, 1630; repr. New York: Burt Franklin, 1967), 103 ("every Countrey").

7. Anonymous letter, c. 1705, Curwen Family Papers, AAS ("the Indians for 100 miles about"); Isaack de Rasières to Samuel Blommaert, 1628, NNN, 113 ("tribes in their neighborhood"). De Rasières believed the Indians near Plymouth were more respectful of English law, and he noted Wampanoag boys endured a coming-of-age ritual that he had never observed among the Munsees; Bragdon, *Native People*, 29 (multilingualism in the region); on the Native geography of this shore, see the essays by Ives Goddard and Bert Salwen in Bruce Trigger, ed., *Handbook of North American Indians*, vol. 15: *Northeast* (Washington: Smithsonian Institution Press, 1978), 70–77, 214–15.

8. The demography of the Northeast is particularly tricky. Looking at the sustained coastal contact between fishermen and Natives, especially near the Maritimes in the sixteenth century, some anthropologists think depopulation from disease in the

region may have begun earlier than 1600, though mainly in areas north of Cape Cod. Shepard Krech III, *The Ecological Indian: Myth and History* (New York: W. W. Norton, 1999), 85. An older, higher-baseline population for this coastal region is argued for by Dean Snow, "Approaches to Cultural Adaptation in the Northeast," in *Foundations of Northeast Archaeology*, ed. Dean Snow (New York: Academic Press, 1981), 112. Kathleen J. Bragdon estimated that seventy-three thousand people lived in the "New England" portion of coast (c. sixty thousand for the Pokanokets/Wampanoags, Pawtuckets, Narragansetts, and Pequots/Mohegans [subtracting her numbers for the more northerly Massachusetts], plus thirteen thousand for the lower Connecticut and central Long Island peoples). That range of figures can then be added to Robert S. Grumet's midpoint estimate of fifteen thousand for the lower Hudson to arrive at a rounded estimate of ninety thousand. Bragdon, *Native People*, 25–26; Grumet, *The Munsee Indians, A History* (Norman: University of Oklahoma Press, 2009), 16.

9. Giovanni da Verrazzano, "Translation of the Cèllere Codex," Susan Tarrow, trans., in *The Voyages of Giovanni Da Verrazzano, 1524–1528*, ed. Lawrence C. Wroth, 138 ("densely populated"), 142 ("highly populated") (New Haven: Yale University Press, 1970); John Mason, *A Brief History of the Pequot War: Especially of the Memorable Taking of Their Fort at Mistick in Connecticut in 1637* (1736; repr. Lincoln: University of Nebraska Press, 2007), 21 ("so populous a Countrey"); Williams, *Key*, 3 ("shall come," density figure); WP 3:246 ("many wigwams" "great Citty").

10. On mobile settlement, see Bragdon, *Native Peoples*, 55–79; Anne-Marie Cantwell and Dianna diZerega Wall, *Unearthing Gotham: The Archaeology of New York City* (New Haven: Yale University Press, 2001), 110–13; on languages, see Ives Goddard, "The Ethnohistorical Implications of Early Delaware Linguistic Materials," in *Neighbors and Intruders: An Ethnohistorical Exploration of the Indians of Hudson's River*, ed. Laurence Hauptman and Jack Campisi (Ottawa: National Museums of Canada, 1978), 88–96; Goddard, "Eastern Algonquian Languages" and "Delaware" and Bert Salwen, "Indians of Southern New England and Long Island: Early Period," in Trigger, ed., *Handbook of North American Indians*, 15:70–77, 214–15.

11. Williams, *Key*, 11 ("invite all Strangers," "*aupúminea-nawsaùmp*"), 114 ("naturall liquor"); Wood, *New England's Prospect*, 79 ("quartered them"); Thomas Morton, *New English Canaan, or New Canaan containing an abstract of New England, composed in three bookes* (London, 1637; repr. Boston, 1883), 137 ("willing that"); Daniel Gookin, *Historical Collections of the Indians in New England* (orig. mss. 1674, repr. Boston: Massachusetts Historical Society, 1792), 153 ("strangers must be"), 150 ("frequently boil"); Adriaen van der Donck, *A Description of New Netherland*, Charles T. Gehring and William Starna, eds., Diederik Goedhuys, trans. (Lincoln: University of Nebraska Press, 2008), 77 ("one can hardly,"

"*sappaen*," "use among"), 78 ("fatty broth"); Johan De Laet, "Nieuwe Wereldt," *NNN*, 57 ("wooden dishes").

12. Williams, *Key*, 114 ("delight in"), 112 ("daintie dish," "for the goodness"), 113 (whale meat); De Rasières, *NNN*, 105–6 ("lascivious"); Van der Donck, *Description*, 77 ("all of them").

13. Wood, *New England's Prospect*, 75 ("dishing it up"); Van der Donck, *Description*, 77 ("have no pride"); Gookin, *Historical Collections*, 150 ("danger of"); "Cèllere Codex," *Voyages of Verrazzano*, 138 ("delicious flavor"); Gookin, *Historical Collections*, 150 ("so sweet"); Williams, *Key*, 11 ("very wholesome"); De Laet, *NNN*, 48 ("excellent eating"); De Rasières, *NNN*, 108 ("good bread"). Early Indian opinions of colonial food were more negative. Perhaps it was the lactose and gluten in the European dairy- and grain-heavy diet that made it "so contrary to their stomachs, that death or a desperate sicknesse immediately accrews." Wood, *New England's Prospect*, 71.

14. Algonquians' cornmeal porridge and fish are prime examples of what the anthropologist Stanley W. Mintz calls the "core complex carbohydrate and flavor-fringe supplement" dietary pattern common to nearly every crop-centered culture (9). As Mintz puts it, "What people eat expresses who and what they are, to themselves and to others. The congruence of dietary patterns and their societies reveals the way cultural forms are maintained by the ongoing activity of those who 'carry' such forms, whose behavior actualizes and incarnates them" (13). Mintz, *Sweetness and Power: The Place of Sugar in Modern History* (New York: Penguin Books, 1985). Lisa Brooks points out that the "common pot" of shared food was a powerful metaphor for Native people throughout the Northeast who were petitioning colonial and state governments, making pantribal alliances, and defending the traditional communal aspects of their economies against market incursions. For an overview, see Brooks, *The Common Pot: The Recovery of Native Space in the Northeast* (Minneapolis: University of Minnesota Press, 2008), 3–8.

15. Christopher L. Pastore, *Between Land and Sea: The Atlantic Coast and the Transformation of New England* (Cambridge: Harvard University Press, 2014), 22–27; Lucianne Lavin, quoted in Cantwell and Wall, *Unearthing Gotham*, 87 ("most productive").

16. Sterling, *Outer Lands*, 21–55; Rachel Carson, *The Edge of the Sea* (1955; repr. Boston: Houghton Mifflin, 1998), 9–39; John Teal and Mildred Teal, *Life and Death of the Salt Marsh* (Boston: Atlantic Monthly Press, 1969), 30–33; Cantwell and Wall, *Unearthing Gotham*, 86–88; Eric W. Sanderson, *Mannahatta: A Natural History of New York City* (New York: Harry N. Abrams, 2009), 136–69.

17. For a more extended analysis of how European writers commodified the shore and land, see William Cronon, *Changes in the Land: Indians, Colonists, and the Ecology of New England* (New York: Hill and Wang, 1983), esp. 19–26; John Smith, *A Description of New England, or the observations, and discoveries, of*

Captain Iohn Smith (Admirall of that Country) in the North of America, in the year of our Lord 1614 (London, 1616), 30 ("their store in the Sea"), 8 ("because I speake"); Wood, *New England's Prospect,* 35 ("There is no countrey"); Nicolaes van Wassenaer, "Historisch Verhael" (1624–30), *NNN,* 81 ("sea fish"); John Brereton, *A Briefe and true Relation of the Discoverie of the North Part of Virginia* (1602; repr., Ann Arbor, 1966), 4–5 (cod, Cape Cod, whales); Francis Higginson, *New-Englands Plantation, or A Short and True Description of the Commodities and Discommodities of that Countrey* (London, 1680), 6 ("The aboundance of Sea-Fish").

18. Wood, *New England's Prospect,* 38 ("Clammes"); Van der Donck, *Description,* 59–60 (oysters, lobsters), 162n106; Ann Griswold to John Winthrop Jr., July 8, 1673, Winthrop Family Papers, MHS ("the Indians think"); Cantwell and Wall, *Unearthing Gotham,* 52–58; Bragdon, *Native People,* 62–63 (Nantucket study), 110–12, 116–17; for a sense of how fishing shaped place naming, see William Wallace Tooker, *Some Indian Fishing Stations Upon Long Island* (New York: Francis P. Harper, 1901).

19. Christopher Levett, "A Voyage into New England" (1628), in *Christopher Levett of York,* ed. James Phinney Baxter (Portland, Me.: Gorges Society, 1893) 119–20 ("leape into the kettle"); Williams, *Key,* 111–17 (fish weirs, spearing, ice fishing); De Rasières, *NNN,* 105 ("wild hemp," "drag-net"); Wood, *New England's Prospect,* 39 (lobster bait); David Pietersz. de Vries, "Korte Historiael Ende Journales Aenteyckninge," *NNN,* 222 ("seventy to eighty fathoms").

20. De Vries, *NNN,* 222–23 ("over the purse" . . . "when the fish swim"); Williams, *Key,* 116 ("Natives take exceeding great paines"), 113 ("in the Sunne"); Wood, *New England's Prospect,* 100 ("very expert" . . . "fitting sundry baites").

21. Wood, *New England's Prospect,* 77 ("who trudge"), 107 ("two or three miles"); Bragdon, *Native People,* 110–12; Robert L. Edwards and K. O. Emery, "Man on the Continental Shelf," and David P. Braun, "Explanatory Models for the Evolution of Coastal Adaptation in Prehistoric Eastern New England," in *The Second Coastal Archaeology Reader: 1900 to the Present,* ed. James E. Truex (Stony Brook, N.Y.: Suffolk County Archaeological Association, 1982), 12–21, 22–34, respectively.

22. For a sweeping summary of this "agricultural revolution" in North America, see Daniel K. Richter, *Before the Revolution: America's Ancient Pasts* (Cambridge: Belknap Press of Harvard University Press, 2011), 12–15.

23. Archaeologists disagree about when the adoption of corn–beans–squash farming along this coast happened, as some argue its adoption across the region was highly spotty, perhaps even in response to contact and trade. That said, the documentary and archaeological records both concur that maize was a presence (the unresolved question being just how significant a presence) on the coast before colonists, and that all coastal peoples had mixed economies that relied heavily on hunting, fishing, and foraging. More recent finds, especially in the Narragansett territory,

have bolstered the assumption that corn was a major part of the coastal Native diet before contact, a fact that most Native oral traditions have long insisted upon. This debate is laid out in Lynn Ceci, "The Effect of European Contact in Coastal New York" (Ph.D. diss., City University of New York, 1977); Bragdon, *Native People*, 80–91; Cantwell and Wall, *Unearthing Gotham*, 110–13; Elizabeth Chilton, "The Origins and Spread of Maize (*Zea mays*) in New England," in *Histories of Maize: Multidisciplinary Approaches to the Prehistory, Linguistics, Biogeography, Domestication, and Evolution of Maize*, ed. John E. Staller, Robert H. Tykot, and Bruce F. Benz, 539–48 (Burlington, Mass.: Academic Press, 2006); Van der Donck, *Description*, 4 ("beans and corn" . . . "before they knew"); Williams, *Key*, 90 ("tradition that the Crow"); a Munsee speaker near Manhattan told a nearly identical story some sixty years later, "that their Corn was at first dropt out of the mouth of a Crow from the Skies." See Wolley, *Two Years' Journal in New York*, 22.

24. William S. Simmons, *Cautantowwit's House: An Indian Burial Ground on the Island of Conanicut in Narragansett Bay* (Providence: Brown University Press, 1970), 50–62 (southwest, grave sites, reverence of crows); Bragdon, *Native Peoples*, 189–99, 233–36 (southwest); Wood, *New England's Prospect*, 104 ("a kind of paradise" . . . "odiferous gardens" . . . "cool streams"); Van der Donck, *Description*, 109 ("one never needs"); De Vries, *NNN*, 224 ("when they die"); Williams, *Key*, 89–90 (crows, killing taboo).

25. De Rasières, *NNN*, 107 ("heaps like molehills"); Williams, *Key*, 99 ("natural howes"); Morton, *New English Canaan*, 42 ("barnes," "greate baskets"); Wood, *New England's Prospect*, 106 ("rinds of trees"); Van der Donck, *Description*, 98 ("corn and green beans," "regard their methods").

26. Edward Winslow, *Good Newes from New-England* (London, 1624; repr. Bedford, Mass.: Applewood Books, 1996), 63 ("The women live a most slavish life"); De Vries, *NNN*, 218 ("compelled to work like asses"); Williams, *Key*, 149 ("above the labour of men," "mighty Burthens"); Daniel Denton, *Description of New-York*, 12 ("their Wives being the Husbandmen"). Kathleen M. Brown unpacks the complexities of this colonial discourse in the "gender frontier" created when Powhatan peoples and English colonists first encountered each other in the Chesapeake Bay region. See *Good Wives, Nasty Wenches, and Anxious Patriarchs: Gender, Race, and Power in Colonial Virginia* (Chapel Hill: University of North Carolina Press, 1996), 42–74. Bragdon lays out this case for Algonquian male dominance rather convincingly in *Native Peoples*, 49–52, 175–83; for concurring analyses, see also Ann Marie Plane, *Colonial Intimacies: Indian Marriage in Early New England* (Philadelphia: University of Pennsylvania Press, 2000), 13–40 (esp. 20–22); Rubertone, *Grave Undertakings*, 152–58; Ann M. Little, *Abraham in Arms: War and Gender in Colonial New England* (Philadelphia: University of Pennsylvania Press, 2006), 13–14; De Rasières, *NNN*, 108 ("thrashes her soundly"); Williams, *Key*, 147 ("before many witnesses"), 146–47 (elite polygamy); Gookin,

Historical Collections, 149 (elite polygamy); Van der Donck, *Description*, 84 (elite polygamy), 85–86 (adultery).

27. Bragdon, *Native Peoples*, 89 (wrist wear); Rubertone, *Grave Undertakings*, 153 (wrist and joint wear, tooth decay, "habitual kneeling"), 155 (tools).

28. Gookin, *Historical Collections*, 149 ("women also leave their husbands"); De Vries, *NNN*, 218 (sexual freedom); Williams, *Key*, 150 (divorce), 99 ("very loving . . . all neighbors . . . joyne," "unless . . . either out of love"); Winslow, *Good Newes*, 64 ("If a woman have a bad husband," "where [women] come"); Van der Donck, *Description*, 84–86 (divorce), 97 ("unless they are"), 98 ("help the women," "under the latter").

29. Van der Donck, *Description*, 21 ("extraordinary and spectacular" . . . "when one sails"); Cronon, *Changes in the Land*, 49–52; Krech, *The Ecological Indian*, 101–10.

30. Williams, *Key*, 118 ("a little Apron," "secret parts"), 118–22 (mantles, stockings, moccasins, turkey coats, tobacco bags), 171 ("general and wonderfull"), 171–77 (hunting details); Wood, *New England's Prospect*, 98–99 (hunting, traps), 108 (moccasins, turkey coats); De Vries, *NNN*, 217 (mantles, turkey coats), 220 (corrals, canoe hunting); Wolley, *Two Years' Journal in New York*, 15 (insulator, repellant, sunblock), 16 ("Adam's Apron"); Van der Donck, *Description*, 78–79 (mantles, whalebone, wampum), 79, 163n8 (*clootlap*); De Rasières, *NNN*, 106 ("smear their bodies," "smell very rankly").

31. Cronon, *Changes in the Land*, 42–49; Bragdon, *Native People*, 102–29.

32. De Rasières, *NNN*, 108 ("reckon consanguinity"); John Davenport, 1649, quoted in Bragdon, *Native Peoples*, 156 ("are carefull to preserve"); Bragdon, *Native People*, 135–36 (language and "intimate possession"), 161–68 (kinship as ideology); see also David J. Costa, "The Dialectology of Southern New England Algonquian" in *The Papers of the 38th Algonquian Conference*, ed. H. C. Wolfart (Winnipeg: University of Manitoba Press, 2007), 81–127.

33. Williams, *Key*, 28–29 ("they hold"), 132 ("similitudes"); Lion Gardiner, "Leift. Gardener his relations of the Pequot Warres," *MHSC*, 3d ser., 3:154 ("calling them bretheren"); on "brothers," see also Strong, *Unkechaug Indians*, 12–13; Bragdon, *Native Peoples*, 156–68 (eastern peoples kinship); Grumet, *Munsee Indians*, 17–23 (western peoples kinship); Cynthia Van Zandt explores this theme fruitfully in *Brothers Among Nations: The Pursuit of Intercultural Alliances in Early America* (New York: Oxford University Press, 2008), esp. 65–85.

34. Bragdon, *Native People*, 169–75; Van der Donck, *Description*, 100 ("Indians recognize some as noble born," "the oldest and foremost," "social differences," "the lowliest person," "the commoners"); Matthew Mayhew, "A Brief Narrative of the Success Which the Gospel Had Among the Indians of Martha's Vineyard," *MHSC*, 2d ser. 119:8–9 ("whose descent . . . yeoman"); Williams, *Key*, 1 ("two sorts").

35. Wood, *New England's Prospect*, 91 ("may have two or three," "Men of ordinary Rank"); see also Williams, *Key*, 146–47 (elite polygamy), 185 ("a special guard");

Gookin, *Historical Collections*, 149 (elite polygamy); Van der Donck, *Description*, 84 (elite polygamy); anonymous, "Journal of New Netherland, 1647," *NNN*, 271 (elite polygamy); Wolley, *Two Years' Journal in New York*, 23 ("Attendants"); Denton, *Description of New-York*, 12 ("a Company of Armed men").

36. Salisbury, *Manitou and Providence*, 37–49; Bragdon, *Native People*, 130–39, 140–55, 200–208; Williams, *Key*, 127 ("doe begin and order their service"), 180 (long house). For an overview of the long theoretical debate over the role of the gift in nonstate societies from Marcel Mauss to Marshall Sahlins and its relevance to Indian and colonial exchanges in early America, see David Murray, *Indian Giving: Economies of Power in Indian–White Exchanges* (Amherst: University of Massachusetts Press, 2000) 15–47.

37. Winslow, *Good Newes*, 13 ("chiefest champion," "without the advice"); Van der Donck, *Description*, 104 ("points being made"), 105 ("gifted with eloquence," "they consider"); Williams, *Key*, 57–58 (speeches, sticks); De Vries, *NNN*, 230 ("bundle of sticks"), 231 ("this laying down").

38. Williams, *Key*, 136 ("feared Mutiny" . . . "a secret Executioner"); Van der Donck, *Description*, 106 (execution), 102 ("amazed that a human society"); De Vries, *NNN*, 217 ("very revengeful"); Patrick M. Malone, *The Skulking Way of War: Technology and Tactics among the New England Indians* (Baltimore: Johns Hopkins University Press, 1993), 9–11; Bragdon, *Native People*, 148–50, 226.

39. Williams, *Key*, 183 ("*Chépewess & Mishittâshin*," "Northerne storm of war"), 85 (*Chepewessin*), 87 (*Mishittâshin*); William Bradford, *Of Plymouth Plantation, 1620–1647*, Samuel Eliot Morison, ed. (New York: Alfred A. Knopf, 1952), 279–80 (hurricane in 1635).

40. Adam J. Hirsch, "The Collision of Military Cultures in Seventeenth-Century New England," *JAH* 74 (March 1988): 1190–92; Malone, *Skulking Way of War*, 9–11; Bragdon, *Native People*, 148–50, 226; for an instance of torture from the Pequot War, see Underhill, *Newes from America*, 20.

41. Underhill, *Newes from America*, 36 ("they might fight"); Denton, *A Brief Description of New-York*, 14 ("it is a great fight"); Williams, *Key*, 50–51 ("their arrow sticks"); Wood, *New England's Prospect*, 95 ("returne [as] conquerours").

42. Williams, *Key*, 50–51 (Timequassin); Simmons, *Cautantowwit's House*, 54–55 ("free," "Southwest"); James Axtell and William C. Sturtevant, "The Unkindest Cut, or Who Invented Scalping?" *WMQ* 37.3 (July 1980): 462–63, 465, 469n52 ("head-skin," 461–62); William Hubbard, *The History of the Indian Wars in New England from the First Settlement to the Termination of the War with King Philip, in 1677*, 2 vols., Samuel G. Drake, ed. (1865; repr., New York: Kaus Reprint, 1969), 2:206 ("when it is too far"). Among scholars who study the origins of Indian dismemberment, Simmons discusses only heads, whereas Axtell suggests that among Indians who favored scalps over heads, the "scalplock" (the tuft of decorated hair that Indian men styled to represent their tribal identities) also

"represented the person's 'soul' or living spirit" (Axtell, "Moral Dilemmas of Scalping," 262). See also Simmons, *Cautantowwit's House*, 52, 54–55; Bragdon, *Native People*, 190–91. The headless woman found by archaeologists is known as Burial 13 and was probably a Narragansett woman more than thirty years old at the time of death. According to Simmons, "her missing skull could not be attributed to modern pot hunters, for the grave had not been disturbed. The woman could only have been beheaded before burial." The objects in her grave and the ones around her date to the postcontact seventeenth century (but not to a particular decade). See Simmons, *Cautantowwit's House*, 102 (quotation), 105–6. For a discussion of Indians' preference for whole heads, see Hubbard, *History of the Indian Wars*, 1:63; Jill Lepore, *The Name of War: King Philip's War and the Origins of American Identity* (New York: Vintage, 1998), 303n103.

43. Williams, *Key*, 51 ("in a trice fetcht off"); Wood, *New England's Prospect*, 95 ("bear home," "true tokens").

44. Anonymous, *MHSC*, 3d ser., 3:164 ("meanes to knitt").

45. Wampum's role in bereavement became more central throughout the Native Northeast only over the colonial period: see Bragdon, *Native People*, 179–81; Daniel K. Richter, *The Ordeal of the Longhouse: The Peoples of the Iroquois League in the Era of European Colonization* (Chapel Hill: University of North Carolina Press, 1992), 32, 276–77; Erik R. Seeman, *Death in the New World: Cross-Cultural Encounters, 1491–1800* (Philadelphia: University of Pennsylvania Press, 2010), 283–88; De Vries, *NNN*, 232 ("constantly wishing . . . as one had lost").

46. Winslow, *Good Newes*, 36 ("brake forth" . . . "My loving Sachem"); Western Niantic or River Indian Petition, c. 1672, Samuel Wyllys Papers, JHL ("we tock him in our bosom . . . we are abused by him").

47. For further thoughts on reading the actions of sachems as reflections on the needs of larger Native communities, see Fisher and Silverman, *Ninigret*, vii–xii, 14–21.

48. Van Wassenaer, *NNN*, 69 ("little authority"); De Laet, *NNN*, 57 ("no government"); anonymous, "Journal of New Netherland," *NNN*, 271 ("not much authority"); De Rasières, *NNN*, 109 ("democratic"); Van der Donck, *Description*, 105 ("public policy in the proper sense" . . . "popular kind"); Gookin, *Historical Collections*, 154 ("mixed"); Mayhew, "A Brief Narrative," *MHSC*, 2d ser., 109:7 ("purely monarchical"); Williams, *Key*, 141 ("that concernes all . . .").

49. For an overview of the contrast between English and Algonquian notions of authority, see Salisbury, *Manitou and Providence*, 37–49; Bragdon, *Native People*, 44–49, 130–39, 140–55; Jenny Hale Pulsipher, *Subjects unto the Same King: Indians, English, and the Contest for Authority in Colonial New England* (Philadelphia: University of Pennsylvania Press, 2005), 1–36; on the Dutch and Munsee, see Evan Haefeli, "Kieft's War and the Cultures of Violence in Colonial America," in *Lethal Imagination: Violence and Brutality in American History*, ed. Michael A. Bellesiles (New York: New York University Press, 1999), 17–40. Some

historians and anthropologists suggest that wampum trade largely created the
coastal tributary networks headed by Tatobem, Canonicus, and Massasoit, but the
multiple sources note that these were sizable powers before the wampum
revolution. Furthermore, the complete lack of any such changes toward the Dutch
or even mild consolidation of power by any coastal sachem west of the Pequots
hints that the regional divide in political cultures existed before the colonial trade
intensified it. The underlying geology and ecology seem relevant to any theory of
why this distinction existed. Communities along the fertile Connecticut and
Hudson valleys had good soil for growing corn and ample woodlands to support a
game population. Peoples on western Long Island, Manhattan, and Staten Island
were closer to the mainland and lived on soil that was not as quite as good as
riverine plains but better than that on the far eastern end of Long Island—their
crop harvests were more secure and their game populations were not as isolated
and thus less vulnerable to overhunting and disease. The local self-sufficiency of
Munsee and Quiripi-Unkechaug peoples to the west would inhibit the forming of
enduring patterns of debts or animosity between nearby communities, thereby
eliminating any basic economic or strategic need for larger confederacies.
Meanwhile, the outlying Mohegan–Pequot, Narragansett, and Wampanoag
peoples along the eastern side of the shore lived on much poorer, sandy soil made
up of glacial till, making them more susceptible to droughts and poor harvests.
Living on islands and peninsulas also made them more vulnerable to Atlantic
hurricanes and overkills of game, suggesting why a small cohort of mainland
sachems, all living along the best estuaries in the region, would be able to build
the loose but real networks of alliance with the peoples on the outer lands that
predated the colonial intrusion. Atlantic hurricanes were also typically less
devastating on the western part of the course, since their southwest-to-east courses
feeding on warmer Gulf Stream waters typically cause them to glance off the
southern mass of Cape Hatteras, effectively shielding the inner part of the coast:
the two recent powerful tropical systems to hit the western side of shore, Irene in
2011 and Sandy in 2012, were notable for their rare east-to-west-curving paths. On
the differences in regional geography, see Cronon, *Changes in the Land*, 29–31;
O'Brien, ed., *A Guide to Nature on Cape Cod*, 74–75; Motzkin and Foster,
"Grasslands, Heathlands and Shrublands in Coastal New England," 1569–90;
Sanderson, *Mannahatta*, 70–72. For a full overview of historic tracks of tropical
systems, the National Oceanic and Atmospheric Administration has a handy
mapping tool online at http://csc.noaa.gov/hurricanes/.
50. William Bradford and Edward Winslow, *A Relation or Journall of the Beginning
and Proceedings of the English Plantation Setled at Plimoth in New England*
(London, 1622; repr., Southport, Conn.: Trustees of the Pequot Library, 1967), 68
("circuits," "Imperial Governour") (hereafter cited as *Mourt's Relation*); Gookin,
Historical Collections, 147–48 ("dominion over divers"); Pulsipher, *Subjects unto*

the Same King, 1–36; John H. Elliott, "A Europe of Composite Monarchies," *Past and Present*, no. 137 (1992), 48–71.

51. "Translation of the Cèllere Codex," in Wroth, ed., *Voyages of Giovanni Da Verrazzano*, 135–36. On the size and significance of these eastern groups before the wampum boom, see also Bradford and Winslow, *Mourt's Relation*, 68 ("larger than"); Winslow, *Good Newes*, 13, 36; Bragdon, *Native People*, 80–102.

52. *Munsee* and the even larger ethnonym *Delaware* would be used by Indians only a century later when many local names had been abandoned; no such clear regional identity existed before colonists. Goddard, "The Ethnohistorical Implications," and Campisi, "Hudson Valley Indians," in Hauptman and Campisi, eds., *Neighbors and Intruders*, 88–96, 171–72, respectively; Grumet, *Munsee Indians*, 3–5.

53. Tom Arne Midtrød, *The Memory of All Ancient Customs: Native American Diplomacy in the Colonial Hudson Valley* (Ithaca: Cornell University Press, 2012), 2–15; Grumet, *Munsee Indians*, 8–23, 8 ("independent-minded"); Strong, *Unkechaug Indians*, 10–15; De Vries, *NNN*, 230 ("asked them"); De Laet, *NNN*, 45 (Manhattans and Sinisinks). Some of the westerly Connecticut-area Indians and central Long Islanders were, at least in the colonial period, occasional tributaries of the Pequots and Mohegans, although those links seemed to be formed mainly by opportunistic raids. See Gookin, *Historical Collections*, 147.

54. For a particularly compelling overview of similarities and contrasts between Europe and America in the late Middle Ages, see Richter, *Before the Revolution*, 11–66, who also experiments with trying to describe Natives and Europeans in similar ways. See also Keith Thomas, *Religion and the Decline of Magic* (1971; repr. New York: Penguin, 1973); Maurice Keen, ed., *Medieval Warfare: A History* (New York: Oxford University Press, 1999); John Laurence, *A History of Capital Punishment*, 3d ed. (New York: Citadel Press, 1960).

55. For a sweeping overview of the rise of larger cities and towns across Europe, see Fernand Braudel, *Capitalism and Material Life, 1400–1800* (New York: Harper and Row, 1975), esp. 373–440 (on towns).

56. On this early stage, see Karen Ordahl Kupperman, *The Jamestown Project* (Cambridge: Harvard University Press, 2007), 12–72; Jonathan Israel, *The Dutch Republic: Its Rise, Greatness, and Fall, 1477–1806* (New York: Oxford University Press, 1995), 307–18.

57. Kenneth Harold Dobson Haley, *The Dutch in the Seventeenth Century* (New York: Harcourt Brace Jovanovich, 1972), 66–68; Israel, *The Dutch Republic*, 276–306.

58. For cultural analysis of this transition and its role in both the Dutch revolt and the English Civil War, see Peter J. Arnade, *Beggars, Iconoclasts, and Civic Patriots: The Political Culture of the Dutch Revolt* (Ithaca: Cornell University Press, 2008); Maarten Roy Prak, *The Dutch Republic in the Seventeenth Century: The Golden Age* (Cambridge: Cambridge University Press, 2005), 75–110; Jacqueline Eales and

Christopher Dunston, eds., *The Culture of English Puritanism, 1560–1700* (New York: St. Martin's Press, 1996).

59. On the English, see J. H. Parry, "Introduction: The English in the New World," and Carole Shammas, "English Commercial Development and American Colonization," in *The Westward Enterprise: English Activities in Ireland, the Atlantic, and America, 1480–1650*, ed. Kenneth R. Andrews (Detroit: Wayne State University Press, 1979), 1–16, 151–62; Kupperman, *The Jamestown Project*, 12–72; Alison Games, *The Web of Empire: English Cosmopolitans in an Age of Expansion* (New York: Oxford University Press), 47–116. On the Dutch, see Prak, *The Dutch Republic in the Seventeenth Century*, 75–110; Jaap Jacobs, *The Colony of New Netherland: A Dutch Settlement in Seventeenth-Century America* (Ithaca: Cornell University Press, 2009).

60. Van der Donck, *Description*, 3 ("They knew not"). For further instructive analysis of the genre of first contact stories, see Simmons, *Spirit of the New England Tribes*, 65–72; Daniel K. Richter, *Facing East from Indian Country* (Cambridge: Harvard University Press, 2001), 11–40; Paul Otto, 'The Origins of New Netherland: Interpreting Native American Responses to Henry Hudson's Visit," *Itinerario* 18.2 (July 1994): 22–39; Evan Haefeli, "On First Contact and Apotheosis: Manitou and Men in North America," *Ethnohistory* 54.3 (Summer 2007): 407–43; Annette Kolodny, *In Search of First Contact: The Vikings of Vinland, the Peoples of the Dawnland, and the Anglo-American Anxiety of Discovery* (Durham: Duke University Press, 2012), 280–326.

61. Wood, *New England's Prospect*, 87 ("they tooke the first ship"); Ezra Stiles, *Extracts from the Itineraries and Other Miscellanies of Ezra Stiles, D.D., LL.D. 1754–1794, With a Selection from His Correspondence* (New Haven: Yale University Press, 1916), 83 ("said at first it was Weetucks"). On the interpretation of strawberries, see Christopher L. Miller and George R. Hamill, "A New Perspective on Indian–White Contact: Cultural Symbols and Colonial Trade," *JAH* 73(1986): 321–22.

62. Van der Donck, *Description*, 3–4 ("they did not know," "strange reports"). For examples of the wide range of artifacts imported and exported from this coast before colonization, see Charles Willoughby, *Antiquities of the New England Indians* (Cambridge, Mass.: Peabody Museum, 1935), 92–112; James Tuck, "Regional Cultural Development, 3000 to 300 B.C.," in Trigger, ed., *Handbook*, 15:28–43; Cantwell and Wall, *Unearthing Gotham*, 109–16; Bragdon, *Native Peoples*, 91–92; Grumet, *Munsee Indians*, 9 ("as Japanese"), 9–12.

63. Williams, *Key*, 4 ("hardly are they brought to believe").

64. This idea is most fruitfully explored by J. H. Elliott in his chapter "America as Sacred Space," in *Empires of the Atlantic World: Britain and Spain in America, 1492–1830* (New Haven: Yale University Press, 2005), 184–218; see also Karen Ordahl Kupperman, ed., *America in European Consciousness, 1493–1750* (Chapel

Hill: University of North Carolina Press, 1995); J. H. Parry, *The Discovery of the Sea* (Berkeley: University of California Press, 1981).

Chapter 2. Watercraft and Watermen

1. Giovanni da Verrazzano, "Translation of the Cèllere Codex," Susan Tarrow, trans., in Lawrence C. Wroth, ed., *The Voyages of Giovanni da Verrazzano* (New Haven: Yale University Press, 1970), 137–39 ("innumerable," "boats," "with only," "go to sea"). Verrazzano explicitly noted that the boats he saw were made from "a single log" and carried ten to fifteen men, making them on average around twenty to thirty feet in length; Roger Williams, *A Key Into the Language of America; Or, An help to the Language of the Natives in that part of America called New-England* . . . (London, 1643; repr., Bedford, Mass.: Applewood Books, 1997), 107 ("twenty, thirty, forty men"); John Winthrop, *The History of New England from 1630 to 1649*, 2 vols., James Savage, ed. (1825; repr. New York: Arno Press, 1972), 1:112 (eighty-person canoe).

2. Some colonial sea-crossing craft discussed in this chapter, such as the bark *Sparrow-Hawk*, were shorter than thirty feet and could hold not more than two dozen people. See Williams, *Key*, 108 (*sepâkehig*, "their owne reason"); John Underhill, *Newes from America; or, A New and Experimentall Discoverie of New England* . . . (1638; repr., Lincoln: University of Nebraska Press, 2007), 16 ("poles").

3. Scholars who do take a close look at Native nautical technology include Horace P. Beck, *The American Indian as a Sea-Fighter in Colonial Times* (Mystic, Conn.: Greenwood Press, 1959); Joyce Chaplin, *Subject Matter: Technology, the Body, and Science on the Anglo-American Frontier* (Cambridge: Harvard University Press, 2001), 208, 213–14; Susanah Shaw Romney, *New Netherland Connections: Intimate Networks and Atlantic Ties in Seventeenth-Century America* (Chapel Hill: University of North Carolina Press, 2014), 148–49; Christopher L. Pastore, *Between Land and Sea: The Atlantic Coast and the Transformation of New England* (Cambridge: Harvard University Press, 2014), 98–100; Katherine Grandjean, *American Passage: The Communications Frontier in Early New England* (Cambridge: Harvard University Press, 2015), esp. 23–34. Works that overlook indigenous maritime culture include Howard Zinn, *A People's History of the United States*, 5th ed. (New York: Harper Collins, 2005), 1 ("naked"), 18 ("peered"); Jenny Hale Pulsipher, *Subjects unto the Same King: Indians, English, and the Contest for Authority in Colonial New England* (Philadelphia: University of Pennsylvania Press, 2005), 1 (bark/dugout conflation, "skirt the coast"). While noting the bark/dugout distinction, Karen Kupperman claims that the rumored eighty-passenger canoe was made of bark. See Kupperman, *Indians and English: Facing Off in Early America* (Ithaca: Cornell University Press, 2000), 166. Ann M. Little interprets an incident in which Pequots used English garments as sails as the

symbolic "mockery" of colonial clothing and not as the practical act of mariners looking for propulsion. The poles used to mount the clothes were a standard feature on Indian great canoes, intended for sailing and not just "making a show of items captured." See Little, " 'Shoot That Rogue, For He Hath an Englishman's Coat On!': Cultural Cross-Dressing on the New England Frontier, 1620–1760," *NEQ* 75 (June 2001): 264.

4. Richard Hakluyt, "Inducements to the liking of the voyage intended towards Virginia in 40. and 42. degrees of latitude, written 1585," in John Brereton, *A Briefe and true Relation of the Discoverie of the North Part of Virginia* (1602; repr., Ann Arbor, 1966), 27 ("lords of navigation"); Thomas Morton, *New English Canaan; or, New Canaan containing an abstract of New England, composed in three bookes* (London, 1637), 40 ("have not the use"), 55. On "common" and "grand" navigation, see J. H. Parry, *The Age of Reconnaissance* (Berkeley: University of California Press, 1963), 83–84. The term *wayfinding*, first used to describe indigenous navigation techniques in the Pacific, has since become a popular term for geographers, cognitive scientists, urban planners, and architects interested in intuitive and vernacular methods of spatial exploration. See David Lewis, *We, the Navigators: The Ancient Art of Landfinding in the Pacific* (Honolulu: University of Hawai'i Press, 1995); Reginald G. Golledge, "Human Wayfinding and Cognitive Maps," in *Wayfinding Behavior: Cognitive Mapping and Other Spatial Processes*, ed. Reginald G. Golledge (Baltimore: Johns Hopkins University Press, 1999), 5–45; Cynthia Van Zandt argues that historians need to see navigation and mapmaking in early America as an intercultural activity, *Brothers Among Nations: The Pursuit of Intercultural Alliances in Early America* (New York: Oxford University Press, 2008), 20–21.

5. Verrazzano, *Voyages*, 137 ("little light boat"); Martin Pring, "A Voyage set out from the Citie of Bristoll," in *Sailors' Narratives of Voyages Along the New England Coast, 1524–1624*, ed. George Parker Winship (Boston: Houghton Mifflin, 1905), 57 ("seeme to bee"); Robert Juet, "Third Voyage of Henry Hudson," NNN, 22 ("sate so modestly"); Christopher Levett, "A Voyage into New England" (1628), in *Christopher Levett of York*, ed. James Phinney Baxter (Portland, Me.: Gorges Society, 1893), 117 ("they call all Masters"); Brereton, *A Briefe and true Relation*, 8–9 ("lord or captain").

6. J. H. Parry, *The Discovery of the Sea* (Berkeley: University of California Press, 1981), 7–13; Parry, *Age of Reconnaissance*, 53–68; Robert Gardiner and Richard W. Unger, *Cogs, Caravels, and Galleons: The Sailing Ship, 1000–1650* (Annapolis: Naval Institute Press, 1994); Kees Zandvliet, *Mapping for Money: Maps, Plans and Topographic Paintings and Their Role in Dutch Overseas Expansion during the 16th and 17th Centuries* (Amsterdam: Batavian Lion International, 1998), 34–37.

7. On the low status and bad manners of sailors, see Jaap Jacobs, *The Colony of New Netherland: A Dutch Settlement in Seventeenth-Century America* (Ithaca: Cornell

University Press, 2009), 40–41; Bernard Bailyn, *New England Merchants in the Seventeenth Century* (New York: Harper and Row, 1955), 2–3; William Bradford, *Of Plymouth Plantation, 1620–1647*, Samuel Eliot Morison, ed. (New York: Alfred A. Knopf, 1952), 111, 58, 146 ("the master . . . his example").

8. William H. Thiesen, "Ship Construction," *Oxford Encyclopedia of Maritime History*, John Hattendorf, ed. (Oxford: Oxford University Press, 2007); Parry, *Age of Reconnaissance*, 60–66; Parry, *Discovery of the Sea*, 7–13; William Baker, *The Mayflower and Other Colonial Vessels* (Annapolis: Naval Institute Press, 1983), 1–7. In addition, my understanding of seventeenth-century European vessels draws from an informative tour of the replica of the Dutch-built, Swedish-run pinnace *Kalmar Nyckel* (1637) out of Wilmington, Delaware, and an extensive interview with Capt. Lauren Morgens on April 5, 2009.

9. Parry, *Age of Reconnaissance*, 60–66; Parry, *Discovery of the Sea*, 7–13; Baker, *Mayflower*.

10. Thomas Dermer to Samuel Purchase, 1619, *Sailors' Narratives*, 255 ("many crooked," "a most dangerous Catwract"); Verrazzano, *Voyages*, 136 ("as often happens"); Charles Wolley, *A Two Years' Journal in New York: And Part of Its Territories in America* (1701, digital repr. Lincoln: University of Nebraska, 2009), 33 ("a rapid violent Stream"); Johan De Laet, "Nieuwe Wereldt," *NNN*, 44n2 (Hellegat).

11. Samuel Argall, "Voyage to Penobscot Bay," *Sailors' Narratives*, 208 ("a very dangerous place"); Isaack de Rasières to Samuel Blommaert, 1628, *NNN*, 110 ("afraid to pass"); Bradford, *Of Plymouth Plantation*, 193 ("dangerous shoals"), 154 (Point Care, Tuckers Terrour). On the early European fishing and its impact on Indians north of Cape Cod, see Neal Salisbury, *Manitou and Providence: Indians, Europeans, and the Making of New England, 1500–1643* (New York: Oxford University Press, 1982), 53–60.

12. Brereton, *A Briefe and true Relation*, 3 ("our barke being weake"); Jasper Danckaerts, *Journal of Jasper Danckaerts, 1679–1680*, Bartlett Burleigh James and J. Franklin Jameson, eds. (New York: Scribners, 1913), 41 ("disorderly," "wretched"). Danckaerts, an obviously finicky fellow, was not the only person with a low opinion of his ship's crew: once arrived in New York, he met a captain who "said he recollected to have seen us" at sea, "but observing us tacking several times, he did not dare follow us, for fear of being misled" (48). *DRCHNY*, 1:11 (great expenses); Oliver Rink, *Holland on the Hudson: An Economic and Social History of Dutch New York* (Ithaca: Cornell University Press, 1986), 27–28 (*De Halve Maen*). A crew digging a tunnel for the southern spur of the IRT Broadway–Seventh Avenue subway line (today's 1 train) may have uncovered part of the *Tijger*'s scuttled hull in 1916 near the present World Trade Center site. A debate continues over the true identity of these remains, though the archaeologists Anne-Marie Cantwell and Dianna diZerega Wall think the tree-ring dating

evidence for it being the *Tijger* remains strong. See Cantwell and Wall, *Unearthing Gotham: The Archaeology of New York City* (New Haven: Yale University Press, 2001), 150–52.

13. Bradford, *Of Plymouth Plantation*, 53 ("over-masted), 58 ("met with"); John Pory, *John Pory's Lost Description of Plymouth Colony in the Earliest Days of the Pilgrim Fathers* (Boston: Houghton Mifflin, 1918), 36 ("dangerous and almost incureable" . . . "he stumbled"); Bradford and Winslow, *Mourt's Relation*, 20 ("be of good cheere"); Dermer to Purchase, *Sailors' Narratives*, 253 ("run on ground").

14. Pring, *Sailors' Narratives*, 55, 60–62 ("very carefull" . . . "very neere"); Edward Winslow, *Good Newes from New-England* (London, 1624; repr. Bedford, Mass.; Applewood Books, 1996), 11 ("many permissions").

15. Juet, *NNN*, 19–20 ("waste boords"), 26 (canoe murder). Waist cloth could also be used in place of waist boards to mask crews' movements from enemies. When the crew of the *Arbella*, bound for Massachusetts Bay in 1630, thought they saw enemy ships, they "heaved out our longe boats, and putt vp our waste Clothes" and sent women and children below. See *WP*, 2:243. Dermer to Purchase, *Sailors' Narratives*, 255 ("many accidents"); Bradford, *Of Plymouth Plantation*, 71 (shallop attack).

16. Thiesen, "Ship Construction," *Oxford Encyclopedia of Maritime History*; on the *fluyt*, see Gardiner and Unger, *Cogs, Caravels, and Galleons*, 115–30; Baker, *Mayflower*, esp. 25–65 (ships), 65–74 (shallops), 75–94 (pinnaces), 95–118 (barks); William Baker, "Vessel Types in Colonial Massachusetts," in *Seafaring in Colonial Massachusetts*, ed. Frederick S. Allis (Boston: Colonial Society of Massachusetts, 1980), 3–15; Richard David, ed., *Hakluyt's Voyages* (Boston: Houghton Mifflin, 1981), 23 ("little more").

17. Van Wassenaer, *NNN*, 86 ("carried out"); David de Vries took note of just how often his men had to row rather than sail their yacht when getting around New York Bay in "Korte Historiael," *NNN*, esp. 188–90; De Laet, "Nieuwe Wereldt," *NNN*, 50 ("tolerable yachts," "the country there abounds," *Onrust*); Isaack de Rasières to Samuel Blommaert, 1628, *NNN*, 110 (shallop); "Grant of Exclusive Trade to New Netherland," October 1614, *DRCHNY*, 1:12–13 (*Onrust*); Bradford, *Of Plymouth Plantation*, 192–93 (commissioning of shallop and fort); *WP*, 2:238nn1, 2 (*Blessings of the Bay*); John Robinson and George Francis Dow, *The Sailing Ships of New England, 1607–1907* (Salem, Mass.: Marine Research Society, 1922), 9–20; Baker, "Vessel Types in Colonial Massachusetts," 14 (shipbuilding); Chaplin, *Subject Matter*, 214 (shipbuilding); Van Wassenaer, *NNN*, 87 ("a large quantity").

18. *NYRPS*, 1:130 ("unserviceable"), 2:197–99 (complaints against boatswain), 4:19 (defection of Gillis Petersen, "rascal"); *CCR*, 1:79–80 (hempseed, ship); Robinson and Dow, *Sailing Ships of New England*, 13 (Mass. laws).

19. Dutch prices are all in Carolus guilders. *NYRPS*, 2:11 (*De Hoop*), 13–14 (two-story house), 73 (yacht sale), 92 (stone house), 4:19; *CCR*, 1:254 (£52 vessel), 474 (£24 boat).

The ratio of home to boat prices remained similar even later in the century: one survey of houses burned in King Philip's War in 1676 put the value of ordinary dwellings in the range of £35–40, while the value of a used bark sold in 1659 was over £90. See Anonymous to Josiah Winslow, January 26, 1676/7, John Davis Papers, MHS (house prices); Inventory of the Estate at Cushnock and Neumkeek, March 28, 1658/9, Winslow Family Papers II, MHS (bark price). Even for repairs, boats were five times more costly than canoes; it cost John Winthrop Jr. £1.6s.0p to have his small boat repaired in 1655, while work on his canoe by the same man cost only 2s.6p. See Bill of John Coit Sr., ca. 1655, Winthrop Family Papers Transcripts, MHS.

20. July 20, 1636, Winthrop, *History*, 1:189–90 ("small pinnace," "full of Indians").

21. De Laet, "Nieuwe Wereldt," *NNN*, 43 (birchbark); Morton, *New English Canaan*, 65 (birchbark); Williams, *Key*, 107–8 (chestnut, pine, birch); William Cronon, *Changes in the Land: Indians, Colonists, and the Ecology of New England* (New York: Hill and Wang, 1983), 45 (chestnut rot resistance); Pring, *Sailors' Narratives*, 58 ("very light," ash and maple); Adriaen van der Donck, *A Description of New Netherland*, Charles T. Gehring and William Starna, eds., Diederik Goedhuys, trans. (Lincoln: University of Nebraska Press, 2008), 23 (tulip trees); John A. Strong, *The Algonquian Peoples of Long Island from Earliest Times to 1700* (Interlaken, N.Y., 1997), 43 ("canoe tree"); certain stands of trees were apparently prized, as one deed from Long Island specifically gave Indians the ongoing right to fell trees on the property for dugouts: see William S. Pelletreau, ed., *Records of the Town of Smithtown, Long Island, N.Y.* (Huntington, NY: Long Islander Print, 1898), 9.

22. Williams, *Key*, 106–7 (canoe making, "burning and hewing"). For the classic and still-illuminating description of Trobriand Islanders' ritual construction and launch of canoes, see Bronislaw Malinowski, *Argonauts of the Western Pacific* (1922; repr. New York: E. P. Dutton, 1932), 105–56; Pring, *Sailors' Narratives*, 58 ("sowed together"); Frank Speck, "Notes on the Mohegan and Niantic Indians" in *The Indians of Greater New York and the Lower Hudson*, ed. Clark Wissler (New York: AMS Press, 1975), 188–89 (canoe knives); Samson Occom, "Account of the Montauk Indians, on Long Island" (1761), in Joanna Brooks, ed., *The Collected Writings of Samson Occom, Mohegan: Leadership and Literature in Eighteenth-Century Native America* (New York: Oxford University Press, 2006), 50 ("making a canoe").

23. Williams, *Key*, 85–86 (winds), 108–10 (winds, tides, nautical verbs, "Sea-fight").

24. Charles Wolley observed that Munsees near New York "have small Boats, which they call Canoes," in *Two Years' Journal in New York*, 32. *Amokol* is Munsee, *mashuee* is Montaukett, *meshwe* is Pequot, *mishoon* is Narragansett, *michseh* is Nauset. Albert Gallatin, "Comparative Indian Vocabulary, 1836," AAS, 22 (*maushee, amokol*); William Cowan, "Pequot from Stiles to Speck," in *Languages and Lore of the Long Island Indians*, ed. Gaynell Stone Levine (Stony Brook, N.Y.: Suffolk

County Archaeological Association, 1980), 131 (meshwe); anonymous, "Indian & English Dictionary," JCBL mss. no. 191, 22 (*michseh*); Williams, *Key*, 106–7 (*mishoon, mishoonémese, mishíttouwand*); Winthrop, *History*, 1:59 (thirty-man canoes), 112 (eighty-man canoes); Bragdon, *Native People*, 105–6 (canoes); Strong, *Algonquian Peoples of Long Island*, 43–44 (canoes); Lion Gardiner, "Leift. Lion Gardener his relation of the Pequot Warres," in *MHSC*, 3d ser., 3:147 ("the nose"); John Mason, *A Brief History of the Pequot War: Especially of the Memorable Taking of Their Fort at Mistick in Connecticut in 1637* (1650) (1736; repr. Lincoln: University of Nebraska Press, 2007), x ("Beak Head"). *Beakhead* was the English name for a decorative protrusion at the bow of many European crafts that served a similar function. See Parry, *Age of Reconnaissance*, 68; Baker, *Mayflower*, 174. Pring, *Sailors' Narratives*, 58 ("sharpe at both ends . . . the beake"). European wooden boats were often kept in the water year-round for the same reason canoes were. For details on the three sunken dugouts found in Lake Quinsigamond in Worcester, Massachusetts, see the Nipmuc Nation Tribal Historic Preservation Office's Project Mishoon site http://projectmishoon.homestead.com/; on the Great Pond dugout, see Chester B. Kevitt, "Aboriginal Dugout Discovered at Weymouth," *Bulletin of the Massachusetts Archaeological Society* 30.1 (1968): 1–5.

25. *MHSC*, 1st ser., 6:86 ("that when any," Niantic canoe loss in 1675); Williams, *Key*, 108 ("before a wind"); Danckaerts, *Journal*, 56 ("scoops"); Pring, *Sailors' Narratives*, 58 ("flat at the end like an oven peel").

26. Van der Donck, *Description*, 13 ("accompanied by his wife . . ."); "Declarations of crew members of the ship the *Fortuyn*, master Henrick Christiaensen," in Simon Hart, *The Prehistory of the New Netherland Company: Amsterdam Notarial Records of the First Dutch Voyages to the Hudson* (Amsterdam: City of Amsterdam Press, 1959), 81 ("with such a speed").

27. Verrazzano, *Voyages*, 139 ("with only the strength"); Wood, *New England's Prospect*, 102 ("will venture"); John Josselyn, *A Critical Edition of Two Voyages to New-England*, Paul J. Lindholdt, ed. (Hanover, N.H.: University Press of New England, 1988), 102 ("They will indure . . . dare to undertake it"); Winslow, *Good Newes*, 67 ("very adventurous").

28. Morton, *New English Canaan*, 19 ("doe divide," "which with them is called Maske"), 20 ("scattered Trojans"), 21 ("a storme"); Williams, *Key*, vi ("draw their Line"); Van der Donck, *Description*, 92–93 ("long ago in legendary times" . . . "the peopling of America").

29. Katherine A. Grandjean, "Reckoning: The Communications Frontier in Early New England" (Ph.D. diss., Harvard University, 2008), 276–82, appendices, 287–348; Nathaniel Sylvester to JW2, April 17, 1658, William Cheseborough to JW2, March 26,1655, Theophilus Eaton to JW2, February 3, 1654/5, Winthrop Family Papers, MHS, reel 5 (Sylvester: "I understand," "promis was great"); (Cheseborough: "he is very possibly" . . . "a great Canow"); (Eaton: "for this intelligence").

30. Danckaerts, *Journal*, 35 ("some of the passengers"); De Vries, NNN, 232 ("the edge was not"), 231 ("for it made"); NYCM, 5:151–53 (East River ferry); Romney, *New Netherland Connections*, 149–50 (East River ferry).

31. On early modern European attitudes toward bathing, swimming, and immersion in water in general, see Kathleen M. Brown, *Foul Bodies: Cleanliness in Early America* (New Haven: Yale University Press, 2009), 15–25; Van der Donck, *Description*, 96, ("from the youngest age"); Williams, *Key*, 109 ("swim a mile," "it hath," "questioned safety," "Feare not").

32. Bradford and Winslow, *Mourt's Relation*, 30 (canoe theft); John Winthrop's son Henry drowned near Salem harbor just days after the *Arbella* arrived: according to an undated family account, he died while attempting to claim an Indian canoe. Entry for July 2, 1630, *Winthrop Papers*, 2:265n2; Pring, *Sailors' Narratives*, 58; Josselyn, *A Critical Edition of* Two Voyages to New-England, 46–47 ("to make large Canows"); Wood, *New England's Prospect*, 48 ("there be more Cannowes"); Roger Williams to John Winthrop Sr., January 10, 1637/8, RWC, 1:140 ("lustie Canow"); NYRPS, 2:425 (canoe in lease); RNA, 1:51 (oystering), 352 (lime); WP, 6:42 ("Canow fell over").

33. William Hubbard, *A General History of New England, From the Discovery to MDCLXXX* (Boston: Little and Brown, 1848), 647 (fisherman), 649 (J.S., Captain Lockwood's wife); Danckaerts, *Journal*, 163 ("to be in such weather"); De Vries, NNN, 226 ("my boat was frozen up").

34. DRCHNY, 3:334 (*f*25 canoe); Johannes Megapolensis, "A Short Account of the Mohawk Indians," NNN, 176 ("wooden canoe"). 1 schepel = ~.75 bushel. Given that the account is focused on the Mohawks, the editor assumes this canoe was used by colonists on the upper Hudson settlement of Rensselaerswyck. Since no other accounts mention such large dugouts upriver or among the Mohawks or Mahicans, it seems more likely the canoe originated from Munsee builders near New Amsterdam and made its way up the Hudson in service as a cargo boat. Indeed, it was probably the "conoe used for a lot of maize" in New Amsterdam mentioned in NYRPS, 1:79; NHCR, 1:211 ("divers cannows"); PCR, 3: 208–9 ("smale and naughty"); CCR, 1:218–19 (Dyer's ferrying).

35. Thomas Minor, *The Diary of Thomas Minor, Stonington, Connecticut: 1653 to 1684* (New London: Press of the Day, 1899), 8 (Sabiantwosucke), 27 (Herman Garrits), 101 ("Calked the Canoow"), 113 ("fecthed home"), 114 (Mr. Chester), 167 ("wife fell"), 182 ("New london"), 185 ("driven away").

36. Willem Beekman to Petrus Stuyvesant, January 14, 1660, Beekman Letterbook, N-YHS ("being intoxicated"); Winslow, *Good Newes*, 48–50 (Weston affair).

37. PCR, 1:110, 151 (canoe disputes); RICR, 1:108 (canoe law); MCR, 1:74, 249 (canoe disputes); John Noble, ed., *Records of the Massachusetts Court of Assistants* (Boston: Suffolk County, 1904), 1:3 (canoe law), 4, 17 (canoe disputes); NHCR, 1:48 (canoe law), 57, 80, 434–35, 2: 3 (canoe disputes); NYCM, 4:67–68, 133 (canoe

disputes); *RNA*, 1:352 (canoe dispute); *NNCM*, 5:12, 55 (canoe disputes); Testimony of Thomas Minor, ca. September 1652, Winthrop Family Papers Transcripts, MHS ("upon the water"); *NYCA*, 134 ("besides a fine," "one of their Ears").

38. *RWC*, 1:118 ("a grievance"); *WP*, 6:6 ("a verie fayer . . . Justies"); John A. Strong, "Wyandanch: Sachem of the Montauks," in *Northeastern Indian Lives, 1632–1816*, ed. Robert S. Grumet (Amherst: University of Massachusetts Press, 1996), 68 ("one of the earliest").

39. Verrazzano, *Voyages*, 139 ("looking at all the ship's equipment"); Nicolaes van Wassenaer, *NNN*, 67 ("when they have seen"), 80–81 ("very much afraid"); on the transit of animals, see Virginia DeJohn Anderson, *Creatures of Empire: How Domestic Animals Transformed Early America* (New York: Oxford University Press, 2004), 99–100.

40. See Thiesen, "Ship Construction," *Oxford Encyclopedia of Maritime History*; Parry, *Age of Reconnaissance*, 60–66; Parry, *Discovery of the Sea*, 7–13; Baker, *Mayflower*, 1–7. My discussion of the ship as a primer on hierarchy is inspired by Greg Dening's reading of space aboard the *RMS Bounty* in *Mr. Bligh's Bad Language: Passion, Power, and Theatre on the* Bounty (Cambridge: Cambridge University Press, 1992), 80–85; Juet, *NNN*, 26 ("Pillow").

41. For examples of Native piloting, see Van Wassenaer, *NNN*, 81n1; Samuel Gardner Drake, "Origin of the Indian Wars," in *The Old Indian Chronicle: Being A Collection of Exceeding Rare Tracts . . . .*, ed. Samuel Gardner Drake (Boston, 1867), 6–17; Levett, "A Voyage into New England," 116–17; Ferdinando Gorges, "A Briefe Narration of the Originall Undertaking of the Advancement of Plantations Into the Parts of America," in *Sir Ferdinando Gorges and His Province of Maine*, 2 vols., ed. James Phinney Baxter, 2:10 ("the opinion . . . understood") (Boston: Gorges Society, 1890); Bradford, *Of Plymouth Plantation*, 81 ("where to take fish"); William Wood, *Wood's New England's Prospect* (London, 1630; repr. New York: Burt Franklin, 1967), 78–79 ("certain intelligence . . . no small advantage").

42. Samuel de Champlain, "Discovery of the Coast of the Almouchiquois," and Thomas Dermer to Samuel Purchase, 1619, *Sailors' Narratives*, 79 ("the course"), 255 ("drew mee a Plot"); Brereton, *A Briefe and true Relation*, 4 (mapping); Gabriel Archer, "The Relation of Captain Gosnold's Voyage," *MHSC*, 3d ser., 8:73 ("with a piece of chalk").

43. Bradford, *Of Plymouth Plantation*, 189–92 (*Sparrow-Hawk*) 190 (quotations); see also Robinson and Dow, *Sailing Ships of New England*, 9–10; Mark C. Wilkins, *Cape Cod's Oldest Shipwreck: The Desperate Crossing of the* Sparrow-Hawk (Charleston, S.C.: History Press, 2011).

44. Winthrop, *History*, 1:39–40 (Garretts), 200 (Flips Jansz.), 208 (Nausets find lost shallop), 182–83 (L.I. plundering); David Pietersz. de Vries, "Korte Historiael Ende Journales Aenteyckninge" (1655), *NNN*, 193–94 (Flips Jansz.); Edmund Bailey

O'Callaghan, *The History of New Netherland, Or New York Under the Dutch* (New York: D. Appleton, 1848), 2:335 (*Prins Maurits*); NYRPS, 1:79 (reward to Munsee man for finding lost yawl); WP, 3:270–71 (L.I. plundering), 276 (Hammond); Gardiner, MHSC, 3d. ser., 3:157 ("killed by a giant-like Indian toward the Dutch").

45. Annette Kolodny, *In Search of First Contact: The Vikings of Vinland, the Peoples of the Dawnland, and the Anglo-American Anxiety of Discovery* (Durham, N.C.: Duke University Press, 2012), 90–92; Sigríður Sunna Ebenesersdóttir et al., "A New Subclade of mtDNA Haplogroup C1 Found in Icelanders: Evidence of Pre-Columbian Contact?" *American Journal of Physical Anthropology* 144.1 (January 2011): 92–99.

46. "Codex" in Wroth, ed., *Voyages of Verrazzano*, 136 ("to carry back to France"), 140 ("where the breakers"), 141n19 ("showing their buttocks"). On Portuguese kidnappers, see Salisbury, *Manitou and Providence*, 53.

47. On early Wabanaki sailing, see John Pory, "A Coppie of a parte of Mr. Poreys Letter to the Governor of Virginia," Champlin Burrage, ed., *John Pory's Lost Description of Plymouth Colony in the Earliest Days of the Pilgrim Fathers* (Cambridge, Mass., 1918), 49 ("as well as"); see also George Popham and Raleigh Gilbert, "The Relation of a Voyage unto New England," *Sailors' Narratives*, 157; on the later fate of the Wabanakis, see also Matthew Bahar, "People of the Dawn, People of the Door: Indian Pirates and the Violent Theft of an Atlantic World," *JAH* 101.2 (September 2014): 401–26.

48. On "Tarentine" raids, see Winthrop, *History*, 1:59,79, and Beck, *The Indian as Sea-Fighter*, 13–19; Josselyn, *A Critical Edition of Two Voyages to New-England*, 23, 102 (birchen pinnace).

49. Brereton, *A Briefe and true Relation*, 3–4 ("shallop with mast," "appareled"); Archer, "The Relation of Captain Gosnold's Voyage," MHSC, 3d ser., 8:73; De Vries, NNN, 203 ("red scarlet mantle"); WP, 3:411 ("dress as an English man"). For a further exploration of how these practices of borrowing clothing mattered in the region, see Little, "Cultural Cross-Dressing," 238–73. On similar "cultural cross-dressing" in a later terrestrial setting, see also Timothy J. Shannon, "Dressing for Success on the Mohawk Frontier: Hendrick, William Johnson, and the Indian Fashion," *WMQ*, 53. 1 (January 1996): 13–42.

50. RICR, 1:26 ("use of my boats"); on Indians commissioning colonial vessels in wartime, see also WP, 3:411 (Pequot War); NYCM, 4:465 (Kieft's War).

51. Van Wassener, "Historisch Verhael," NNN, 73 ("would kill"); Juet, NNN, 19–20, 25–36 (*Halve Maen*); Hart, *Prehistory*, 30 (Pieter Fransz.), 18–19, 51–52 (*Swarte Beer*); Jacobs, *New Netherland*, 26–27 (*Swarte Beer*).

52. Hart, *Prehistory*; also Alfred A. Cave, "Who Killed John Stone? A Note on the Origins of the Pequot War," *WMQ* 49.3 (July 1992): 509–21; Andrew C. Lipman, "Murder on the Saltwater Frontier: The Death of John Oldham," *EAS* 9.2 (May 2011): 268–94; De Vries, NNN, 208 (Raritan attack); Johannes Bogaert to

Hans Bontemantel, 1655, *NNN*, 386 (Van Beeck); *DRCHNY*, 13:300 ("constantly cruise"); Romney, *New Netherland Connections*, 174–75 (Esopus raiding and piloting); *MCR*, 4:277 (ban on selling colonial vessels to Indians).

53. William Thompson to JW2, January 15, 1661, Winthrop Family Papers, MHS, reel 6 ("struck his hatchet"); *DRCHNY*, 3:84 ("murdered and pillaged"), 168–70, 168 ("all due furniture"), 170 ("these Indians"); on the Naushon Island piracy, see also *NYGE* 1:17.

Chapter 3. The Landless Borderland

1. For interpretations of how epidemics in general and this one in particular shaped both the colonization of New England and how the narratives of colonization were written, see Francis Jennings, *The Invasion of America: Indians, Colonialism, and the Cant of Conquest* (New York: W. W. Norton, 1975), 15–31; Cristobal Silva, *Miraculous Plagues: An Epidemiology of Early New England Narrative* (New York: Oxford University Press, 2011); on the Narragansett explanation for how they were spared, see Julie A. Fisher and David J. Silverman, *Ninigret, Sachem of the Niantic and Narragansetts* (Ithaca: Cornell University Press, 2014), 26–28.

2. Various summaries of this early phase are found in Bernard Bailyn, *New England Merchants in the Seventeenth Century* (New York: Harper and Row, 1955), 2–3; Oliver Rink, *Holland on the Hudson: An Economic and Social History of Dutch New York* (Ithaca: Cornell University Press, 1986), 69–80; Donna Merwick, *The Shame and the Sorrow: Dutch-Amerindian Encounters in New Netherland* (Philadelphia: University of Pennsylvania Press, 2006), 63–65; *DRCHNY*, 1:56 ("surrounded on all sides"); Thomas Morton, *New English Canaan, or New Canaan containing an abstract of New England, composed in three bookes* (London, 1637), 45 ("corslets . . . in harnesse"); Edward Winslow and William Bradford reported many instances of the early colonists suiting up in armor, and noted that two lost Plymouth colonists brought "a great Mastiffe bitch with them and a Spanell," *Mourt's Relation*, 27.

3. Ferdinando Gorges, "A Briefe Narration of the Originall Undertaking of the Advancement of Plantations Into the Parts of America," in *Sir Ferdinando Gorges and His Province of Maine*, 2 vols., ed. James Phinney Baxter (Boston: Gorges Society, 1890), 2:25 ("more zealous"). Bernard Bailyn emphasizes the importance of these early adventurers, whom he describes as "almost to a man outcasts from the respectable world of the English middle class." Bailyn, *New England Merchants*, 13 (quotation), 13–15. Cynthia Van Zandt explores the related processes of alliance building in this period of early contact, and she argues convincingly that "intercultural alliances in seventeenth-century North America were fundamentally based on an Indian logic rather than a European one." *Brothers*

Among Nations: The Pursuit of Intercultural Alliances in Early America (New York: Oxford University Press, 2008), esp. 6–16, 15 (quotation).

4. For a sweeping overview of the rise of larger cities and towns across Europe, see Fernand Braudel, *Capitalism and Material Life, 1400–1800* (New York: Harper and Row, 1975), esp. 373–440 (on towns); on London, see Ian Mortimer, *The Time Traveller's Guide to Elizabethan England* (New York: Viking, 2013), esp. 2–71; on Amsterdam and Dutch cities in general, see Simon Schama, *The Embarrassment of Riches: An Interpretation of Dutch Culture in the Golden Age* (New York: Vintage Books, 1997).

5. Phil Withington, "Public Discourse, Corporate Citizenship, and State Formation in Early Modern England," *AHR* 112 (October 2007): 1016–38; Patrick McGrath, "Bristol and America, 1480–1631," and Carole Shammas, "English Commercial Development," in *The Westward Enterprise: English Activities in Ireland, the Atlantic, and America, 1480–1650*, ed. Kenneth R. Andrews (Detroit: Wayne State University Press, 1979), 81–102, 151–162, respectively.

6. Jonathan Israel, *The Dutch Republic: Its Rise, Greatness, and Fall, 1477–1806* (New York: Oxford University Press, 1995), 307–18; Maarten Roy Prak, *The Dutch Republic in the Seventeenth Century: The Golden Age* (Cambridge: Cambridge University Press, 2005), 75–110; David Armitage, *The Ideological Origins of British Empire* (Cambridge: Cambridge University Press, 2000), "Introduction," esp. 20–23; Anthony Pagden, "The Empire's New Clothes: From Empire to Federation, Yesterday and Today," *Common Knowledge* 12.1 (2006): 36–46; Withington, "Public Discourse, Corporate Citizenship, and State Formation," 1016–38.

7. Other major English trading groups formed in the late sixteenth century included the Eastland Company (for Baltic trade) in 1579, the Levant Company (for Middle Eastern trade) in 1581, and the Africa Company in 1588. See Richard David, ed., *Hakluyt's Voyages* (Boston: Houghton Mifflin, 1981), 30–32.

8. Bailyn, *New England Merchants*, 1–15; Benjamin Schmidt, "Mapping an Empire: Cartographic and Colonial Rivalry in Seventeenth-Century Dutch and English North America," *WMQ* 54.3 (July 1997): 549–78; Rink, *Holland on the Hudson*, 29–30. The colonization of New Netherland itself was directed by the West India Company's Amsterdam chamber, though some of the early trade missions were sponsored by investors from Hoorn and Zeeland who would resent Holland's dominance in the fur trade. The East and West India Companies were each made up of seven chambers (one for each of the provinces) in an attempt to divvy up areas of trade to different cities, much like the division of the Virginia Company into Plymouth and London arms. This was in part a means to resolve the intense competition between Dutch ships that flared up in numerous spots, including along the Hudson. However, both the East and West India Companies built their headquarters in Amsterdam, and the city's dominant role in running the

companies and reaping their profits was never really in doubt. See Henk Den Heijer, "The Dutch West India Company, 1621–1791," Victor Enthoven, "An Assessment of Dutch Transatlantic Commerce, 1585–1817," and Wim Klooster, "An Overview of Dutch Trade with the Americas, 1600–1800," in *Riches from Atlantic Commerce: Dutch Transatlantic Trade and Shipping, 1585–1817*, ed. Johannes Postma and Victor Enthoven (Leiden: Brill, 2003), 77–112 (Heijer), 385–445 (Enthoven), 365–84 (Klooster); Wim Klooster, "The Place of New Netherland in the West India Company's Grand Scheme," in *Revisiting New Netherland: Perspectives on Early Dutch America*, ed. Joyce D. Goodfriend (Leiden: Brill, 2005), 57–70; Prak, *The Dutch Republic*, 111–34.

9. See David, *Hakluyt's Voyages*, 17–32; McGrath, "Bristol and America," 81–102; Shammas, "English Commercial Development, 151–62; Postma and Enthoven, eds., *Riches from Atlantic Commerce*, 77–112, 385–445, 365–84.

10. Shammas, "English Commercial Development," 151–62; David Harris Sacks, "Discourses of Western Planting: Richard Hakluyt and the Making of the Atlantic World," and Benjamin Schmidt, "Reading Ralegh's America: Texts, Books, and Readers in the Early Modern Atlantic World," in *The Atlantic World and Virginia, 1550–1624*, ed. Peter C. Mancall (Chapel Hill: University of North Carolina Press, 2007), 410-53, 454–88, respectively; Benjamin Schmidt, "The Dutch Atlantic: From Provincialism to Globalism," in *Atlantic History: A Critical Appraisal*, ed. Jack P. Greene and Philip D. Morgan (New York: Oxford University Press, 2009), 163–90.

11. Van Zandt, *Brothers Among Nations*, 52–53, 57 ("obvious" . . . "did not lead"); Bradford and Winslow, *Mourt's Relation*, 114 ("judged to be" . . . "shee was deprived"); Council for New England Records, 1622–1623, AAS, 7 ("upon the Sands . . . the Savages"); see also Edward Arber, *The Story of the Pilgrim Fathers, 1606–1623, As Told By Themselves, their Friends, and their Enemies* (Boston: Houghton Mifflin, 1897), 392–94.

12. The most compelling study of how captive taking could forge lasting bonds between peoples in borderlands is James F. Brooks, *Captives and Cousins: Slavery, Kinship, and Community in the Southwest Borderlands* (Chapel Hill: University of North Carolina Press, 2002). Scholars who point out the oddly destructive yet also creative nature of captive taking in New England include Neal Salisbury, "Squanto, Last of the Patuxets," in *Struggle and Survival in Colonial America*, ed. David J. Sweet and Gary B. Nash (Berkeley: University of California Press, 1988), 228–46; Alden T. Vaughan, *Transatlantic Encounters: American Indians in Britain, 1500–1776* (Cambridge: Cambridge University Press, 2006), 57–77. George Waymouth, "A True Relation of Captaine George Waymouth his Voyage, made this present yeere 1605; in the Discouerie of the Northpart of Virginia," in *Sailors' Narratives of Voyages Along the New England Coast, 1524–1624*, ed. George Parker Winship (Boston: Houghton Mifflin, 1905), 148 (quotation), 147–49; Gorges, *Sir Ferdinando Gorges*, 2:10.

13. Scholars who give Epenow close attention include Vaughan, *Transatlantic Encounters*, 65–67, 73; Van Zandt, *Brothers Among Nations*, 54–55, David J. Silverman, *Faith and Boundaries: Colonists, Christianity, and Community among the Wampanoag Indians of Martha's Vineyard, 1600–1871* (Cambridge: Cambridge University Press, 2005), 1–5.

14. Philip L. Barbour, ed., *Complete Works of Captain John Smith*, 3 vols. (Chapel Hill: University of North Carolina Press, 1986), 2:399 ("warres of Bohemia"); Gorges, *Sir Ferdinando Gorges*, 2:20–21 ("stout and sober," "as to bid").

15. Vaughan, *Transatlantic Encounters*, 66 (Epenow and Shakespeare); Alden T. Vaughan, "Trinculo's Indian: American Natives in Shakespeare's England," in *The Tempest and Its Travels*, ed. Peter Hulme and William H. Sherman (Philadelphia: University of Pennsylvania Press, 2000), 49–59; Coll Thrush, " 'Meere Strangers': Indigenous and Urban Performances in Algonquian London," in *Urban Identity and the Atlantic World*, ed. Elizabeth Fay and Leonard Von Morzé (New York: Palgrave Macmillan, 2013), 195–213; Gorges, *Sir Ferdinando Gorges*, 2:21 ("grown out," "adventurers").

16. Gorges, *Sir Ferdinando Gorges*, 2:24 ("conduct the adventurers . . . communed").

17. Ibid., 2:23–25 ("Epenow privately . . . Musquetteers aboard").

18. *Ibid.*, 2:29 ("met with Epinew"); Dermer to Purchase, *Sailors' Narratives*, 255 ("With him").

19. Nicolaes van Wassenaer, "Historisch Verhael," (1624–30), NNN, 78 ("two sons"), 81. The best modern version of the text is Shira Schwam-Baird, *Valentin et Orson: An Edition and Translation of the Fifteenth-Century Romance Epic* (Tucson: Arizona Center for Medieval and Renaissance Studies, 2011). The story was apparently undergoing a revival of popularity in England at the same time; in *Twelfth Night, or What You Will* (1602), Shakespeare gave Duke Orsino a servant named Valentine.

20. Michel Pastoureau, *The Bear: History of a Fallen King*, trans. George Holoch (Cambridge: Harvard University Press, 2011), 208–12.

21. Van Wassenaer, NNN, 78 ("though very dull men"), 81 ("a thoroughly wicked fellow," "was paid").

22. Simon Hart, *The Prehistory of the New Netherland Company: Amsterdam Notarial Records of the First Dutch Voyages to the Hudson* (Amsterdam: City of Amsterdam Press, 1959), 75 ("mulatto"); Ira Berlin, *Many Thousands Gone: The First Two Centuries of Slavery in North America* (Cambridge: Harvard University Press, 1998), 17; Lois E. Horton and James Horton examine Rodrigues as an exemplary creole in *Slavery and the Making of America* (New York: Oxford University Press, 2005), 34.

23. On sexuality/intimacy with visitors among Hudson-area Indians, see De Vries, NNN, 218; Van der Donck, *Description*, 84–88; Susanah Shaw Romney, *New Netherland Connections: Intimate Networks and Atlantic Ties in Seventeenth-*

Century America (Chapel Hill: University of North Carolina Press, 2014), 135–45.

24. Hart, *Prehistory*, 75, 80. Adriaen Block would claim that Mossel had purposefully dispatched Rodrigues as contact with Munsees, but Rodrigues' later insistence that he was not bound to Mossel suggests that the Dominican had departed more on his own terms than those of his captain's.

25. Ibid., 80–82.

26. Ibid., 17–32 (internal rivalry), 80–82 ("took away" . . . "black rascal"); on early inter-Dutch trade rivalries, see also Rink, *Holland on the Hudson*, 33–49; Jaap Jacobs, *The Colony of New Netherland: A Dutch Settlement in Seventeenth-Century America* (Ithaca: Cornell University Press, 2009), 22–27.

27. William Bradford, *Of Plymouth Plantation, 1620–1647*, Samuel Eliot Morison, ed. (New York: Alfred A. Knopf, 1952), 81 ("a special instrument"). For various readings of Squanto's story, including the question of when he was first taken captive, see Salisbury, "Squanto, Last of the Patuxets," 228–46; Vaughan, *Transatlantic Encounters*, 57–77; Van Zandt, *Brothers Among Nations*, 52–53; Daniel K. Richter, *Before the Revolution: America's Ancient Pasts* (Cambridge: Belknap Press of Harvard University Press, 2011), 152–56.

28. Samuel de Champlain, "Discovery of the Coast of the Almouchiquois as far as the Forty-Second Degree of Latitude, and Details of this Voyage," in *Sailors' Narratives*, 83 ("a great many"); Gorges, *Sir Ferdinando Gorges*, 1:20. These events and the evidence for them are weighed and examined in detail in Salisbury, "Squanto, Last of the Patuxets," 234–237; Vaughan, *Transatlantic Encounters*, 70–72.

29. Salisbury, "Squanto, Last of the Patuxets," 234–37; Vaughan, *Transatlantic Encounters*, 70–72.

30. Richter, *Before the Revolution*, 154–56, 155 ("it was less").

31. For detailed analysis of Squanto's complex role as a translator, see Salisbury, "Squanto, Last of the Patuxets," 236–40; Vaughan, *Transatlantic Encounters*, 70–75; Bradford, *Of Plymouth Plantation*, 99 ("Squanto sought").

32. As Donna Merwick puts it: "Even when [Indians] came into view as customers, they were formless shapes: objects, seldom subjects, and never personalized." *The Shame and the Sorrow*, 49. Jonas Michaëlius, NNN, 128 ("a made-up, childish language," "signs," "half sentences").

33. Ives Goddard, "The Use of Pidgins and Jargons on the East Coast of North America," in *The Language Encounter in the Americas, 1492–1800: A Collection of Essays*, ed. Edward G. Gray and Norman Fiering (New York: Berghahn Books, 2000), 61–73; see also Lois M. Feister, "Linguistic Communication between the Dutch and Indians in New Netherland, 1609–1664," *Ethnohistory* 20. 1 (Winter 1973): 25–38.

34. Goddard, "The Use of Pidgins and Jargons, 73–75 (limited English fluency); Van der Donck, *Description*, 94 ("can understand").

35. *DRNN*, 200–203 (*vrientschap*, "each according" . . . "one must"). On De Rasières's policy, see also Romney, *New Netherland Connections*, 135–36; Bailyn, *The Barbarous Years*, 210–11. On Dutch–Native land transactions, see Jacobs, *New Netherland*, 64–65; Merwick, *The Shame and the Sorrow*, 61–76.

36. Hart, *Prehistory*, 37 (*Witte Duyf*); Susanah Shaw Romney offers a deeper reading into this incident in *New Netherland Connections*, 131–33.

37. Van Wassenaer, *NNN*, 86 ("in his yacht . . . "small beads"). Although van Wassenaer identifies the Indians as "Sickenanes," scholars suggest that was an alternate term for Pequots. See Neal Salisbury, *Manitou and Providence: Indians, Europeans, and the Making of New England, 1500–1643* (New York: Oxford University Press, 1982), 277n14. The incident is also discussed in Lynn Ceci, "Wampum as a Peripheral Resource," in *The Pequots in Southern New England: The Fall and Rise of an American Indian Nation*, ed. Laurence M. Hauptman and James D. Wherry (Norman: University of Oklahoma Press, 1990), 52–58.

38. On wampum's form, see Kathleen Bragdon, *Native People of Southern New England, 1500–1650* (Norman: University of Oklahoma Press, 1996), 97–98, 179–81; Lynn Ceci, "The Effect of European Contact and Trade on the Settlement Pattern of Indians in Coastal New York, 1524–1665: The Archeological and Documentary Evidence" (Ph.D. diss., City University of New York, 1977); Christopher L. Miller and George R. Hamill, "A New Perspective on Indian–White Contact: Cultural Symbols and Colonial Trade," *JAH* 73 (1986): 318; Elizabeth Shapiro Peña, "Wampum Production in New Netherland and Colonial New York: The Historical and Archaeological Context" (Ph.D. diss., Boston University, 1990), 23–30. Purple wampum was not common in early trade, as indicated in a description from 1646 of a land transaction when Roger Williams commented that the mid-1630s was "a time when white wampum only was current." *RICR*, 1:33.

39. William Wood, *Wood's New England's Prospect* (London, 1630; repr. New York: Burt Franklin, 1967), 74 ("a rare kind of decking").

40. John Brereton, *A Briefe and true Relation of the Discoverie of the North Part of Virginia* (London, 1603; repr. Ann Arbor: University Microfilms, 1966), 9–10 ("about their bodies" . . . "offered"); Champlain, *Sailors' Narratives*, 91 ("little shell beads"); Robert Juet, "The Third Voyage of Master Henry Hudson," *NNN*, 22, 24 ("stropes of beads").

41. Van Wassenaer, *NNN*, 87 ("can understand").

42. For overviews of the colonial adoption of wampum, see *DRNN*, 223–31; Ceci, "The Effect of European Contact," 191–276; Salisbury, *Manitou and Providence*, 147–52; Alfred A. Cave, *The Pequot War* (Amherst: University of Massachusetts Press, 1996), 49–51.

43. *DRNN*, 227–28; Bradford, *Of Plymouth Plantation*, 202; Van Wassenaer, Isaac de Rasières to Samuel Blommaert, 1628, *NNN*, 86, 109–12.

44. Bragdon, *Native People*, 100–101 ("revolution"), 239–40; Ceci, "The Effect of European Contact," 191–276; Miller and Hamill, "A New Perspective," 311–28; Cave, *The Pequot War*, 61–63; David Murray, *Indian Giving: Economies of Power in Indian–White Exchanges* (Amherst: University of Massachusetts Press, 2000), 116–40.

45. Miller and Hamill, "A New Perspective," 311–28; Laurier Turgeon, "The Tale of the Kettle: Odyssey of an Intercultural Object," *Ethnohistory* 44.1 (1997): 1–29; Jacobs, *New Netherland*, 137–39.

46. Christopher L. Pastore, *Between Land and Sea: The Atlantic Coast and the Transformation of New England* (Cambridge: Harvard University Press, 2014), 27–34; Bragdon, *Native People*, 110–12 (mollusk habitats); J. T. Carlton, Donald P. Cheney, and Geerat J. Vermeij, Conveners [editors], "A minisymposium and workshop: Ecological effects and biogeography of an introduced marine species: the periwinkle, Littorina littorea." Abstracts of Papers presented at the Littorina Minisymposium and Workshop. First North American Symposium on Littorina, August 28–30, 1981, Nahant. *Malacological Review* 15:143–50.

47. Roger Williams, *A Key Into the Language of America; Or, An help to the Language of the Natives in that part of America called New-England . . .* (London, 1643; repr., Bedford, Mass., Applewood Books, 1997), 114–15; Wood, *New England's Prospect*, 69 (men as beadmakers), 113 (women and children as shellfishers); William S. Simmons, *Cautantowwit's House: An Indian Burial Ground on the Island of Conanicut in Narragansett Bay* (Providence: Brown University Press, 1970), 69–75, 82–89 (wampum and tools in burials). On the general thesis that men were minters, see Peña, "Wampum Production," 27. Kathleen Bragdon argues that both men and women minted wampum in *Native People*, 112.

48. On bead making and units, see Peña, "Wampum Production," 13–35; Ceci, "The Effect of European Contact," 15–30. Ceci, "Wampum as a Peripheral Resource," 62 (tribute figures from 1657).

49. Peña, "Wampum Production," 61, 67 (counterfeiting); Morton, *New English Canaan*, 41 ("Salvages have found"); Williams, *Key*, 217 ("I never knew"), 218 ("beate all markets"); Wood, *New England's Prospect*, 69–70 ("make a double profit").

50. Bradford, *Of Plymouth Plantation*, 203–4 ("strange it was"). On the rise of the other coastal tributary networks, see Van Wassenaer, Isaack de Rasières to Samuel Blommaert, 1628, NNN, 87, 103; Wood, *New England's Prospect*, 69–70; Ceci, "Wampum as a Peripheral Resource," 48–63; Ceci, "The Effect of European Contact," 192; Bragdon, *Native People*, 25; Cave, *The Pequot War*, 53–54.

51. WP, 2:224–25 (fleet departure), 243–45 ("small ships," "man of warre," "prize he had"); John Winthrop, *The History of New England from 1630 to 1649*, 2 vols., James Savage, ed. (1825; repr. New York: Arno Press, 1972), 1:2 ("manned with fifty-two seamen").

52. Virginia DeJohn Anderson, *New England's Generation: The Great Migration and the Formation of Society and Culture in the Seventeenth Century* (Cambridge: Cambridge University Press, 1991), 12–46, 21 (quotation). Alison Games has found that migration within New England was also common: two-thirds of her sample of the cohort of New England migrants of 1635 moved from their initial place of settlement at least once, some heading back to England. See Games, *Migration and the Origins of the English Atlantic World* (Cambridge: Harvard University Press, 1999), 163–89, esp. 168 (table 6.1); other region-specific summaries of this migration include David Cressy, *Coming Over: Migration and Communication Between England and New England in the Seventeenth Century* (Cambridge: Cambridge University Press, 1987), 1–144; Frank Thistlethwaite, *Dorset Pilgrims: The Story of West Country Pilgrims Who Went to New England in the 17th Century* (London: Barrie and Jenkins, 1989), 1–78.

53. WP, 2:105–6 ("Plantations ar for . . . this long vyadge"), 145 ("diverse plantations," "ill condicions").

54. WP, 2:113 (quotations); Thomas Tillam, "Uppon the first sight of New-England," June 29, 1638, John Davis Papers, MHS ("hayle holy-land").

55. Morton, *New English Canaan*, 23 ("Plague . . . small number of Salvages"); Jennings, *The Invasion of America*, 15–31 (virgin/widowed); Bradford and Winslow, *Mourt's Relation*, 68 ("common land," "we have it"); WP, 2:113 ("these savage people . . . ther is more").

56. Winthrop, *History*, 1:62 ("walked out . . . safe home"); Williams, *Key*, 31–32 (menstrual hut). My thanks to Robert Blair St. George for pointing out the likely type of structure Winthrop had invaded.

57. The intellectual history of these ideas is discussed at greater length in Jennings, *The Invasion of America*, 134–37; Armitage, *The Ideological Origins*, 61–99; Daniel K. Richter, "The Strange North American Colonial Career of *Terra Nullius*," in *Frontier, Race, Nation: Henry Reynolds and Australian History*, ed. Bain Attwood and Tom Griffiths (Melbourne: Australian Scholarly Publishing, 2009), 159–84. A representative quotation that disparaged Native possession came from the Salem preacher Francis Higginson, who wrote, "The Indians are not able to make use of the one fourth part of the Land, neither have they any settled places, as Townes to dwell in, nor any ground as they challenge for their owne possession, but change their habitation from place to place." *New-Englands Plantation, or A Short and True Description of the Commodities and Discommodities of that Countrey* (London, 1680), 12. This notion of proper landscape use equaling proper possession has been discussed in many places, most trenchantly in William Cronon, *Changes in the Land: Indians, Colonists, and the Ecology of New England* (New York: Hill and Wang, 1983), esp. 51–53, and Patricia Seed, *Ceremonies of Possession in Europe's Conquest of the New World, 1492–1640* (Cambridge: Cambridge University Press, 1995), 31–36. On Winthrop's purchase, see also Jennings, *Invasion of America*, 138.

58. As Francis Jennings pointed out, the Williams banishment also illustrated tensions between the "Old Planters" population in Salem and Boston Puritans. Jennings, *Invasion of America*, 138–44. On the larger legal context of the Williams banishment, see Nan Goodman, "Banishment, Jurisdiction, and Identity in Seventeenth-Century New England: The Case of Roger Williams," *EAS* 7.1 (2009): 109–39.

59. This transition is well described in Cronon, *Changes in the Land*, 55–81; Braudel, *Capitalism and Material Life*, 373–440.

60. Rink, *Holland on the Hudson*, 69–94; DRCHNY, 1:35–36 (budget numbers).

61. Den Heijer, "The Dutch West India Company," 78–80.

62. Merwick, *The Shame and the Sorrow*, 65–76; Seed, *Ceremonies of Possession*, 167–69. The struggle of private citizens to take establishment of *staplerecht* ("staple right," the authority to be the local hub of commodities) away from the company in Nieuw Amsterdam is discussed trenchantly by Simon Middleton in " 'How It Came that the Bakers Bake No Bread': A Struggle for Trade Privileges in Seventeenth-Century New Amsterdam," *WMQ* 58.2 (2001): 347–72, and Dennis J. Maika, "Securing the Burgher Right in New Amsterdam: The Struggle for Municipal Citizenship in the Seventeenth-Century Atlantic World," in Goodfriend, ed., *Revisiting New Netherland*, 93–128.

63. Adriaen van der Donck, "Vertoogh van Nieu-Neder-land" (1650), NNN, 309 (Cape Cod), 315 (Philadelphia—referred to as "above Maghchachansie, near the Sankikans," corresponding with the place where the Dutch colonist Andries Hudde bought land in 1646, on what is now Philadelphia's Delaware River waterfront). See NNN, 315n2; Seed, *Ceremonies of Possession*, 67 (quotation), 66–69. For further elaborations on the Dutch method of taking possession, see Faren R. Siminoff, *Crossing the Sound: The Rise of Atlantic American Communities in Seventeenth-Century Eastern Long Island* (New York: New York University Press, 2004), 34–55; Merwick, *The Shame and the Sorrow*, 59–98.

64. Schama, *The Embarrassment of Riches*, 70–71 (lion images); John H. McCashion and Theodore Robinson, "The Clay Tobacco Pipes of New York State Under the Sidewalks of New York: Archaeological Investigations Near the U.S. Customs House on Manhattan Island, New York," in Gaynell S. Levine, ed., *The Coastal Archaeology Reader: Selections from the New York State Archaeological Association Bulletin, Readings in Long Island Archaeology and Ethnohistory*, vol. 2 (Stony Brook, N.Y.: Suffolk County Archaeological Association, 1976), 394–411.

65. On Swanendael, see also Amy C. Schutt, *Peoples of the River Valleys: The Odyssey of the Delaware Indians* (Philadelphia: University of Pennsylvania Press, 2007), 10. In 1646 New Sweden colonists removed the plaque that the Dutch had posted near present-day Philadelphia, and the English similarly showed contempt for the States' Arms at Kievets-hoeck, the spit of land at the mouth of the Connecticut River that the English called Saybrook Point. Van der Donck, NNN, 309

(English removal of arms), 313 ("mischievous savages"), 315 (Swedish removal of arms).

66. Hugo Grotius, *The Freedom of the Seas, or the Right Which Belongs to the Dutch to take part in the East Indian Trade*, trans. Ralph van Deman Magoffin (New York: Oxford University Press, 1916), 8 ("does not the ocean"), 42 ("the sea is common to all"); Prak, *The Dutch Republic*, 111–34; Philip E. Steinberg, *The Social Construction of the Ocean* (Cambridge: Cambridge University Press, 2001), 89–109.

67. Not all English believed in *mare clausum*. As early as 1580 William Camden had anticipated Grotius by arguing that "all are at liberty to navigate the vast ocean, since the use of sea and the air are common to all," and Samuel Purchas later agreed that sea was free to all because "by Nature all the Earth was common Mother, and in equall community to be enjoyed of all hers." But others also lay the groundwork for Selden's side, in particular when it came to fishing grounds. John Dee articulated this notion of *imperium* over territorial waters in his "General and Rare Memorials Pertayning to the Perfect Arte of Navigation" (1577), and his thoughts were later echoed by the Anglo-Scots king James I and his supporter William Welwood, who in 1613 argued for fishing-based mare clausum on the basis of Genesis 1:28: "God said unto them . . . have dominion over the fish of the sea." See Armitage, *The Ideological Origins*, esp. 103–10 (quotations); Mónica Brito Vieira, "*Mare Liberum* vs. *Mare Clausum*: Grotius, Freitas, and Selden's Debate on Dominion over the Seas," *Journal of the History of Ideas* 64.3 (2003): 370–71.

68. MCR, 1:3–4 ("To have and hould"); DRCHNY, 1:51–52 (colonial bounds), 56 ("from all time").

69. John Underhill, *Newes from America; or, A New and Experimentall Discoverie of New England* . . . (1638; repr., Lincoln: University of Nebraska Press, 2007), 17 ("Glance your eye"); Morton, *New English Canaan*, 100 ("a greate trade . . . commodious Country").

70. On the Plymouth moves against the Dutch, see Bailyn, *New England Merchants*, 49–53; Salisbury, *Manitou and Providence*, 150; Cave, *The Pequot War*, 54–55; Rink, *Holland on the Hudson*, 119–22; DRNN, 224 (quotations of Dutch requests); DRCHNY, 1:38 ("by friendly alliance").

71. DRCHNY, 1:45, 48–49, 56 ("five thousand beaver skins"); Merwick, *The Shame and the Sorrow*, 79–85.

72. DRCHNY, 1:72 ("quarrel with the Dutch"), 71–81; Hart, *Prehistory*, 55 (Eelkens).

Chapter 4. Blood in the Water

1. John Mason, *A Brief History of the Pequot War: Especially of the Memorable Taking of Their Fort at Mistick in Connecticut in 1637* (1650; repr. Lincoln: University of Nebraska Press, 2007), (dog bark, "Owanux!"); John Underhill, *Newes from America; or, A New and Experimentall Discoverie of New England* . . .

(1638; repr., Lincoln: University of Nebraska Press, 2007), 32 ("bred in them," "brake forth").

2. Underhill, *Newes from America*, 34 ("some through," "many courageous"), 35 ("blazed . . . so many soules"); Mason, *A Brief History*, 8 ("WE MUST BURN THEM"). Historians offer varying numbers of Pequots in the fortified Mystic village, citing as few as three hundred and as many as seven hundred. But the evidence favors the lower end of the range. All sources written at the time of the war place the number at three or four hundred. Only John Mason's account, which was written much later and defended the necessity of the attack because of the Pequots' overwhelming numerical superiority, offered the suspicious outlier of "six or seven hundred" (Mason, *A Brief History*, 10). For a richly detailed analysis of the fighting and its complexities, see Kevin McBride and David Naumec, "Battle of Mystic Fort Documentation Plan: A Technical Report," GA-2255–07–011 (Mashantucket, Conn.: National Park Service American Battlefield Protection Program, 2009), http://pequotwar.org/wp-content/uploads/2010/04/Technical -Report-Short.pdf.

3. David Pietersz. de Vries, "Korte Historiael Ende Journales Aenteyckninge" (1655), NNN, 227 ("a great shrieking"), 228 ("forty Indians"), 227–28 (atrocities).

4. De Vries, NNN, 228 ("some with," "they had done"), 229 ("indeed a disgrace"); for other accounts of the attacks, see anonymous, "Journal of New Netherland," NNN, 277; DRCHNY, 1:151, 200, 412.

5. Scholarship on the Pequot War builds from a decades-long debate between the self-confessed Puritan hater Francis Jennings and the reluctant Puritan apologist Alden T. Vaughan. Jennings argued that the war was motivated by geopolitics and land hunger, whereas Vaughan at first highlighted Pequot aggression but eventually came to agree with Jennings's overall take. See Vaughan, "Pequots and Puritans: The Causes of the War of 1637," *WMQ* 21.2 (April 1964): 256–69; Vaughan, *The New England Frontier: Puritans and Indians, 1620–1675* (Boston: Little, Brown, 1965), 93–154; Jennings, *The Invasion of America: Indians, Colonialism, and the Cant of Conquest* (New York: W. W. Norton, 1975), 177–227; Vaughan, "Pequots and Puritans: The Causes of the War of 1637," in *Roots of American Racism: Essays on the Colonial Experience* (New York: Oxford University Press, 1995), 177–99. The most detailed treatment to date is Alfred A. Cave, *The Pequot War* (Amherst: University of Massachusetts Press, 1996), which emphasizes the religious fervor of Puritan rhetoric and the terrifying intent of the massacre. Steven T. Katz rejects the possibility of genocidal intent in "The Pequot War Reconsidered," *NEQ* 64.2 (June 1991): 206–24; Adam J. Hirsch, Ronald Dale Karr, and Guy Chet debate the degree to which the war entailed an "Americanization" of colonial warfare: Hirsch, "The Collision of Military Cultures in Seventeenth-Century New England," *JAH* 74.4 (March 1988): 1187–1212; Karr, " 'Why Should You Be So Furious?' The Violence of the Pequot War," *JAH* 85.3 (December 1998): 76–909; Chet, *Conquering the*

American Wilderness: The Triumph of European Warfare in the Colonial Northeast
(Amherst: University of Massachusetts Press, 2003), 14–38. Katherine A. Grandjean
emphasizes how colonists' literal hunger, not just land hunger, inspired their
aggression in "New World Tempests: Environment, Scarcity, and the Coming of
the Pequot War," *WMQ* 68.1 (January 2011): 75–100. The Mashantucket Pequot
tribe even shot a widescreen film about the conflict for its museum in Connecticut.
Based on the same Puritan accounts all other historians use, the film presents a
cautious, semifictionalized cinematic telling of the Pequot War that is quite
accurate, though it offers (understandably) sinister portrayals of the English military
leaders. *The Witness*, prod. Mashantucket Pequot Museum and Research Center,
dir. Keith Merrill, 20 min., 1997, 70 mm film.
The scholarship on Kieft's War is a lot thinner, reflecting the general
historiographical neglect of New Netherland. In recent accounts of the conflict,
most scholars still use the title "Kieft's War," indicating that they agree with the
director's contemporaries who alleged that Kieft had been too eager to start the
war, too inept to command it, and too arrogant to admit his mistakes. But they also
point out that the war can be attributed to the cultural chasm between the
colonists and Natives, as a series of isolated murders and the resulting
misunderstandings turned into an all-out war. Blame still falls on the director,
though, for being needlessly provocative. The cultural conflict thesis dates to Allen
W. Trelease's monograph on Dutch–Indian relations and is revisited in Evan
Haefeli's essay on the war. Trelease, *Indian Affairs in Colonial New York: The
Seventeenth Century* (Ithaca: Cornell University Press, 1960), 60–84; Haefeli,
"Kieft's War and the Cultures of Violence in Colonial America," in *Lethal
Imagination: Violence and Brutality in American History*, ed. Michael A. Bellesiles
(New York: New York University Press, 1999), 17–40. Two recent popular syntheses
wholly fault Kieft for his eponymous war: Edwin G. Burrows and Mike Wallace,
Gotham: A History of New York City to 1898 (New York: Oxford University Press,
1999), 37–40; Russell Shorto, *The Island at the Center of the World: The Epic Story
of Dutch Manhattan and the Forgotten Colony That Shaped America* (New York:
Doubleday, 2004), 110–45. Most recently, Jaap Jacobs analyzes the war as a crisis of
colonial administration; Paul Otto emphasizes the intergenerational struggle in
Munsee communities as a catalyst; Donna Merwick explains the war as the
confluence of many "ominous" cultural and historic factors. See Jacobs, *New
Netherland: A Dutch Colony in Seventeenth-Century America* (Leiden: Brill, 2005),
133–39; Paul Otto, *The Dutch–Munsee Encounter in America* (New York:
Berghahn Books, 2006), 106–26; Donna Merwick, *The Shame and the Sorrow:
Dutch–Amerindian Encounters in New Netherland* (Philadelphia: University of
Pennsylvania Press, 2006), 101–69.

6. Though connections between the two wars were pointed out by John Underhill's
biographer in 1932, in recent years, as scholars increasingly move toward a

historians-without-borders approach to early America, several have pointed out that the conflicts were connected in both subtle and obvious ways. Henry C. Shelley, *John Underhill: Captain of New England and New Netherland* (New York: D. Appleton, 1932), 170–94 (Pequot War), 306–20 (Kieft's War); Michael Leroy Oberg, " 'We are all the Sachems from East to West': A New Look at Miantonomi's Campaign of Resistance," *NEQ* 77.3 (September 2004): 478–99; Faren R. Siminoff, *Crossing the Sound: The Rise of Atlantic American Communities in Seventeenth-Century Eastern Long Island* (New York: New York University Press, 2004), 34–55; Otto, *The Dutch–Munsee Encounter*, 106–26; and three articles in *EAS*: Mark Meuwese, "The Dutch Connection: New Netherland, Pequots, and the Puritans in Southern New England"; Sabine Klein, " 'They Have Invaded The Whole River': Boundary Negotiations in Anglo-Dutch Colonial Discourse"; and Katherine A. Grandjean, "The Long Wake of the Pequot War," *EAS* 9.2 (Spring 2011): 295–323, 324–47, 379–411, respectively.

7. Many interpretations note the geopolitical motives of the colonial aggressors, though they seldom place the two conflicts side by side. Francis Jennings and Alfred Cave emphasize the importance of the rivalry with the Dutch in sparking the Pequot War, but they completely overlook the aftermath of the war in New Netherland and Indian country. Scholars of the Dutch–Indian conflict are generally more likely to link the two conflicts, such as Merwick, *The Shame and the Sorrow*, 33–42; Otto, *The Dutch–Munsee Encounter*, 106–26; scholars who place events on this coast in a more global context include Benjamin Schmidt, "Mapping an Empire: Cartographic and Colonial Rivalry in Seventeenth-Century Dutch and English North America," *WMQ* 54.3 (July 1997): 549–78; Cynthia Van Zandt, *Brothers Among Nations: The Pursuit of Intercultural Alliances in Early America, 1580–1660* (Oxford: Oxford University Press, 2008), 108–11; Alison Games, "Anglo-Dutch Connections and Overseas Enterprises: A Global Perspective on Lion Gardiner's World," *EAS* 9.2 (Spring 2011): 435–61. For two recent rereadings that highlight the watery character of these wars, see Katherine Grandjean, *American Passage: The Communications Frontier in Early New England* (Cambridge: Harvard University Press, 2015), 26–31 (Pequot War); Merwick, *The Shame and the Sorrow*, 33–42, 101–69 (Pequot War and Kieft's War). On the events that sparked the war, see Alfred A. Cave, "Who Killed John Stone? A Note on the Origins of the Pequot War," *WMQ* 49.3 (July 1992): 509–21; Andrew C. Lipman, "Murder on the Saltwater Frontier: The Death of John Oldham," *EAS* 9.2 (May 2011): 268–94.

8. Miantonomi's role is the least explored aspect connecting the wars, though two fairly recent articles take a good look at it: Oberg, " 'We are all the Sachems from East to West,' " 478–99; Grandjean, "The Long Wake of the Pequot War," 409–10.

9. On the founding of the Huys de Goede Hoop, see *DRCHNY*, 1:287, 2:139–40. On the Connecticut rivalry, see William Bradford, *Of Plymouth Plantation, 1620–1647,*

Samuel Eliot Morison, ed. (New York: Alfred A. Knopf, 1952), 257–60 (Dutch–Plymouth trade rivalry), 270 ("three or four . . . did rot"); John Winthrop, *The History of New England from 1630 to 1649*, 2 vols., James Savage, ed. (1825; repr., New York: Arno Press, 1972), 1:113, 153; Salisbury, *Manitou and Providence*, 206–9; Oliver Rink, *Holland on the Hudson: An Economic and Social History of Dutch New York* (Ithaca: Cornell University Press, 1986), 121–25. Francis Jennings speculates that the Puritans in Boston had ulterior motives for avoiding a partnership: "they declined to share Connecticut with Plymouth because they hoped to make it Massachusetts's exclusive possession." Though Jennings reflexively saw the most nefarious motives behind every Puritan action, he seems to have a point here. *Invasion of America*, 189.

10. Underhill, *Newes from America*, 16 ("a place of"); on the English belief in the principle of *vacuum domicilium* on the Connecticut, see WP, 4:454; Bradford, *Of Plymouth Plantation*, 280 ("the fear of").

11. Cave, *The Pequot War*, 57–58; Salisbury, *Manitou and Providence*, 210–11; DRCHNY, 1:287 (free trade policy); Underhill, *Newes from America*, 9–10 ("demanded of," "much exasperated").

12. Winthrop, *History*, 1:104, 111 ("upon pain of death"), 123 ("killed such"), 148 ("bound them," "suddenly blew"). The most complete analysis of Stone's death is found in Alfred A. Cave, "Who Killed John Stone?" *WMQ* 49.3 (July 1992): 509–21. Cave was responding to the argument made by Francis Jennings and others that Stone's killers were Western Niantics (a group of Pequot tributaries). Cave suggests that perhaps two attack parties, one Pequot, the other Niantic, were responsible for Stone's death. For the Western Niantic argument, see Mason, *A Brief History*, viii–ix; Jennings, *Invasion of America*, 190–94. On confusion between the Dutch and English (a claim that some colonists dismissed as a thin excuse but seems quite plausible given that Stone was headed to a Dutch fort and that the English presence on the river was still rare in 1634 compared to the continued Dutch traffic), see Underhill, *Newes from America*, 10–11.

13. Winthrop, *History*, 1:189 ("cleft to the brains"); another account of this murder, remembered over forty years later by John Gallop's son and recorded by the Ipswich preacher Thomas Cobbet, differs on several key details. The younger Gallop recalls that his father actually beheaded one of the Native assailants once on board, and he also misremembers that Pequots, not Narragansetts, were responsible for Oldham's death. As luck would have it, the younger Gallop would also, like Oldham, die at Narragansett hands forty years later as a soldier in King Philip's War. See Thomas Cobbet, "A Narrative of New England's Deliverances" (1677), *NEHGR*, 7:211.

14. In 1634 the Narragansett sachems offered Oldham the entire thousand-acre island of "Chippacursett" in Narragansett Bay "upon condition, as it should seem, that he would dwell there near unto them." The island is now known as Prudence Island.

Winthrop, *History*, 1: 147 ("Chippacursett," size), 189 ("set up sail . . . stood ready"); WP, 3:503 ("upon condition"), 504n1; Bradford, *Of Plymouth Plantation*, 166 ("strangely recovered"); Lipman, "Murder on the Saltwater Frontier," 285–91 (Oldham's murderers' motives).

15. Underhill, *Newes from America*, 1–13 (voyages to Block Island and Pequot River), 8 ("Ambassadour"), 13 ("for bootie"); Gardiner, "Relation of the Pequot Warres," *MHSC*, 3d ser., 3:141; Winthrop, *History*, 1:194–96.

16. Winthrop, *History*, 1:191 ("seventeen canoes").

17. WP, 4:409 ("when we undertook"); Jennings, *Invasion of America*, 190–91; Salisbury, *Manitou and Providence*, 207–15; Cave, *Pequot War*, 57–68; Eric S. Johnson, "Uncas and the Politics of Contact," and Paul A. Robinson, "Lost Opportunities: Miantonomi and the English in Seventeenth-Century Narragansett Country," in *Northeastern Indian Lives, 1632–1816*, ed. Robert S. Grumet (Amherst: University of Massachusetts Press, 1996), 1–16, 29–33, respectively.

18. For examples of colonists stating their grounds for war, see Mason, *A Brief History*, viii–ix; Bradford, *Of Plymouth Plantation*, 292; William Hubbard, *The History of the Indian Wars in New England from the First Settlement to the Termination of the War with King Philip, in 1677*, 2 vols., Samuel G. Drake, ed. (1865; repr., New York: Kaus Reprint, 1969), 1:38, 2:7–11; Increase Mather, *Early History of New England; Being a Relation of Hostile Passages Between the Indians and European Voyagers . . .*, Samuel G. Drake, ed. (Boston, 1864), 114–16.

19. Grandjean also makes the point that "the Pequot War was a water war" in "Reckoning: The Communications Frontier in Early New England" (Ph.D. diss., Harvard University, 2008), 49–53, 49 (quotation); the early raiding is well chronicled in McBride and Naumec, "Battle of Mystic Fort," WP, 3:270 ("cutting off," "for as soon"), 298 ("Pequts heare," "comfort them selves"), 321 ("the Indians are"); Underhill, *Newes from America*, 20 ("One Master Tillie"); Mason, *A Brief History*, x ("made a shot," "drew their Canoes").

20. Mason, *A Brief History*, 1 ("sailing down"); WP, 3:411 ("direct the Pinnace," "without landing").

21. Underhill, *Newes from America*, 32 ("deluding the Pequeants"); Mason, *A Brief History*, 9 ("Exulting and Rejoycing"); Hubbard, *The History of the Indian Wars*, 1:25 ("were secure").

22. There are several historians who have given trophy exchanges more than a passing glance. See James Axtell and William C. Sturtevant, "The Unkindest Cut, or Who Invented Scalping?" WMQ 37.3 (July 1980): 451–72; Axtell, "The Moral Dilemmas of Scalping," in *Natives and Newcomers: The Cultural Origins of North America* (New York: Oxford University Press, 2001), 259–79. Evan Haefeli examines trophies' place within two different "cultures of violence" in an essay on a contemporary Dutch–Indian war. See Haefeli, "Kieft's War," 17–40. Jill Lepore analyzes the meanings embedded in severed body parts for both cultures during

King Philip's War, though she emphasizes display rather than exchange. See Lepore, *The Name of War: King Philip's War and the Origins of American Identity* (New York: Vintage, 1998), 148, 173–80, 190, 303n103. Discussing the bounties for wolves' heads in New England, Jon T. Coleman makes connections between colonists' and Indians' uses of human parts and their uses of animal parts. See Coleman, "Terms of Dismemberment," *Common-place* 4.1 (October 2003), http://www.common-place.org/vol-04/no-01/coleman/. Few historians have emphasized cultural accommodation as a major feature of the English victory, though that appears to be changing. Jenny Hale Pulsipher points out the large degree of negotiation and flexibility in the early stage of Indian–English relationships in New England and argues that the years after the war of 1637 were a turning point. See Pulsipher, *Subjects unto the Same King: Indians, English, and the Contest for Authority in Colonial New England* (Philadelphia: University of Pennsylvania Press, 2005), 8–36.

23. Regina Janes, *Losing Our Heads: Beheadings in Literature and Culture* (New York: New York University Press, 2005), 1–9; Thomas Churchyard, *A Generall Rehearsall of warres, called Churchyardes Choise* (London, 1579), n. p. (quotations). For further discussions of English notions of a just war, see Karr, *JAH* 85:880–88, esp. 885–88; Lepore, *Name of War*, 105–13. An overview of how the colonization of Ireland influenced the colonization of America is found in Nicholas P. Canny, "The Ideology of English Colonization: From Ireland to America," *WMQ* 30.4 (October 1973): 575–98; For a discussion of Standish's actions at Plymouth, see Salisbury, *Manitou and Providence*, 130; Axtell and Sturtevant, *WMQ* 37:464; John Laurence, *A History of Capital Punishment*, 3d ed. (New York: Citadel Press, 1960), 11 ("godly butchery"). George Lee Haskins cautions that the Bible "was an indispensable touchstone, but not the cornerstone, of Puritan legal thinking," yet he also notes that New England colonists closely adhered to scriptural definitions of capital crimes. Some Massachusetts capital statutes were nearly word-for-word transcriptions of biblical passages. See Haskins, *Law and Authority in Early Massachusetts: A Study in Tradition and Design* (New York: Macmillan, 1960), 118, 141–53, 162 (quotation).

24. For an expanded version of this argument, see Andrew Lipman, " 'A meanes to knitt them togeather': The Exchange of Body Parts in the Pequot War," *WMQ* 65.1 (January 2008): 3–28.

25. Underhill, *Newes from America*, 24–25 ("five Pequeats heads," 25); Winthrop, *History*, 1:223 ("set all their heads"). In his account, Lion Gardiner mentions that the Pequots killed only four men. See Gardiner, *MHSC*, 3d ser., 3:131–60, esp. 149.

26. RW to John Mason and Thomas Prence, June 22, 1670, in Glenn W. LaFantasie, ed., *The Correspondence of Roger Williams*, 2 vols. (Providence: Brown University Press, 1988), 2:609–23 ("to pieces," 2:611). Tutoring his countrymen in the ways of Native gift giving, Williams hinted to the Massachusetts colonists that a Pequot spy

would like a new coat, and he advised them that "For any gratuities or tokens," one Narragansett sachem "desires Sugar," whereas the other preferred "powder." WP, 3:410–12 (quotation, 412).

27. Winthrop, *History*, 1:190, 195 ("crept into a swamp"); Gardiner, *MHSC* 3:142 ("thus began the war"). In his summary of the war, Gardiner repeated his claim that this scalp triggered it, remarking that all the bloodshed of the war happened "only because Kichamokin [Cutshamakin], a Bay Indian, killed one Pequit." See Gardiner, *MHSC*, 3:151 (quotation); Salisbury, *Manitou and Providence*, 218.

28. Gardiner, *MHSC*, 3:150 (quotations); Mason, *A Brief History*, 14.

29. Mason, *A Brief History*, 17 ("Pequots now became"); Winthrop, *History*, 1:237 ("still many Pequods' heads"). For accounts of other Indian groups supplying heads, see WP, 3:450–52.

30. Winthrop, *History*, 1:235 ("part of the skin"); Bradford, *Of Plymouth Plantation*, 297 ("to satisfy the English"); Vincent, *True Relation of the Late Battell*, 17 ("wily Mowhacks"). For a larger analysis of the Mohawks' role on the New England frontier, see Neal Salisbury, "Indians and Colonists in Southern New England after the Pequot War: An Uneasy Balance," in *Pequots in Southern New England: The Fall and Rise of an American Indian Nation*, ed. Laurence Hauptman and James Wherry (Norman: University of Oklahoma Press, 1990), 81–95; Salisbury, "Toward the Covenant Chain: Iroquois and Southern New England Algonquians, 1637–1684," in *Beyond the Covenant Chain: The Iroquois and Their Neighbors in Indian North America, 1600–1800*, ed. Daniel K. Richter and James H. Merrell (Syracuse: Syracuse University Press, 1987), 61–74; WP, 3:446–48, esp. 447–48, 450. Lynn Ceci makes the point that wampum from Indians funded English expansion. See Ceci, "Native Wampum as a Peripheral Resource in the Seventeenth-Century World-System," in Hauptman and Wherry, *Pequots in Southern New England*, 48–63. For a discussion of the war's aftermath, see Salisbury, "Indians and Colonists in Southern New England after the Pequot War," 81–95.

31. "Appendix II: Articles Between the Inglish in Connecticut and the Indians Sachems," in Vaughan, *New England Frontier*, 340–41 ("theirs," "shall as soon," 341); Cave, *Pequot War*, 159 ("branded on the shoulder"); Michael L. Fickes, " 'They Could Not Endure That Yoke': The Captivity of Pequot Women and Children after the War of 1637," *NEQ* 73.1 (March 2000): 58–81, 61n13; Andrea Robertson Cremer, "Possession: Indian Bodies, Cultural Control, and Colonialism in the Pequot War," *EAS* 6.2 (2008): 295–345

32. Gardiner, *MHSC*, 3d. ser., 3:150 ("we will give"); WP, 3:452 ("as Long Iland").

33. Bradford, *Of Plymouth Plantation*, 312 (Dutch purchase of Stone's booty); Gardiner, "Relation," 147 (£10 reward), 152 (Dutch purchase of Oldham's gold); Underhill, *Newes from America*, 26–27 (redemption of captives).

34. Winthrop, *History*, 1:217 ("to keep"). Another party of Dutch traders took the wife of the Pequot sachem hostage, probably to extort a payment in wampum, but

before they could collect a ransom English soldiers "violently" stole the captive. See *WP*, 3:419 (Dutch captive taking), 479 ("so excellent").

35. Henk Den Heijer, "The Dutch West India Company, 1621–1791," in *Riches from Atlantic Commerce: Dutch Transatlantic Trade and Shipping, 1585–1817*, ed. Johannes Postma and Victor Enthoven (Leiden: Brill, 2003), 79–80 (Usselincx); *DRCHNY*, 1:69, 70–71, 83–88, 103, 104 (colonists v. company trade disputes); 106 ("not seasonably"), 107 ("by what right"). On attitudes among the company toward colonists, see also Merwick, *The Shame and the Sorrow*, 62–64.

36. Wim Klooster, "The Place of New Netherland in the West India Company's Grand Scheme," in *Revisiting New Netherland: Perspectives on Early Dutch America*, ed. Joyce D. Goodfriend (Leiden: Brill, 2005), 57–70; Den Heijer, "The Dutch West India Company," 92–94. Jonathan I. Israel has offered the most comprehensive interpretation of the second half of the Dutch Revolt, which he sees more as an imperial contest than as a continuation of the battle for independence. See Israel, "A Conflict of Empires: Spain and the Netherlands, 1618–1648," *Past and Present* 76 (August 1977): 34–74. On the crash of 1638, see Anne Goldgar, *Tulipmania: Money, Honor, and Knowledge in the Dutch Golden Age* (Chicago: University of Chicago Press, 2007); Simon Schama, *The Embarrassment of Riches: An Interpretation of Dutch Culture in the Golden Age* (New York: Vintage, 1997), 350–66; Burrows and Wallace, *Gotham*, 60.

37. *DRCHNY*, 1:111–23. For more on *ziekentroosters* and the early Reformed Church in the colony, see Gerald F. De Jong, *The Dutch Reformed Church in the American Colonies* (Grand Rapids: Eerdsmans, 1978), 11–27.

38. *DRCHNY*, 1:104 (appointment of Kieft), 151 ("Woter, Woter"), 13:7 (Raritans); De Vries, *NNN*, 187 ("unruliness"); Bradford, *Of Plymouth Plantation*, 369 ("he could scarce"). Quoted in Otto, *The Dutch–Munsee Encounter*, 92 ("the Indians came"). Otto found the reference in the Notarial Archives of the Amsterdam Gemeentearchief (GAA NA 1283, July 13, 1641, 114). He notes that "the statement in the original document was crossed out, but since the statement does not relate to the main business of the deposition, it nevertheless is likely a true report." Ibid., 103n60; Alan Trelease discusses the cryptic evidence of the Raritan conflict of 1634 in *Indian Affairs*, 45–46. There is no direct mention of a gift exchange, but given the customs and expectations of Munsee leaders there is no way a peace could have been settled without ceremonial presents.

39. For an examination of Kieft's early career, his social milieu, and the patronage networks that contributed to his appointment, see Willem Frijhoff, "Neglected Networks: Director Willem Kieft (1602–1647) and His Dutch Relations," in Goodfriend, ed., *Revisiting New Netherland*, 147–204; "Copie of a letter from New Netherland, out of the Fort Amsterdam, on the Manhavens of Guillame Kieft — Spring 1638," an intercepted letter, possibly translated and transcribed by William Boswell, the English ambassador to the Dutch States General. My thanks to Jaap

Jacobs for alerting me to the existence of this letter. BNA, State Papers 84/154 1638–1639, f. 267.

40. Trelease, *Indian Affairs*, 60–61; Otto, *The Dutch–Munsee Encounter*, 108; discussion of this disorganized settlement process can be found in DRCHNY, 1:135–36 (letter to Heren XIX); anonymous, "Journal of New Netherland, 1647," NNN, 271, 273 ("contrary to"); De Vries, NNN, 226, 271–73; NYCM, 4:186.

41. DRCHNY, 1:150 ("the liberty . . . father of hate"); anonymous, "Journal of New Netherland," NNN, 273 ("the liberty to trade," "stole much more"); NYCM, 4:42 ("guns, powder, and lead"), 70 ("against which," ordinance on containing livestock).

42. On the disruptive nature of sailors, see also Jacobs, *New Netherland*, 40–41; Winthrop, *History*, 1:299, 2:6, 316 ("sober," "discreet," "prudent"); NYCM, 4:4 ("must refrain"); 8 ("evil and mischief," ordinance on lodging sailors), 31 (ordinance keeping soldiers on Manhattan).

43. NYCM, 4:29–30 (trial of Cors Pietersen for assault and theft from an Indian), 52 (trial and punishment of Jan Dondey and Claes), 61 (ordinances on fair trade with Indians), 65 (another trial of a soldier for stealing wampum), 73 (reprimand regarding loose livestock). For all other crimes not discussed in detail, see NYCM, 4:17–18, 24, 51, 62 (knife fights); 24–25, 66 (manslaughter cases); 4, 23, 25, 29, 30–34, 65 (fraud/theft); 4, 26, 33, 43–45, 46–47, 122 (sex crimes).

44. Jan Gysbertsen killed Gerrit Jansen on Saturday, May, 15, 1639. The ban on casks was issued immediately after the Sabbath on Monday, May 17, 1639. A couple of months after the attempted mutiny, when the deputy sheriff arrested sailors from *Den Harinck* for smuggling liquor, the men lured him below decks and beat him bloody with a crowbar and then heaved an iron cannonball at him as he fled the ship. NYCM, 4:54 (work strike by nine soldiers), 55 (Gregoris Pieterson trial and execution order), 60 ("great expense," ordinance taxing Indians), 62–63 (*Den Harinck*).

45. De Vries, NNN, 209 ("must be").

46. A similar act also occurred at Kievets-hoeck later that same decade: the Dutch accused the English of again tearing down the arms and replacing the plate with "a ridiculing picture of a face." On the imagery of fooling, see Schama, *The Embarrassment of Riches*, 362–65, 365 ("graphic satire"); when the Prince of Arragon eagerly opened a chest expecting silver, he groaned when he found "the portrait of a blinking idiot . . . a fool's head" inside. Shakespeare, *The Merchant of Venice*, 2.4:54; NYCM, 4:71 (new seals), 75–76 ("torn off"), 76–85, 77 ("make a strong protest," "above all," "eight men"), 79 ("Lt. Daniel Houw," "Mr. Foret"), 80–81 ("fool's face"), 84 ("without the director's").

47. See NYCM, 4:29–30 (trial of Cors Pietersen). The best account of the *De Vreede* incident (and all quotations) comes from the "Declaration of Harmen

Meyndertsen van den Bogaert and others respecting an attack by the Raritan Indians," given several years later to the provincial secretary, in *NYRPS*, 2:409–10. For other summaries of the incident, see *DRCHNY*, 13:6–7; De Vries, *NNN*, 208.

48. *NYCM*, 4:87 ("orders to attack"); De Vries, *NNN*, 208–9 ("negro's house," colonial plundering, "the troop wished," "on account of the pertinacity," "the troop killed," Van Tienhoven's unpaid trading debt, "standing at the mast," "such acts of tyranny"). Though some historians question the accuracy of de Vries's account, pointing out his heavy animosity toward Kieft, this incident seems credible, not least of which because it paints Van Tienhoven and Kieft as more restrained than the soldiers themselves.

49. De Vries, *NNN*, 208, 211 (Raritan counterattacks), 211 ("in a great triumph"). As Paul Otto notes, Pachem "may not have really considered the Dutch his 'best friends,' but he probably believed survival in the new world of European colonization required cultivating their friendship." Otto, *Dutch–Munsee Encounter*, 116–17; Interrogatories to be proposed to Dr. Johannes de la Montaigne, October 1643, Interrogatories to be proposed to Secretary van Tienhoven, July 21, 1650, *DRCHNY*, 1:199, 410; *NYCM*, 4:126 ("came to a standstill").

50. Accounts of Smits's murder can be found in De Vries, *NNN*, 213; anonymous, "Journal of New Netherland," ibid., 274–75 (quotations); Report of the Board of Accounts on New Netherland, 1644, *DRCHNY*, 1:150.

51. *NYCM*, 4:124–25 (plan for war), 126 ("deaf man's door," "lull the Indians to sleep," "ship to come from the fatherland").

52. *NYCM*, 4:30 ("that he well knew"), 126 ("the war cannot"); De Vries, *NNN*, 213 ("there was no profit"). Realizing that an attack of this magnitude would require colonial volunteers in addition to the company soldiers, the council pointed out that since Kieft was "our [commander] as well as the soldiers' chief, therefore, in order to prevent all disorder, the honorable director shall personally lead this expedition." This request could be taken either as a veiled criticism of Van Tienhoven's permitting "disorder" during the raid on Staten Island or as a frank acknowledgment that rallying the young, impulsive company soldiers without an authoritative leader could lead to trouble. Though no new threats of mutiny had occurred since 1639, the men were still regularly committing mischief and showing worrisome symptoms of boredom and unrest. Just weeks earlier, a company sailor and gunner had drunkenly loaded and fired one of the fort's cannon, damaging the house of a colonist. *NYCM*, 4:121–22, 125.

53. On Miantonomi's career as a diplomat, see Robinson, "Lost Opportunities," in Grumet, ed., *Northeastern Indian Lives, 1632–1816*, 1–16.

54. Williams to Winthrop, August 20, 1637, in LaFantasie, ed., *The Correspondence of Roger Williams*, 1:113 ("*Chenock*," emphasis added); Oberg, " 'We are all the Sachems from East to West,' " 478–99; Jennings, *Invasion of America*, 265–70; Salisbury, *Manitou and Providence*, 225–34.

55. Lion Gardiner, "Leift. Lion Gardener his relation of the Pequot Warres," and anonymous, "Relation of the Indian Plott," in *MHSC*, 3:154 ("you know . . ."), 163 ("the english did gett").

56. Gardiner, "Relation of the Pequot Warres," *MHSC*, 3:153 ("are no Sachems")

57. Ibid. Anonymous, "Relation of the Indian Plott," *MHSC*, 3:155 ("men, women, and children"), 154 ("we all Indians"), 162 ("the English were . . . It is true," "all the Sachems"), 164 ("would kill"); *WP*, 3:440 ("the only lords").

58. De Vries, *NNN*, 213–14 (Van Dyck expeditions), 215 ("villainous Swannekens"); anonymous, "Journal of New Netherland," *NNN*, 275–76; *DRCHNY*, 1:199, 410.

59. Anonymous, *NNN*, 276 ("soliciting them," "some of the neighboring Indians").

60. *PCR*, 10:440 ("offered to mediate . . . they questioned not").

61. For descriptions of the Munsee counterattacks, see *DRCHNY*, 1:416–17; anonymous, *NNN*, 277–78; *PCR*, 10:440 ("that first," "saw their flames"); De Vries, *NNN*, 229 ("wondered . . . why should").

62. De Vries, *NNN*, 232 ("could have").

63. De Vries, Anonymous, "Journal of New Netherland," Van der Donck, "Vertoogh," *NNN*, 232 ("many of," "kill these," "laughed within"), 279 ("ran through").

64. Van der Donck, "Vertoogh," *NNN*, 334–35 (Long Island attacks); Winthrop, *History*, 2:135–36 (mainland fighting); *NYRPS*, 2:170–71 (Newark Bay attacks), 175 ("the great number"), 200–201 (blue arrows).

65. On the influence of the Dutch Revolt on European fighting in America, see Shelley, *John Underhill*, 98–110, 290–92, 302–20; Merwick, *The Shame and the Sorrow*, 108–10, 127–28; Gardiner, *MHSC*, 3:149 ("we old soldiers"). In a paragraph waxing on the role of fate in war, John Mason made a passing reference to the "great Commander in Belgia" named "Grubbendunk" (a reference to the Baron of Grobbendonk, Antoine Schetz), who died taking a city. Mason, *A Brief History*, 3. The revolt itself was a key conflict in driving a larger transformation of warfare in early modern Europe, one that the historian Michael Roberts called "the military revolution," though more recently scholars have revised that formulation. Now they characterize the changes as a sometimes gradual, sometimes rapid evolution of military techniques in the seventeenth century that was highly dependent on print culture. John Childs promotes the term *evolution* over *revolution*, arguing that "advances in technology during the later Middle Ages resulted in new weapons that gradually modified all aspects of war between 1450 and 1700, but revolutions are sharp, sudden events: they do not occur across 350 years, or even a century." Childs, *Warfare in the Seventeenth Century* (London: Cassell, 2001), 16–17, 17 (quotation); on print culture and seventeenth-century "military evolution," see David R. Lawrence, *The Complete Soldier: Military Books and Military Culture in Early Stuart England, 1603–1645* (Leiden: Brill, 2009), esp. 313–61.

66. Anonymous, *NNN*, 280–84 (quotations); Trelease, *Indian Affairs*, 76–80; Haefeli, "Kieft's War," 31–33; *DRCHNY*, 14:56 (Underhill's attacks); on the winter feast, see

Kathleen Bragdon, *Native People of Southern New England, 1500–1650* (Norman: University of Oklahoma Press, 1996), 227–28.

67. *NYCM*, 4:216 ("they will not"), 265 ("embark in one"); *PCR*, 10:440 ("After vast expenses"). Goelet Treaty Index, 1643–45, N-YHS.

68. *WP*, 4:419–20, 428 ("spet . . . fell down dead"); *NYRPS*, 2:206 ("Onderhill . . . strike at random"). Katherine Grandjean also explores the legacy of wartime trauma among New England's fighting men in "The Long Wake of the Pequot War," 379–411.

69. Mason, *A Brief History*, 11 ("and beholding"); Underhill, *Newes from America*, 40 ("wee are a people"); De Vries, *NNN*, 234 ("come daily").

70. Roger Williams, *A Key Into the Language of America; Or, An help to the Language of the Natives in that part of America called New-England* (London, 1643; repr., Bedford, Mass., Applewood Books, 1997), 186 (*aumánsk* or *waukaunòsint*); Adriaen van der Donck, *A Description of New Netherland*, eds. Charles T. Gehring and William Starna, trans. Diederik Goedhuys (Lincoln: University of Nebraska Press, 2008), 82–83 ("high or steep," "to shelter"). For further discussion of coastal Algonquian forts and defensive behavior during war, see Bragdon, *Native People*, 96, 148–50, 169–83; Gaynell Stone, "Introduction" and Ralph Solecki, "Native Forts of the Mid-17th Century," *in Native Forts of the Long Island Sound Area*, ed. Gaynell Stone (Stony Brook, N.Y.: Suffolk County Archeological Association, 2006), vii–viii, 1–2, respectively.

71. Van der Donck, *Description*, 83 ("think highly," "they do not," "of little consequence"); Mason, *A Brief History*, 6 ("almost"); Wood, *New England's Prospect*, 85 ("naked assailants"). Some foreigners who witnessed these structures were complimentary. The colonist Philip Vincent marveled that although Pequots lacked "mathematicall skill, or use of yron toole," their "naturall reason and experience hath taught them to erect" a sizable "military fortresse." Vincent, *True Relation of the Late Battell*, 13 ("mathematicall").

72. For summaries of the excavations discussed in this paragraph and the following one, see William Wallace Tooker, "The Indian Fort at Montauk," Edward J. Johannemann, "Fort Hill and Vicinity, Montauk," Kevin McBride, "Fort Island: Conflict and Trade in Long Island Sound," Christine N. Reiser, "Safeguarding the 'Mint': Wampum Production and the Social Uses of Space at Fort Island," Charlotte C. Taylor, "The History and Archaeology of Fort Ninegret, a 17th Century Eastern Niantic Site in Charlestown, R.I.," Bert Salwen, "European Trade Goods and the Chronology of the Fort Shantok Site," McBride, "The Pequots in King Philip's War," in Stone, ed., *Native Forts*, 243–305, 323–36; Anne-Marie Cantwell and Dianna diZerega Wall, *Unearthing Gotham: The Archaeology of New York City* (New Haven: Yale University Press, 2001), 135–42; entry for February 16, 1664, Goelet Treaty Minutes, N-YHS ("a small cannon").

73. For larger context around the murder of Miantonomi, see Oberg, " 'We are all the Sachems from East to West,' " 478–99; Oberg, *Uncas: First of the Mohegans*

(Ithaca: Cornell University Press, 2004), 87–109; Julie A. Fisher and David J. Silverman, *Ninigret, Sachem of the Niantic and Narragansetts* (Ithaca: Cornell University Press, 2014), 47–53.

74. For a discussion of Kieft's fate and the war's aftermath, see Merwick, *The Shame and the Sorrow,* 170–79.

Chapter 5. Acts of Navigation

1. On Anglo–Dutch competition and proximity, see Benjamin Schmidt, "Mapping an Empire: Cartographic and Colonial Rivalry in Seventeenth-Century Dutch and English North America," *WMQ* 54.3 (July 1997): 549–78; Joshua W. Lane, ed., *The Impact of New Netherlands upon the Colonial Long Island Basin: Report of a Yale–Smithsonian Seminar Held at Yale University, New Haven, Connecticut, May 3–5, 1990* (New Haven: Yale–Smithsonian, 1993); on the larger Anglo–Dutch Atlantic in this period, see Christian Koot, *Empire at the Periphery: British Colonists, Anglo–Dutch Trade, and the Development of the English Atlantic, 1621–1713* (New York: New York University Press, 2011), 47–116; see also the special issue of *Early American Studies* edited by Ned Landsman and Andrew Newman titled "The Worlds of Lion Gardiner, c. 1599–1663: Crossings and Boundaries," *EAS* 9.2 (Spring 2011), esp. the articles by Mark Meuwese, Kim Todt, Sabine Klein, and Alison Games. The Dutch were expelled from their eponymous island in Narragansett Bay in 1652. *RICR*, 1:243–44.

2. "Concerning the United Provinces and there [*sic*] relation to this crown" (1633), BNA, State Papers 84/147, f. 222 ("grounded upon"); John Winthrop Jr. to Petrus Stuyvesant, June 17, 1663, Winthrop Family Papers, MHS, reel 7 ("friendly peace"); *MHSC,* 5th ser., 1:396 ("neighbourhood").

3. *NNC,* 11:169 ("would be glad"); *DRCHNY,* 2:157 ("neither nation"); *RNA,* 4:331 ("on the one side"); *PCR,* 10:23–24 ("by the duch").

4. Antipas Newman to John Winthrop Jr., July 17, 1660, Winthrop Family Papers, MHS, reel 6 ("taken a canooe . . . before the evening"); Alden T. Vaughan, *Early American Indian Documents: Treaties and Laws, 1607–1789,* 20 vols. (Bethesda: University Publications of America, 1979–2004), 17:313 ("barbarouse and inhumaine").

5. *RWC,* 1:234 ("lyes are frequent"); *MHSC,* 4th ser., 7:468 ("I understand not"); Leicester Bradner, "Ninigret's Naval Campaigns Against the Montauks," in *Rhode Island Historical Society Collections* 18.1 (January 1925): 14–20.

6. John Eliot to William Steele, December 8, 1652, *NEHGR,* 36:294 ("Unkas and Nenecrot"); Bradner, "Ninigret's Naval Campaigns Against the Montauks," 14–20; Robert Grumet, ed., *Northeastern Indian Lives, 1632–1816* (Amherst: University of Massachusetts Press, 1996); Uncas and Ninigret have each been the subject of two fine biographies that cover the complexity of their lives and quarrels in depth. See

Michael Leroy Oberg, *Uncas: First of the Mohegans* (Ithaca: Cornell University Press, 2004); Julie A. Fisher and David J. Silverman, *Ninigret, Sachem of the Niantic and Narragansetts* (Ithaca: Cornell University Press, 2014).

7. *RWC*, 1:146 ("he hath drawn"); *WP*, 6:20 ("univerall monarky," "desire they might").

8. *WP*, 6:20 ("new monarkes"); Robert Lay to John Winthrop Jr., March 23, 1658/9, Winthrop Family Papers, MHS, reel 6 ("doune from the backline . . . dun murder"); for further details on the Lay family, see *NEHGR*, 62:172–78, 238–41.

9. John Mason to John Winthrop Jr., June 1657, Thomas Welles to John Winthrop Jr., Francis Newman to John Winthrop Jr., March 17, 1658/9, Winthrop Family Papers, MHS, reel 5 (Mason: "continually ly," "truly sir"), reel 6 (Welles: "I feare the Indians," Newman: "Such Insolent cariag"); Katherine A. Grandjean, "Reckoning: The Communications Frontier in Early New England" (Ph.D. diss., Harvard University, 2008), 276–82, appendices, 287–348.

10. *WP*, 6:28 ("Nenékunat now with me); William Cheseborough to John Winthrop Jr., March 26,1654/5, William Thomson to John Winthrop Jr., January 3, 1660/1, Edward Rawson to John Winthrop Jr., March 1660/1, Daniel Lane to John Winthrop Jr., June 17, 1665, Winthrop Family Papers, MHS, reel 5 (Cheseborough: "I could get no quiet"), reel 6 (Thomson: "I am Importuned," Rawson, "Indains comme yesterday"); reel 8 (Lane: "your friend unchcage").

11. On Native literacy and letter writing, see Jill Lepore, "Dead Men Tell No Tales: John Sassamon and the Fatal Consequences of Literacy," *American Quarterly* 46.1 (December 1994): 479–512; *WP*, 3:442 ("to augment"), 6:20 ("new monarkes"); Francis Newman to JW2, April 14, 1659, Winthrop Family Papers, MHS, reel 6 ("not knowing").

12. For various accounts of Dutch colonists using Native couriers, see *DRCHNY*, 2:460–63, 465, 467, 13:96, 305, 333; Willem Beekman to Petrus Stuyvesant. September 12, 1659, December 16, 1659, January 25, 1660, Beekman Letterbook, N-YHS ("I could not . . . disappointed me again").

13. *PCR*, 10:49 ("as well as most Duch"); quoted in Susanah Shaw Romney, *New Netherland Connections: Intimate Networks and Atlantic Ties in Seventeenth-Century America* (Chapel Hill: University of North Carolina Press, 2014), 249–69, 263 (*kinterhaye*), 266 ("that she was").

14. Quoted in Romney, *New Netherland Connections*, 187 (translation by Romney: "good and needful," "they allow"); an inferior eighteenth-century translation of this schooling agreement is found in the entry for February 1660, Goelet Treaty Minutes Microfilm, N-YHS. On the failures of Dutch missionaries, see Jaap Jacobs, *New Netherland: A Dutch Colony in Seventeenth-Century America* (Ithaca: Cornell University Press, 2009), 176–79; on missionaries and translators, see William Wallace Tooker, *John Eliot's First Indian Teacher and Interpreter Cockenoe-De-Long Island and the Story of His Career from the Early Records*

(London: Henry Stevens' Son and Stiles, 1896); Lois M. Feister, "Linguistic Communication between the Dutch and Indians in New Netherland, 1609–1664," *Ethnohistory* 20.1 (Winter 1973): 25–38; Ives Goddard, "The Use of Pidgins and Jargons on the East Coast of North America," in *The Language Encounter in the Americas, 1492–1800: A Collection of Essays,* ed. Edward G. Gray and Norman Fiering (New York: Berghahn Books, 2000), 61–73; James Axtell, "Babel of Tongues: Communicating with the Indians," in *Natives and Newcomers: The Cultural Origins of North America* (New York: Oxford University Press, 2001), 46–78; NNCM, 6:145 (Adam), 204 (Joseph). The complexity of translation and communication in this zone is explored by Katherine Grandjean in *American Passage: The Communications Frontier in Early New England* (Cambridge: Harvard University Press, 2015), 76–109.

15. Romney, *New Netherland Connections,* 151–61.

16. For a representative sample of sex cases from 1638–40, see NYCM, 4:4, 26, 33, 43–45, 46–47, 122; David Pietersz. de Vries, "Korte Historiael Ende Journales Aenteyckninge," *NNN,* 231 ("had given them"), Megapolensis, *NNN,* 174 ("the women are"); Van der Donck, *Description,* 86 ("as if it were," gifts for sex); Romney, *New Netherland Connections,* 177–80, 177 ("ensured that sex"). A tantalizing and exceedingly rare case of an extramarital affair between a European woman and a Native man is hinted at in the letter from 1654. John Cullick gossiped about the supposed infidelities of one Martha Groves, writing, "I am allso Informed that the wife of one Grover within your Libberties liveth very scandalously, and hath unmeete society with the natives or at least some of them which cannott but be a great Abomination to the Lord, and a blemish to our Nation and profession." John Cullick to John Winthrop Jr., November 2, 1654, Winthrop Family Transcripts, MHS.

17. Robert S. Grumet, *The Munsee Indians: A History* (Norman: University of Oklahoma Press, 2009), 20–22; RTH, 1:40.

18. DRCHNY, 1:366 ("great numbers"); NNCM, 6:145 ("done no harm").

19. NYCM, 4:265–66 (Kieft's War); DRCHNY, 14:60 (Kieft's War); Grumet, *Munsee Indians,* 60–62, 70–71, 74, 77, 99–100.

20. Neal Salisbury, "Indians and Colonists in Southern New England after the Pequot War: An Uneasy Balance," in *Pequots in Southern New England: The Fall and Rise of an American Indian Nation,* ed. Laurence Hauptman and James Wherry (Norman: University of Oklahoma Press, 1990), 81–95; Salisbury, "Toward the Covenant Chain: Iroquois and Southern New England Algonquians, 1637–1684," in *Beyond the Covenant Chain: The Iroquois and Their Neighbors in Indian North America, 1600–1800,* ed. Daniel K. Richter and James H. Merrell (Syracuse: Syracuse University Press, 1987), 61–74.

21. Thomas Stanton to John Winthrop Jr., May 2, 1653, Winthrop Family Transcripts, MHS ("There bee a sperit"); NNC, 11:230 ("whole world").

22. The concurrent Thirty Years' War came to a formal end the following October with the Peace of Westphalia. For overviews of Stuyvesant's pre–New Netherland career, see Oliver Rink, *Holland on the Hudson: An Economic and Social History of Dutch New York* (Ithaca: Cornell University Press, 1986), 223–26; Russell Shorto, *The Island at the Center of the World: The Epic Story of Dutch Manhattan and the Forgotten Colony That Shaped America* (New York, 2004), 146–55.

23. PCR, 9:62 ("to fasten," "we know"), 64 ("English were fooles"), 179 ("various and unsertaine"); quoted in Rink, *Holland on the Hudson*, 247 ("in New Netherland").

24. Declaration of the Commissioners of the United Colonies, September 10, 1648, YIPP 1648.09.10.00 (*St. Beninjo*); Stuyvesant to Eaton, May 4, 1649, NNC, 11:46 ("I doe reallie"); PCR, 9:107 ("shall enjoy"), 112–15 (1649 meeting), 171–73, 188–90 (Treaty of Hartford). Ironically, given that the English were soon to pass the Navigation Acts, Puritans alleged it was the Dutch who wanted a *mare clausum*, grousing about "the dutch Imposicions and restraints by which english Marchants are burthened and much discouraged in their trade." *PCR*, 9:128.

25. Rink, *Holland on the Hudson*, 235–47; Gehring, "Introduction," NNC, 11:xiv–xx.

26. The summary of Anglo–Dutch hostilities in this and the following three paragraphs draws from Kenneth Harold Dobson Haley, *The Dutch in the Seventeenth Century* (New York: Harcourt Brace Jovanovich, 1972), 75–82; Maarten Roy Prak, *The Dutch Republic: The Golden Age* (Cambridge: Cambridge University Press, 2005), 45–51; John Morrill, "Postlude: Between War and Peace, 1651–1662," in *The Civil Wars: A Military History of England, Scotland, and Ireland, 1638–1660*, ed. John Kenyon and Jane Ohlmeyer (Oxford: Oxford University Press, 1998), 312–17; Jonathan Israel, *The Dutch Republic: Its Rise, Greatness, and Fall, 1477–1806* (New York: Oxford University Press, 1995), 713–34, 766–74. Countering the economic interpretation of the wars posited by Israel and others, Steven A. Pincus offers a more nuanced and contingent reading of English motives as stemming from "an unusual political alliance between apocalyptic Protestants and classical republicans." See Pincus, *Protestantism and Patriotism: Ideologies and the Making of English Foreign Policy, 1650–1668* (Cambridge: Cambridge University Press, 2002).

27. Anonymous, *The Character of Holland* (1652; repr. London, 1672), 1 ("ingested Vomit"), 4 ("Hogs"), 5 ("Sea-sick Courage"); Morrill, "Postlude: Between War and Peace 1651–1662," in Kenyon and Ohlmeyer, eds., *The Civil Wars*, 312–17, 317 (derogatory prints).

28. On Amboyna and the war itself, see Benjamin Schmidt, *Innocence Abroad: The Dutch Imagination and the New World, 1570–1670* (Cambridge: Cambridge University Press, 2001), 292–98; Rink, *Holland on the Hudson*, 255–56.

29. Though previous disputes between the colonies had been brought to the attention of high-level ambassadors and King Charles I, European diplomats made scant mention of either nation's respective "New" provinces during most of the First

Anglo–Dutch war. This would change in the Second Anglo–Dutch War, though, as the takeover of New Amsterdam did attract a fair amount of European notice. See Dutch Treaty Papers, 1651–65, BNA SP 103/46, and more generally the Anglo–Dutch State Papers for 1649–65, BNA SP 84/159–175. Alison Games, "Anglo-Dutch Connections and Overseas Enterprises: A Global Perspective on Lion Gardiner's World," *EAS* 9.2 (Spring 2011): 435–61, esp. 459–60; NNC, 11:155 ("be on guard") 191 ("pleased to learn").

30. NNC, 11:168–69 ("sade news," "a vast wilderness"); RNA, 1:65–66 ("Fort Amsterdam").

31. *PCR*, 9:148 ("strengthening and animating"), 10:3 ("Att a meeting . . . hiddius a plot"), 12 ("that the Duch . . . left naked").

32. *PCR*, 10:5 ("three of the"), 8–10 ("he went" . . . "lett me in").

33. *PCR*, 10:8–9 ("What doe the English . . . by the dore of the English").

34. *PCR*, 10:10 ("said there was"), 43–45 ("Indians whoe dwell"), 47 ("Coco").

35. NYCM, 5:143 ("we be visited"); Stuyvesant also was under strict orders to "apply all honest and equitable means to continue the previous harmony and to cultivate commerce" with his English neighbors. NNC, 11:191. The biographers of Uncas and Ninigret suspect that some sort of limited Narragansett–Dutch partnership was real, if strategically exaggerated by Uncas and others enemies of Ninigret, while another historian looking at the episode as an example of intertwined colonial and Native news networks refrains from taking a side. Oberg, *Uncas*, 132–38; Fisher and Silverman, *Ninigret*, 73–79; Grandjean, *American Passage*, 76-109.

36. *PCR*, 10:47.

37. NNC, 11:229–30 ("frivolous and false" . . . "up against us"), 234 ("stirred by presents" . . . "meeting houses").

38. Oliver Cromwell to Robert Sedgwick and John Leverett, February 8, 1653/4, Saltonstall Papers, MHS ("shall by way"); Robert Sedgwick and John Leverett Jr. to the Comm. of the United Colonies, June 5, 1654, Misc. Bound Mss. Book 1, MHS ("how things are").

39. *MHSC*, 2d ser., 6:549 ("with their vessels"); WP, 6:20 ("universall").

40. NNCM, 6:121 ("at a very early," "almost before"), 122 (damage and death toll), 205 ("robbed under threat"); NNC, 12:103 (peach theft); Johannes Bogaert to Hans Bontemantel, 1655, NNN, 386 ("pleasure excursion"); for this compelling reinterpretation, see Cynthia Van Zandt, *Brothers Among Nations: The Pursuit of Intercultural Alliances in Early America, 1580–1660* (Oxford: Oxford University Press, 2008), 171–86.

41. "Articles of Agreement betwixt the Governor of the New Netherlands and Tackpausha, March the 12, 1655/6," *RTH*, 1:40–42; September, 2, 1660, Goelet Treaty Minutes Microfilm, N-YHS ("he & his Indians," "Indians should be Molested"); on Narragansetts attacks on Western Long Island, see also *DRCHNY*,

13:58; Grumet, *Munsee Indians*, 71, 327n8. On the Massapequas as wampum producers, see Kevin McBride, "Fort Island: Conflict and Trade in Long Island Sound," Christine N. Reiser, "Safeguarding the 'Mint': Wampum Production and the Social Uses of Space at Fort Island," in Stone, ed., *Native Forts*, 243–305, 323–36, respectively; Grumet, *Munsee Indians*, 70–71, 74, 77.

42. *RTH*, 1: 40 (quotations); Ralph Solecki, "The Archaeology of Fort Neck and Vicinity, Massapeaqua, Long Island, New York," McBride, "Fort Island: Conflict and Trade in Long Island Sound," Reiser, "Safeguarding the 'Mint': Wampum Production and the Social Uses of Space at Fort Island," in Stone, ed., *Native Forts*, 157–64, 243–305, 323–36, respectively; Anne-Marie Cantwell and Dianna diZerega Wall, *Unearthing Gotham: The Archaeology of New York City* (New Haven: Yale University Press, 2001), 135–42; Grumet, *Munsee Indians*, 70–71, 74, 77.

43. West India Company to States General, December 20, 1663, State Papers 84/168, f. 194, BNA ("16 or 18 men . . . all manner of Violence"); *DRCHNY*, 2:401–2 ("sounding trumpet . . . unblushing shamelessness"); Petrus Stuyvesant to John Winthrop Jr., October 12, 1663, New York–Connecticut Correspondence, N-YHS ("the silly and common," "to recover al," "great Murther & Bludsheade"); on the temporary resolution of this standoff, see "English and Dutch on Long Island Articles of Agreement," January 4, 1663/4, Winthrop Family Transcripts, MHS.

44. *DRCHNY*, 13:7 (Raritan attack); De Vries, *NNN*, 208–11 (Raritan attacks); Grumet, *Munsee Indians*, 75–76 (Raritan fights); *NYCM*, 5:97 ("sorceror," "he has poisoned"); *MHSC*, 5th ser., 1:398 ("to purchase").

45. *MHSC*, 5th ser., 1:398 ("the Governour . . . in the sand"); for the Dutch take on these events, see *DRCHNY*, 2:231, 397.

46. *DRCHNY*, 2:446 ("the English"); Megan Lindsay Cherry, "The Imperial and Political Motivations behind the English Conquest of New Netherland," *Dutch Crossing* 34.1 (March 2010): 77–94; Koot, *Empire at the Periphery*, 89–106.

47. On the actual events of the standoff and capitulation, see *NYGE*, 1:1–5, 29–39; *DRCHNY*, 2:248–50, 365–70; Letter of the Town Council of New Amsterdam, September 16, 1664, *NNN*, 451–53.

48. Grumet, *Munsee Indians*, 117 (quotation); *DRCHNY*, 3:67–68.

49. Hubbard, "General History," *MHSC*, 2d ser., 6:323 ("molestations"); Petrus Stuyvesant, "Report on the Surrender of New Netherland," October 19, 1665, *DRCHNY*, 2:365–70; *RNA*, 4:331 ("on the one side").

50. *PCR*, 10:440 (Williams quotations); Hubbard, *The History of the Indian Wars in New England from the First Settlement to the Termination of the War with King Philip, in 1677*, 2 vols., Samuel G. Drake, ed. (1865; repr., New York: Kaus Reprint, 1969), 1:15. For a more lengthy exegesis of this phrase, see Jill Lepore, *The Name of War: King Philip's War and the Origins of American Identity* (New York: Vintage Books, 1998), 3–18.

51. *MHSC*, 1st ser., 6:200 ("fighting with Indians").

52. WP, 6:34 ("a great blacspottd sow . . ."); for similar incidents, see NYCM, 5:23; Virginia DeJohn Anderson, *Creatures of Empire: How Domestic Animals Transformed Early America* (New York: Oxford University Press, 2004), 175–208; Romney, *New Netherland Connections*, 143–44.

53. Anderson, *Creatures of Empire*, 60, 186 (islands and peninsulas); Christopher L. Pastore, *Between Land and Sea: The Atlantic Coast and the Transformation of New England* (Cambridge: Harvard University Press, 2014), 50–81; for representative examples of encouraging Indians to plant "necks," especially on the shores of Long Island Sound, see New London Town Grants, 1650, WP, 6:61–65; RTS, 1:2, 39, 202–3, 230–31, 356; *RTEH*, 1:96–97, 156, 172, 261; on coastal sales in New Netherland, see Grumet, *Munsee Indians*, xxi–xxiv (Staten Island), 82–106 (other sales, renegotiation); RICR, 1:464 ("the priviledge"); PCR, 9:266 ("free libertie"); William S. Pelletreau, *Records of the Town of Smithtown, Long Island, N.Y.* (Huntington, N.Y.: Long Islander Print, 1898), 9 (canoe trees).

54. Western Niantic or River Indian Petition, c. 1672, and Western Niantic Petition, c. 1672, Samuel Wyllys Papers, JHL ("to hunt by" . . . "we will be radey"); Anderson, *Creatures of Empire*, 211–14.

55. An Agreement between Uncas and Arramanet, c. 1666, YIPP, 1666.08.03.00; Niantic Petition to Connecticut Assembly, October 1667, Samuel Wyllys Papers, JHL (Uncas/Joshua); RICR, 1:460 ("most of the Coweset"); Samuel Gorton et al. to the Lord Chancellor Hyde, April 1662, America Collections, Unbound Mss., JCBL ("theese men").

56. West Indies Company to States General, December 20, 1663, BNA State Papers 84/168, f. 194 ("Masters of the Whole Country"); Robert Carr to Lord Arlington, 1666, YIPP, 1666.04.09.00. On this transformative moment and the complicated back-and-forth between the rival colonies and the crown, see Jenny Hale Pulsipher, *Subjects unto the Same King: Indians, English, and the Contest for Authority in Colonial New England* (Philadelphia: University of Pennsylvania Press, 2005), 37–100; Daniel K. Richter, *Before the Revolution: America's Ancient Pasts* (Cambridge: Belknap Press of Harvard University Press, 2011), 241–64.

57. Much of this paragraph and the ones that follow drew their inspiration from the work of Jenny Hale Pulsipher and Daniel K. Richter. Both argue that shifts in the larger Atlantic and continent help explain the outbreak of King Philip's War. Pulsipher, *Subjects unto the Same King*, 70–118; Richter, *Before the Revolution*, 265–94.

58. On the late boom in the Dutch colonial population, see Rink, *Holland on the Hudson*, 164–71; Jacobs, *New Netherland*, 32–61.

59. "Letter of Reverend Jonas Michaëlius, 1628," NNN, 130; DRCHNY 1:87–88 ("in a manner"), 303 ("the payment in Wampum"); Donck, *Description*, 95 ("everything one needs"); MCR, 1:303 (wampum limits), 323 (Harvard); Charles Wolley, *A Two Years' Journal in New York: And Part of Its Territories in America* (1701, digital repr. Lincoln: University of Nebraska, 2009), 42 ("was said"). For a representative

sample of Dutch inventories and transactions in wampum from a single volume of Provincial Secretary records, see *NYRPS*, 3:45, 243, 319, 320, 327, 423; on wampum's ubiquity, see also Jacobs, *New Netherland*, 107–9.

60. *MCR*, 1:302, 329 (establishment of mint); Shepard Krech III, *The Ecological Indian: Myth and History* (New York: W. W. Norton, 1999), 174–77 (beaver population crashes).

61. *RNA*, 1:41 ("payment in wampum"); *MHSC*, 5th ser., 1:396–97 ("wampon falenge"); *DRCHNY*, 14:450–51 (mint request); Lynn Ceci, "The First Fiscal Crisis in New York," *Economic Development and Cultural Change* 28.4 (July 1980): 845–47; Elizabeth Shapiro Peña, "Wampum Production in New Netherland and Colonial New York: The Historical and Archaeological Context" (Ph.D. diss., Boston University, 1990), 61–62.

62. See Krech, *The Ecological Indian*, 174–77 (beaver population crashes); Daniel K. Richter, *The Ordeal of the Longhouse: The Peoples of the Iroquois League in the Era of European Colonization* (Chapel Hill: University of North Carolina Press, 1992), 57–74; for the effects of the Haudenosaunee campaigns along the Great Lakes, see Richard White, *The Middle Ground: Indians, Empires, and Republics in the Great Lakes Region, 1650–1815* (Cambridge: Cambridge University Press, 1991), 1–49; for the wars' impact on the evolving captive trade, see Brett Rushforth, *Bonds of Alliance: Indigenous and Atlantic Slaveries in New France* (Chapel Hill: University of North Carolina Press, 2012), 24–26.

63. Patrick M. Malone, *The Skulking Way of War: Technology and Tactics among the New England Indians* (Baltimore: Johns Hopkins University Press, 1993), 42–51 (firearm trade); *DRCHNY*, 2:157 ("Indians will"); *RICR*, 1:324 ("The barbarians"); Increase Mather, *A Brief History of the Warr with the Indians* (Boston: John Foster, 1676), 42–43 (guns from Albany).

64. William Coddington to Josiah Winslow, December 15, 1675, Winslow Family Papers II, MHS ("a ship from Holland . . . the enemies hands"); John Allyn and Connecticut Council to Edmund Andros, January 13, 1675/6 ("the Dutch people"), John Allyn to Edmund Andros, January 31, 1675/6 ("the enemie do boast"), New York–Connecticut Correspondence, N-YHS.

65. *PCR*, 4:164–65 ("readiness to comply" . . . "a meer plot"); other records of this supposed conspiracy and colonists' concerns are found in *RICR*, 2:192–95, 198. On the 1673–74 reconquest of New York and its general erasure by historians, see Rink, *Holland on the Hudson*, 164–71.

66. *RICR*, 2:184 (Dutch warships), 207 ("for the erectinge"), 274 ("soe farr"), 488 ("the danger"); Alexander Bryan to John Winthrop, August 1673, Winthrop Family Transcripts, MHS ("men from Rye" . . . "Dutch against the English"); Edward Rawson to Josiah Winslow, September 6, 1673 ("the whole emergency"), Edward Rawson to Josiah Winslow, March 14, 1673/4 ("present insolency"), Winslow Family Papers II, MHS.

67. James D. Drake, *King Philip's War: Civil War in New England, 1675–1676* (Amherst: University of Massachusetts Press, 1999), 75–109; George Denison to John Winthrop Jr., February 17, 1664/5, Winthrop Family Papers, MHS, reel 7 ("in hazard of stinking"); address from the Massachusetts Governor and Council to the Narragansett Indians, September 5, 1668, YIPP 1668.09.05.00 ("as they rode"); Josiah Winslow to Rhode Island, August 1671, Winslow Family Papers II, MHS ("very high and insolent").

68. John Eliot to Thomas Prince, June 16, 1671, John Davis Papers, MHS ("with speede and vigor . . . have cause to be"); on the controversy in 1670–71 between Philip and Plymouth, centered mostly on the issue of Philip's increasing stockpile of guns and Plymouth's attempts to bring the Wampanoags within their jurisdiction. It ended in a wary stalemate, though memories of the standoff informed Plymouth's response to the murder of John Sassamon in 1675. On the trial and Native reactions, see Lepore, *Name of War*, 21–26; Yasuhide Kawashima, *Igniting King Philip's War: The John Sassamon Murder Trial* (Lawrence: University of Kansas Press, 2001), 112–24.

Chapter 6. Sea Changes

1. John Freeman to Josiah Winslow, July 10, 1675 ("any Indeans . . . passing over"), Winslow Family Papers II, MHS; Josiah Winslow to Governor Leverett, June 28, 1675 ("smalle bote"), John Davis Papers, MHS; NYGE, 2:69 ("an armed Sloope," "so no ill Indyans").

2. NYCA, 168–69 ("to prevent . . . bee destroyed"); William Coddington to Josiah Winslow, December 15, 1675, Winthrop Family Papers II, MHS ("all the Indians Cannoos"); DRCHNY, 3:264 ("wee kept good"), 14:721 (the eventual repeal of the canoe bans in 1676).

3. Mary Rowlandson, "A True History of the Captivity and Restoration of Mrs. Mary Rowlandson," in *Colonial American Travel Narratives*, ed. Wendy Martin (New York: Penguin Books, 1994), 42 ("they would").

4. On King Philip's War as a turn, not an end, see Colin G. Calloway, ed., *After King Philip's War: Presence and Persistence in Indian New England* (Hanover: University Press of New England, 1997); Jean M. O'Brien, *Dispossession by Degrees: Indian Land and Identity in Natick, Massachusetts, 1650–1790* (Cambridge: Cambridge University Press, 1997); Daniel R. Mandell, *Behind the Frontier: Indians in Eighteenth-Century Massachusetts* (Lincoln: University of Nebraska Press, 2000); David Silverman, *Faith and Boundaries: Colonists, Christianity, And Community Among the Wampanoag Indians of Martha's Vineyard, 1600–1871* (Cambridge: Cambridge University Press, 2005); Lisa Brooks, *The Common Pot: The Recovery of Native Space in the Northeast* (Minneapolis: University of Minnesota Press, 2008); Linford Fisher, *The Indian Great Awakening:*

Religion and the Shaping of Native Cultures in Early America (New York: Oxford University Press, 2012); Christine DeLucia, "The Memory Frontier: Uncommon Pursuit of Past and Place in the Northeast After King Philip's War," *JAH* 98.4 (2012): 975–97.

5. Nathaniel Saltonstall, *The Present State of New-England with Respect to the Indian War* (London: Dorman Newman, 1675), 15 ("a most violent Storm," "it blew up," "it broke down"); John Hull to Philip French, September 2, 1675, John Hull's Letterbook, AAS ("put severall Vessells," "Hirocane").

6. Nathaniel Saltonstall, "A Continuation of the State of New England, 1676," in *Narratives of the Indian Wars*, ed. Charles H. Lincoln (New York: Scribners, 1913), 73 ("tasted of the same Cup"); Increase Mather, *A Brief History of the Warr with the Indians* (Boston: John Foster, 1676), 57 ("a cold Euroclidon," "by the storm"); Edward Wharton, *New England's Present Sufferings Under Their Cruel Neighboring Indians* (London, 1675), 6 ("there seems to"); Roger Williams, *A Key Into the Language of America; Or, An help to the Language of the Natives in that part of America called New-England . . .* (London, 1643; repr., Bedford, Mass., Applewood Books, 1997), 183 ("*Chépewess & Mishittâshin,*" "Northerne storm of war"); Saltonstall, *The Present State*, 15 ("Pawwaw," "They farther say"); on the hurricane of 1635, see also Katherine Grandjean, *American Passage: The Communications Frontier in Early New England* (Cambridge: Harvard University Press, 2015), 20–22. A bad drought hit New England at the close of King Philip's War, leading to another showdown between pawwaws and preachers in whose prayers could truly bring rain. See Fisher, *The Indian Great Awakening*, 13.

7. Works that present major interpretations of the causes and consequences of King Philip's War include Francis Jennings, *The Invasion of America: Indians, Colonialism, and the Cant of Conquest* (New York: W. W. Norton, 1975); Stephen Saunders Webb, *1676: The End of American Independence* (Syracuse: Syracuse University Press, 1995); Jill Lepore, *The Name of War: King Philip's War and the Origins of American Identity* (New York: Vintage, 1998); James D. Drake, *King Philip's War: Civil War in New England, 1675–1676* (Amherst: University of Massachusetts Press, 1999); Jenny Hale Pulsipher, *Subjects unto the Same King: Indians, English, and the Contest for Authority in Colonial New England* (Philadelphia: University of Pennsylvania Press, 2005); Daniel K. Richter, *Before the Revolution: America's Ancient Pasts* (Cambridge: Belknap Press of Harvard University Press, 2011); Grandjean, *American Passage*; John Easton, *A Relation of the Indian War, by Mr. Easton, of Rhode Island, 1675* (digital repr., Lincoln: University of Nebraska Digital Commons, 2006), 8 ("if they kept by the watersides").

8. William Hubbard, *The History of the Indian Wars in New England from the First Settlement to the Termination of the War with King Philip, in 1677 . . .*, Samuel G. Drake, ed. (1865; repr., New York, 1969), 1:39 ("A gallant Neck"); Mather, *A Brief*

History, 82 ("a very substantial"); Easton, *A Relation of the Indian War*, 8 ("the English wear afraid . . . bine veri frequent"). Christopher L. Pastore also zeroes in on these peninsulas as the heart of a larger borderlands space and details their continued contestation by the colonies of Rhode Island, Plymouth, and Massachusetts Bay in *Between Land and Sea: The Atlantic Coast and the Transformation of New England* (Cambridge: Harvard University Press, 2014), 82–129.

9. John Brown to Josiah Winslow, June 11, 1675, Winslow Family Papers II, MHS ("in a posture of war"); Easton, *A Relation of the Indian War*, 12 ("why thay shot . . . begun with philop"); Mather, *A Brief History*, 10 ("this fire which"). Mather's account included a letter by Josiah Winslow and Thomas Hinckley that gave a different account of the break-in written over a year later, dating it to June 19 and leaving out the entire murder and insult (85–86). Seeing as Easton lived much closer to Sowams and Swansea than Winslow and Hinckley, wrote his account earlier and not for publication, and generally provided a more evenhanded account of Indians' motives, I consider him the more reliable source.

10. *MHSC*, 1st ser., 6:86 (Niantics in Buzzards' Bay); Saltonstall, *The Present State of New-England*, 5 ("their Cannoues . . . Burnt all"); on "Cornelius the Dutchman," see also anonymous, "Soldiers in King Philip's War," *NEGHR* 37 (April, 1883): 173–74; Easton, *A Relation of the Indian War*, 13 ("hunt[ing] Philop," "seased sum Cannos"); Josiah Winslow to Gov. Leverett, June 28, 1675, John Davis Papers, MHS ("We have taken").

11. Edmund Andros to William Leete, October 10, 1675, New York–Connecticut Correspondence, N-YHS; *PCR*, 10:455 ("deafe to all" . . . "never get ashoare"); *RICR*, 2:550–51 (travel restrictions); William Coddington to Josiah Winslow, December 15, 1675, Winslow Family Papers II, MHS ("when the blow" . . . "all their Cannoes").

12. John Leverett to Josiah Winslow, July 18, 1675, Winslow Family Papers II, MHS ("on owre narrow neck"); Rowlandson, "A True History," 19 ("They quickly fell . . . this River"); Mather, *A Brief History*, 65 ("on two Rafts"), 71 ("furnished Philip").

13. Benjamin Church, *A Diary of King Philip's War*, Alan and Mary Simpson, eds. (Little Compton, R.I.: Lockwood, 1975), 84 ("the hill seemed . . . to attend him"), 88–89 ("numerous enemies . . . bullet holes").

14. Hubbard, *The History of the Indian Wars*, 1:145–47 ("a Kind of Island . . . the said work"); Patrick M. Malone, *The Skulking Way of War: Technology and Tactics among the New England Indians* (Baltimore: Johns Hopkins University Press, 1993), 73–75; Stonewall John is also discussed in Samuel Gardner Drake, *Biography and History of the Indians of North America* (Boston, 1837), 75–76; on other known Native blacksmithing sites, see Kevin McBride, "The Pequot in King Philip's War," in *Native Forts of the Long Island Sound Area*, ed. Gaynell Stone (Stony Brook, N.Y.: Suffolk County Archeological Association, 2006), 323–36.

15. Rowlandson, "A True History," 23 ("peck and a half"), 41–43 ("driven from"); Church, *Diary*, 33 (Canochet), 121 ("to eat clams"); Saltonstall, "A New and Further Narrative," in *Narratives of the Indian Wars*, 91 ("as a Token . . . at Hartford").

16. Church, *Diary*, 109–10 ("was forced . . . coasts were clear").

17. For a more detailed discussion of female sachems, see Ann Marie Plane, "Putting a Face on Colonization: Factionalism and Gender Politics in the Life History of Awashunkes, the 'Squaw Sachem' of Saconet," in *Northeastern Indian Lives, 1632–1816*, ed. Robert S. Grumet (Amherst: University of Massachusetts Press, 1996), 128–53; Ann M. Little, *Abraham in Arms: War and Gender in Colonial New England* (Philadelphia: University of Pennsylvania Press, 2006), 29–34; Susanah Shaw Romney, *New Netherland Connections: Intimate Networks and Atlantic Ties in Seventeenth-Century America* (Chapel Hill: University of North Carolina Press, 2014), 269–86; Rowlandson, "A True History," 34 (wampum belts).

18. John Almy to Thomas Prince, March 16, 1670/1, Winslow Family Papers II, MHS ("hath a young Child"); Rowlandson, "A True History," 34 (maids); Plane, "Putting a Face on Colonization," 137–39 (Awashonks infanticide charges); Malone, *The Skulking Way of War*, 75 (Quaiapen's Fort).

19. Rowlandson, "A True History," 34 ("severe and proud . . . Gentry of the land"), 39 ("a Kersey Coat . . . always before Black").

20. Church, *Diary*, 114 ("all armed with").

21. Ibid., 115–17 ("good hearty dram . . . corn be ripe"), 125–27 (seaside meeting).

22. Andros's alliance with the Mohawks is best detailed in Webb, 1676. Church, *Diary*, 112, 118, 152 (Peter), 137, 143, 158, 160 (Lightfoot), 128–76 (final campaigns), 150 ("mirey swamp"), 153 ("fell upon"); Mather, *A Brief History*, 72 ("in that very place").

23. On the Wabanakis' complex wars with both the English and the French, see Christopher J. Bilodeau, "The Economy of War: Violence, Religion, and the Wabanaki Indians in the Maine Borderlands" (Ph.D. diss., Cornell University, 2006); Matthew Bahar, " 'The Sea of Trouble We Are Swimming In': People of the Dawnland and the Enduring Pursuit of an Atlantic World" (Ph.D. diss., University of Oklahoma, 2012); Mather, *A Brief History*, 46 ("some rude English"); James Axtell, "The Vengeful Women of Marblehead: Robert Roules's Deposition of 1677," *WMQ* 31.4 (1974): 650–52 (fleet, pirate subterfuge).

24. Increase Mather, *Remarkable Providences, Illustrative of the Earlier Days of American Colonization* (repr. London: John Russel Smith, 1856), 44 ("none came").

25. WP, 6:63 ("Expressing themselves").

26. WP, 3:455 (male and female), 465 ("first request was"), 5:164 ("Indean mayde"); on various dispersals of the Pequots among Connecticut and Massachusetts, see also WP, 3:435–36, 480–83. See also Michael L. Fickes, " 'They Could Not Endure That Yoke': The Captivity of Pequot Women and Children after the War of 1637,"

NEQ 73.1 (March 2000): 58–81; on interracial rape in New England in 1638, see Wendy Anne Warren, " 'The Cause of Her Grief': The Rape of a Slave in Early New England," *JAH* 93.4 (2007): 1031–49.

27. Jacobs, *New Netherland*, 54–56 (black population), 211–12 ("wilde Indiaen," "to the Bermudas"); John Richard II to John Winthrop Jr., April 13, 1660, Winthrop Family Papers, MHS, reel 6 ("to send them"); NYCM, 4:115 ("1 Indian Child").

28. Joshua Micah Marshall, " 'A Melancholy People': Anglo-Indian Relations in Early Warwick, Rhode Island," and John A. Sainsbury, "Indian Labor in Early Rhode Island," in *New England Encounters: Indians and Euroamericans ca. 1600–1850*, ed. Alden T. Vaughan (Boston: Northeastern University Press, 1999), 84–109, 98 ("sould as a slave"), 259–75, respectively; Margaret Ellen Newell, "Indian Slavery in Colonial New England," in *Indian Slavery in Colonial America*, ed. Alan Gallay (Lincoln: University of Nebraska Press, 2009), 33–61, 51 ("judicial enslavement"); PCR, 9–10 ("Incurragement"), 252 ("one coate"); RICR, 2:264 ("six Indyans servants"), 534–35 (curfew, minding of servants); deposition of Samuel Cheesebrough, July 21, 1669, YIPP, 1669.07.21.00 (Ninigret hosting runaways).

29. Easton, *Relation*, 9 ("sold all but"); PCR, 10: 451–52 ("an effectual . . . the land"); Daniel Gookin, "An Historical Account of the Doings and Sufferings of the Christian Indians in New England, in the years 1675, 1676, 1677," in *Collections of the American Antiquarian Society* (Cambridge, Mass.: University Press, 1836), 516–17 ("It was intended . . . wigwams were mean"); Lepore, *Name of War*, 136–41.

30. For general overviews of Indian slavery in King Philip's War and the debate over the legality of slavery from the perspective of both New England and the larger Atlantic, see Lepore, *Name of War*, 150–70; Newell, "Indian Slavery in Colonial New England," in Gallay, ed., *Indian Slavery in Colonial America*, 33–61; Linford D. Fisher, " 'Dangerous Designes': The 1676 Barbados Act to Prohibit New England Slave Importation," WMQ 71.1 (January 2014): 99–124, 99 ("too subtle, bloody"); Easton, *Relation*, 11–12 (Great Swamp Fight); letter to Philip French, September 2, 1675, Letterbook of John Hull, AAS (Calais, Cadiz); MHSC, 3:183 (Tangier letter).

31. Jace Weaver, *The Red Atlantic: Indigenes and the Making of the Modern World* (Chapel Hill: University of North Carolina Press, 2014), 17–18, 17 ("reverse middle passage"), 282n31 ("blue water transhipment"); on the Carolina slave trade, see Alan Gallay, *The Indian Slave Trade: The Rise of the English Empire in the American South, 1670–1717* (New Haven: Yale University Press, 2002); Christina Snyder, *Slavery in Indian Country: The Changing Face of Captivity in Early America* (Cambridge: Harvard University Press, 2011).

32. Virginia DeJohn Anderson, *Creatures of Empire: How Domestic Animals Transformed Early America* (New York: Oxford University Press, 2004), 240–46; on population numbers, Robert Grumet estimates roughly one thousand Munsees living near the lower Hudson in 1767, while Linford Fisher tallies approximately

twenty-six hundred on Long Island, Rhode Island, and Connecticut in 1725, while David Silverman counts thirty-five hundred Christian Wampanoags in 1676. Assuming some continued losses to disease in postdating Fisher and Silverman's figures to 1750, I arrived at the approximate figure of five thousand. See Robert S. Grumet, *The Munsee Indians: A History* (Norman: University of Oklahoma Press, 2009), 273; Fisher, *The Indian Great Awakening*, 31; Silverman, *Faith and Boundaries, Colonists, Christianity, and Community among the Wampanoag Indians of Martha's Vineyard, 1600–1871* (Cambridge: Cambridge University Press, 2005), 80. Robin Cassinomin to Conn. General Court Oct. 1, 1676, Samuel Wyllys Papers, JHL ("connews"); Charles Wolley, *A Two Years' Journal in New York: And Part of Its Territories in America* (1701, digital repr. Lincoln: University of Nebraska, 2009), 32 ("Oysters and other fish"); on early fishing, see Kelly K. Chaves, "Before the First Whalemen: The Emergence and Loss of Indigenous Maritime Authority in New England, 1672–1740," *NEQ* 87.1 (2014): 46–71.

33. Sarah Kemble Knight, "The Journal of Madam Knight," Alexander Hamilton, "The Itinerarium of Dr. Alexander Hamilton," in *Colonial American Travel Narratives*, 64–65 ("every where"), 64 (oysters), 55–56, 74 (canoo ferries), 54, 67 (Indian bread), 218 ("medley"), 220–21 (canoes), 244 (Montauketts), 297 (Western Niantics), 305 ("stark naked"); James H. Merrell cites some of these same sources and makes a similar point about Natives' ubiquity in "Some Thoughts on Colonial Historians and Indians," *WMQ* 46.1 (Jan. 1989): 94–119.

34. Eric Jay Dolin, *Leviathan: A History of Whaling in America* (New York: W. W. Norton, 2007), 21–22, 31–32 (right whales).

35. Williams, *Key*, 113 (*pótop-pauog, tatackommmàuog*, "farre and neere"); John A. Strong, *The Unkechaug Indians of Eastern Long Island: A History* (Norman: University of Oklahoma Press, 2011), 33 (mica tablet); Massachusetts Archaeological Society, *A Handbook of Indian Artifacts from Southern New England* (Middleborough: Massachusetts Archaeological Society, 1976), 46–48, 58; William Pynchon of Springfield on Quinetticot River, April 20, 1641, Misc. Bound Mss., Book 1, MHS ("Misquis alias Weekoshawen").

36. William Bradford, *Of Plymouth Plantation, 1620–1646*, Samuel Eliot Morison, ed. (New York: Alfred A. Knopf, 1952), ("cutting up"); Adriaen van der Donck, *A Description of New Netherland*, Charles T. Gehring and William Starna, eds., Diederik Goedhuys, trans. (Lincoln: University of Nebraska Press, 2008), 12 (Hudson whale); another whale was apparently found near the Hudson at some point in the mid-1650s: see "Petition of Hans Jongh for Trane Oil," *NNCM*, 6:294. On the early drift whale fishery, see Dolin, *Leviathan*, 43 ("early-warning system"); W. Jeffrey Bolster, *The Mortal Sea: Fishing the Atlantic in the Age of Sail* (Cambridge: Harvard University Press, 2012), 69–72; Elizabeth Alden Little and J. Clinton Andrews, "Drift Whales at Nantucket: The Kindness of Moshup," in *Nantucket and Other Native Places: The Legacy of Elizabeth Alden Little*, ed.

Elizabeth S. Chilton and Mary Lynne Rainey (repr. of 1982 article; Albany: State University of New York Press, 2010), 63–77.

37. Dolin, *Leviathan*, 43–45; *RTS*, 1:34 ("fins and tayles"); *NYGE*, 1:157 (beached whale in 1668), 479 (beached whale in 1672); Bolster, *The Mortal Sea*, 70 ("all the whal fish," tax evasion); for other examples of drift whale disputes, see also *NYCA*, 52–54.

38. Dolin, *Leviathan*, 45–47 (attempts at shore whaling); Thomas Prince, Simon Lynde, Nathanell Newgate, Charter of Whaling Partnership, December 5, 1659, Winslow Family Papers II, MHS ("joynte partnership"); *DRCHNY*, 3:197 ("they had endeavored . . . 2 or 3 years past").

39. T. H. Breen, *Imagining the Past: East Hampton Histories* (Reading, Mass.: Addison-Wesley, 1989), 168 ("no one was"); Dolin, *Leviathan*, 47–50 (start of shore whaling), 47–48 ("not as teachers"); on the Dutch whale fishery, see Jonathan Israel, *The Dutch Republic: Its Rise, Greatness, and Fall, 1477–1806* (New York: Oxford University Press, 1995), 622–23.

40. On the various tasks of shore whaling, see Wolley "Two Years' Journal," 24–25; Breen, *Imagining the Past*, 155–60; Dolin, *Leviathan*, 48–52.

41. *NYGE*, 1:265 ("sell some"), 389–91 (orders on liquor sales, Shinnecocks, and Montauketts); 440, 477, 491 (powder and liquor sales license renewals, 1671–72), 477 ("the Indyans on those parts"); *NYCA*, 134 ("Strangers coming").

42. *NYGE*, 1:388 ("one of the first"), 388–89 (order in 1670 regarding Natives honoring contracts), 402 (order in 1670 allowing Elnathan Topping and Benjamin Hand to employ Indian whalers), 516–17 (trade cloth and blubber), 2:91 ("of Civill").

43. This system of debt peonage has been explored by many scholars, starting with Daniel Vickers, "The First Whalemen of Nantucket," *WMQ* 40.4 (October 1983): 560–83; see also John A. Strong, "The Pigskin Book: Records of Native-American Whalemen, 1691–1721," *Long Island Historical Journal* 3.1 (Fall 1990): 17–29, 18 (items sold to whalers on credit); Breen, *Imagining the Past*, 168–81; Mandell, *Behind the Frontier*, 48–76; Mark A. Nicholas, "Mashpee Wampanoags of Cape Cod, the Whalefishery, and Seafaring's Impact on Community Development," *American Indian Quarterly* 26.2 (2002): 165–95; Silverman, *Faith and Boundaries*, 185–222; Chaves, "Before the First Whalemen," 46–71.

44. *AP*, 1:374 (Unkechaug petition); Strong, *Unkechaug Indians*, 95; Obed Macy, *History of Nantucket: A Compendious Account of the First Settlement of the Island by the English Together With The Rise and Progress of the Whale Fishery* (Boston: Hilliard, Gray, 1835), 48 (conspiracy of 1738); Paul Quaab quoted in Chaves, "Before the First Whalemen," 71 ("English will leave"); Quaab's protests are also discussed by Vickers, "The First Whalemen of Nantucket," 580–81.

45. *RTS*, 2:247 ("to use and Improve . . . to our management"); Wolley, *Two Years' Journal*, 24–25 ("as soon as . . . over-sets the Boat"); Breen, *Imagining the Past*, 202 (drownings in 1719).

46. Macy, *The History of Nantucket*, 42 (learning English); on the gendered appeal of seafaring, see Ruth Wallis Herndon and Ella Wilcox Sekatau, "The Right to a Name: The Narragansett People and Rhode Island Officials in the Revolutionary Era," in *After King Philip's War: Presence and Persistence in Indian New England*, ed. Colin G. Calloway (Hanover, N.H.: University Press of New England, 1997), 123–24; Nancy Shoemaker, "Mr. Tashtego: Native American Whalemen in Antebellum New England," *Journal of the Early Republic* 33.2 (Spring 2013): 109–32; James Deetz, *In Small Things Forgotten: An Archeology of Early American Life*, 2d ed. (New York: Anchor Books, 1996), 44–45 (tavern site).

47. Bolster, *The Mortal Sea*, 70–71; Breen, *Imagining the Past*, 200–203; Edouard A. Stackpole, *The Sea-Hunters: The New England Whalemen During Two Centuries, 1635–1835* (New York: Bonanza Books, 1953), 22 (Delaware Bay drift whales).

48. DRCHNY, 5:59 ("Some years"); 474–75 ("the native Indians," "undergo the hardship," "fishery at present"), 498 ("if the Whale fishing," "freight away"); quoted in Bolster, *The Mortal Sea*, 70 ("fished out"); Obed Macy indicates that shore whaling remained viable on Nantucket to 1760 but had been declining since the 1730s. Macy, *The History of Nantucket*, 31.

49. Ezra Stiles, *Extracts from the Itineraries and Other Miscellanies of Ezra Stiles, D.D., LL.D. 1754–1794, With a Selection from His Correspondence* (New Haven: Yale University Press, 1916), 167-69; quoted in Deetz, *In Small Things Forgotten*, 46 ("as easily driven"); MHSC, 6th ser., 5:55 ("all the boates").

50. See Shepard Krech III, *The Ecological Indian: Myth and History* (New York: W. W. Norton, 1999); Andrew Isenberg, *The Destruction of the Bison: An Environmental History, 1750–1920* (Cambridge: Cambridge University Press, 2001); on the problematic nature of Tashtego, see Shoemaker, "Mr. Tashtego," 118–19.

51. On the pivot to offshore whaling and the pioneering role of whalers, see Stackpole, *The Sea-Hunters*; Dolin, *Leviathan*, 90–135, 135 ("from an idea"); Bolster, *The Mortal Sea*, 70–75.

52. J. Hector St. John de Crèvecoeur, *Letters from an American Farmer and Sketches of Eighteenth-Century America* (New York: Penguin Classics, 1981), 134–35 ("five of the . . . Indians and master"); Charles R. Foy, "Seeking Freedom in the Atlantic World, 1713–1783," *EAS* 5.1 (Spring 2006): 46–76; Shoemaker, "Mr. Tashtego," 109–32.

53. Samson Occom, "Autobiographical Narrative, Second Draft," September 17, 1768, in *The Collected Writings of Samson Occom, Mohegan: Leadership and Literature in Eighteenth-Century Native America*, ed. Joanna Brooks (New York: Oxford University Press, 2006), 53 ("Extraordinary Ministers"); Fisher, *The Indian Great Awakening*, 5–12; on the Atlantic phenomenon of Indian and black missionaries, see Edward E. Andrews, *Native Apostles: Black and Indian Missionaries in the British Atlantic World* (Cambridge: Harvard University Press, 2013).

54. Fisher, *The Indian Great Awakening*, 5–6 (bible page and bear paw), 11 ("thriving, largely underground"), 130–33 (rain prayers, dreams, holidays); Macy, *The History of Nantucket*, 269 ("tawpoot").

55. Fisher, *The Indian Great Awakening*, 43–51, 56–57, 66–67, 73, 149–54 (Indian schools); Nicholas, "Mashpee Wampanoags of Cape Cod," 180 ("more ambitious"), 181 (widow support); quoted in David J. Silverman, *Red Brethren: The Brothertown and Stockbridge Indians and the Problem of Race in Early America* (Ithaca: Cornell University Press, 2010), 56 (knife parable); Jason Eden, " 'Therefore Ye Are No More Strangers and Foreigners': Indians, Christianity, and Political Engagement in Colonial Plimouth and on Martha's Vineyard," *American Indian Quarterly* 38.1 (Winter 2014): 36–53.

56. Grumet, *The Munsee Indians*, 273–86; Tom Arne Midtrød, *The Memory of All Ancient Customs: Native American Diplomacy in the Colonial Hudson Valley* (Ithaca: Cornell University Press, 2012), 191–209.

57. Stiles, *Itineraries*, 164 ("a little unhappy . . . the sea side"); Priscilla Wakefield, *Excursions in North America: described in letters from a gentleman and his young companion, to their friends in England* (London, 1806), 207 ("chiefly employed . . . to Long Island"), 230–31 ("inhabited the Atlantic shores").

58. Hamilton, "The Itinerarium of Dr. Alexander Hamilton," 249 ("King George"); Committee Report on Mashantucket Lands, YIPP, 1761.05.20.00 ("the Indian Familys"); quoted in Laura J. Murray, ed., *To Do Good to My Indian Brethren: The Writings of Joseph Johnson, 1751–1776* (Amherst: University of Massachusetts Press, 1998), 288 ("they would suffer"); quoted in Fisher, *The Indian Great Awakening*, 187 ("well enough . . . good fishing!"), 211 ("gain the salt water"). For a detailed history of the Stockbridge and Brothertown movements, see Silverman, *Red Brethren*.

59. Silverman, *Faith and Boundaries*, 226 (shipwreck death toll); Russel Lawrence Barsh, " 'Colored' Seamen in the New England Whaling Industry: An Afro–Indian Consortium," in *Confounding the Color Line: The Indian–Black Experience in North America*, ed. James F. Brooks (Lincoln: University of Nebraska Press, 2002), 86 (smallpox in 1732, mast fall in 1744); Herndon and Sekatau, "The Right to a Name," 123 (Primus Thompson); William Apess, "A Son of the Forest," in *On Our Own Ground: The Complete Writings of William Apess, A Pequot*, ed. Barry O'Connell (Amherst: University of Massachusetts Press, 1992), 24 ("the devil would").

60. Nicholas, "Mashpee Wampanoags of Cape Cod," 180 (Babcock's tavern/brothel); Samson Occom to the Long Island Presbytery, [January 4, 1769], "A Sermon, Preached at the Execution of Moses Paul," [1772], Occom, Journal 4, June 14, 1761, *Collected Writings of Samson Occum*, 87 ("I have been Shamefully"), 194–95 ("confirm[ing] those evil . . . unsteady Way"), 260 ("Drunkards . . . Heathen English"); Fisher, *The Indian Great Awakening*, 119 (Ashpo's relapse).

61. W. Jeffrey Bolster, *Black Jacks: African American Seamen in the Age of Sail* (Cambridge: Harvard University Press, 1997), 96 (Crispus Attucks); Ezra Stiles, *The Literary Diary of Ezra Stiles*, Franklin Bowditch Dexter, ed. (New York: Charles Scribners' Sons, 1901), 1:335–37 (Aaron Briggs).

62. On racial mixing, acceptance, and exclusion among New England Algonquians, see Barsh, " 'Colored' Seamen in the New England Whaling Industry"; Tiffany M. McKinney, "Race and Federal Recognition in Native New England," *Crossing Waters, Crossing Worlds: The African Diaspora in Indian Country*, eds., Tiya Miles and Sharon P. Holland (Durham: Duke University Press, 2006), 57–79; Silverman, *Red Brethren.*

63. Hawley quoted in Mandell, *Behind the Frontier*, 197 ("The long whaling"); John Adams to Thomas Jefferson, June 28, 1812, quoted in Calloway, "Introduction," *After King Philip's War*, 8 ("But the Girls"); John Milton Earle, *Report to the Governor and Council concerning the Indians of the Commonwealth, Under the Act of April 16, 1859* (Boston: William White, 1861), 6 ("near the seaboard").

64. Quoted in Mandell, *Behind the Frontier*, 197 ("their favourite employ"); Malchizedick Howwoswe to his parents, July 16, 1807, Miscellaneous America Manuscripts, JCBL ("I embrace this"); Paul Cuffe Jr., *Narrative of the Life and Adventures of Paul Cuffe, A Pequot Indian: During Thirty Years Spent At Sea, and in Travelling in Foreign Lands* (Mt. Vernon, N.Y.: Horace N. Bill, 1839), 3 ("This was new'); Betsey Chamberlain, "Recollections of My Childhood," in *The Lives and Writings of Betsey Chamberlain: Native American Mill Worker*, ed. Judith A. Ranta (Boston: Northeastern University Press, 2003), 211–12 ("queer stories," "marvellous tales"). Old Bill's ethnicity is not clear—Chamberlain relates that neighborhood "boys called him 'the wandering Jew' and 'my man Friday,' because he had no home." Both of these racialized terms and the youths' insolence toward him suggest that Bill was not white and likely had indigenous ancestry.

65. Joseph Johnson, Diary, January 2, 1772, *The Writings of Joseph Johnson*, 126 ("Altho I have been . . . the mighty Waters").

Epilogue

1. On Tecumseh and his larger movement, see Richard White, *The Middle Ground: Indians, Empires, and Republics in the Great Lakes Region, 1650–1815* (Cambridge: Cambridge University Press, 1991), 511–19; Gregory Dowd, *A Spirited Resistance: The North American Indian Struggle for Unity, 1745–1815* (Baltimore: Johns Hopkins University Press, 1993); Colin Calloway, *The Shawnees and the War for America* (New York: Penguin, 2007); Adam Jortner, *The Gods of Prophetstown: The Battle of Tippecanoe and the Holy War for the American Frontier* (New York: Oxford University Press, 2011).

2. Quoted in Horatio Bardwell Cushman, *A History of the Choctaw, Chickasaw, and Natchez Indians* (Greenville, Tex.: Headlight Printing House, 1899), 311. This speech was relayed by a Scots translator named John Pitchlynn to the historian Horatio Cushman. There is little doubt that the transcript was partially or mostly embellished by these white men, who held romantic ideas about Indian eloquence. Yet it cannot be completely dismissed. Tecumseh's overture to the Chickasaws and Choctaws in 1811 did happen, and the basic thesis of the speech is broadly consistent with other accounts of the Shawnee leader's rhetoric. Indeed, if Tecumseh, whose entire movement hinged on a radically purist view of indigenous culture, meant to declare these nations as "vanished," perhaps he was referring to their adoption of Christianity and English as an abrogation of their Native identities. On the caution needed when citing this text, see Jortner, *The Gods of Prophetstown*, 282n74.

3. On the westward migrations of Munsees, see Robert S. Grumet, *The Munsee Indians, A History* (Norman: University of Oklahoma Press, 2009) 273–86; Tom Arne Midtrød, *The Memory of All Ancient Customs: Native American Diplomacy in the Colonial Hudson Valley* (Ithaca: Cornell University Press, 2012), 191–209.

4. My thinking in this paragraph and the two following is largely inspired by many sources, including the essays in Laurence M. Hauptman and James D. Wherry, eds., *The Pequots in Southern New England: The Fall and Rise of an American Indian Nation* (Norman: University of Oklahoma Press, 1990); Philip J. Deloria, *Indians in Unexpected Places* (Lawrence: University Press of Kansas, 2004); Tiffany M. McKinney, "Race and Federal Recognition in Native New England," *Crossing Waters, Crossing Worlds: The African Diaspora in Indian Country*, eds., Tiya Miles and Sharon P. Holland (Durham: Duke University Press, 2006), 57–79; Jean M. O'Brien, *Firsting and Lasting: Writing Indians Out of Existence in New England* (Minneapolis: University of Minnesota Press, 2011), esp. xi–xxvi; Jace Weaver, *Red Atlantic: Indigenes and the Making of the Modern World* (Chapel Hill: University of North Carolina Press, 2014). Weaver's pathbreaking work builds off and engages with Paul Gilroy's *Black Atlantic: Modernity and Double Consciousness* (Cambridge: Harvard University Press, 1993).

5. Weaver, *Red Atlantic*, 1–34; on the ocean as a point of connection between Native American and African histories, see Tiya Miles and Sharon P. Holland, *Crossing Waters, Crossing Worlds: The African Diaspora in Indian Country* (Durham: Duke University Press, 2006), esp. 1–23; on traditional maritime peoples, see also Greg Dening, *Islands and Beaches: Discourses on a Silent Land, Marquesas 1774–1880* (Honolulu: University Press of Hawai'i, 1980); Marshall Sahlins, *Islands of History* (Chicago: University of Chicago Press, 1985); Philip E. Steinberg, *The Social Construction of the Ocean* (Cambridge: Cambridge University Press, 2001), esp. 39–67; Bernhard Klein and Gesa Mackenthun, *Sea Changes: Historicizing the Ocean* (New York: Routledge, 2004); Isaiah Helekunihi Walker, *Waves of*

Resistance: Surfing and History in Twentieth-Century Hawai'i (Honolulu: University of Hawai'i Press, 2011).

6. William Apess, "A Son of the Forest," in *On Our Own Ground: The Complete Writings of William Apess, A Pequot*, ed. Barry O'Connell (Amherst: University of Massachusetts Press, 1992), 14 ("I saw, as I thought"), 24 ("the devil would"), 62 ("doubly wronged"); for further work on Apess, see O'Connell, "Introduction," xiii–lxxvii; Jill Lepore, *The Name of War: King Philip's War and the Origins of American Identity* (New York: Vintage, 1998), 215–20; Lisa Brooks, *The Common Pot: The Recovery of Native Space in the Northeast* (Minneapolis: University of Minnesota Press, 2008), 163–218; O'Brien, *Firsting and Lasting*, 180–91; Arnold Krupat, *"That the People Might Live": Loss and Renewal in Native American Elegy* (Ithaca: Cornell University Press, 2012), 122–25.

7. Apess, "A Son of the Forest," 19–20 ("a tempest-tossed mariner"); for other examples of Apess using oceanic metaphors, mostly drawn from hymns, see O'Connell, ed., *On Our Own Ground*, 40–41, 52, 112, 146.

8. Apess, "Eulogy on King Philip," 296 ("every Indian heart"); Nancy Shoemaker, "Race and Indigeneity in the Life of Elisha Apes," *Ethnohistory* 60.1 (Winter 2013): 27–50.

9. On Apess's long shadow, see Brooks, *The Common Pot*, 219–46; on Native women writers in the nineteenth century, see Judith A. Ranta, ed., *The Lives and Writings of Betsey Chamberlain: Native American Mill Worker* (Boston: Northeastern University Press, 2003), 3–14; on Paul Cuffe the elder and younger, see Weaver, *Red Atlantic*, 87–98. The anthropologist Jack Campisi argues that the younger Apess was not a Pequot (Weaver, 94–95). Seeing as his mother's maiden name was Alice Pequitt and that she and her son probably had a better sense of their ancestry than modern scholars do, I defer to Cuffe on this matter. On Alice (Pequitt) Cuffe, see Rosalind C. Wiggins, "Introducing Captain Paul Cuffe, Friend," in *Captain Paul Cuffe's Logs and Letters, 1808–1817*, ed. Rosalind C. Wiggins (Washington: Howard University Press, 1996), 46–48.

10. Wiggins, "Introducing Captain Paul Cuffe," and Paul Cuffe, Account Book, 1811, *Cuffe's Logs and Letters*, 45–69.

11. On Cuffe's biography and larger historical context, see Rhett S. Jones, "Introduction: The African Diaspora in British North America in the Time of Paul Cuffe," and Wiggins, "Introducing Captain Paul Cuffe," in *Cuffe's Logs and Letters*, 1–45, 46–48, 99 ("peopel of Colour"); Jeffery A. Fortin, "Cuffe's Black Atlantic World, 1808–1817," *Atlantic Studies* 4.2 (October 2007): 245–66; Russel Lawrence Barsh, " 'Colored' Seamen in the New England Whaling Industry: An Afro–Indian Consortium," in *Confounding the Color Line: The Indian–Black Experience in North America*, ed. James F. Brooks (Lincoln: University of Nebraska Press, 2002), 96–99.

12. Paul Cuffe to William Allen, April 22, 1811, *Cuffe's Logs and Letters*, 115 ("Encouragement . . . Sierra Leone"), 119 ("Severall hundred miles . . . . righting

Arabeck"); on the Kru/Krumen, see Fortin, "Cuffe's Black Atlantic World,"
253–54, 254n43; Jane Martin, "Krumen 'Down the Coast': Liberian Migrants on
the West African Coast in the 19th and Early 20th Century," *International Journal
of African Historical Studies* 18.3 (1985): 401–23; on the beginnings of the Sierra
Leone project, see also Maya Jasanoff, *Liberty's Exiles: American Loyalists in the
Revolutionary World* (New York: Alfred A. Knopf, 2011), 279–312.

13. Cuffe to Allen, April 22 and 24, 1811, *Cuffe's Logs and Letters*, 119–20 ("People of
the Colony" . . . "a Servisable Subject among them").

14. Olivia Ward Bush-Banks, "Driftwood," in *The Collected Works of Olivia Ward
Bush-Banks* (New York: Oxford University Press, 1991), 52 ("a gleam of light").

INDEX

Adams, John, 242

African Americans, 7, 235, 240–42, 249

African slaves, 117, 219, 235, 241, 250

alcohol, 73–74, 147–48, 156, 228–29, 239–40, 247–48, 303(n44)

Algonquians: Anglo–Dutch conflict and, 6–7 (*see also* English–Dutch conflict); and boats (*see* seafaring and boating; ships, European; watercraft; whales and whaling); captured/enslaved, 7, 79–80, 91–100, 105–6, 131–32, 141, 217–22, 301–2(n34) (*see also* slavery; Squanto); clothing, 3, 34, 81–82, 214, 229; conflict between, 5, 38–41, 104–5, 125–26, 135, 168–71, 207, 271–72(n42) (*see also* trophies; *and specific conflicts and groups*); conversion to Christianity, 174, 235–37, 247–49; cultural similarities, 22–24; demographics, 25, 222, 265–66(n8), 319–20(n32); diet, 26–34, 267(nn13–14), 268–69(n23) (*see also* corn; fish and fishing; shellfish); disease's impact on, 85, 100, 115, 131, 222, 239; diversity of colonial experiences, 10; economic exploitation of, 219, 229–30, 233; economies, 105, 109, 189, 197–98 (*see also* trade; wampum); and the English king, 196; European vs. Native culture, 48–49; first encounters with Europeans, 51–56, 77; forest management and hunting, 33–34, 66, 154, 195; gender roles, 27, 29–33, 56–57, 231; gods and spirits, 19–20, 29, 31, 35, 38–39; government, politics, and intertribal relationships, 35–38, 40–48, 111 (*see also* sachems; sachemships; *and specific groups and individuals*); graves, 110; hospitality valued, 25–26; kinship and social class, 35–37; letters commissioned, 172; literature of, 11–12, 248–49; mapmaking, 78; maritime history of (as field of study), 11–13; marriage, 7, 33, 37, 240–42; mobile settlements, 25; modern communities and reservations, xi–xiii, *xxi*, 222, 238; names and terms for, 15; origin theories, 70–71; place names, 16, 17; pre-colonial travel and trade, 52; psychological effects of war on, 161; relations with colonists (*see* colonial–Native conflict; Dutch colonists; English colonists); sexual customs, 33, 37, 98, 175; sovereignty surrendered, 195; struggle to control coast, 1–4; swimming ability, 72, 227; traditional stories, 19–20, 22, 52, 223–224; transportation services, 71–72, 74, 172–73; as "vanished" people, 244–46, 325(n2). *See also* colonial–Native conflict; land use and landownership; languages; women, Native; *and specific topics, groups, and individuals*

Allerton, Isaac, 127
Andros, Edmund, 203–4, 209, 216, 228–30
Anglo–Dutch Wars, 166, 181–84, 187,
    190–93. *See also* English–Dutch
    conflict
Apess, William, 239, 247–48, 251, 326(n9)
Arbella (ship), 72–73, 112–13, 279(n15),
    282(n32)
Atlantic Ocean, 10–11, 52–53. *See also*
    sea, the
Attucks, Crispus, 241
Awashonks, 213–15
Axtell, James, 271–72(n42)

Bailyn, Bernard, 285(n3)
Barentsen, Pieter, 107–8
beheading, 39–40, 137–38, 168–69, 212,
    271–72(n42). *See also* trophies
Berlin, Ira, 97
Block, Adriaen, 61, 64, 96–97, 289(n24)
Block Island, 17, 66, 83, 112, 132–34, 219
Bolton, Herbert Eugene, 9–10
Borsum, Egbert von, 72
Bradford, William, 58, 78, 101–2, 112, 131,
    140–41, 285(n2)
Bradgon, Kathleen, 35, 266(n8)
Brereton, John, 106–7
Brooks, Lisa, 267(n14)
Bush-Banks, Olivia, 11–12, 249, 251

Camden, William, 294(n67)
Canochet, 212
canoes. *See* watercraft
Canonicus, 44–46, 100, 112, 139, 153,
    273(n49). *See also* Narragansett peoples
Cape Cod: name, 16, 17, 28; sailing
    hazardous near, 60–61, 78–79, 217; and
    whaling, 224, 229, 231, 233 (*see also*
    whales and whaling). *See also* Mashpee
    Wampanoag people; Nauset people
captives: Algonquians, 79–80, 91–100,
    105–6, 131–32, 217–18, 301–2(n34) (*see
    also* slavery); Europeans, 136, 143, 173,
    204, 211–12, 217; Native treatment of, 39
Chamberlain, Betsy, 243, 249, 324(n64)
Champlain, Samuel de, 78, 100, 107

Charles I, 43, 113, 121–22, 180
Charles II, 180, 191, 196
Cheshanamp, 171
Christiaensen, Hendrick, 82, 96–97, 98
Christianity, conversion to, 174, 235–37,
    247–49. *See also* missionaries
Church, Benjamin, 210–16
clothing, 3, 34, 81–82, 214, 229
coastal geology and geography, 15–22, 17,
    21, 27, 60–61, 194–95, 265(n5).
    See also maps
Coginaquam, 195
Coke, Sir Edward, 138
colonial–Native conflict, 5–6; 1650s–1660s,
    177, 187–88; and Anglo–Dutch conflict,
    166–68, 193; colonial vessels attacked,
    62–63, 77, 82–83, 97, 132–34, 149–50,
    188, 216–17; English fears of, 199–201;
    Native captives, 79–80, 91–100, 105–6;
    Natives massacred, 125–26, 211; numbers
    killed, 126–27; over beached whales,
    226; over canoes, 75–76, 203–4, 208–9;
    over land deeds/use, 193–95; Wabanaki
    war, 216–17. *See also* Kieft's War; King
    Philip's War; Pequot War; warfare
colonization of North America: early years,
    1–7, 85–86; first encounters, 51–56, 77;
    origins of, 88–91; Turner's frontier thesis
    and critiques, 8–11. *See also* colonial–
    Native conflict; Dutch colonists;
    English colonists; English–Dutch
    conflict; *and specific colonies and topics*
"common pot" metaphor, 27, 267(n14)
Concord (Gosnold's ship), 51, 52, 61, 78, 81
Connecticut, 16, 195–96, 200, 205, 209. *See
    also* English colonists; New England
Connecticut River, 130–31, 136, 143, 167,
    205, 298(n9). *See also* Fort Saybrook
Cooper, John, 226, 228
Coppin, Robert, 61–62
corn, 25–27, 30–33, 35, 212, 267(n14),
    268–69(n23)
Crèvecoeur, J. Hector St. John, 235
Cromwell, Oliver, 168, 180–81, 187
Cuffe, Paul, Jr., 242, 249
Cuffe, Paul, Sr., 249–51, 326(n9)

Cullick, John, 309(n16)
currencies, 197–98. *See also* wampum
Cutshamakin, 139, 301(n27)

Daily, Jeremy, 76
Dauphine (Verrazzano's ship), 51, 52, 76
deer, 34, 108, 154, 229
de Graeff, Cornelis, 181
Delaware Indians, 237–38. *See also* Munsee
    peoples
de Rasières, Isaack, 104, 108, 265(n7)
Dermer, Thomas, 62–63, 96, 100, 101
De Vries, David, 149–52, 157, 158, 161,
    304(n48)
de Witt, Johan, 181
diet, Native, 26–34, 267(nn13–14),
    268–69(n23). *See also* corn; deer; fish
    and fishing; shellfish
disease, 85, 100, 115, 124, 131, 222, 239
Dondey, Jan, 148
"Driftwood" (Bush-Banks), 12–13, 251
Dutch colonists: arrival of, 1–4, 3;
    currencies, 197–98 (*see also* wampum);
    diet, 267(n13); disgruntled with sailors,
    ships, 61, 278(n12); and Esopus pirates,
    83; guns traded, 175, 177, 183, 199–200;
    Hellegat named, 60; house and ship
    prices, 65, 279–80(n19); on Indian
    government/politics, 43, 46–47;
    landownership, 105, 118–19; and
    maritime claims, 121–24; Native attacks
    on ships of, 82, 97, 149–50, 188; and
    Native languages, 173–74; on Natives'
    appearance, 34; place names used, 16,
    17; recruiting, 117–18, 145; relations with
    Indians, 86, 102–5, 129–30, 142–53,
    155–58, 163, 173–78, 183–89, 193,
    289(n32), 304(n48) (*see also* Kieft's
    War); shipbuilding, 65; and slavery, 117,
    218–19, 221 (*see also* slavery); terms for,
    15; territory claimed/controlled, 86–88,
    87, 117–22, 120, 131–32, 135, 143–44, 149,
    165–66, 167, 179–80, 303(n46); trade in
    seagoing skills, 6; trade restrictions
    flouted, 144; travel by water, 71–72; and
    the wampum trade, 105–8, 197–98; and

whales and whaling, 225–26, 228. *See
    also* colonial–Native conflict; English–
    Dutch conflict; New Amsterdam; New
    Netherland; ships, European; trade;
    watercraft; West India Company;
    women, European; *and specific
    settlements and individuals*

Earle, John Milton, 242
East India Company (Dutch), 89–90, 122,
    286–87(n8)
ecology of the coastal region, 27–29,
    109–10, 231–33, 273(n49). *See also* fish
    and fishing; shellfish; whales and
    whaling
economy: economic exploitation of Indians,
    219, 229–30, 233 (*see also* slavery);
    wampum trade and, 105–12, 197–98 (*see
    also* wampum). *See also* trade
Eelkens, Jacob, 105–6, 124
Eendracht (Dutch ship), 123
Eliot, John, 170, 201, 220, 221, 315(n68)
England: and the Anglo–Dutch Wars, 166,
    181–82, 187 (*see also* Anglo–Dutch
    Wars); civil war, 113, 180, 310(n26);
    dismemberment in, 137–38, 300(n23);
    Dutch ship held, 123; history and
    culture, 49–51; Indians displayed in,
    94–95; landownership, 117; and *mare
    clausum*, 121–22, 294(n67), 310(n24);
    New Netherland seized, 196–97; roots
    of colonial enterprise, 88–91 (*see also*
    Virginia Company); seafaring by, 49–51;
    taxes, 232
English colonists: alliances with
    Algonquians, 86, 101–2, 125, 129, 134–36,
    138–42, 177–78, 195–96 (*see also*
    Massasoit; Pequot War; Squanto);
    arrival of, 1–4, 2, 112–17; diet, 32,
    267(n13); on fish and shellfish, 28–29;
    guns traded, 199–200; Indians enslaved,
    7, 141, 217–22 (*see also* captives; slavery);
    living in New Netherland, 180, 190; and
    maritime claims, 121–24; migration
    within New England, 292(n52); on
    Native appearance, 34; Native attacks

English colonists (*continued*)
on ships of, 62–63, 77, 82–83, 132–34, 216–17; on Native government/politics, 43–44; and Native letters, 172–73; Native methods of rule impersonated, 138–42, 154–55; origins of, 89; outnumbered in early years, 85–86, 285(n2); place names used, 16, 17, 28; religious motivation/justification, 113–14, 117, 121; tensions between, 293(n58); terms for, 15; territory claimed/controlled, 86–88, 87, 115–17, 122–24, 131, 135, 143–44, 149, 165–66, 167, 179–80, 190–92, 196, 205, 292(n57), 303(n46); and tribal conflicts, 171–72; and the wampum trade, 108–9; and whales and whaling, 224–35. *See also* colonial–Native conflict; English–Dutch conflict; seafaring and boating; ships, European; trade; watercraft; women, European; *and specific colonies and individuals*

English–Dutch conflict (colonial), 6–7; and the Anglo–Dutch Wars, 183–84, 187, 190–93, 310–11(n29); and the Dutch States' Arms, 149, 293(n65), 303(n46); English fears, 183–86, 200–201; Hudson colonies recaptured by Dutch, 200; Indians and, 166–68; maritime claims, 121–24, 294(n67); New Netherland invaded by English, 6–7, 190–92, 196–97; and the Pequot War, 143, 297(n7), 301–2(n34); territorial claims, 6–7, 122–24, 128–31, 135, 143–44, 149, 165–66, 179–80, 303(n46); wampum trade and, 108–9, 112

Epenow, 94–96, 99

Esopus people, 47, 83, 130, 177, 193, 218

farming: in Europe, 49; fences needed, 194; Native practices, 25, 27, 30–33, 116, 268–69(n23); Puritan emphasis on, 114, 116; surplus sold/traded, 32, 109

fish and fishing, 26–30, 35, 78, 109–10, 154, 222, 238. *See also* shellfish; whales and whaling

Fisher, Linford, 235

forests and trees, 33–34, 66, 195, 222, 280(n21). *See also* hunting

Fort Amsterdam, 119, 123–24, 147–48, 183, 185. *See also* New Amsterdam

Fort Orange, 87, 104–5, 108, 167, 199

forts, Native, 161–63, 189, 211, 214, 306(n71)

Fort Saybrook, 128, 136, 139

Fortuyn (Dutch ship), 98–99, 105

"frontier" narrative, 8–9

fur trade, 108, 122, 123, 141, 144, 198–99

Gallop, John, 133, 298(n13)

Gardiner, Lion, 139–40, 159, 300(n25), 301(n27)

geology and geography of the coastal region. *See* coastal geology and geography

giant story, 19–20, 22, 52

Gilbert, Sir Humphrey, 137–38

Goddard, Ives, 103

Gorges, Ferdinando, 94, 95

Gosnold, Bartholomew, 51. See also *Concord*

Grandjean, Katherine, 71

Great Swamp Massacre, 211, 220

Grotius (Groot, Hugo de), 121

guns, Native acquisition of, 110, 175, 177, 183–86, 199–200, 207

Hakluyt, Richard, 55

Halve Maen, De (Hudson's ship), 51, 52, 61, 77, 82, 122

Haudenosaunee peoples, 199

Hawley, Gideon, 239

heads. *See* trophies

hemp, 29

Higgenson, Francis, 292(n57)

Hobson, Nicholas, 95

Hontom, Willem, 105

houses, Native, 25, 37

How, Ephraim, 217

Howwoswe, Malchizedick, 242

Hubbard, William, 73, 192–93, 211

Hudson, Henry, 51, 61, 62, 107, 122

Hudson River: English colonists and, 122–23, 179; names for, 17; Native attacks along, 187–88; and the Pequot and Kieft's Wars, 128; piracy on, 83; settlements along, 87, 167, 205
Hunt, Thomas, 92, 100
hunting, 33–34, 154. *See also* deer; fur trade
hurricanes, ix–x, 39, 206, 273(n49)
Hutchinson, Anne, 127

indentured servitude, 219. *See also* Apess, William
interracial marriage, 7, 240–42, 249
Iroquois Five Nations (Haudenosaunee), 199

James, Duke of York (James II), 6, 191–92
Jennings, Francis, 115, 293(n58), 295(n5), 298(nn9, 12)
Johnson, Joseph, 235, 243
Jones, Thomas, 93
Jonge Tobias (Dutch ship), 97, 98–99
Josselyn, John, 73, 81

Kieft, Willem, 145–46; and Anglo–Dutch relations, 179; crackdown on company employees, 147–48; death, 164; and Dutch–Native relations, 147–53, 156, 186, 304(nn48, 52); on Indian ancestry, 70; and Kieft's War, 126, 142–43, 156–57; and shipbuilders, 65. *See also* Kieft's War
Kieft's War, 127–30, 163; aftermath, 160–61, 163–64; major events, 126, 128, 157–61; Massapequas and, 176, 177; origins, 142–53, 155–56, 296(n5), 304(n52)
Kierstede, Sara, 173–74, 176
King Philip's War, 7; beheading during, 40; Dutch guns used in, 200; major events, 207–12, 216, 317(n9); and Native enslavement, 220–21; origins, 193, 201–2, 208, 315(n68); and the sea, 203–4, 206–11, 216–17. *See also* Metacom

land use and landownership: conflicts over, 193–94; Dutch views and ownership,

105, 118–21 (*see also* Dutch colonists: territory claimed/controlled; New Netherland); English views and ownership, 115–16, 120–22, 190–91, 292(n57) (*see also* English colonists: territory claimed/controlled); land sales agreements, 190–91, 193–95; Native practices, 33–35, 116, 194–95, 292(n57); Native rights, 105, 115, 154
languages, 22–25, 23, 35–36, 68, 93, 102–4, 107–8, 173–74
Lay, Robert, and family, 171
letters (mail), 71–72, 172–73
livestock, 48, 77, 112, 154, 155, 194, 222
Long Island: agriculture, 273(n49); beached whales on, 226; English land purchases, 190–91; Europeans "discovery" of, 78; forest rights, 280(n21); Kieft's War and, 128; names for, 16; Treaty of Hartford and, 188; tribal relations on, 45, 47, 111–12, 168–69, 176–77, 188, 273(n49), 274(n53); and the wampum trade, 105, 109; and whales and whaling, 226–27, 232
Long Island Sound, xi, 27–29, 60, 109, 123–24, 140, 149, 203. *See also* Pequot War
Loper, Jacobus (James), 228
Lubbertsen, Frederick, 152

Manhattan (island): agriculture, 273(n49); canoe theft, 76; colonial arrival, 54; colonial presence on, 117–18, 146–48; drunkenness on, 240; Dutch and English claims, 2–4, 3, 7, 179, 183, 187, 201; Dutch–Native relations on, 102–4, 157, 158, 183–84, 187–88, 192; and the Hell's Gate, 60; Hurricane Sandy and, ix–x; and Kieft's War, 126, 130, 145–48, 157 (*see also* Kieft's War); and trade, 108, 112. *See also* Dutch colonists; New Amsterdam; New Netherland
Manhattan people, 46, 47, 98
Manisses people, 45, 132–34
manitou, 20, 29, 35, 51. *See also* Algonquians: gods and spirits

maps: colonial presence, 87, 167, 205; Dutch map (1635), 120, 224; glacial advance, 21; indigenous and colonial place-names, 17; modern tribal communities, *xii*; Native dialects, 23; Pequot and Kieft's Wars, 128; sachemships, 45, 47

marine wayfinding (navigation), 55, 58, 60–62, 277(n4)

marriage, 7, 33, 37, 170, 240–42, 249

Mashpee Wampanoag people, 236–37, 239, 248

Mason, John, 140, 159, 171, 295(n2)

Massachusett people, 75, 85, 103

Massachusetts Bay, 115–17

Massachusetts Bay Colony, 167, 205; beheading and dismemberment, 138, 300(n23); charter, 122; conflict with Plymouth colony, 298(n9); Connecticut River settlements, 131; currencies, 197; relations with Native Americans, 196, 220 (*see also* Pequot War); and the Wabanaki war, 216–17; and whales and whaling, 224 (*see also* whales and whaling). *See also* English colonists; English–Dutch conflict; New England; *and specific individuals*

Massapequa people, 46, 47, 87, 175–76, 188–89, 205. *See also* Tackapousha

Massasoit, 41–42, 44, 86, 100–102, 115, 273(n49). *See also* Wampanoag peoples

Mayflower, 58, 61–62, 72–73, 224

Melijn, Cornelis, 190

Merwick, Donna, 289(n32)

Metacom (King Philip), 7, 200–202, 204, 207, 209–11, 216, 248, 315(n68). *See also* King Philip's War

methodology, 13–18, 261(n18)

Miantonomi: and Canonicus, 44–46, 112; death, 163, 170; and Kieft's War, 36, 128, 155–56, 163, 202; and Oldham's death, 134; and the Pequot War, 81–82, 128, 136, 142, 153–54. *See also* Narragansett peoples

Michaëlius, Jonas, 102

Minor, Thomas, 74–75

Mintz, Stanley W., 267(n14)

missionaries, 103, 170, 174, 235–37, 239–40. *See also* Apess, William; Eliot, John; Johnson, Joseph; Occom, Samson

Moby-Dick, or the Whale (Melville), 234

Mohawk people, 108, 140–41, 199, 216

Mohegan people: demographics, 266(n8); dialects, 22, 23; giant story, 19; vs. Narragansetts, 168–71; and the Pequot War, 136–42; political structure and relationships, 45, 48, 130, 135, 273(n49), 274(n53); territory, 205, 238. *See also* Uncas

Montaukett people, 11–13, 45, 87, 169, 172, 188, 223, 228, 238. *See also* Bush-Banks, Olivia; Wyandanch

Morton, Thomas, 55, 70, 122–23

Mossel, Thijs Volckertsen, 97–98, 289(n24)

Munsee peoples: and colonial–Native wars, 126, 128, 129–30, 156–61, 218 (*see also* Kieft's War); diet, 26; Dutch relations with, 86, 102–5, 126, 145, 147–53, 174–75, 185, 304(n48) (*see also* Dutch colonists); and English–Dutch conflict, 190–91; enslaved, 218; first encounters with Europeans, 51, 62, 77; giant story, 19; language and dialects, 22, 23, 103–4, 173–74; Manhattan raided, 187–88; migration and amalgamation, 237–38; names for, 46, 274(n52); piracy by, 82, 83, 97; political relationships among, 46–48, 47, 273(n49); Rodrigues and, 98–99, 289(n24); taken captive, 96–97; territory, 87, 205; watercraft, 79, 280(n24), 282(n34) (*see also* watercraft). *See also specific Native American groups*

Mystic massacre, 125–26, 128, 140. *See also* Pequot War

Nantucket: colonial–Native relations on, 226, 229–30, 236; colonial presence, 196, 205; Native diet, 29; origin myth, 19; piracy on, 83; and sea level rise, 22; shipwreck deaths, 239; and whales and whaling, 226, 229, 230, 234–35

Narragansett Bay: colonial presence, 165; ecology, 27–29; European arrival in, 54; and King Philip's War, 207–11, 216; name origin, 16; Native boat travel banned, 203; origin myth, 19; and wampum, 109–10, 112

Narragansett peoples: conflict with Mohegans and Montauketts, 168–71; and crows, 31; demographics, 266(n8); diet, 26; and the Dutch, 183–85, 311(n35); and English encroachment, 154, 201; feared by Massapequas, 188–89; giant story, 19; and King Philip's War, 207, 211–12; land use agreements, 195; language and dialects, 22, 23, 103; and Oldham, 132–34, 298(nn13–14); and the Pequot War, 128, 135, 137, 139–42, 153–54; and the Plymouth colony, 101; political structure/relationships, 44–46, 45, 48, 273(n49); scalping and beheading by, 40; territory, xxi, 25, 87, 205, 238; uprising contemplated, 154–55, 202; and the wampum trade, 112; watercraft, 54, 68; and Williams, 81, 153–54. See also Canonicus; Miantonomi; Ninigret

Native Americans. See Algonquians

Nauset people, 45, 78–79, 92, 100–101, 233

Navigation Acts, 181

Netherlands, the: and the Anglo–Dutch Wars, 166, 181–82 (see also Anglo–Dutch Wars); history, government, and culture, 49–50, 118–19, 159, 178–79, 181, 305(n65); Indians displayed in, 97; interest in New Netherland, 117–18, 144–45; roots of colonial enterprise, 88–91 (see also West India Company); and sovereignty over the sea, 121, 310(n24)

New Amsterdam, 56, 167; defenses, 7, 165, 183, 185; Dutch fleet and, 147–48; English takeover of, 187, 191–92, 311(n29); Kieft's War and, 128; tradespeople in, 146; and the wampum trade, 123. See also Dutch colonists; Manhattan; New Netherland; New York

New England, 90; communication within, 172; competition between colonies, 196; economy, 197–98; growth of, 154, 165–66, 191; migration within, 292(n52); territorial claims, 86–88, 87, 115–17, 122–24, 154, 165–66, 167, 196, 292(n57) (see also Massachusetts Bay Colony; Plymouth Plantation); United Colonies Commissioners, 165–66, 179–80, 183–84. See also colonial–Native conflict; English colonists; English–Dutch conflict; and specific colonies and individuals

Newman, Antipas and Elizabeth, 168–69

New Netherland, 90–91, 286–87(n8); Dutch (lack of) interest in, 117–18, 144–45; economy, 197–99; English invasions of, 190–92, 196–97; English migrants in, 180, 190; growth of, 144–47, 154, 165–66; slavery in, 117, 145, 218–19; territorial claims, 86–88, 87, 117–21, 120, 122–24, 143–44, 149, 167, 303(n46). See also Dutch colonists; English–Dutch conflict; Kieft, Willem; Manhattan; New Amsterdam; West India Company

New York, 192, 203, 205, 216, 226–29, 232. See also Andros, Edmund; New Amsterdam; New Netherland

New York City, 240

New York Harbor, 27, 82, 188

Niantic people: canoe wrecked, 69, 208; and colonial–Native conflicts, 132, 140, 298(n12); and Connecticut, 195–96; and English–Dutch relations, 184–85; hogs slaughtered, 194; political structure/ relationships, 48; territory, 45, 223. See also Ninigret

Nicolls, Richard, 192, 196

Ninigret, 169–72, 176, 183–84, 188, 200, 211, 219

Occom, Samson, 235, 237, 240

Oldham, John, 66, 83, 128, 132–35, 143, 298(nn13–14)

Orson and Valentine (Munsee teens), 96–97, 99

Pachem, 151, 158, 304(n49)

Parry, J. H., 53

Patrick, Daniel, 159, 160

peacemaking, 41, 105–6, 132, 156–58, 229–30, 272(n45). *See also* Treaty of Hartford; *and specific conflicts*

Peach War, 187–88

Penhawitz ("One Eye"), 176

Pequots: canoes requested, 222; demographics, 266(n8); first encounters with Europeans, 52; giant story, 19; language and dialects, 22, 23; after the Pequot War, 129–30, 141, 161, 170–71, 217–18; political structure/relationships, 44, 45, 48, 135, 273(n49), 274(n53); relations with Dutch colonists, 105–8, 131–32; sailing by, 276–77(n3); and Stone's death, 132–34; territory, *xxi*, 87, 205; and the wampum trade, 111–12. *See also* Pequot War; Tatobem

Pequot War, 127–42; boats and, 76, 81–82; colonial–Native alliances, 125, 129, 134–36, 138–42, 153, 163; map, 128; Mystic massacre, 125–26, 136–37, 161, 295(n2); origins, 83, 129–37, 295–96(n5), 297(n7), 301(n27); trophies taken, 137–42, 300(n25)

Philip. *See* Metacom (King Philip)

Pietersen, Cors, 149–50, 152

piracy, 82–84, 97, 132–34, 149–50, 216–17. *See also* colonial–Native conflict: colonial vessels attacked

place names, 15–18, 17

Plymouth Plantation: colonists' arrival, 2, 2–4; colonists attacked, 63; colonists' origins, 89–90; conflict with Boston Puritans, 298(n9); first Thanksgiving, 3, 101; and King Philip's War, 201–2, 207–10, 220, 315(n68) (*see also* King Philip's War); shallop, 79; Squanto and, 78, 99–103; territory, 87, 167, 196, 205; trade, 64, 108–9, 123; waters closed to Native boats, 203. *See also* colonial–Native conflict; English colonists; *Mayflower; and specific individuals*

Protestants, 6–7, 50. *See also* Christianity, conversion to

Puritans, 15, 112–13. *See also* English colonists; Plymouth Plantation

Quabb, Paul, 230

quahogs (hard-shell clams), 30, 106, 109–10. *See also* wampum

Quaiapen, 213, 214

Quiripi-Unkechaug peoples, 23, 46–48, 47, 87, 273(n49). *See also* Unkechaug people

Raritans: conflict with the Dutch, 76, 128, 130, 145, 149–51, 155–56, 190–91, 304(n48); and English–Dutch conflict, 168, 190–91; territory, 46, 47

reservations, 222, 238

Rhode Island, 196, 200–201, 203–4, 205, 209, 219. *See also* English colonists; New England

Richter, Daniel, 101

Rockaway people, 47, 157

Rodrigues, Juan, 97–99, 104, 289(n24)

Romney, Susanah Shaw, 173–74

Rowlandson, Mary, 204, 211–12, 214

Rubertone, Patricia, 261(n18)

Ryece, Robert, 114

sachems, 107; and Anglo–Dutch conflict, 168; and colonial–Native wars, 129–30; colonists' gifts to, 300–301(n26); communication between, 171–72; customs appropriated by English, 138–42; difficulty of assessing, 42–43; and Dutch colonists, 104; female sachems, 37, 209, 213–15; and Kieft's War, 157–58, 160; political relationships between, 36, 41, 44–46, 138, 155, 169; power and role of, 37–38, 41–44, 111, 154–55, 169–70, 272–73(n49); shipmasters as, 57; traditions appropriated by English, 138–42, 154–55; and the wampum trade, 111–12. *See also* sachemships; *and specific individuals*

sachemships, 43–48, 45, 47, 196, 273(n49). *See also* sachems

Sakaweston, 94
Sakonnet people, 45, 210, 212–16. *See also*
    King Philip's War
Samoset, 101
Sassacus, 128, 135, 140–41
scalping, 40, 139–41, 271–72(n42), 301(n27).
    See also trophies
Schama, Simon, 119
sea, the: Bush-Banks on, 12–13; dangers of,
    230–31, 239; ignored by historians, 9;
    King Philip's War and, 203–4, 206–11,
    216–17; Native beliefs about, 19–20; as
    primary stage of colonial encounters,
    6–8; sovereignty over, 121–24, 181, 203–4,
    294(n67), 310(n24) (*see also* Anglo–
    Dutch Wars); war likened to storms,
    5–6, 12. *See also* ecology of the coastal
    region; seafaring and boating; ships,
    European; watercraft; whales and
    whaling
seafaring and boating: coastal region's
    hazards, 60–61; and colonial–Native
    wars, 129, 132–33; dangers of, 69–70,
    73–74, 230–31, 239; Dutch traders, 49,
    50; European sailors, 58–59; Indians
    barred from, 203–4; as male province,
    56–57; marine wayfinding, 55, 61–62,
    78, 277(n4); Native encounters with
    colonists, 54–57, 62–63, 66; Native
    naval battles, 67–68, 136; Native pilots
    used, 78, 83, 93; Native skills and
    techniques, 6, 7, 55, 67, 69–70, 78,
    80–81, 93, 227–28, 239; seafaring's effect
    on Native communities, 239–43;
    transportation services, 71–72, 74;
    whaling, 226–35 (*see also* whales and
    whaling); wrecks and capsizings, 69–70,
    73–74, 78–79, 282(n32). *See also* sea,
    the; ships, European; watercraft
Sedgewick, Robert, 187
Seed, Patricia, 119
Selden, John, 121
Shakespeare, William, 94, 149, 288(n19)
shell beads. *See* wampum
shellfish, 26–30, 35, 109–10. *See also*
    quahogs; whelks

ships, European: Anglo–Dutch conflict and,
    123, 179; design and technology, 57–60,
    279(n15); first indigenous encounters
    with, 51–56, 77; off Manhattan, 54, 56; as
    metaphor, 12–13, 251; Native attacks on,
    62–63, 77, 82–83, 97, 132–34, 149–50, 188,
    216–17; and Native captives, 92–100;
    Native-owned, 249–50; Native sailors on,
    79, 227–31, 234–35, 239–40, 242–43,
    247–48 (*see also* whales and whaling);
    Puritan armada, 112–13; seaworthiness,
    60–61; shipbuilding, 50, 64–65;
    shipwrecks, 239; size, 276(n2); smaller
    vessels, 63–66, 64, 80–81, 83, 136,
    281(n24); whaling ships, 234–35 (*see also*
    whales and whaling). *See also* seafaring
    and boating; watercraft; *and specific
    ships and captains*
Shoemaker, Nancy, 242
Sierra Leone, 250–51
Simmons, William S., 271–72(n42)
slavery: abolished, 241; African slaves, 117,
    219, 235, 241, 250; Native Americans
    enslaved, 7, 141, 217–22; in New
    Netherland, 117, 145, 218–19. *See also*
    captives
Smith, John, Capt., 28, 94, 100, 226
Smits, Claes, 151–52, 156
Southwest, the, 30–31
sovereignty: Native vs. European ideas
    of, 154–55 (*see also* land use and
    landownership; sachemships); over
    the seas, 121–24, 181, 203–4, 294(n67),
    310(n24); surrendered by Algonquians,
    195
Sparrow-Hawk (boat), 64, 78–79
Speedwell (ship), 62, 73
Squanto, 78, 99–103
Stanton, Thomas, 76, 184
Staten Island, ix, 74, 151, 190, 192, 195,
    273(n49), 304(n52)
States' Arms (Dutch), 119–20, 149, 293(n65),
    303(n46)
St. Beninjo (English ship), 179
Sterling, Dorothy, 22
Stiles, Ezra, 233, 238

Stone, John, 81, 83, 128, 132, 134, 143, 298(n12)
Strong, John, 230
Stuyvesant, Petrus (Pieter), 177–79, 183, 186, 188–93, 198, 218, 311(n35)
Susquehannock people, 177, 180, 193
Swarte Beer, De (Dutch ship), 82, 97
Sybrants, Aeltie, 173

Tackapousha, 175–77, 186, 188–89, 192
Tankiteke people, 46, 47, 128, 130, 159–60. *See also* Pachem
Tatobem, 44, 105–8, 111–12, 131–32, 142, 273(n49). *See also* Pequots
Tecumseh, 244–45, 325(n2)
Tijger (Dutch ship), 61, 278–79(n12)
trade: via boat, 64, 66, 71–72, 112; Dutch territorial claims and, 118–21; English–Dutch conflict re, 122; fur trade, 108, 122, 123, 141, 144, 198–99; guns, 110, 175, 177, 183, 185–86, 199–200, 207; Native economies and, 109; and New Netherland's growth, 144, 147; wampum trade, 44, 105–12, 123, 144, 189, 197–98, 207, 290(n38); West India Company's focus on, 117–18, 144
trading companies, 86, 89–91, 285–86(n3). *See also* Virginia Company; West India Company
Traveller (Cuffe's ship), 249–51
Treaty of Hartford, 141, 167, 179–80, 188
trophies (heads/body parts), 40–41, 137–42, 151, 212, 216, 300(n25)
Turner, Frederick Jackson, 8–10, 12

Uncas: alliance with the English, 135, 138–39, 142, 154, 163, 211; feud with Ninigret, 168–72, 211; historical records, 176; Miantonomi killed, 163, 170; Niantics afraid of, 195; rumors spread by, 185, 187; sachemship of, 130, 163, 169–70. *See also* Mohegan people
Underhill, John (Jan Onderhill), 127, 133–34, 138–39, 159–61
United Colonies Commissioners, 165–66, 179–80, 183–84. *See also* New England

Unkechaug people, 46, 47, 87, 205, 226, 229–30, 238. *See also* Long Island; Quiripi-Unkechaug peoples
Usselincx, Willem, 118

Valentin et Orson (medieval romance), 96–97
van der Donck, Adriaen, 103, 180
Van Tienhoven, Cornelius, 147, 149, 150, 185–86, 304(n48), 304(n52)
Van Twiller, Wouter, 145
Van Zandt, Cynthia, 285–86(n3)
Vaughan, Alden T., 295(n5)
Verrazzano, Giovanni da, 44, 51, 60, 76, 80, 276(n1)
Vikings, 70–71, 79–80
violence. *See* colonial–Native conflict; peacemaking; slavery; trophies; warfare; *and specific conflicts*
Virginia Company, 89–90, 122
Vreede, De (Dutch ship), 149–50

Wabanaki people, 80–81, 216–217
Wampanoag peoples: coming-of-age ritual, 265(n7); demographics, 266(n8), 320(n32); disease's impact on, 85, 100, 115; and the Dutch, 200–201; early encounters with Europeans, 57; giant story, 19; hurricane seen as prophecy, 206; and King Philip's War, 7, 201–2, 207–16, 220, 315(n68) (*see also* King Philip's War); language and dialects, 22, 23, 103; piracy by, 83–84; political structure/relationships, 44, 45, 48, 273(n49); relations with English colonists, 86, 100–102; territory, xxi, 87, 205; and wampum, 106–7, 112; and whaling, 242. *See also* Epenow; Massasoit; Metacom; *and specific tribes*
wampum: and the composite sachemships, 272–73(n49); creation of, 30, 106, 110–11, 189; description and uses, 6, 106–7, 107, 110; as peacemaking gift, 41, 105–6, 132, 156, 229–30, 272(n45); during the Pequot War, 139, 141–42; wampum

trade, 44, 105–12, 123, 144, 189, 197–98, 207, 290(n38)

warfare, 125–64, 208; among tribes, 38–41, 67–68, 199; in the Anglo–Dutch wars, 182; colonists' fear of, 177–78; European style, 49, 159–60, 305(n65); maritime vs. land attacks, 136–37, 169; and Native–colonial partnerships, 125, 129; Native metaphors for, 38–39, 206; Native style, 161–63, 306(n71); naval warfare, 169, 191, 208–11, 216–17 (*see also* colonial–Native conflict: colonial vessels attacked; King Philip's War); psychological effects, 160–61; and slavery, 7, 141, 217–18; trophies, 40–41, 137–42, 151, 212, 216, 300(n25). *See also* colonial–Native conflict; Kieft's War; King Philip's War; Pequot War

watercraft: bark vessels, 66–70, 81; boatbuilding, 64–65, 73, 75; colonial control over, 203–4, 208–9, 222, 230; colonists' use of Native craft, 71–76, 84; cost of, 65–66, 74; dugout canoes, 34, 54–57, 56, 66–74, 68, 84, 136, 224, 276(n1), 280(n21), 282(nn32, 34); indigenous use of sails, 54, 69, 276–77(n3); Natives and colonial craft, 76–84, 136; naval warfare, 169, 191, 208–11, 216–17; small colonial vessels, 63–66, 64, 80–81, 83, 136, 281(n24). *See also* seafaring and boating; ships, European

weather, ix–x, 39, 74, 206, 273(n49), 316(n6)

Weaver, Jace, 246–47

Weeks, William, 83–84

Welles, Thomas, 171

West India Company (Dutch), 90, 91, 108, 286–87(n8); and colonial–Native relations, 147–49, 174–75, 188–89; colonization project, 102, 117–18, 144–45; and currency, 198; employees unruly, 147–48, 303(n44), 304(n52); and English–Dutch conflict, 124, 183, 186, 191–92; fur trading, 108, 198–99 (*see also* fur trade); guns traded, 199–200; land purchase preferred, 105; and maritime

claims, 122, 123; and New England, 143–44; territorial claims, 117–21, 131–32, 135 (*see also* New Netherland). *See also* Dutch colonists; Kieft, Willem; New Amsterdam; New Netherland; Stuyvesant, Petrus

Weston, Thomas, 75

whales and whaling, 20, 26, 223–35, 239, 242

whelks, 30, 106, 109–10. *See also* wampum

Wiechquageseck people, 46, 47, 130, 151–52, 155–56

Willet, Thomas, 198

William (English ship), 123–24

Williams, Roger: banished, 117, 153, 293(n58); diplomacy of, 139, 177, 193, 300–301(n26); on Indian affairs, 169; on Indian gun acquisition, 199–200; and Kieft's War, 127, 156–57, 160, 193; on King Philip's War, 209; and the Narragansetts, 81, 153–54, 170; and Native boats and seafaring, 66–68, 72, 73, 76; and Ninigret, 170, 172; and the Pequot War, 135–36, 139, 142, 153, 193; Rubitone on, 261(n18); on wampum, 110, 290(n38); on whale meat, 224

Winthrop, John, Jr., 217, 280(n19)

Winthrop, John, Sr.: colonization undertaken, 112–14; death, 179; and English land use, 115–16; on Kieft, 147; and the Pequot War, 134–35, 140; relations with Native Americans, 171–72, 177, 218; son's death, 282(n32); and wampum, 198

women, European, 57, 136, 143, 173, 204, 211–12, 309(n16)

women, Native: enslaved, 218; and European men, 98, 148, 175, 240; female sachems, 37, 209, 213–15; gender roles, 27, 30–34, 110; kept apart from early encounters, 56–57; menstruation retreat, 115; rights and power of, 33; sons taken captive, 92–93, 100

Wood, William, 73

Wyandanch, 76, 140–42, 177

Zinn, Howard, 55